THE STAGECRAFT AND PERFORMANCE OF
ROMAN COMEDY

A comprehensive survey of Roman theatrical production, this book examines all aspects of Roman performance practice, and provides fresh insights into the comedies of Plautus and Terence. Following an introductory chapter on the experience of Roman comedy from the perspective of Roman actors and the Roman audience, addressing among other things the economic concerns of putting on a play in the Roman republic, subsequent chapters provide detailed studies of troupe size and the implications for role assignment, masks, stage action, music, and improvisation in the plays of Plautus and Terence. Marshall argues that Roman comedy was raw comedy, much more rough-and-ready than its Hellenistic precursors, but still fully conscious of its literary past. The consequences of this lead to new conclusions concerning the dramatic structure of Roman comedy, and a clearer understanding of the relationship between the plays-as-text and the role of improvisation during performance.

C. W. MARSHALL teaches Greek and Latin literature at the University of British Columbia, Canada. His work has been published in many books and journals, including the *Journal of Hellenic Studies* and *Classical Quarterly*.

THE STAGECRAFT
AND PERFORMANCE OF
ROMAN COMEDY

C. W. MARSHALL

CAMBRIDGE
UNIVERSITY PRESS

CAMBRIDGE UNIVERSITY PRESS
Cambridge, New York, Melbourne, Madrid, Cape Town, Singapore, São Paulo

Cambridge University Press
The Edinburgh Building, Cambridge CB2 2RU, UK

Published in the United States of America by Cambridge University Press, New York

www.cambridge.org
Information on this title: www.cambridge.org/9780521861618

First published 2006

Printed in the United Kingdom at the University Press, Cambridge

A catalogue record for this publication is available from the British Library

Library of Congress Cataloguing in Publication data

Marshall, C. W., 1968–
The stagecraft and performance of Roman comedy / C. W. Marshall.
p.   cm.
Includes bibliographical references and index.
ISBN-13: 978-0-521-86161-8 (hardback)
ISBN-10: 0-521-86161-6 (hardback)
1. Latin drama (Comedy) – History and criticism. I. Title.

PA6069.M28 2006
872.01–dc22   2006003307

ISBN-13 978-0-521-86161-8 hardback
ISBN-10 0-521-86161-6 hardback

For Jonah
you got a face with a view

Contents

Figures

Preface

Books on *The Stagecraft of Plautus* and *Roman Theatre Production* seem beyond our capabilities.

Goldberg (1998) 2

This book is about comedy, and, like most books about comedy, it does not contain nearly enough jokes; for that I apologise. I hope the book contains enough of interest to convey something of the excitement Plautus and Terence have brought me over the past several years. Stagecraft and performance are a challenge to document, and the separation of twenty-two centuries has done little to make it easier. I have attempted to present a consistent, credible, and comprehensive picture of how the mechanics of the Plautine stage functioned, and in most respects the picture remains true for Terence. I have tried to remain grounded in the text of the plays, but a lack of evidence has meant that some speculation has been necessary, and I know that not all readers will accept all the conclusions. It is possible to isolate various claims – to agree with what I say about masks, but not about improvisation, for example – but taken together, it is hoped that the resulting picture remains true to what we understand of the text of Plautus, even given the necessary limits that such a claim must entail.

Roman comedies were intended for production. My purpose is to examine a number of aspects of the performance and stagecraft of Roman comedy, with an emphasis on Plautus. The term 'performance' concentrates on the experience of the play as presented to an audience. Performance is the event where actor and audience meet. Peter Brook has reduced this idea to its rawest form in his famous dictum at the beginning of *The Empty Space* (1968, 11): 'I can take any empty space and call it a bare stage. A man walks across this empty space whilst someone else is watching him, and this is all that is needed for an act of theatre to be engaged.' 'Stagecraft' takes a step back, and examines the resources

available to the playwright as he crafts his play, and the decisions made by
playwright and director to facilitate communication with the audience.
Stagecraft concerns the often gritty backstage reality of mounting a play,
and the restrictions and opportunities offered to performers that creating
a narrative for a live audience presents. Together stagecraft and
performance create a direct line of communication from the playwright
to the director to the actors to the audience.

For some, these are modest concerns: Aristotle notoriously makes ὄψις
('spectacle'), the least of the parts of Greek tragedy (*Poetics* 1450b16–20).
Many of my concerns are addressed in George E. Duckworth's *The
Nature of Roman Comedy* (1952; a 'second edition' appeared in 1994, but
since Duckworth's text remains unaltered, I continue to refer to
Duckworth (1952) and use Hunter (1994) only when referring to the
bibliographic appendix that was added) and William Beare's *The Roman
Stage* (3rd edn, 1964). Both works are infused with an understanding of
the theatre, and represent the ground on which I hope to build. Several
advances since their publication have dated their conclusions. In
particular, Niall Slater's *Plautus in Performance* (1985; 2nd edn, 2000)
altered the landscape for interpreting Plautine comedy by providing a
vocabulary for metatheatre. 'Metatheatre', as Slater uses the term, is a
dramatic technique whereby characters on stage acknowledge their status
as characters in a play. Euanthius calls it *vitium Plauti frequentissimum* (*de
Fabula* 3.8: 'Plautus' most frequent fault') – and it was not seen as a virtue
of Plautus' dramaturgy until an article by M. Barchiesi in 1970, after
Duckworth and Beare were writing. Each of my six chapters contributes
to this perspective. The first three describe the resources available to a
Roman comic playwright c. 200 BC. The last three address different ways
that Plautus patterns his narrative so that his desired effect will be
maximised.

I have tried to write for both students and professionals in Classics and
Theatre, but many disclaimers are needed. This is not a 'how-to' manual
for directing Plautus today, though it would be possible to use the ideas
here to create exciting, funny performances that have Plautine elements in
them. Unattributed translations are my own, but I cite others when I am
concerned about slanting translations so that they are favourable to my
argument. The manuscripts divide the plays into acts and scenes, but
since such divisions had no meaning for the Roman playwrights, I have
resorted to reckoning by line number, which at least has the virtue of
precision. Over the past century, Plautus has remained in need of textual
criticism. None of the editions by Leo (1895–96), Lindsay (1904–05, rev.

1910), and Ernout (1932–61) is completely satisfactory, and Plautinists eagerly await the completion of a new text, the *Editio Plautina Sarsinates*, beginning with Questa (2001). For Terence I have consulted Kauer and Lindsay (1926, with additions 1958) and Barsby (2001). My citations reflect the eclectic state of the text, though I have normalised orthography. While Lindsay is not the best version available for Plautus, it is the most accessible, and so I have used it exclusively when presenting statistics or surveying the entire corpus. Other options were available, but this seemed the most transparent. At times I use statistics because they can help one to see unexpected patterns. There is a danger that this will appear to present a pseudo-scientific degree of certainty greater than the data in fact warrant. When included, statistics principally offer transparency (so that the reader may see the basis for a conclusion). Ancient works are referred to by Latin or English title depending on what seems most natural to me, but the result will not please everyone. Throughout I assume a relatively sophisticated economic model for the functioning of *ludi scaenici*. It is not possible to account for all variables, but I have tried to ground what I say in the real-world pressures that would affect an itinerant troupe working in and around Rome.

If *Asinaria*, *Curculio*, and *Miles Gloriosus* receive particular attention, it is because of the casts and crews of the Plautine productions I have directed: *Curculio* (Trent University, Peterborough, Ontario; March 1996); *Asinaria* (University of Victoria, Victoria, BC; March 1997); *Miles Gloriosus* (Memorial University of Newfoundland, St. John's, Newfoundland; October, 1999). All three were produced through Modern Actors Staging Classics (MASC), with translations by Peter L. Smith. I see these productions as experiments, testing hypotheses about ancient performance, allowing me to corroborate and modify conclusions that would otherwise have remained theoretical. Because an effect worked (or failed to work) in my productions does not prescribe how Plautus must have staged the play. Student actors were masked and the outdoor performances ran for several days in the early afternoon, in all weathers. Audiences did not buy tickets, but often had to be drawn away by the performance from other distractions (lunch, friends, classes). Seats were available, and a minimal set of empty doorframes was used in a found-space performance area (always a high-traffic location on campus). Roles were doubled and improvisation encouraged. All of these factors correspond in some degree to what I believe transpired on the Roman stage. Rehearsing and watching the performances taught me a great deal about what is possible with Roman comedy. At times, this experience strengthened my convictions, while at others it sent me back to the text to reconsider. The casts endured completely unreasonable requests, performing in snow, rain, and (literally) gale-force winds. At times, actors are amazing. They know when a scene is not working, and they let you know when an explanation or decision is not coherent. Since in no case did any of the actors have more than a year of Latin, they could not be expected to adopt scholarly solutions on principle. In other contexts, Mary-Kay Gamel and Amy Richlin gave me a chance to perform in *Persa* and George Adam Kovacs gave me a chance to act in masks when he directed *Rhesus*. Both experiences corrected misapprehensions I had.

Since 1987, many hundreds of hours of my life have been mis-spent improvising on stage and in workshops, and this has taught me more than anything else about theatre, performance, and making an audience laugh. It has made me a better actor, and perhaps helped me perceive things in scripted comedy I would otherwise have missed. Thanks are due to the many people I have shared a stage with, but in particular I am grateful to my improv groups in Montreal, Edinburgh, and Sackville, New Brunswick.

Much of this research was funded by a Standard Research Grant from the Social Sciences and Humanities Research Council of Canada. Other funding was received from the University of Victoria, the Memorial University of Newfoundland, the University of British Columbia, and from an Overseas Research Fellowship at the University of South Africa. Parts of Chapter 3 appeared in *Social Identity*, and I am grateful to the editors for permission to use them here.

Many individuals have helped me, too. Peter Smith has helped me appreciate Plautus more than anyone else, and I cannot repay him for his kind offer to translate *Curculio* and *Asinaria* for my productions. Had he not done so, this book would not exist. Tim Moore, Fred Franko, David Creese, John Starks, and Jim Russell read portions of the manuscript and saved me from at least some of my gaffes. George Adam Kovacs, Michael J. Griffin, and Michael S. Leese were exceptional research assistants, and I was lucky to benefit from their skills, which are many. Niall Slater and Sander Goldberg have given me continued encouragement, and have taught me much about Plautus, and so I trust they will forgive my temerity when I disagree with them. Elaine Fantham, David Wiles, Susanna Braund, Ian Storey, John Porter, Lyn Rae, Mary-Kay Gamel, Mark Damen, George Harrison, Annette Teffeteller, Rob Ketterer, Paul Wilson, Jim Butrica, and Mark Joyal have also (in some cases unknowingly) given me encouragement in various forms at various stages, which has helped a great deal, as have my wonderful parents.

Victoria Cooper at Cambridge University Press, along with Elizabeth
Davey, Rebecca Jones, Nancy-Jane Rucker and no doubt many others,
has provided valuable help and support. Students at Trent University,
Concordia University, the Memorial University of Newfoundland, and
the University of British Columbia have read plays with me in class, and
forced me to answer questions I otherwise would not have touched.

My wife Hallie challenges me and charms me with her perception and
insight, and she has given much of her time to me reading drafts, making
masks, and listening to jokes when she had better things to do. Jonah
Franklin Marshall works harder at making people laugh than anyone I
know, and he can always make me smile.

The deaths of Jim Butrica and Peter Smith in the summer of 2006
mark a great loss for Latin studies in Canada. I was honoured to have
both men as colleagues and friends, and I shall miss wisdom and wit.

Introduction

Titus Maccius Plautus was one of several comic playwrights writing in Latin c. 200 BC. Victorious in the Second Punic War, and flexing its military muscles in North Africa and in Greece, Rome had begun to establish itself as an ancient superpower. The development of Roman New Comedy (the *fabulae palliatae*, or 'plays in Greek dress' as they came to be called, from *pallium*, a Greek cloak) coincided with this growth, and reflected a sophisticated, cosmopolitan attitude shared by the Hellenistic Greek world. Rome was also consciously cultivating a sense of 'literature' for the Latin language, and theatre was at the forefront in this cultural programme.[1]

Plautus is the best-represented playwright from antiquity, with twenty plays surviving more or less complete, plus significant fragments. Though much of his work is lost, Plautus remains the earliest Latin author whose complete literary works survive. Even dating the plays of Plautus is notoriously uncertain, though it is generally thought they were written between c. 205 and 184 BC.[2] A generation later, Publius Terentius Afer (Terence) wrote six *palliatae*, also surviving, produced between 166 and 160. The plays of Plautus continued to be performed at least until the end of the republic, and there are indications Terence was performed into the fourth century AD. Both authors have influenced modern European comic playwrights from Elizabethan times until the present, and the humour has

---

[1] Representative but somewhat dated accounts in English of the historical and literary background to Roman comedy can be found at Duckworth (1952) 3–72, Bieber (1961) 129–60, Beare (1964) 10–158.

[2] Two plays are securely dated by *didascalia* ('production notices'): *Stichus* to 200 BC and *Pseudolus* to 191 BC. Much has been written on dating the plays, but the schemes proposed are all questionable. For rival proposals, all of which have adherents today, see Buck (1940), Sedgwick (1949), Schutter (1952), and De Lorenzi (1952). Not enough is known for any confidence, however. Even the principle that the amount of lyric *cantica* increases over time, proposed by Sedgwick (1925), has been questioned: see Dumont (1997) 45 and n. 26.

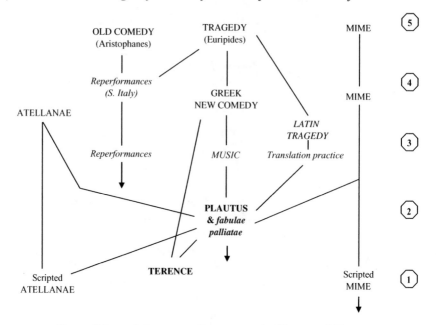

Fig. 1   Primary influences on Roman comedy: Plautus and Terence.

proved resilient and capable of crossing linguistic and cultural borders.[3] By examining the plays as works intended for performance – asking what they expect of actors, directors, and audiences – it becomes possible to understand Roman comedy and its performance culture better (see Fig. 1).

The plays agree as to where Plautus' literary debts lie. The prologue may tell a Roman audience that there is a Greek original, and that this is an adaptation of it: e.g. *huic Graece nomen est Thensauro fabulae:* | *Philemo scripsit, Plautus vertit barbare* (*Trinummus* 18–19: 'The name of this play in Greek is *Thensaurus*, "The Treasure"; Philemon wrote it, Plautus made it Latin').[4] There is a sense already that self-deprecating irony colours this picture. Accepting for the moment that Plautus can choose to refer to himself as either 'Plautus' or (as in *Asinaria*) 'Maccus', the change from Greek to Latin is represented with the words *vertit barbare*. *Barbare* ('into barbarian') is a funny way of speaking about one's own language. The prologue is here adopting a Greek perspective, one

---

[3] Study of the afterlife of Roman drama has been limited, though see Lefèvre (1997) 115–50, Baier (1998), (1999b), Lefèvre (2001) 157–201, Götte (2001), and Elm (2001). For a general overview, see Duckworth (1952) 396–433.

[4] There are similar claims at *Asinaria* 10–11, *Mercator* 9–10, *Vidularia* 6–7. See Wright (1974) 93–4.

still within the ostensible world of the play,[5] as he jokingly sneers at his Roman audience.

The publication in 1968 of a substantial papyrus fragment of Menander's *Dis Exapatôn* ('The Double Deceiver') gave for the first time a clear sense of how Plautus appropriated and reinterpreted source material.[6] The surviving lines of *Dis Exapatôn* correspond directly to Plautus' *Bacchides* ('The Bacchis Sisters') lines 494–561. Some phrases are rendered almost verbatim, so that it is possible in places to use the Greek to restore the Latin text. There are also large-scale additions and alterations. This discovery confirmed the theory that Plautus introduced large amounts of additional material into his versions of Greek plays.[7] Because this is a familiar and much-discussed example, here I merely list six types of change evident in this overlap. (1) Stylistic and rhetorical flourishes (assonance and wordplay) are regularly introduced. Names of characters are changed. (2) Where the Greek verse is spoken (iambic trimeters), Plautus alternates between a chanted metre (Latin trochaic septenarii) to a spoken meter (Latin iambic senarii, at *Bacchides* 500–25) and back again. (3) This metrical change has other performative implications, as the trochaic lines would be accompanied by music on the *tibia*, played by a piper standing at the side of the performance area. While Menander's play also had a piper, he did not play in the passage represented by the *Dis Exapatôn* fragment. (4) Menander's play almost certainly possessed four act divisions, creating five acts; Plautus' play was performed continuously. The *Dis Exapatôn* fragment shows that Plautus has smoothed over Menander's act division by combining two speeches of a character separated by a choral interlude into a single speech. Not insignificantly, the single speech is the unaccompanied passage. (5) Characterisation has changed: 'where Menander's characterisation is complex, subtle, and realistic, Plautus' is simple, bold and comic'.[8] (6) Whole speeches are omitted and others are invented, and this affects the narrative flow. In addition, there must have been many more alterations not obvious from the text.[9] Audience expectations change as the performance venue

---

[5] It is only ostensible, though: there exist many Roman elements in this supposedly Greek world. See Moore (1998b) 50–66.

[6] There is an immense bibliography on this. In particular, see Handley (1968), Questa (1970), Bain (1979), Schönbeck (1981), Primmer (1984), Zwierlein (1990) 24–40, Anderson (1993) 3–29, and Damen (1995).

[7] Fraenkel (1960), an Italian translation with addenda to the German original of 1922.

[8] Barsby (1986) 140.

[9] Another parallel passage (surviving in Aulus Gellius, *Attic Nights* 2.23) compares about fifteen lines from *Plocium* ('The Necklace') by Caecilius, a rival of Plautus writing in the early second century,

changes, and a successful performance in a large, Greek stone theatre will necessarily require alteration if it is to be equally successful in the smaller, temporary Roman venue. Vocal delivery, acting style, the vocabulary of gesture, and the scale of movement are all products of an actor's relationship with the stage and the audience. When any factor is changed, the others shift to accommodate it. This degree of alteration was typical.

Further, Terence, *Adelphoe* 6–11, shows scenes could be omitted or transferred from one play into another:

> *Synapothnescontes Diphili comoediast;*
> *eam Commorientis Plautus fecit fabulam.*
> *in graeca adulescens est qui lenoni eripit*
> *meretricem in prima fabula: eum Plautus locum*
> *reliquit integrum, eum hic locum sumpsit sibi*
> *in Adelphos; verbum de verbo expressum extulit.*

Synapothnescontes is a Greek comedy by Diphilus; Plautus rendered it as his play 'Partners in Death'. At the beginning of the Greek play there is a young man who abducts a girl from her pimp. Plautus left that scene untouched; that scene Terence has taken over for his *Brothers*; he has reproduced and rendered it word for word.[10]

Terence provides his play's pedigree. He claims to render at least one scene in his play *verbum de verbo* ('word for word'), though 'This cannot be literally true.'[11] Plautus' playwriting is described with the prosaic word *fecit* ('made'); Terence has no reason to present another playwright from a previous generation favourably. Terence also claims Plautus could omit whole scenes, not just speeches: line 10 must mean this, since Terence presents his own practice (*verbum de verbo*) as contrast.

Where Plautus streamlines, Terence incorporates a scene from another play into a Latin version of a Greek comedy. Terence uses the verb *contaminare* ('to pollute') to describe this practice at *Andria* 16, *Heauton Timoroumenos* 17, and *Eunuchus* 552, and the name *contaminatio* continues to be used.[12] Terence grafts a neglected scene by Diphilus – i.e. one Plautus did not translate – onto his version of Menander's *Adelphoe B* (his second version of 'The Brothers'). In his prologue Terence admits

with his Menanderean source (see J. Wright (1974) 120–23; for other examples, see Law (1922) 3–4). Caecilius changes the spoken metre of Greek comedy into a polymetric monody.
[10] Text and translation, Gratwick (1999) 60–61, slightly adapted.
[11] Gratwick (1999) 179. Compare Cicero, *de Finibus* 1.2.4.
[12] See Duckworth (1952) 202–8 for the practice generally, and Fantham (1968), Grant (1980), and Gratwick (1999) 34–6 for *Adelphoe*.

this is part of a defence against an accusation of plagiarism. This provides insight into the concept of intellectual property rights in the second century, and shows that Terence sees his activity as an acceptable practice for playwrights.[13]

These techniques are part of the Roman comic translation practice, a practice Plautus describes with the verb *vertere* (*vortere* at *Asinaria* 11) which means 'to twist', like a screw. 'Plautus twists [the Greek play] into barbarian' gives a much rougher image of translation than we might typically assume, but it does more closely reflect his observed practice. The double meaning of the English word 'render' might capture the spirit of *vertere*. The bare-bones information the prologue provides is probably meant to close down inquiry concerning Greek originals, rather than to invite audience speculation: 'We need not suppose that the audience demanded or expected close fidelity to Greek originals, or that they would have bothered to ask what changes Plautus had made to them.'[14] But there were other literary debts, too, and by examining them it is possible to identify the influence exerted on Plautus' compositional practice by contemporary performance traditions. An understanding of these other genres will help to define many aspects of Roman comic stagecraft, but it will also identify key ways in which the *palliata* remained distinct from them.

The *fabulae Atellanae* ('Atellan farces') were, in the time of Plautus and Terence, unscripted, improvised plays performed in and around Rome in the Oscan dialect, native to Campania in Southern Italy. Umbria used a related dialect, and the ancient biographical tradition asserts that Plautus came from Umbria.[15] Oscan continued as the language of Atellan performance throughout its history, even into the Augustan period (Strabo 5.233).[16] The plays used a set of stock characters, represented by traditional masks: Pappus the old man, Maccus the clown, Bucco the fool, Dossennus the glutton, and Manducus the ogre. Characters were put into stock situations, as indicated by surviving titles: *Pappus the Farmer, Maccus the Maid, Maccus the Soldier, Bucco Adopted, The Twin*

---

[13] Gratwick (1982) 98–103 argues that Plautus similarly grafts a scene from Menander's *Sicyonians* into his *Poenulus*. Other examples of Plautine contamination have been suspected but remain unproved (e.g. *Miles Gloriosus*, with the supposedly extraneous duping of Sceledrus). Terence, *Andria* 18, implies Naevius, Plautus, and Ennius all practised *contaminatio*.

[14] Brown (1995) 678.

[15] There is no good reason to doubt this claim: it cannot derive solely from *Mostellaria* 770, where a joke about an Umbrian girl is made, for example.

[16] Only rarely does Roman comedy joke about accent or dialect. This was a feature of Greek New Comedy, as with the Doric doctor from Cos in Menander's *Aspis*.

Dossennuses (Manducus is not attested as a title character). There were also mythological titles that suggest the same approach applied to other familiar faces: *Hercules the Tax Collector*, for example.[17] A small performance troupe would present these plays and would travel to local festivals to offer entertainments.[18] Because the *Atellanae* at this time were improvised, no scripts can survive, and we cannot know how long a performance would have lasted, but a rough guess might be half an hour or more.[19] In an improvised performance, actors draw on stock routines that they have performed before to extend the narrative when it is working well, or to shorten it when the weather turns sour, for instance. It is a pre-literary form of entertainment.[20]

In the late 90s BC, however, a century after Plautus flourished, certain individuals began to script *Atellanae*. The literary *Atellana* of Pomponius and Novius in some ways continued the traditions of the unscripted genre, and from these authors many verse fragments survive, most of which are *sententiae*, gnomic maxims.[21] The titles seem to suggest continuity with the earlier improvised forms, and the plays continued to be performed in Oscan long after it would have ceased to be the native tongue of even part of the audience. Claims cannot extend beyond this, however, and Beare is right to treat the scripted and unscripted *Atellanae* in separate chapters.[22] Consequently, the extant fragments of the *fabulae Atellanae*, which postdate all extant Roman comedy, cannot tell us

---

[17] Surviving fragments and titles are collected and translated in Frassinetti (1967). See also Kamel (1951) and Lowe (1989).

[18] Professional Atellan troupes still existed in the time of Tiberius: Tacitus, *Annals* 4.14.

[19] Duckworth (1952) 11 guesses they were 'perhaps about three or four hundred verses' but bases this on the much later testimony that they were *exodia* ('afterpieces'), which would follow a main entertainment. While this was the custom for later, literate *Atellanae* (Livy 7.2.11; Cicero, *ad Fam.* 9.16.7; Suetonius, *Tiberius* 45, *Domitian* 10), it need not have been the case for the plays Plautus knew. Similar difficulties exist in determining the length of an improvised performance of the *commedia dell'arte*.

[20] 'Pre-literary' is not a completely satisfying term, but seems preferable to its rivals ('sub-literary'? 'illiterate'?). I use it to designate three aspects of the genre's social context. First, the term emphasises that the genre does not depend upon the literacy either of its practitioners or of its audience. Second, the term locates the genre in a later, transitional period where the literacy rates in Rome were beginning a substantial increase, which coincides to a large degree with the development of Latin literature. Third, the term avoids establishing a hierarchy among genres, with a presumed privileging of 'literate' or scripted entertainment.

[21] Frassinetti (1967).

[22] Beare (1964) 137–42, 143–8. Beare does raise the possibility that the literary stage was short-lived: 'We hear practically nothing of literary *Atellanae*, or of the authors of such *Atellanae* as were performed on stage. Perhaps after the time of Pomponius and Novius this type of farce had returned to its sub-literary, semi-improvised form' (238–9). I am not certain that the mechanism for such a reversion is effectively paralleled, but this remains a possibility. The point is that we cannot know.

anything certain about the improvised *Atellanae* (in terms of themes addressed, sententious style, metre used, or narrative development, etc.) because all of these features may have been imported into first-century literary *Atellanae* from Plautus and other Roman comic playwrights. The improvised *Atellanae* did affect the writers of the *palliata*, but we cannot use later fragments of literary *Atellanae* for evidence of this performance tradition any more helpfully than the *monostichoi* ('one-line maxims') of Menander can shed light on Greek New Comedy. So much uncertainty remains.

Plautus was also influenced by the Hellenistic mime, a genre that was performed throughout the Greek world, including Alexandria (where literary imitations of it were produced by Theocritus), Greece, and the Greek cities in Southern Italy and Sicily.[23] Literary forms of the genre survive in the work of Herodas, whose Greek mimiambs (mimes written in iambic verse, another distinctive Hellenistic conflation of genres, like the *palliatae*) were probably written in Alexandria in the 270s or 260s.[24] The term 'mime' was applied to a wide variety of performance styles in antiquity, none of which, it should be noted, coincide with the modern western tradition of unspeaking solo mime.

The information that survives about mime resists integration, and apparently aberrant facts need not refer to the same sort of performance. Mimes were variously performed in public, in theatres and amphitheatres, and at symposia. For at least part of their history, they had scripts, but apparently allowed for some degree of improvisation. Examples survive in prose, in verse, and in combination ('prosimetric' mimes). Performers of mime have scurrilous reputations, but could consort with the highest levels of Roman society: one of Sulla's companions was a mime (Plutarch, *Sulla* 36) and Augustus' reported last words compare his life to that of a mime (Suetonius, *Augustus* 99). No single performance context for the mime existed and the imprecise use of the term in antiquity means that certain knowledge will continue to elude us. A type of unmasked performance involving men and women is apparently suggested by the bulk of the evidence, and this may be thought to characterise the Greco-Roman mime for most sources.

Mime (like Roman satire) was fundamentally an urban genre. Its defining feature was that performances were unmasked. The actor's

---

[23] Surviving fragments and titles are collected and translated in Bonaria (1965) and Cunningham in Rusten and Cunningham (2002) 178–421. See also Reich (1903), Wüst (1932), Cunningham (1971) 3–11, Wiemken (1972), Benz, Stärk and Vogt-Spira (1995) 139–225.

[24] Cunningham in Rusten and Cunningham (2002) 179–283.

physical face, pulled into a variety of exaggerated expressions, imitated ('mimicked') a range of emotions and at times perhaps even multiple characters. A second defining feature was the sex of the performers, which (again, unlike other ancient performance genres) was not restricted only to men. At the end of the fifth century Sophron of Syracuse was writing 'women's mimes' and 'men's mimes'.[25] This may mean actors would only play their own sex: unlike the regular practice elsewhere of male actors playing both sexes, there is no clear indication this ever happened in mime, though references to mimes wearing a *ricinium* ('shawl') may suggest they did at times impersonate women in mourning.[26] Perhaps appropriate *mimêsis* of the other sex was thought to require masks. Inscriptions attest that the lead actor of a mime troupe could be called an *archimimus* ('head-mime', masculine) or an *archimima* (feminine).[27] Troupe size could vary considerably.[28] Venue was not fixed – mime did not need a formal stage – and opportunities for performance could come at formal and informal occasions for professional and non-professional performers. For male professional mimes, visual representations and literary descriptions regularly present the mime as bald (*calvus*) and barefoot (*planipes*; see Festus 342 L); there seem to have been no distinctive costumes used (*scholion* to Juvenal 3.177), despite references to a multi-coloured jacket (*centunculus*).

It seems likely that in at least some cases mimes wore tights that simulated nudity. For men, of course, this is a well-established Greek tradition reaching back to the days of Aristophanes with the padded bodysuits (*de rigueur* for comic actors) with a distended belly and buttocks, and an oversized phallus dangling between the actor's legs: vase illustrations demonstrate that the representation of naked women on the comic stage was also accomplished by 'genital tights' with artificially

---

[25] Cunningham in Rusten and Cunningham (2002) 287–351. Sophron's work may have been in prose (a scholion to Gregory of Nazianzus, *PCG* I, Sophron *testimonium* 19 KA, says it was rhythmical prose), or in a combination of verse and prose.

[26] For this and other terms, see Beare (1964) 369–70, nn. 16 and 17. Athenaeus, *Deipnosophistae* 620e and 621c–d, identifies 'Magode' and 'Lysiode' as specialists in playing the other sex; while the sung solos of these individuals could be lumped with 'mime' in casual speech, they are different from the type of performance discussed here.

[27] *Archimimus*: *CIL* 14.2408, and see Seneca, fr. 26 (Haase, p. 426), Suetonius, *Vespasian* 19.2, and in Greek, Plutarch, *Sulla* 36. *Archimima*: *CIL* 6.10106.

[28] Some mimes apparently performed individually. The 'adultery mime', a standard plot apparently, required at least three performers, and perhaps many more. The 'Charition mime' (to be discussed shortly) needed many more, though most have minor parts. An inscription from AD 169 records sixty names of members of a mime troupe (*CIL* 14.2408) though this may be better thought of as a guild than a troupe; see Nicoll (1931) 85–86.

represented pubic hair.[29] Given that adultery and other sexual themes
became synonymous with the mime in the Roman Empire, it seems the
simulated sex of the mime would be represented with this degree of
realism. The erotic component is present in descriptions of mime from
the very beginning: Xenophon, *Symposium* 9, concludes his Socratic
dinner party with a sexy mythological mime recounting the story of
Dionysus and Ariadne. Mime was indecent enough for Cato to leave a
performance so his fellow citizens could enjoy the show without his
moralising presence. When we are later told that mime actresses could
appear naked on stage (Valerius Maximus 2.10.8, *scholion* to Juvenal
6.250, Seneca, *Letter* 97.8, Lactantius, *Institutes* 1.20), this is likely what
was meant, though no doubt private performances may at times have
used real nudity. Augustine, *Confessions* 3.2, describes the simulated sex in
some sort of performance. In some circles, the fact that the emperor
Justinian's wife Theodora had been a successful mime actress was a
permanent blot on her character.

Not surprisingly, the adultery theme was common in mime narratives:
Ovid, *Tristia* 2.497–514, describes a mime featuring a wife, her husband,
and her lover, and this pattern is found illustrated and appropriated by
elegy and the Latin novel.[30] While the pattern of the 'adultery mime' has
been studied,[31] the desire to determine a single cast and number of scenes
for the mimic presentation of an adultery tale is misguided. The basic
narrative is familiar, but different performances will emphasise different
aspects of what is essentially the same basic situation, employing
different permutations of characters, different numbers of scenes, and
different settings. Some adultery mimes might have the lovers arranging a
rendezvous, some might have the lovers caught in the act, some might be
set at a subsequent trial, and some might present a combination of scenes.
All would be 'adultery mimes', yet individual examples would possess
enough variation and interest to ensure the ongoing presence of repeat
audiences from one show to the next.

While the genre clearly could appeal to a range of tastes and found
audiences at all levels of society, the plots possessed an earthiness
that could include vulgarity.[32] Narratives could appear disjointed and
episodic. Cicero describes the arbitrariness of the endings of mime plots
in his day: *mimi ergo est iam exitus, non fabulae; in quo cum clausula non*

---

[29] Marshall (2000a) 19–20.
[30] Apuleius, *Golden Ass* 9.5–6 and 10.2–12 both may be derived from the plots of popular mimes.
[31] See particularly Reynolds (1946), McKeown (1979), and Kehoe (1984).
[32] Rawson (1993).

invenitur, fugit aliquis e manibus, deinde scabilla concrepant, aulaeum tollitur ('This, then, is now the end of a mime, and not of a play, in which, when an ending cannot be found, someone flees from another's hands, then the clappers rattle and the curtain is pulled', *pro Caelio* 65). Mime could have an acrobatic component and musical accompaniment and songs may have featured (Petronius, *Satyricon* 35.6). Few properties were required, and nothing beyond a curtain for a set. Dogs could appear in mimes, as on the Elizabethan stage (Plutarch, *Moralia* 973e). Perhaps during a performance someone moved through the crowd collecting change, as continues to happen with street theatre and buskers today.[33]

It is very difficult to identify the degree of scriptedness of these per-formances, and perhaps it is safest to remain agnostic. As with the *Atel-lanae*, in the first century BC there seems to have been a move to make literary what had been improvised previously, and the names of Decimus Laberius (a Roman knight born 106 BC) and Publilius Syrus (a freedman from Syria) are given as those who first wrote Roman mimes. Macrobius, *Saturnalia* 2.7.1–10, describes a contest between these two authors of literary mimes, instigated by Julius Caesar. Ashamed at being asked to perform in his own work at a time when acting on stage made an indi-vidual *infamis* ('without political rights'), Decimus Laberius appeared on stage as a Syrian slave and exclaimed, *porro Quirites! libertatem perdimus* ('Arise, citizens! We lose our freedom!'), and later added *necesse est multos timeat quem multi timent* ('He whom many fear must fear many') – clear warnings to Caesar concerning abuse of power in the time of the civil war (as Seneca notes, *On Anger* 2.11.3). Caesar awarded victory to Publilius Syrus, but rewarded Laberius sufficiently to restore his political rights. This anecdote reveals much about the performance context of mimes in 46 BC: the competitive aspect, the presumption that normally Decimus would not act in his own mimes, his choice to appear in a costume that evokes his rival, and the insertion of politically motivated sentiments into an already scripted play. This last point suggests a blending of scripted and improvisational elements may have been an expected feature of lit-erary mime. We have other fragments of the mimes of Decimus Laberius and Publilius Syrus, and we might expect them to exist in the same relationship with previous Latin mimes as literary *Atellanae* do with improvised *Atellanae*. However, since mimes did possess an earlier literary form in Greek, perhaps the innovation of these men was to write mimes in Latin.

---

[33] Reich (1903) 540.

An incredibly valuable papyrus excavated at Oxyrhynchus in Egypt, *P. Oxy.* 413,[34] enriches the picture. One side (*verso*) presents an adultery mime, meant to be performed by an *archimima* and six or seven others (all in very minor roles, as seems to have been the norm).[35] While the dialogue is concentrated on the female lead, a lot of movement from the other characters is required. The mistress is in love with her slave Aesopus, who has a girlfriend; the plot turns to poisoning and several bodies lie on the ground before the papyrus breaks off. It falls into eight short scenes. The first seven consist of a single speech from the mistress. The final scene has her in dialogue with up to four other characters. It is very hard to imagine this work in performance, but it is possible, with other characters responding appropriately to the lines of the female lead and perhaps offering minor (unscripted?) vocal responses, to make sense of it. Further, a gap of more than forty lines at the beginning of the text means that the lost introductory material may have further clarified things.

The other side of the same papyrus (*recto*), written in a different hand and possibly dating as late as the second century AD, is even more exciting. Drawing on Euripides' tragedy *Iphigeneia among the Taurians* (written c. 413 BC), the *Charition* mime relates the rescue of a young girl from barbarian captors, who speak polysyllabic nonsense purporting to be an Indian dialect (the closest parallel for this scene in extant drama is the Punic spoken by Hanno in Plautus' *Poenulus*, 'The Little Carthaginian', which draws on the same sort of audience response).[36] The mime is prosimetric: lines 88–91 and 96–106 are verse; the rest is prose.[37] The text provides stage directions for music, percussion, and farting noises, which provides some indication of the tone. Nor is the debt to Euripides unique. Mime regularly invoked or depicted elevated cultural values, and we know of mime performances of the poetry of Ovid (*Tristia* 2.519–20) and Vergil (Macrobius, *Saturnalia* 5.17.4).

---

[34] Grenfell and Hunt (1903) 41–57, Cunningham in Rusten and Cunningham (2002) 376–401.

[35] Reference is made to mime actors *secundarum partium* ('of second parts'; see Horace, *Epistles* 1.18.10–14, Festus 438.22 L, and Cicero, *Divinatio in Q. Caecilium* 48), a term which is probably best thought of as meaning 'supporting actor' in a mime context.

[36] It does not matter for my purposes how authentic the Indian and Punic in these passages are. Certainly there are reasons to believe that the author has drawn on an actual understanding of the languages, but for the vast majority of the audience, we should not expect this degree of multilingualism.

[37] Mime therefore connects with other examples of prosimetricity, such as Seneca's *Apocolocyntosis*, Petronius' *Satyricon*, and *P. Oxy.* 3010. While these are generally treated under the rubric of ancient fiction or the novel, they all may have had a mimic performance tradition as well.

The relationship between these genres is, for the most part, agreed.[38] Yet most would accept the claim that 'there are scenes ... which Plautus has rewritten so thoroughly that a neat separation of his additions from original Greek material is impossible':[39] at times, the Greek source play may be unrecoverable, but this does not mean (as some have suggested) it was non-existent.[40] Plautus wanted his audience to think it was getting a Greek play, and the simplest way for him to do that would be to adapt a Greek play, rather than risk a claim about one's work ('this is a Greek play') that was falsifiable and produced no clear comic benefit.

It is possible to overstate Roman comedy's debts to Italian performance genres. Plautine verse is distinguished by its metrical variety, which necessarily attests to a musical variety. Aulus Gellius, *Attic Nights* 1.24.3, preserves an epigram that Varro from his *De poetis* ('On the Poets'), attributed to Plautus himself:

> *postquam est mortem aptus Plautus, Comoedia luget,*
> *scaena est deserta, dein Risus Ludus Iocusque*
> *et Numeri innumeri simul omnes conlacrimarunt*
>
> After the death of Plautus, Comedy mourned.
> The stage was bare. Then Laughter, Play, Jest,
> And countless Measures all cried together.

The *cantica mixtis modis* ('songs in various modes', a term evoking the *numeri innumeri* of the epigram) constitute a development of these Hellenistic Greek musical innovations.[41] The *Dis Exapatôn* fragment demonstrated that Plautus felt free to change the metre of his Greek originals, and add accompaniment to scenes or parts of scenes that had been unaccompanied in Greek.

Nevertheless, Plautus is not doing something unique to him, but is building on an established Greek Hellenistic performance tradition. Menander's comedies contained much less music than did Aristophanes'. The fragments suggest that only the first act break was signalled to any degree in the text, with a departing character calling attention to the arriving chorus, who in Menander are typically drunken youths (e.g. *Dyskolos* 230–32). A chorus (perhaps of five to seven) would arrive, sing a

[38] See, e.g., Gratwick (1993) 6–16, esp. 7.
[39] Lowe (1992) 174.
[40] See, e.g., Goldberg (1978) and Lefèvre, Stärk, and Vogt-Spira (1991). 'Demophilus,' for example, is unknown except for the reference to him at *Asinaria* 11.
[41] Leo (1897) was the first to discuss this connection.

song (μέλος χοροῦ, 'song of the chorus'), and leave. The manuscripts signal subsequent act divisions only with the word χοροῦ. This musical component may have been important to the original audience's experience of Greek comedy: there was an *aulos*-player who would provide music for short songs within the narrative or for festive scenes, as at the end of *Dyskolos*.[42] The metre for such scenes is the trochaic tetrameter;[43] generally, the verse of Menander was spoken and unaccompanied, written in the iambic trimeter standard for dramatic narrative.[44]

A change took place in the later performance of New Comedy. Gentili suggests that in Hellenistic times Greek drama was performed in excerpts, with iambic trimeters set to music[45] (indeed, a musical papyrus from the third century AD, *P. Oxy.* 3705, preserves a line of Menander written with four different musical settings). At some point, the metre that had been reserved for spoken verse could be accompanied, and, with as much certainty as we can ever expect to have, we can say they were sung.[46] The musical presence in Menander can be understated, and it seems likely that when the plays were re-performed (still in Greek, in the years following Menander's death) the sung component was actively increased.[47]

Further, Plautus' metrical variety exists within a larger context of Latin translation practice.[48] Literary production was still relatively new in Plautus' time, and the debts to Greece were always explicit in the first centuries of Latin literature. The fragments of Livius Andronicus, who in 240 BC staged a tragedy and a comedy at the *ludi Romani*, use both iambic and trochaic verse, a choice that coincides with the practice of Greek drama. More relevant for the study of Plautus, however, is Livius' translation of Homer's *Odyssey*, of which twenty-one verses survive, providing a gauge for 'acceptable' translation practice. Of interest are the

---

[42] The piper is referred to in the text of *Dyskolos* at lines 432–3, 880 and 910, as the *aulos*-player for the performance is integrated into the world of the characters.

[43] Dumont (1997) 47 n. 40.

[44] It has also been observed that Latin translations of Ennius diminished the lyric content that had been in Euripides; see Fraenkel (1960) 320–23, Dumont (1997) 45.

[45] Gentili (1979) 22–45, Huys (1993).

[46] Pöhlmann and West (2001) 185 provide an unparalleled alternative: 'If we had found a continuous piece of Menandrian dialogue with musical notation, we should have been obliged to believe it. What this papyrus offers, however, is something different. It seems possible that the intention was to illustrate different ways in which an actor might *speak* the verse, the musical notation being used in an attempt to describe speech intonations.' Not only does this posit a new use for musical notation, but it fails to account for why a single line would receive this treatment any better than the hypothesis that it was sung.

[47] Dumont (1997) 45–8. See Duckworth (1952) 376 and Dumont (1997) 46–7 for the influence of Hellenistic song on the music of Plautus.

[48] Weissinger (1940) 62 discusses some single-line examples of translations that have survived.

observable differences: gods and heroes are given local names (it is with Livius that the Latin 'Ulixes' for 'Odysseus' originates). Descriptions were simplified, or toned down, and Greek idioms were replaced with more straightforward local descriptions. The language was also set in a consciously exalted style. The metre used is surprising: Homer's dactylic hexameters are translated into saturnians. Saturnians are a distinctively Latin verse form; all later Latin verse is made to fit metres that were originally designed for Greek. Gnaeus Naevius also wrote both comedies and tragedies, and at one point Plautus in his drama refers to Naevius' imprisonment (*Miles Gloriosus* 210–12). Naevius also wrote epic, a seven-book poem on the First Punic War in saturnians. It is not until Quintus Ennius, in fact, writing in the decade after Plautus, that Latin epic begins to use the Greek hexameter for Latin verse, a practice which was to become the standard in Vergil and all subsequent Latin epic poets.

Whatever Plautus understood by the concept of 'Latin literature,' it included translations exhibiting localised vocabulary and new metrical forms that could be substituted for the Greek original. It is within this tradition of verse translation that we may localise several important features of Plautine style that might otherwise be attributed to another source: the use of Roman terms for parts of the Greek city (such as *forum*, found more than eighty times in Plautus' plays), characteristic of his boisterous exuberance of language; and the change of metre as spoken Greek iambic trimeters are recast as passages of recitative or song with musical accompaniment.

Even more shadowy performance genres may have had a significant impact on the developing *palliatae*: Fescennine verses,[49] *satura* ('satire'), whatever is properly meant by the term *phlyax* (Pollux' *Onomasticon* 9.149, Athenaeus 621f), the *hilarotragoediae* ('mock tragedies') of Rhinthon, Etruscan dancers at Rome, acrobats and wheel-dancers at symposia (Xenophon, *Symposium* 7), and solo singers, including Lysiodes and Magodes. Pantomime, the masked ballets of mythological scenes by unspeaking performers dancing to musical accompaniment, becomes very significant by the mid-first century AD, but seems to have existed in some form in the fifth century BC (Xenophon, *Symposium* 7). Other genres of stage drama existed in parallel with the *palliatae*: comedies set in Roman domestic contexts, the *fabulae togatae* ('plays in Roman dress'), which may or may not have been the same as *fabulae tabernariae* ('plays in

---

[49] Horace, *Epistles* 2.1.139–63, and see Duckworth (1952) 7–8, Beare (1964) 11–18. This may also be connected to the contest between Publilius Syrus and Decimus Laberius.

private houses'), in addition to *tragoediae* adapted from Greek myth (and often Greek drama) and plays on aspects of Roman history (*fabulae praetextae/praetextatae*, 'plays with a purple border').[50] All of these were fair game for a playwright seeking to create a hybrid performance style that would entertain all levels of Roman society.

This picture does not hold for Terence. What is seen as 'Plautine' style is in fact characteristic of the *palliatae* as a whole.[51] There exists a 'stylistic unity of the *comoedia palliata*', which Terence deliberately eschews. Within the more nuanced picture of Plautine literary debts, the radicalism of Terence's poetry shines through (see Fig. 1). Terence minimises collaborative effects, and instead seeks to Latinise Greek New Comedy directly. Indeed, it is not even the living performance tradition of Menander that Terence adopted, but the earlier, less ornamented version known from the book tradition. Even here, though, the practice of Latin translations before him, which is now a tradition that includes Plautus and his musical virtuosity, led Terence to change metres, to add scenes, and to add or expand musical accompaniment. For the most part, though, Terence successfully resists the traditions of the *palliatae* and in doing so establishes his own niche in the history of western theatre.

---

[50] See Beare (1964) 264–6 and Fantham (1989a). Genre categories are defined by the costume worn by the actors, and it is clear that class divisions were seen as a defining feature of the characters of serious and comic plays. *Praetexta* refers to the purple border on the Roman noble's toga.

[51] Wright (1974); see, e.g., 195: 'Above all, the critic must resist the temptation to judge Plautus by how well or how poorly he appears to *escape* the tradition. Such statements ... betray a serious lack of understanding of what Plautus is doing.' Compare Sheets (1983) 208, 'A rendering into Latin of Hellenistic New Comedy ought not to be thought the central goal of Plautus' comedic interests', and see 206.

CHAPTER I

The Experience of Roman Comedy

OPPORTUNITIES FOR PERFORMANCE

Romans enjoyed the *palliatae*. Adaptations of Greek drama constituted one of the principal forms of entertainment at the *ludi* ('games'). *Ludi* were public religious festivals that offered the only opportunity for dramatic performance in Rome.[1] Combining sacrifices and other religious practices[2] with public entertainments such as chariot events at the circus, *ludi* were the significant celebrations in the religious year of Rome. The evidence for the early history of the *ludi scaenici* ('theatrical shows') is confused,[3] but, for the period of Plautus' plays, the situation is relatively stable. There were four major festivals at which comedies could be presented, each administered by magistrates under the authority of the senate. The *ludi Romani*, administered by the curule aediles and held in September, were the first site of Roman literary performance: Livius Andronicus staged a tragedy and a comedy in 240 BC.[4] In 214 the number of days for *ludi scaenici* was fixed at four.[5] The *ludi Plebeii*, administered by the plebeian aediles and held in November, had at least three days for performance.[6] It was here that *Stichus* was performed in 200.[7] The *ludi Apollinares*, administered by the *praetor urbanus* and held in July, were first celebrated in 212 and became annual in 208:[8] they were the first of a wave of new festivals inaugurated during the Second Punic War, reflecting both an increased awareness of the societal value served by *ludi* and a genuine sense that there were theological benefits to be realised from such celebrations. They offered at least two days for *ludi scaenici*.

---

[1] Taylor (1937), Duckworth (1952) 76–9, Beare (1964) 162–3.
[2] Probably involving processions: see Taylor (1935) 127–8, Hanson (1959) 81–6.
[3] Contrast Bernstein (1998) with e.g. Wiseman (1995) 129–44.
[4] Cicero, *Brutus* 72, Cassiodorus *Chronicle* p. 128M. Livy 1.35.9, 4.27.1, etc., calls the games *magni*, and at 6.42.12 he calls them *maximi*.
[5] Livy 24.43.7.   [6] Taylor (1937) 288.   [7] *Stichus, didascalia.*
[8] Cicero, *Brutus* 78, assumes these were *ludi scaenici*.

The *ludi Megalenses*, administered by the curule aediles and held in early April, were first celebrated in 204 and were made annual by 194, when for the first time *ludi scaenici* were introduced.[9] The evidence for the number of performance days at this festival is ambiguous, but there were at least two and may have been as many as six, the number it would later have in the empire.[10] It was here that *Pseudolus* was performed in 191, *Hecyra* in its initial appearance in 165, and, likely, *Trinummus* at some uncertain date.[11]

The months in which festivals were celebrated can be misleading. At this time, the Romans used a 355-day year, and therefore required regular intercalations to match the actual seasons. After a period of considerable laxity, efforts to fix the calendar were advanced by a *lex de intercalando* in 191, by which time the calendar was four months ahead of the sun.[12] The April of the *ludi Megalenses* was in Plautus' time experiencing short, cold, wet days typical of December weather; the *ludi Apollinares* were held in March by modern reckoning; the *ludi Romani* were in practice a spring festival celebrated in May, and the *ludi plebeii* were celebrated in the heat of July.

As for other festivals, there is no evidence that the Floralia (the *ludi Florales*, instituted in 238 and made annual in 173) ever included plays, though mime performances did take place. Similarly, while there were seven days for dramatic performances at the *ludi Cereales* by the time of Augustus, there is no evidence for *ludi scaenici* there during the republic.[13] Thus, for the first half of Plautus' career, there were at least nine performance days at three festivals for *ludi scaenici*, and this increased to perhaps fifteen performance days at four festivals in 194. This growth coincides with an increased cosmopolitan sophistication and awareness of Greek drama among many Roman men associated with their military experience in South Italy, Sicily, and Greece.

It is unlikely that these festivals alone could support many theatrical troupes. There were, however, other opportunities to perform in Rome. These were of four types. The first are *ludi magni* ('great games'), which

---

[9] Livy 29.14.14, 34.54.3. For the introduction of the Magna Mater (Cybele) to Rome, see Gruen (1990) 5–33.

[10] Livy 34.54.3, Taylor (1937) 289–90, Duckworth (1952) 77. The dedication of the temple took place during the celebration of the *ludi Megalenses* in 191.

[11] *Pseudolus, didascalia*; *Trinummus* 990 refers to *novi aediles*, a reference that only makes sense at a spring festival, since the aediles' term of office began on 15 March. See Taylor (1937) 89–91, Duckworth (1952) 77, Slater (2000) 176.

[12] Macrobius 1.13.21. See Briscoe (1981) 17–26, Gratwick (1982) 81, Goldberg (1998) 15. It was still two and a half months out in 168.

[13] Taylor (1937) 289 believes 'there were probably at least two days in the theatre', but this is a guess.

were irregular and not held annually.[14] Held five or ten years following a vow made by a magistrate, these *ludi* were likely theatrical, especially if the length of ten days (mentioned in vows made in 191 and 172[15]) was typical. Second, there were other *ludi votivi* ('votive games'), beginning with those celebrated by Scipio in 205.[16] In this category too may be placed the *ludi Iuventatis*, which, despite Cicero's confusion concerning their date, were theatrical.[17] Plays may have been common at the *ludi* associated with the dedication of other temples, too.[18] Third, there were private *ludi*, and in particular *ludi funebres* ('funeral games'). Four days of *ludi scaenici* were held during the funeral of T. Quinctius Flamininus in 174,[19] and two of Terence's plays were performed at the *ludi funebres* of L. Aemilius Paullus in 160 (this is the only indication we have of a troupe performing more than one play at a given festival, and it is significant that one of them is a revival).[20]

Finally, the institution of *instauratio* complicates the matter further. *Instauratio* was a religious practice, which provided that the day of a given festival would be repeated if a defect in ritual was noticed. The relationship between the entertainments and the more traditionally conceived religious elements of the *ludi* are here bound tightest. Servius describes an instance of *instauratio* avoided, in 211, at the first *ludi Apollinares*:

denique cum ludi circenses Apollini celebrarentur et Hannibal nuntiatus esset circa portam Collinam urbi ingruere, omnes raptis armis concurrunt. reversi postea cum piaculum formidarent, invenerunt saltantem in circo senem quendam. qui cum interrogatus dixisset se non interupisse saltationem, dictum est hoc proverbium 'salva res est, saltat senex'.

Finally, when the circus games for Apollo were being celebrated and Hannibal had been announced to be attacking the city near the Colline gate, everyone grabbed their weapons and ran there. Later, when they returned and were concerned about the necessary sacrifice, they found a certain old man dancing in the circus. When asked, he told them he had not stopped dancing, and so the proverb goes: 'All is well, the old man is dancing.'[21]

---

[14] Taylor (1937) 296–7. Such games were held in 217 and 207 (Livy 27.33.8), in 203 (Livy 30.27.12), and 194 (Livy 34.44.6, where he calls them *ludi Romani votivi*).

[15] Livy 36.2.2–5, 42.28.8.

[16] Taylor (1937) 297–98. Such games were held in 205 (Livy 28.38.14, 28.45.12), in 200 (Livy 31.49.4), in 191 (Livy 36.36.1–2), and in 186 (Livy 39.22.1–3, 8–10, where the presence of *artifices ex Graecia* and *ex Asia* implies the usual presence of local theatre troupes).

[17] Cicero, *Brutus* 73.   [18] Taylor (1937) 298.   [19] Livy 41.28.11.

[20] *Ludi scaenici* are not explicitly attested in every account of *ludi funebres* (Livy 23.30.15, 28.21.10, 31.50.4, 39.46.2), and we cannot assume their existence, despite Taylor (1937) 299–300. Nevertheless, plays were performed at some *ludi funebres*.

[21] Servius, *ad Aeneidis* 8.110. See also Taylor (1937) 294–5 and n. 26 citing Festus 436–8 L.

While the connection with *instauratio* is not explicit (though it is when Cicero alludes to the story at *de Haruspicum Responso* 23), the theological benefits resulting from the successful continuation of the celebrations are clear. Because the old man (or a mime imitating an old man?) had not stopped his performance, the need for the expiation that the Romans had dreaded (*piaculum formidarent*) was averted.[22] These stories contrast with the more usual accounts of *instaurationes*, which make one almost suspect *instaurationes* were used as a ploy to extend the length of a dramatic run.[23] Livy documents the large number of *instaurationes* between 216 and 179 leading to additional dramatic performances, which by Taylor's calculations added an average of five performance days per year. Livy only records *instaurationes* at the *ludi Romani* and *ludi Plebeii*, but an *instauratio* could likely be declared at other public *ludi* as well, and Livy may simply be omitting references to lesser festivals.[24]

When *instauratio* was invoked, it is unlikely to have benefited the acting troupe itself. Certainly, the audience had another chance to see the show, but it is unlikely the troupe would receive additional payment for the performance: the contract would have been for the festival, and the voided day would be excluded. If we remove the religious associations of the performance, we can identify plausible motivations for the audience to seek *instauratio*, and perhaps for the magistrates to do so as well (e.g. to increase returns on their investment, and to demonstrate to the people their authority and that of the senate). But to suggest that the magistrates would deliberately spoil an aspect of their own festival overlooks both the religious dynamic and their personal investment (of both finances and prestige). The *ludi* were religious, and it does them a disservice to minimise this, but the spirit of their celebration would no doubt appear to us to be very secular. Even if the religious aspect of the *ludi* were relaxed somewhat, default public morality would expect and support a conservative, pious position.

While the combined benefits of these additional factors cannot be fully assessed, a total of twenty-five to thirty performance days in Rome

---

[22] Livy 27.23.5–7 shows it was not foolish to associate an epidemic with the failure to hold *ludi*. The ability to maintain one's culture during a military attack no doubt provided a great psychological boost; compare Glenn Miller and his orchestra playing through the bombings in London in the summer of 1944.

[23] See Duckworth (1952) 78; Beacham (1991) 158–9. Pansiéri (1997) 144 ties *Miles Gloriosus* to the year 205 because of the large number of *instaurationes*.

[24] A catalogue of Livy's *instaurationes* can be found at Cohee (1994) 466–8.

annually seems to be a fair guess, and more would not surprise. If these did not offer enough to sustain a troupe, there was always the possibility of travelling to other cities – Diodorus Siculus 37.12 has an Italian actor claiming never to have worked in Rome – or to subcontract oneself for a different kind of performance (as seems to be envisaged by the joke at *Rudens* 535). Such subcontracting need not involve the whole troupe: the troupe's *tibicen* ('piper') could probably secure additional contracts throughout the year. However, even thinking in terms of 'twenty-five to thirty performance days' is to consider the matter from the perspective of the audience. In many ways a more important figure is the number of different plays a troupe would be expected to mount, and the number of plays the magistrates would expect from a successful troupe over the course of a year. Here, too, is guesswork, but thinking in terms of three or four fixed contracts a year, with possibly one to three more for *ludi votivi* or *ludi funebres*, provides a reasonable approximation of the opportunities a successful troupe could be given for dramatic performances in Rome. There will not be many troupes able to flourish under such conditions, but a few could, particularly if these same troupes also provided entertainments for smaller cities in Latium and Campania, which also had flourishing theatrical cultures.

THE BUSINESS OF COMEDY

The administration of the *ludi* was one of the chief responsibilities of certain magistrates, and by this time the aedileship at least was open to patricians and plebeians. There was no admission charge for the plays, and no tickets: the audience was gathered from the assembled festival crowd and had no direct financial investment in the performance. Comedy was, however, a business, and given the limited number of contracts available from a relatively fixed set of funds (all entertainments would come from the same budget, which was fixed for each festival by the senate), each troupe was obliged to seek as many profitable contracts in a year as it could. There is certainly a political dimension to this: the senate controls funds, and, since it was responsible for the regular re-building of the temporary performance spaces, it also exerted ultimate control over artistic matters.[25] But the *ludi* did not provide a venue for overt political

---

[25] Gruen (1992) 209–10.

campaigning, due perhaps to the social inversion that characterised these events.[26] Consequently, an economic perspective proves more informative.

The economic pressures were different for the different parties involved. The magistrates were concerned to offer a full selection of entertainments, of great variety. It is suspected that they would typically supplement the state allowance for the *ludi* from their private funds, since 'It was a basic tenet of ancient political theory that political influence could be gained or asserted by the provision of spectacles.'[27] In doing so, their cash investment was used to create a different type of capital that nevertheless could prove just as valuable for an ambitious politician.[28] For some playwrights, those not actively involved in the play's production, the number of performance days is of little consequence. A manuscript is sold, and with it came the rights to produce the play. Perhaps a playwright could think in terms of a new play for each festival. Here perhaps lies the reason for the emphasis on new plays in the prologues of Terence (e.g. *Adelphoe* 12), which seem to concern Plautus less – probably, this is because Plautus was part of his troupe.

Still, the language for this dimension of economic activity requires examination. Ovid indicates that in his day there was money to be made: *scaena est lucrosa poetae,* | *tantaque non parvo crimina praetor emit* (Ovid, *Tristia* 2.507–8: 'The stage is profitable for the poet, and the praetor does not buy these immoralities cheaply').[29] When we are told Plautus sold his comedies (*fabulas solitus … vendere*),[30] is it a performance that is sold, or merely the manuscript? Confusion has existed because of an apparent inconsistency in the prologues of Terence. *Eunuchus* 20 refers to a time *postquam aediles emerunt* ('after the aediles bought [the play]'). Nevertheless, Ambivius Turpio, speaking the second prologue to *Hecyra* (lines 9–57), claims the plays were 'purchased at my own expense' (57: *pretio emptas meo*).[31]

---

[26] Gruen (1992) 188–93. Segal (1987) discusses the social inversion of Roman comedy.

[27] Potter (1999) 320.

[28] For the competitive environment at this level, compare the accounts of Millar (1984) 12 and Gruen (1992) 190. Wilson (2000) explores this dynamic among Athenian *chorêgoi*.

[29] We may observe in passing that Ovid specifies the praetor, which points to the *ludi Apollinares*, games which certainly by the Augustan period were celebrated with six days of *ludi scaenici*. They therefore likely represented theatrical contracts of considerable expense.

[30] Jerome, *Chronicle ann. Abr.* 1817; and see Aulus Gellius 3.3.14. It is this language that lies behind Horace's prejudice at *Epistles* 2.1.170–76. Ennius too *fabulas vendavit* (Jerome, *Chronicle ann. Abr.* 1863/64: 'sold his plays'). See Lebek (1996) 31–2.

[31] Different views are given by Carney (1963) 35 n. 57, and Lebek (1996) 32–3, but it will be clear that I find these less convincing. Lebek (1996) 32 associates this disruption with *instauratio*, but without reason. The confusion comes from equating Terence the playwright with the troupe and the actor delivering the prologue in particular. It is the troupe's perspective that is being represented in the prologue. Nowhere is this clearer than in the rival accounts of sums involved, none of which, I

The aediles have purchased the play (that is, a performance of the play) from this troupe. In anticipation of this, Ambivius Turpio has purchased the play (that is, the manuscript from which he can begin rehearsals) from the playwright, because Terence, and Caecilius before him, are not members of the troupe. This represents an initial outlay that Turpio hopes will be offset by the monies gained through the production, and is what he stands to lose.[32] Turpio seems to have made a career of fostering young playwrights and bringing their work to the stage. However, a generation earlier, when the opportunities for performance were considerably fewer, there would be a strong incentive to have a playwright on the payroll as a sharer in the production, rather than as an independent agent requiring an initial financial outlay.

It is probably anachronistic to think of Turpio purchasing production rights along with the manuscript. While today's society is very concerned with abstract rights of intellectual property, the pressures on a performing troupe in the early second century would probably have been much more pedestrian. Without at least one copy of 'the script' (itself a problematical concept) a new play cannot be staged. It is this technical restriction in a world without a printing press that ties ownership of the manuscript with rights of production, and we shall see ways this control could be maintained. After an initial performance, it becomes less easy to control a script, which could lead to unauthorised productions.

A consequence of this financial dimension is that the plays themselves must be flexible in their construction. Since a functioning troupe will be regularly looking forward to future bookings, a playwright in all likelihood does not know at which festival a given play will be produced. If for whatever reason a new play is not contracted at a given festival, work on the play will nevertheless have begun. We cannot know what the lead-in time for a production was at every occasion, but the troupe has an incentive to be ready to perform a new play with minimal time for rehearsals. The *ludi Megalenses* provides the clearest timetable. Since

---

suspect, may be fully trusted. Turpio does not ask for a high price from the magistrates (*Hecyra* 49, a line written by Terence), but Suetonius, *de Poetis* ('Terence' 3), says it was the highest price ever paid for a comedy. Donatus (*ad Eunuchum praefatio* 6, Wessner (1902–8) vol. I: 266) believed this represents Terence's take – 8,000 denarii = 32,000 HS, as Wessner (1902–8) notes. Suetonius is however discussing the performance, and this price may be seen to represent the troupe's price from the aediles; Gilula (1985–8) 77 and n. 11 hints at this possibility. *Hecyra* 49 is therefore disingenuous, but it may be that the audience was not concerned with the backroom finances, and such a pose of modesty was considered customary or at least polite.

[32] The *Eunuchus* prologue distinguishes the *poeta* in lines 3 and 28, which shows that the speaker represented is not Terence but a member of the troupe; see *Andria* 1, *Heauton Timoroumenos* 2, *Phormio* 1, *Hecyra* 13, *Adelphoe* 1.

aediles began their term of office on 15 March it is implausible that contracts could be drawn before that date. Even assuming this was the first matter addressed by the new magistrates, there is still less than three weeks' time before the *ludi scaenici* at the *Megalenses*. This is less time than an Elizabethan theatre company would have spent in rehearsal,[33] and clearly we must assume that at least the writing of the play is done in anticipation of a contract; probably some of the rehearsals are as well. *Eunuchus* 20–26 seems to envisage some sort of preliminary performance, after the play has been purchased, but before the festival.[34] Whatever the situation, the magistrates were present, as somehow was Terence's enemy Luscius Lanuvinus,[35] whose denunciation was intended to invalidate the dramatic contract. Luscius' motivations remain mysterious, but it may be that his play (or his troupe) had been overlooked by the magistrates selecting plays for the festival. Plays cannot be venue-specific, and, since the celebrations for the different *ludi* were held in different locations, the system required a fair degree of flexibility. With only a minimum effort, each performance site would in the normal course of events be able to house most plays.

Only two extant plays preclude a generic performance space. The Choragus at *Curculio* 462–84 seems to require performance in the *forum Romanum*. The play is, however, easily adaptable. *Curculio* 462–84 could be replaced by another context-specific speech as the venue changed (or, indeed, it could be simply omitted, though that would entail the loss of a powerful scene).[36] The speech as it exists happens to describe one location, but that does not mean that the play was never performed elsewhere, or that another speech never was delivered at this point in the play. The other context-specific play is *Amphitruo*, which requires the actors to stand on the roof of the stage building. Line 1008 is explicit, as Mercurius says he will ascend *in tectum* ('onto the roof') and fragments IV and V make reference to dropping things *in caput* ('onto [Amphitruo's] head'). No other comedy has this requirement.

The troupe is not the only professional group hired by the magistrates. There are other entertainers, of various types. Contracts could be issued for performances of other theatrical genres. Further, seventy-four

---

[33] Potter (1999) 270 discusses some first-century BC occasions where the rehearsal time was as short as a week, but these are not for new plays.

[34] Could *occeptast agi* (*Eunuchus* 22) refer to the beginning of the rehearsal period?

[35] See Duckworth (1952) 62–5, Garton (1972) 41–72, and J. Wright (1974) 78–9.

[36] In my production of *Curculio*, the speech was re-written to accommodate known haunts of students at the university campus where the play was performed.

gladiators fought at the *ludi funebres* of Flamininus in 174 (Livy 41.28.11), and, in other contexts, we hear of events such as chariot races, mimes, Atellan farces, acrobats, boxers, tightrope walkers, and dancing bears.[37] Some of these may not have been paid by the festival, but would be busking, relying on the goodwill of citizens enjoying the atmosphere of the games. Other indirect employment may well have come from food vendors and the like, and we may imagine that much of this secondary activity is focused around the forum, even when the principal entertainment was held elsewhere.

We cannot be certain about the nature of timetabling events, but there is some indication that principal entertainments were presented serially and not simultaneously.[38] The prologues to the second and third performances of Terence's *Hecyra* (lines 1–8, 9–57) provide the best test case.[39] In 165, *Hecyra* was performed at the *ludi Megalenses*. In 160, it was presented at the *ludi funebres* of Aemilius Paullus along with *Adelphoe*. Because both of these performances had been interrupted, Terence felt he could still describe his play as new later that same year, when the play was mounted at the *ludi Romani* (and presumably met its deserved success). The prologue claims audience noise was the problem with the first two performances (*Hecyra* 29–30), in both cases because of rival entertainments.[40] The failure at the *ludi funebres* of Paullus is straightforward (lines 39–42):

quom interea rumor venit datum iri gladiatores, populus convolat, tumultuantur, clamant, pugnant de loco. ego interea meum non potui tutari locum.

But then a rumour arose that there was going to be a gladiatorial show: crowds rushed in, with much confusion, shouting, and fighting for places, and in these circumstances I couldn't preserve my place.[41]

---

[37] For bears, see Horace, *Epistles* 2.1.185–6, and Macrobius 2.7.12–16; for gladiators in the forum, see Valerius Maximus, *Memorabilia* 2.4.7, Livy 23.30.15 and 39–46. *P. Oxy.* 2707, a sixth-century AD circus programme, includes singing tightrope walkers among the entertainments, and Suetonius, *Galba* 6.1, mentions tightrope-walking elephants; for other performers of 'minor' arts, see Potter (1999) 276.

[38] Duckworth (1952) 81–2 and 173 and Beare (1964) 161 argue for simultaneous performances; Gilula (1978) for serial performances.

[39] See Gilula (1978), (1981), and Sandbach (1982).

[40] We cannot of course know the real reasons for the play's lack of success, which need not be what we are told. Duckworth (1952) 378 n. 41 suggests 'various other factors also were responsible for the rejection of this play by the spectators, e.g., its unusually serious theme and Terence's unconventional treatment of plot and character'.

[41] Text and translation, Barsby (2001) vol. II: 150–51.

As Donatus correctly recognised,[42] *Hecyra* and the gladiatorial combat shared a venue, and the actors felt compelled to leave the stage when those expecting the next event would not listen to the play.[43] The celebration of Anicius' triumph in 167 provides another example of a performance degenerating because of rival entertainments. In this case, musicians began an impromptu mock battle, and were joined by dancers and boxers.[44]

Less clear are the reasons provided for the initial failure of *Hecyra*. The first prologue relates how *ita populus studio stupidus in funambulo | animum occuparat* ('the audience took a foolish fancy to a tightrope walker who claimed their attention', lines 4–5).[45] A fuller account is provided in the second prologue (lines 33–36):

> *quom primum eam agere coepi, pugilum gloria*
> *(funambuli eodem accessit expectatio),*
> *comitum conventus, strepitus, clamor mulierum*
> *fecere ut ante tempus exirem foras.*

The first time I tried to perform the play, I was forced off the stage early; there was talk of boxers – and added to that the promise of a tightrope walker – crowds of supporters, general uproar, and women screaming.[46]

Two rival entertainments interfered with Terence's play. The praise of boxers (*pugilum gloria*) need not mean that they were next on the bill as the gladiators would be in 160, though this remains possible. The audience could be discussing boxers who had performed earlier that day (in the same performance venue, or at another) or indeed at some other time. Gilula insists that the promise of the tightrope walker (*funambuli ... expectatio*) means this performance was next,[47] but this is not a necessary conclusion. Assuming the two accounts are both honestly representing

---

[42] Donatus, *ad Hecyra* 39 (Wessner (1902–8) II: 200): *hoc abhorret a nostra consuetudine, verumtamen apud antiquos gladiatores in theatro spectabantur* ('This is inconsistent with our custom, nevertheless in olden times gladiators were seen in the theatre'). This position will be refined below.

[43] This further suggests *Adelphoe* was not presented on the same day back-to-back as *Hecyra* as a 'double bill' at the *ludi funebres*, but instead took place at a different time, with the two plays as it were 'in repertory'. This inference is based on the prologue's silence: we may presume that the prologue would mention the successful performance of another of the author's plays immediately preceding *Hecyra*, and it could not have followed immediately, since it is clear that gladiators had been scheduled.

[44] Polybius 30.22, quoted by Athenaeus 615b–d.

[45] Text and translation, Barsby (2001) vol. II: 148–9.

[46] Text and translation, Barsby (2001) vol. II: 150–51.

[47] Gilula (1978) and see Gilula (1981), and Sandbach (1982).

the event, Gilula's hypothesis would mean the distraction (line 4) occurred as he was setting up in the venue where Terence was performing (or that the rope was set up before Terence's play, which seems unlikely if the magistrates were not actively trying to sabotage the performance). It is equally possible that some of the audience could see the *funambulus* performing elsewhere, and that the *expectatio* accompanied an intention to move to that location. The actors left the stage because of the noise and possibly a departing crowd. Regardless, the *Hecyra* prologues demonstrate certainly that gladiators and actors could perform in the same venue (a 'main stage' location) and that perhaps secondary venues existed and secondary types of performance could occur in parallel with main stage attractions.

Also employed were other individuals essential to the smooth running of the games. Indeed, there was a whole section of the urban economy that would cater specifically to those individuals celebrating the *ludi*, the existence of many of whom cannot be recovered.[48] Among these professionals are at least two people specifically concerned with the *ludi scaenici*: the *choragus* and the *praeco*. The Athenian *chorêgos* provided the financial resources for the production of choruses, both dramatic and non-dramatic (dithyrambic). He was, in modern theatre parlance, the producer.[49] In the Roman republic, the Latinised form *choragus* had assumed a very different meaning.

Plautus makes two references to the *choragus*, and at *Curculio* 462–84 introduces one as a character. At *Persa* 159–60, Saturio seeks a source for his daughter's disguise:

SAT.   πόθεν ornamenta?

TOX.   abs chorago sumito;
        dare debet: praebenda aediles locaverunt.

SAT.   Whence the costume?

TOX.   I got them from the *choragus*.
        He has to give them: the aediles hired him to provide!

Toxilus here makes a metatheatrical joke about the backstage reality of a Roman performance, and this brief mention provides sufficient data to suggest that 'the aediles ... defrayed the production's extra costs separately and paid the supplier of these extras directly, and this on top of

---

[48] Potter (1999) 293 describes the great many types of 'hidden' professionals involved in the chariot races in Rome.
[49] The *chorêgia* is discussed in detail by Wilson (2000).

the payment made to the troupe and the poet'.[50] Similarly, at *Trinummus* 858, the *sycophanta* claims of his employer, *ipse ornamenta a chorago haec sumpsit suo periculo* ('he himself got the costume from the *choragus*, at his own risk'). *Suo periculo* suggests that the costumes are rented and that a deposit has been paid against their return, and this is confirmed by the *choragus* in *Curculio*, when he refers to *ornamenta quae locavi* (464: 'the costumes I rented'). Gilula argues that the *choragus* 'belongs to the off-stage fictional setting of *Trinummus*',[51] i.e. that the reference to the *choragus* maintains the dramatic stage world and is not metatheatrical.[52] Rather, this is an entirely typical Plautine blurring of the play's frame of reference, and that any reference to the *choragus* will be understood in the most immediate sense for the Roman audience, the theatrical context.[53]

The *choragus* therefore provides *ornamenta* ('costumes'), which are among the things that may be classified as *choragium*.[54] When it is remembered that in Elizabethan theatre, the costs of costumes and their maintenance was the major expense for a permanent company, the presence of such a professional could greatly enhance the possibility for spectacle for an itinerant troupe. The *choragus* was a professional, no doubt working with a group of employees, and seems to have had contracts both with the aediles as well as with individual performers (it may be that with the performers, only a deposit was required).[55] It is possible in any case that the *choragus'* responsibilities do not end with this. The magistrates had to hire someone to build the stage building itself in the days before the festival. This too may have been the responsibility of

[50] Gilula (1996) 482, with discussion at 481–2.

[51] Gilula (1996) 480, with discussion at 480–81. The claim seems to be contradicted, however, on 482. Similarly, in *Pseudolus* 1184–5 when Simo and Ballio tease Harpax, believing him to be someone claiming to be Harpax, they ask the cost of his cloak (*chlamys*) and blade (*machaera*). I take this to be a metatheatrical reference to the backstage presence of the *choragus*.

[52] Perhaps Gilula believes this because the *Curculio* Choragus says he dealt with Phaedromus, the character, rather than the actor; *Curculio* 467–8. My reading would suggest that Plautus is here deliberately blurring the theatrical reality with the fictional dramatic world.

[53] This also shows that the *choragus* is not normally considered to be part of the troupe (i.e. 'the stage manager' *vel sim.*) – though obviously this is a troupe member playing the role. This seems to be the assumption of Donatus' obscure comment *ad Eunuchus* 967, *choragi est administratio, ut opportune in proscaenium* ('the *choragus* is the management, so that the *proscaenium* runs smoothly', Wessner (1902–8) vol. I: 471), though perhaps the meaning had changed since Plautus' day.

[54] Festus, *Gloss. Lat.* 45 L defines *choragium* as *instrumentum scaenarum* ('stage apparatus'). There is no need to assume that the *choragus* is the play's director, or is the stage manager, as is sometimes claimed, following Weinberger (1892) 127; see Gilula (1996) 484 n. 12. Indeed, that he is contracted separately makes this fundamentally implausible.

[55] In this sense he is exactly like his Hellenistic Greek counterpart, the *himatiomisthês*. Sifakis (1967) 81–2 provides the sources for both types of financial arrangements, but does not consider that both might be operating at once.

the *choragus* and his team, and would then constitute his principal obligation to the aediles, and leave him free to make separate contracts with the performers for *ornamenta*. *Captivi* 61–2 demonstrate that the *choragium* of a comedy is different from that of a tragedy, and that the tragic *choragium* allows battles to be presented on stage but the comic one does not.[56] Gilula argues that *choragium* must include the set, interpreting Festus' definition in the broadest possible way.[57] This is a possible but not a necessary conclusion, and it could be that *choragium* and *ornamenta* are synonyms, both meaning costumes. Regardless, someone is building a set, and the set will be used by a variety of troupes, performing a variety of plays (*Menaechmi* 72–6):

> *haec urbs Epidamnus est, dum haec agitur fabula;*
> *quando alia agetur, aliud fiet oppidum.*
> *sicut familiae quoque solent mutarier:*
> *modo hic habitat leno, modo adulescens, modo senex,*
> *pauper, medicus,*[58] *rex, parasitus, hariolus.*[59]

> This city is Epidamnus, while this play is acted.
> When another is acted, it will become another town.
> Households, too, are typically changed the same way:
> Now a pimp lives here, now a young man, now an old man,
> Poor man, doctor, king, parasite, seer.

While all of the figures listed in line 75 are from comedy, at least some of those listed in line 76 point to figures more often found on a tragic stage. If this passage then is properly interpreted (that the same set building is used for all types of play), then it follows that *Captivi* 61–2 shows that *choragium* and *ornamenta* are essentially synonymous, with *choragium* perhaps being used more broadly to include stage properties.

Rather than undergoing this expense at each festival, the creation of a permanent theatre was contemplated from time to time throughout the second century. Livy 40.51.3 records a contract being let for the construction of a theatre and stage at the *ludi Apollinares* in 179.[60] These

---

[56] Vitruvius 5.6.9 describes three different kinds of stages, for tragedy, for comedy, and for satyr drama; perhaps this is what he means.

[57] Gilula (1996) 487, and see 479–80, 484–7.

[58] I suggest *medicus* ('doctor') in place of *mendicus* ('liar'): the word then describes a function in society like the rest of the words in the line, rather than a character trait. A *medicus* appears later in *Menaechmi* as a character, and Plautus has a fragmentary play called *Parasitus Medicus* ('Dr. Feedme'). See also *Rudens* 1304–06 where the wordplay is explicit.

[59] Gratwick (1993) transposes these lines from the end of the prologue to follow line 10, which removes the need for a lacuna of a line or two, which otherwise is likely.

[60] Livy refers to *theatrum et proscaenium ad Apollinis*, and see 41.27.5 for the next attempt in 174.

theatres were always to be wooden constructions (a permanent theatre need not be stone; see Vitruvius 5.5.7); nor is it accidental that the initiative in 179 came during a festival controlled by the praetors, where more elevated political reputations were at stake.

Arising from this was the issue of rehearsal. While we cannot know how long a play would be rehearsed (though, given the regular festival timetable, I expect it was typically only a few weeks), it is improbable there would be opportunity for rehearsals *in situ* – all preparations would take place at other locations, in contexts that will not necessarily bear any resemblance to the final performance space, since (at least in one sense) the venue did not yet exist.[61] There is no evidence concerning the nature of actors' scripts for republican Rome, but a later papyrus and some reasonable inferences drawn from it point to further uncertainty and need for flexibility. *P. Oxy.* 4546 is the remains of a first-century actor's script found in Roman Egypt.[62] The actor played Admetus in Euripides' *Alcestis*. So much about this performance remains obscure to us, but it is clear that the actor had been given a 'part' – only his lines were written down (arguably like the role of the mistress in most of the adultery mime, *P. Oxy.* 413 *verso*), with perhaps a mark to indicate speech divisions. Lacking even his cue lines, this actor apparently learned the lines of Admetus from this text, and worked out the performance dynamics in rehearsal. We do not know that this was the rehearsal technique employed by Plautus' troupe, but it is a good bet that it was. Writing out any lines would constitute an investment of both time and resources for the troupe, and again we can see the pressure to economise. When a troupe bought a play, as did Ambivius Turpio's troupe from Terence, it would have received a single copy from the playwright. Copying parts rather than full scripts streamlines the rehearsal process, allowing a quicker dispersal of lines to the actors, and further provides a safeguard against the unlawful selling of the troupe's investment.[63] It also represents

---

[61] My actors experienced the same situation as they prepared for the outdoor performances I directed, with the only opportunity to perform at the site being a 'dress rehearsal' the day before the run began. There were always spectators – as with the *ludi*, the location had been selected because it was a high-traffic thoroughfare. The actors at least never felt over-rehearsed. Throughout the run, they availed themselves of new opportunities as they learned to react and respond both to the performance space and to the audience.

[62] Obbink (2001), Marshall (2004).

[63] These motivations also lie behind the use of parts in Elizabethan theatre. Arnott (1967) 44–6 suggests that ancient rehearsals were in fact accomplished without any physical text, but were all learned with the aid of a 'prompter', as is still done in some countries today. Certainly such a technique is possible, and may have been used for those actors not carrying the bulk of the play. It does seem to be the system used in the rehearsal of Greek choruses (Plutarch, *Moralia* 813e).

a financial saving, as the costs of papyrus and of a scribe could accumulate quickly. But it also changes the nature of the interaction between actors, and should at least be considered as a possibility when we try to imagine a Roman stage performance.

The other professionals contracted by the aediles did not operate backstage. Plautus has his prologue address the *praeco* ('herald') twice.[64] The prologue in *Asinaria* 4–5 says,

> *face nunciam tu, praeco, omnem auritum poplum.*
> *age nunc reside, cave modo ne gratiis.*

> Now, herald, provide the audience with ears.
> (*The herald delivers his proclamation.*)
> O.K., sit down – and don't forget your fee.   (tr. Smith)

In *Poenulus* 11–15, the same joke is extended:

> *exsurge praeco, fac populo audientiam.*
> *iam dudum exspecto si tuom officium scias:*
> *exerce vocem quam per vivisque et colis.*
> *nam nisi clamabis, tacitum te obrepet fames.*
> *age nunc reside, duplicem ut mercedem feras.*

> Herald, get up and make an audience of this crowd.
> For a while now I've wanted to know if you knew your job.
> Stretch your voice, through which you live and thrive.
> For, unless you shout, you will silently starve.
> (*The herald again makes an announcement.*)
> Come now, sit back down, if you want your pay doubled.

Both passages make it clear that the *praeco* is sitting during the prologue, that he receives instructions from the prologue speaker to make the audience more attentive, and that he receives a wage.

Praecones were used in many contexts to provide information to large numbers of Romans, and due to literacy levels were presumably more efficient at disseminating information than written notices. Like the *choragus*, the herald's financial arrangements were apparently both with the magistrates and with the troupe. There is at least the pretence that the

---

However, the metatheatrical comment at *Poenulus* 550–54, where the actors acknowledge they learned their parts together, need not refer to anything beyond the fact that rehearsals took place.
[64] See Gilula (1993) and Slater (2000) 154–5.

fee received for his services came from the company. While the smooth running of the venue is clearly important (*Hecyra* 4–5 and 33–41 describe what happens when things do not go well), the offer of pay demonstrates that the *praeco* was not in the company but was an official appointed by the magistrates. A *praeco* was 'a junior and uncoveted apparitorial post'[65] through which there might be some hope of advancement. It would seem his duties were to silence or at least to quiet the crowd, and in doing so no doubt he also served to help draw the audience to the performance area. Livy 33.32.4 refers to *praeco cum tubicine* ('a herald with a trumpet'), and perhaps the use of a horn assisted in his task. This is likely to have been more than a simple fanfare, which the troupe itself could provide.[66] The presence of an independent contractor with this job suggests not only that under normal conditions the task filled several minutes' time, but also that there were related duties as the *praeco* helped effect the transition from one performance to another. Perhaps he announced the title of the play to the audience (Donatus, *de Comoedia* 8.11, though this passage is confused). He was, in effect, the front-of-house manager, responsible to the magistrates for the smooth running of the *ludi scaenici* or (more likely) of a single performance venue.[67] If this is correct, then we may equally believe that the *dissignator* ('usher,' mentioned only at *Poenulus* 19), who stays near the front of the theatre (19: *praeter os*) and helps people find their seats, works with the *praeco*, perhaps as an assistant. The force of the whole sentence suggests that there would be more than one *dissignator* working with the *praeco*.[68]

PERFORMANCE SPACES

There was no permanent theatre, of stone or wood, in Rome until the theatre of Pompey was built in 55 BC, though several others followed soon afterwards. A number of attempts were made to create a permanent

---

[65] Purcell (1983) 147. For the *praecones* generally, see Hinard (1976), and Purcell (1983) 147–8.

[66] Further, the use of the *praeco* does argue against the presence of musical overtures provided by the *tibicen*, despite Cicero, *Lucullus* 20 (Moore (forthcoming), ch. 2).

[67] Terence's problems with staging *Hecyra* may therefore have arisen due to a particularly weak or disorganised *praeco*.

[68] The references to the *praeco* jokingly imply that he failed to draw the audience as expected, and dismissively suggest he is a mere employee. In response, the *praeco* may be good-natured, and happily become the actor's stooge (Slater (2000) 155 n. 77). Alternately, any hesitation will serve to make the audience louder, forcing the *praeco* to stand and re-silence them. In contrast, Gilula (1993) 286–7 argues that the individual being addressed is not a real *praeco* (who having done his job is now sitting down), but a member of the troupe playing the part of the *praeco*. This seems to me an odd joke, and one that risks alienating the audience who, we must suspect, can still see the real *praeco* sitting before them (*praeter os*?).

theatre before this, but all were unsuccessful and postdate Plautine production. When theatres were built, they possessed a distinctive shape, with a semicircular orchestra and a long thin stage space in front of a multi-levelled *scaenae frons*. It is unlikely however that the earlier, temporary stages upon which the extant comedies were performed ever had that shape. Part of the reason for this is architectural: temporary constructions made out of wood, constructed hastily in the days before the *ludi*, would possess neither the structural strength nor occupy sufficient space to anticipate the proportions of the later permanent performance venues. There are no indications that the temporary theatres looked like or were used like scaled-down versions of the later ones. Indeed, the topographical discussion below will suggest that the opposite is true, that performances took place in a variety of venues of different shapes. The situation therefore parallels the development of the Greek theatre, where the fifth-century *orchêstra* was not always circular but was usually an irregular polygon.[69]

Those considering early Roman performance venues look to two artistic sources, both of which are problematic. First is the collection of later Roman wall paintings with theatrical motifs. Beacham believes these temporary wooden stages provide a 'missing link' between the stone theatres of Hellenistic Greece and the stone theatres Rome began to build in the first century:[70] these are paintings of actual Roman performance spaces, and the advent of permanent theatres did not affect the visual representation of Roman theatre architecture. This is not credible. The combination of imperial wall painting, incorporating features found on temporary South Italian stages, and employing Greek *trompe l'oeil* painting techniques[71] is too complex a combination to posit without corroboration. It presumes a fixed relationship between audience and performance space over time, which is not supported by the literary or archaeological record. The second source is the illustrations of stages on fourth-century South Italian red-figure vases.[72] Though much earlier than Plautus' plays, these stages show a wooden stage approximately 1 metre high, sometimes fronted with banners (which serve to increase the appearance of permanence), and accessed by a low wooden staircase. It is

[69] See Wiles (1997) 23–62.   [70] Beacham (1991) 56–7.
[71] Beacham (1991) 64–7, 69–85, and 227–30.
[72] For a duly cautious sample formulation, see Richardson (1992) 380: 'At first plays were given on simple stages run up for the occasion, and the spectators stood in a crowd before these. This, one gathers, must have been the way the Etruscan dancers were presented when their art was first introduced to Rome (Livy 7.2.3–7) and the way Atellan farces were traditionally performed.'

typically suggested that these South Italian stages are like the temporary stages upon which *phlyakes* and Atellan farces would have been performed, and, following them, the plays of Plautus and Terence. There are three problems with this claim. First, it is no longer believed that these scenes depict the native Italian performance tradition exclusively. As the influence of fifth-century Athenian comedy on these illustrations becomes increasingly apparent, there exists less reason to assume that any Italian traditions used such stages,[73] to say nothing of the chronological disparities. Second, the illustrations depict a performance space that gives access to the *orchêstra*, with steps creating two levels of performance that may be used simultaneously, as on a Greek stage.[74] The demands of Roman comedy are different. All plays are set on a (level) street in front of one, two, or three doors. No play employs a split-level main stage area. Third, the stage on the vases mandates a particular relationship with the audience. Every performance space creates a relationship between *scaena* ('performance space')[75] and *cavea* ('auditorium')[76] – between actors and audience. Consequently, 'We do not know exactly what the stage wall used in Plautus and Terence looked like'.[77] The architecture defines this relationship, and it does so in a way that tends towards an ideal. This claim bears some examination.

Any culture with theatre will create a venue that is ideally suited to the drama it produces. This is not a causative relationship, but a recognition that there exists a nexus around which the venue, the work performed

---

[73] See Taplin (1993) for these vases and their Athenian connection generally.

[74] As on the 'New York Goose Play' vase: New York, Metropolitan Museum of Art, 24.97.104 (Fletcher Fund, 1924), *PhV*² 84 (Trendall (1967) 53–4).

[75] Plautus' Latin terms for 'stage' are surprisingly elusive. Properly, *scaena* should be the wooden, temporary backdrop, and *proscaenium* the area directly in front of it. Thus at *Amphitruo* 91, a character recalls what happened *in proscaenio hic* ('on this very stage'), and at *Poenulus* 17, prostitutes in the audience are not to sit *in proscaenio* ('on the stage') – the term is then a straight Latinisation of Greek *proskênion*, about which see Sifakis (1967) 126–30. Even in English, though, there is ambiguity, as 'stage' can mean either the whole performance area, or the raised part of the performance area, between the stage building and the *orchestra* (this is how the *Oxford Latin Dictionary* defines it). *Captivi* 60 emphasises that battles take place *extra scaenam* (which must mean 'outside of the performance area'). *Poenulus* apparently distinguishes *proscaenium* from *scaena*, but *in scaena* at line 20 could mean either 'before the stage building' (as the etymology of *proscaenium* should suggest) or 'in the performance area' (as at *Captivi* 60). Consequently, neither term can be reduced to a single meaning apart from performance context. Some of these difficulties persist in the Augustan period and afterwards, where there is always an *orchestra* in the permanent theatres. See also Beacham (1991) 60.

[76] *Amphitruo* 66; however, *Truculentus* 931 has an actor speaking *in cavea*, suggesting the term can mean the theatre in general, since the point does not seem to depend on him physically being among the audience (which I believe was not an inconceivable mode of delivery).

[77] Wiles (1991) 55.

(or the playwright), and the performers will collaborate to yield an optimal result for the ideal audience. Experimental theatre will push these limits and in time alter the parameters of performance, thereby creating a new set of audience expectations of what the theatre can do. In republican Rome, all three of these were variables, and any one could be changed according to demands of any other. Shaw's lengthy and detailed stage directions imply an understanding of naturalism that could only be created on the picture-window stage of Victorian England.[78] They imply an acting style that maintains a fourth wall, creating a rigid separation between the audience and the actors. Similarly, the structure of the *agôn* and *stichomythia* and the use of messenger speeches in Greek tragedy presume delivery to a much larger audience by actors wearing masks: these techniques developed as a means to facilitate audience comprehension in the vast Athenian theatre.[79] To alter the intended performance spaces of any of these works – to perform Shakespeare in a proscenium arch or in a black box theatre, for instance – changes the variables and the nature of the performance that is possible.[80] This is not a judgment – it is not 'wrong' to perform a play in a venue for which it was not intended – but it is ahistorical, and requires a number of adaptations ('translations') to the script and its means of presentation to create effective theatre. This is a truism among theatre practitioners, but, since it allows for so many permutations and no clear 'best answer', it is still easily overlooked. Changes may even be introduced subconsciously, as actors and directors work to create meaning out of the text.

Further, one element in this nexus can point to significant features of another. A raised stage, such as is found in the Globe and on the temporary stages seen on South Italian vases, means that at least some of the audience will be positioned below the stage, and therefore will be looking up at the performance. In Shakespeare's Globe Theatre, this creates an area for the (low-paying) groundlings, and keeps sightlines clear for all those in the more expensive seats surrounding the stage. Similarly, if Aeschylus had been writing for a black box, the use of masks is unlikely to have developed as it did.[81] While there will certainly be a period of growth and experimentation, performance practice will quickly realise an ideal means of delivery, which creates a standard with which future texts

---

[78] One aspect of this is evoked by Bennett (1997) 143–7.   [79] Arnott (1961) 87–9.
[80] This is one benefit of the reconstructed Globe Theatre in London; it allows discoveries about the intended performance space that have been forgotten.
[81] Marshall (1999b) 190.

may engage.[82] For any type of entertainment, this nexus of influences will exert itself.

Tacitus attests to a change over time in Roman theatrical venues: *nam antea subitariis gradibus et scaena in tempus structa ludos edi solitos, vel, si vetustiora repetas, stantem populum spectavisse, ne, si consideret theatro dies totos ignavia continuaret* (*Annals* 14.20: 'Before, the games had usually been exhibited with the help of improvised tiers of benches and a stage thrown up for the occasion; or, to go further into the past, the people stood to watch: seats in the theatre, it was feared, might tempt them to pass whole days in indolence').[83] Tacitus' concern is the moral condition of the audience, but he points to a three-stage development in actor–audience relations at Rome. At first, the audience stood. If the performers were to hold the attention of more than two or three rows of spectators, this would require a raised stage to allow for effective sightlines: the audience were at this point like Shakespeare's groundlings, and the actors would need a venue similar to what is seen on the South Italian vases, though perhaps without the staircase and the two levels of performance.[84] The second stage Tacitus describes, with its 'hurriedly built tiered seats and a stage built for the occasion', represents a development whereby the audience can now look down on the performance space. The term *scaena* need not imply a raised stage (rather than just 'performance area' or 'backdrop'). This architectural change would necessarily be associated with a different kind of performance style. The third stage, the 'modern' stone theatres of late republican Rome, lead to a different performance style again.[85] The first two stage types Tacitus describes allow for the creation of intimacy between actor and audience. Only the third, with the audience positioned only on one side of the stage space, leads to a separation between the two – as in the proscenium arch.[86] Indeed, the huge *scaenae frons* and the long narrow stage of the permanent theatre

---

[82] Similarly, one may look at films in the 1920s and early 1930s and observe that actors are framed as if they were on stage: the audience is shown whole bodies, and faces are restricted to the very top of the screen. This however soon gave way to close-ups and (again) a different style of acting, which was better suited to the new medium.

[83] Text and translation, Jackson (1962) 136–9.

[84] There is no need to infer from this, incidentally, that shows were necessarily short 'sketches'. Modern audiences stand for more than two hours regularly at the reconstructed Globe, myself among them. But when this is the case, both the physical environment and the actors are working to keep the audience members present, and prevent them from wandering off. Vitruvius 5.6.2 suggests Roman stages were never higher than 5 feet, out of consideration for the Roman senators sitting in the front (Goldberg (1998) 19).

[85] Rome was very late in this development, though, and other Roman cities in Italy did have permanent performance venues earlier.

[86] Marshall (2000b) 30–33.

serve to reinforce this separation, and such features have no place in the earlier performance contexts Tacitus describes. They are also not going to foster drama that creates a rapport between actor and audience, such as is accomplished by the metatheatrical plays of Plautus.[87]

Leaving aside the issue of later performances (the venues played by Roscius were no doubt very different from the original locations, and would have required a different performance style and, likely, alterations of the text), even in Plautus' day there is no need to assume a single venue type. Different *ludi* were celebrated in different parts of Rome, and at each occasion a different performance venue might be found. Flexibility becomes central for both plays and players, since a given play may end up in any of a number of performance venues. In fact, the one location where we can feel confident we know a Plautine play was performed corresponds to none of the performance spaces described by Tacitus.[88]

Each festival was associated with a particular part of Rome. The *ludi Romani* and the *ludi Plebeii* were centred on the forum, as apparently were *ludi funebres*.[89] The bulk of the celebrations for the *ludi Apollinares* were probably celebrated on the other side of the Capitoline hill in the Circus Flaminius, and the *ludi Megalenses* were probably celebrated above the Circus Maximus at the top of the Palatine cliff in front of the temple of the Magna Mater.[90] At a minimum, then, we should expect three separate locations for theatrical performances. These places, where the set was constructed (which too might vary by some degree each year), need not be similar in shape to one other. Indeed, there is every reason to believe that they were not.

The situation is clearest for the *ludi Megalenses*. Cicero explicitly refers to those games *quos in Palatio nostri maiores ante templum in ipso Matris Magnae conspectu Megalesibus fieri celebrarique voluerunt* (*de Haruspicum Responso* 24: 'which on the Palatine our ancestors wished to establish and celebrate as "Megalensian" before the temple in the sight of the Great Mother herself').[91] *In . . . conspectu* can only mean directly in front of the temple, so that the cult figure housed within can be thought to see the

---

[87] Slater (2000) and Moore (1998b) 67–90.

[88] Given such flexibility and our ignorance of techniques of ancient actor training, I do not believe we need to accept specific limitations on the ability to project, as, for example, does Goldberg (1998) 17. I prefer to look for indications of the physical dynamics of the performance venues and to assume that actor training in antiquity was capable of producing performers with sufficient histrionic ability to meet the technical needs of the performance spaces.

[89] Gilula (1978) 48–9 n. 11.

[90] Goldberg (1998). The Circus Maximus is also a possible (earlier?) location: Gilula (1978) 47–8 n. 9.

[91] Goldberg (1998), building on the work of, particularly, Saunders (1913) and Hanson (1959) 9–26.

events. The *ludi* were first celebrated in 194, and the temple itself was dedicated on 10 April 191 – celebrations that included performances of Plautus' *Pseudolus*. Excavations demonstrate the nature of the space: '[it] is too small (and probably too irregular) a space to accommodate a complete theatre structure, i.e. both a *cavea* and a *proscaenium*, of any size. A freestanding building, however temporary ... is impossible.'[92] The greatest pressures for space come not from the stage but from the *cavea*, which holds the audience. Goldberg's solution is elegant and convincing: the audience sat on the temple steps, and looked down, not at a raised stage but to the narrow and irregular trapezoidal podium in front of the temple, which constituted the performance area. The goddess is in a position to watch directly, from the same perspective as the majority of spectators, as the play is performed in the temple's forecourt:[93]

A plausible reconstruction of the original Temple of the Magna Mater ... suggests seven steps, each c. 40 m long in the lower, wider tier and eighteen steps of c. 20 m length in the upper staircase leading directly to the temple ... This yields a crowd of just under 1,300, plus those who might gather on the nearby Temple of Victory or stand elsewhere on or by the podium ... To imagine any audience of over 2,000 gathering for a performance of *Pseudolus* at the dedication in 191 or fidgetting through the beginning of *Hecyra* in 165 therefore becomes very difficult.[94]

I will return to the size of the audience later, but for now we may note that Cicero speaks of *constrictum spectaculis* (*de Haruspicum Responso* 22: 'the small area for the spectators').[95] The performance space at the *ludi Megalenses* bears no real relationship to theatres in Greek cities, but rather is seamlessly incorporated into the landscape of Rome.

A similar venue probably developed for the *ludi Apollinares*. In 179, M. Aemilius Lepidus attempted to construct a *theatrum et proscaenium ad Apollinis* (Livy 40.51.3: 'a theatre and stage-building at Apollo's [temple]'), at the north end of the *forum Boarium*. The archaeology of this site is complex, and there is no way of knowing precisely what existed there in the republic. Lepidus' intended construction was part of a larger building programme, which included among other things the construction of a portico *ad aedem Apollinis Medici* (Livy 40.51.6: 'at the temple of Apollo

---

[92] Goldberg (1998) 6, incorporating results from the recent excavations at the site by Pensabene.
[93] Tacitus' use of *gradibus*, literally 'steps', suggests that temples perhaps were used for theatres from the earliest days.
[94] Goldberg (1998) 13–14, with illustration on 6, from Praeneste.
[95] OLD s.v. *spectaculum* 3 cites this passage and *Curculio* 647.

Medicus'). While apparently the games were first held in the Circus Maximus,[96] it need not still be used for theatrical performances in Plautus' day. When the Theatre of Marcellus (*theatrum Marcelli*) was built in the Augustan period, the area immediately adjoining the temple of Apollo Medicus was thought to have theatrical connotations, and Livy 41.28.11 confirms that the Circus Flaminius, slightly further to the west, could be used for theatrical *ludi funebres* in 174. It is not likely that Lepidus, as *censor* and *pontifex maximus* (Livy 40.51.1), would be innovating in his selection of a site for theatrical activity, which of course falls under the auspices of the god. Indeed, the *ludi Apollinares* commemorated the date of the temple's foundation, 13 July. At some point, then, perhaps soon after 212 (so the practice could be seen to be accustomed by 179), the site for the *ludi Apollinares* seems to have been moved closer to the area of the temple, near to it but still separate. Space was therefore restricted for the building of either a theatre or a temple in the 170s, but a connection is certainly present in Livy's mind. The site later occupied by the theatre of Marcellus was the obvious place for theatrical activity dedicated to Apollo.

It is tempting in this light to attempt to reinterpret certain passages in Plautus. When a character addresses Apollo, as Euclio does at *Aulularia* 393–5 and Chrysalus does in *Bacchides* 170–73, it is possible that reference is not being made to a stage altar. While it would be natural in a Greek context to have a character address the shrine to Apollo Aguieus that was part of the front of a typical Greek house,[97] this would make no sense in a Roman context. The Latin may point to an aspect of the Greek original for these plays, but the reference would still need to be naturalised in the Roman context. If these plays were performed at the *ludi Apollinares*, the result would be a striking and amusing metatheatrical joke, as the actors evoke the god whose presence can be seen by the audience sitting in the area where the theatre of Marcellus was later built. Indeed, *Bacchides* 170–73 then masterfully blurs the dramatic setting of Athens with the theatrical context in Rome:

> *erilis patria, salve, quam ego biennio,*
> *postquam hinc in Ephesum abii, conspicio lubens.*

---

[96] Livy 25.12.14, Macrobius, *Sat.* 1.17.27–29. Indeed, whether the Circus Maximus was ever used may be open to question: Macrobius 1.17.29 says merely *in circo*, and it remains possible that in Livy 25.12.14 *ludos praetor in circo maximo cum facturus esset*, the adjective *maximo* represents a false inference by Livy or an interpolator.

[97] Saunders (1911) 93–6.

> *saluto te, vicine Apollo, qui aedibus*
> *propinquos nostris accolis . . .*

Land of my master, greetings. It's two years
Since I left for Ephesus, and I rejoice to see you.
I salute you, neighbour Apollo, you who dwell
Beside our house . . . (tr. Barsby)

The words *vicine Apollo* do not require a physical altar on stage, and emphasise the performance area's proximity to the Roman temple. While it is generally assumed that the stage altar has a 'default' affiliation with Apollo,[98] in fact only one other passage makes such a connection explicit. Dorippa and her 84-year-old slave Syra have arrived home, whereupon Dorippa wishes to make an offering (*Mercator* 675–78):

> DOR.   *aliquid cedo*
> *qui hanc vicini nostri aram augeam.*
> *da sane hanc virgam lauri. abi tu intro.*
> SYRA.   *eo.*
> DOR.   *Apollo, quaeso te, ut des pacem propitius . . .*

> DOR.   Give me something
> That I may offer on our neighbour's altar here.
> Good – give me this laurel branch. You go inside.
> SYRA.   I go.
> DOR.   Apollo, I beseech you, kindly grant your peace . . .

In the Greek context, this would be interpreted as an offering at a household shrine. We cannot know what Plautus' source, Philemon's *Emporos*, had at the point corresponding to *Mercator* 675–8. In *Mercator*, however, it may represent the use of the stage altar (in which case we must believe Syra happens coincidentally to be carrying a laurel branch)[99] or it may be another metatheatrical evocation of *vicinus Apollo*. Might we imagine the actor playing Syra actually leaving the performance area, going towards the real altar of Apollo and finding a pre-set laurel bough to be used by Dorippa? Whatever the answer, these passages are not

---

[98] Duckworth (1952) 83.

[99] Indeed, the exchange between the two characters at 670–75 would suggest that Syra is not carrying anything. Dorippa's question at 673, *quid oneris?*, then sets up the joke answer. Nixon in his translation assumes she carries 'a few parcels'.

enough to warrant maintaining the Greek custom of the Apollo Aguieus altar on the Roman stage.

The third likely location for theatrical performances in Rome is the *forum Romanum*, probably used at the *ludi Romani*, some *ludi funebres*, and possibly the *ludi Plebeii*, with equestrian events celebrated in the Circus Maximus.[100] Where precisely the theatrical activity was located in the forum cannot be determined, but there are good reasons to believe that more than one area could be used: the forum and Rostra were the focal points for *ludi funebres* (Polybius 6.53.1; gladiatorial fights also featured, Livy 23.30.15, 31.50.4, and Cicero, *pro Sestio* 124). The forum was not nearly as built-up as it would be in the Augustan period: 'at the end of the third century BC the Forum Romanum remained an irregular open space marked by nothing more monumental than a handful of average-sized temples' (see Fig. 2).[101] Major constructions were begun after Plautus' active career, including basilicas in 184, 179, and 169, though the burning of many shops had led to the rebuilding of the *atrium Regium* during wartime in 209 (Livy 26.27.2, 27.11.16).[102]

The Choragus' speech in *Curculio* isolates almost a dozen individual locations in the forum.[103] Further, each Roman space is connected in

---

[100] See Saunders (1913) 94–6 and, for the forum generally, see Coarelli (1983), (1985).

[101] Stambaugh (1988) 110. The illustration comes from Welch (1994) 29, fig. 11. I am grateful to K. Welch and the editors of *The Journal of Roman Archaeology* for permission to reproduce the image, which was drawn by Philip Stinson. K. Welch now believes that numismatic evidence shows that the temple of Vesta was not at this date a columnar tholos but preserved something of its original hut-like character.

[102] Welch (2003) 7 and 17, and see Coarelli (1977) and Welch (2003) 17 n. 47: 'It was only after the first decade of the 2nd c., when money began to flow into Rome after the defeat of Hannibal and the Seleucids, that such large, public projects were undertaken'.

[103] The first five locations follow the northern edge of the forum, from west to east:
1. the Comitium, line 470, attracts perjurers (*periurum*);
2. the temple of Venus Cloacina, line 471, attracts liars and braggarts (*mendacem et gloriosum*);
3. the basilica, lines 472–3, attracts husbands (*damnosos maritos*) and prostitutes (*scorta exoleta*; Moore (1998b) 220 n. 26 demonstrates that they are male); *quique stipulari solent* ('and those who strike bargains') probably refers back to the husbands;
4. the Forum Piscarium ('fish market'), line 474, probably refers to the Macellum, the great food market northeast of the forum; it attracts dining-club members (*conlatores symbolarum*).

The next three locations pass through the middle of the forum, from east to west:
5. the lower forum (*foro infumo*), line 475, attracts rich notables (*boni homines atque dites*);
6. the open culvert of the Cloaca (*in medio propter canalem*), line 476, attracts show-offs (*ostentatores*); it was to be covered by 179 (Richardson (1992) 172);
7. *supra lacum*, lines 477–9, must therefore refer to the Lacus Curtius (not the Lacus Iuturnae); it attracts the confident, the talkative, and the ill-willed (*confidentes garrulique et malevoli*).

Finally, the description proceeds along the south side of the forum, from west to east:
8. the *veterae tabernae*, line 480, attracts moneylenders (*qui dant quique accipiunt faenore*);
9. the temple of Castor, line 481, attracts the untrustworthy (*quibus credas male*);

Fig. 2   *Forum Romanum*, late 3rd–early 2nd centuries BC.

some way with the world of Comedy, and this is part of a larger series of references blurring the divisions between the world of the play and Rome itself.[104] Here is Moore's conclusion for the location of the *Curculio* performance:

> The *choragus*'s tour is both restricted and orderly. It includes only places in the immediate vicinity of the forum, east of the western end of the comitium. It is most unlikely that, if the play were performed at some other location, Plautus would have discussed only this small area, or that the *choragus* would have been so careful to lead his spectators from the comitium east along the north side of the forum to the fish market, then back through the middle of the forum to the west of the Lacus Curtius, then along the south side of the forum to the Temple of Castor and Pollux, and finally south a little to the Velabrum. Given, then, that the *choragus* does not mention such places farther west in the forum as the temples of Saturn or Concordia, there is every indication that he speaks from a stage just south of the comitium, facing east.[105]

10. the Tuscan *vicus*, line 482, attracts 'those who sell themselves' (*homines qui ipsi sese venditant*; as in 473 the group of prostitutes is at least partly male);

11. the Velabrum, lines 483–4, attracts various merchants known to cheat – bakers, butchers, and soothsayers (*vel pistorem vel lanium vel haruspicem*).

(Line 485 is deleted as a doublet of line 472.)

[104] Moore (1991) and Moore (1998b) 126–39, 219–22.   [105] Moore (1998b) 137.

Many aspects of this interpretation are convincing, and precisely this location would later be used for the Rostrum Augusti in the first century. However, by suggesting that the actor faces east, Moore places the audience in the bulk of the forum, essentially filling it. He describes how this compounds the joke, as individual spectators are physically positioned in at least some of the locations specified, and incorporated into the world of the play, and indeed, this is how the Rostrum Augusti is generally thought to have been used.[106]

Several factors suggest that Plautus' audience would instead be positioned in the much smaller area to the west, and that an actor delivering the Choragus' speech would face in that direction. This has an effect on the dynamics of the scene: the actor gesticulates beside and behind himself, beginning stage right with the Comitium and with each location pointing further upstage; he refers to directly behind the stage building as he refers to the Cloaca and the Lacus Curtius (476–9), and then points stage left and begins working his way upstage with gestures along the south side of the forum. The chief advantage of this orientation is that the spectators are already facing the indicated direction without having to crane their necks. The Choragus' metatheatrical speech asks the audience to look beyond the limits of the theatre (in some cases over whatever temporary set has been constructed). There are indications that at least part of the audience must be able to see (or at least look in the direction of) the named locations clearly, since, having pointed to the *tabernae veterae* and the temple of Castor and Pollux (480–81), the Choragus then does not continue further east beyond the sightlines possible, but instead points to the road that lies between these two, the Tuscan *vicus* (482–3) which then leads to the Velabrum (line 483).[107] This is the only interruption in the smooth S-curve the Choragus has been following, and it is explained best by taking advantage of the physical position of the entire audience. Even if not every spectator can actually see the road, all know where it is. As discussed below, Lyco the *danista* ('banker') in the scenes framing the Choragus' speech, arrives from stage left, which corresponds with where *Curculio* 480 places moneylenders. If the audience faces east, this limits the area allotted for the theatre space as a whole, and perhaps allows the steps of the temples of Saturn and Concordia to be used for

---

[106] See Dio Cassius, epitome of Book 74.4.4, for Pertinax's funeral in AD 193, held in the forum. Women sit in the porticoes, men under the open sun, which implies a similar orientation.

[107] For the authenticity of this line, see Moore (1991) 354–5.

audience seating. The forum is not overwhelmed with a single comic performance.

Hecyra 39–42 demonstrated that gladiatorial combats and *ludi scaenici* could share a venue. Jory believes there is 'a certain amount of evidence for gladiatorial combats in the theatres at Rome, that is at venues where *ludi scaenici* were performed'.[108] The reverse is just as likely: that *ludi scaenici* could be performed in venues designed for gladiatorial combat. Temporary wooden amphitheatres were built in the Roman forum:[109]

> The *cavea* of such a temporary wooden amphitheatre could have been supported by a truss-like system of beams (which could have been constructed in a day or two, if the temporary seating for the Palio in Siena today is any indication). If the *cavea* was 5 to 10 m high it could have had between 10 and 20 rows of seats and accommodated up to 10,000 spectators. The audience could still have watched the games from the second storeys of the basilicas ... [110]

Even if this overestimates the speed of construction (which I suspect it does, despite *subitariis* in Tacitus, *Annals* 14.20), a temporary gladiatorial venue would fill the eastern two-thirds of the forum, with a diagonal stretching from the Rostra to the temple of Castor and Pollux. Such a space would not necessarily be built at all festivals. When constructed, this represented a further significant cost for the magistrates. Plutarch describes how, later in the second century, some administrators attempted to defray these expenses: τῶν ἀρχόντων οἱ πλεῖστοι θεωρητήρια κύκλῳ κατασκευάσαντες ἐξεμίσθουν (*Gaius Gracchus* 12.3: 'Most of the magistrates, having built spectator seats in a circle, were renting them out') – but Gracchus insisted the seats be removed.[111]

If a wooden amphitheatre were in place during the performance of *Curculio*, then the *ad hoc* theatre space could occupy the remaining part of the forum, as described. But it is also possible that the amphitheatre itself could be used for theatre, as at the *ludi funebres* of Paullus in 160. Once the expense of an amphitheatre had been undertaken, it is possible the space would be used for all performances, including *ludi scaenici*. In some ways, this represents the clearest means of explaining what happened to the second performance of *Hecyra*. A temporary *scaena frons* placed within the arena would effectively reduce the seating capacity for a

---

[108] Jory (1986) 537. This was Donatus' interpretation, *ad Hecyra* 39.
[109] Welch (1994) 69–78. Livy 1.35.8–9 describes temporarily erected bleacher-type seating in Rome's earliest days.
[110] Welch (1994) 76, and see the figure on p. 75.
[111] Welch (1994) 77 associates this passage specifically to the wooden amphitheatre because of κύκλῳ.

play by two-thirds (we can imagine the audience seated along the minor axis of the ellipse on the western side, again facing east, so they are not looking into the afternoon sun). An audience entering such a space with the intention of seeing gladiators – it is an amphitheatre, after all – would indeed cause confusion (*Hecyra* 41: *tumultuantur, clamant, pugnant de loco*) particularly since a gladiatorial audience would expect to be able to fill all the seats, and not merely those at one end. This is speculative, but it does suggest another possible performance venue. It was not used for *Curculio*, however. The presence of the extensive wooden superstructure changes the amount of available space in the forum. Despite the audience being in the centre of the forum, most of the imaginative effects created by the Choragus' tour would be eliminated, since most of the spaces listed lie beneath the sightlines of the seated audience (regardless of where they sit).

In addition, a number of factors point towards the use of the Comitium as a site of theatrical activity within the forum. No archaeological record of the republican Comitium survives, but it seems certain that at this time 'it was a circular amphitheatre of steps, on which the Romans stood in their assemblies, leading up to the curia or the senate on the north side'.[112] There was a speaker's platform, the Rostra, slightly built up, from which magistrates would address the assembly and on which the praetor held his tribunal, facing the Curia (see Fig. 2).[113] The Rostra physically created a barrier that blocked the view of some of the rest of the forum for those present in the Comitium, but its precise dimensions cannot be determined. Perhaps we can imagine a temporary set being built directly in front of the Rostra, connecting two points of the circle of the Comitium, with the performance space facing north to the Curia, where the audience was situated on the steps.[114] This produces a much

---

[112] Richardson (1992) 170, in light of which it is hard not to recall Tacitus, *Annals* 14.20, *stantem populum spectavisse*. The circular shape is assumed on analogy with Cosa and Paestum, and has led many to comment on the theatrical space created. These cities copied the circular shape of the *ekklēsiastērion* which served a similar purpose in South Italian Greek colonies. See also Hanson (1959) 37–9, Taylor (1966) 21–3, Russell (1968) 307–8.

[113] That this was the usual orientation is shown in later republican history 'when Licinius Crassus in 145 and Gaius Gracchus in 123 BC made a political issue of the spatial arrangements by turning their backs on the senators in the Curia and speaking directly to the people out in the *forum Romanum*, in violation of parliamentary etiquette' (Cicero, *de Amicitia* 96; Plutarch, *Gaius Gracchus* 5), cited in Stambaugh (1988) 113, though see also Taylor (1966) 23–8.

[114] If so, then we can imagine at least one way that the required second level for *Amphitruo* could be achieved, with the actor physically climbing onto the Rostra, and appearing above the temporary set built on the packed-earth floor of the Comitium. Such a solution is venue-specific, and is not the only possible one; if this were the site, it would be the natural solution. Christenson (2000) 20 suggests 'a ladder behind the façade led to scaffolding near the top' on which the actor could

smaller *cavea*, though it is one largely isolated from forum distractions. This seems to be the situation presumed by Livy 27.36.8: *eo anno primum ex quo Hannibal in Italiam venisset comitium tectum esse memoriae proditum est, et ludos Romanos semel instauratos ab aedilibus curulibus Q. Metello et C. Servilio* ('In that year [208 BC], for the first time since Hannibal had entered Italy, it is recorded that the Comitium was covered, and that the *ludi Romani* were repeated for one day by the aediles Q. Metellus and C. Servilius'). The end of the sentence suggests that the context for the beginning is the *ludi Romani*. This surprising claim is very important, for the covering of the Comitium almost certainly indicates that the space was being used as a performance venue.

The use of *vela* ('sails') as sunscreens becomes standard much later: according to Pliny the Elder, *Natural History* 19.23, Caesar covered the whole forum with *vela*.[115] While Livy indicates he has a sure source for the antiquity of the practice, Pliny and Valerius Maximus date the innovation much later, to 69 BC: *Q. Catulus … primus spectantium consessum velorum umbraculis texit* (Valerius Maximus 2.4.6: 'Q. Catulus was the first to cover the sitting spectators with a shady awning').[116] This might mean that the coverings provided in 211 were not (technically) *vela* but were made of some other material, or that Catulus reinstated a practice that had again fallen into disuse, or that there is some other distinction to be made. In any case, though it becomes a standard practice in the first century, there is no reason to doubt Livy's claim. Pliny also mentions the bright colours of theatrical awnings, which are also evoked by Lucretius, *On the Nature of Things* 4.72–84:

> nam certe iacere ac largiri multa videmus,
> non solum ex alto penitusque, ut diximus ante,
> verum de summis ipsum quoque saepe colorem.
> et volgo faciunt id lutea russaque vela
> et ferrugina, cum magnis intenta theatris
> per malos volgata trabesque trementia flutant;
> namque ibi consessum caveai subter et omnem
> scaenai speciem, patrum turbamque decoram
> inficiunt coguntque suo fluitare colore.

stand, with his upper torso appearing above the set. However, the plot of the play is exceptional in so many ways that we may even imagine it was written for a completely non-Roman context – perhaps for a Greek theatre in South Italy, where a *skênê*-roof was part of the theatre architecture?

[115] Welch (1994) 71 rightly relates this to an oversize but temporary wooden amphitheatre in the forum. See also Dio 43.24.2. Several inscriptions from Pompeii attest the use of *vela* with gladiatorial hunts (*Corpus Inscriptionum Latinarum* 4.1189, 1190, *Inscriptiones Latinae Selectae* 5145).

[116] Text and translation, Shackleton Bailey (2000) 158–9. Valerius is evidently Pliny's source.

et quanto circum mage sunt inclusa theatri
moenia, tam magis haec intus perfusa lepore
omnia conrident correpta luce diei.
ergo lintea de summo cum corpore fucum mittunt....

For assuredly we see many things cast off particles with lavish bounty, not only from the depths and from within (as we said before) but from the outermost surface, amongst others colour not seldom. This is often done by yellow and red and dark purple awnings, when outspread in the public view over a great theatre upon posts and beams they tremble and flutter; for then they dye, and force to flutter in their own colour, the assembly in the great hollow below, and all the display of the stage, and the glorious throng of the fathers; and the more the walls of the theatre are enclosed all round, the more all within laughs in the flood of beauty when the light of day is thus confined. Therefore, since canvas throws off colour from its outermost surface ... [117]

While Lucretius' description is meant to evoke the theatre in his day (and is used to clarify his atomistic theory of colour), many details coincide with what is known of Plautus' theatre, and we are given a fleeting image of the effects of lighting within one of the Roman performance spaces. When linen *vela* were set up, they not only offered shade and protection from the heat for the spectators, but a joyous and festive series of colours that bathed both the audience and the stage space. Modern theatres typically use lighting to separate the audience from the stage, directing attention towards the actors. Lucretius suggests Rome instead separated the whole theatre from the outside world. This was a special space, awash with colour and encouraging a collective response to a comic performance (4.83: *conrident*). Rather than use lighting to create specific effects to complement an aspect of the dramatic narrative, in at least some outdoor venues specific lighting effects were sought to heighten the playful theatricality of the event. The double reference to the wind on the *vela* (4.77: *flutant*, 80: *fluitare*) suggests that the awnings had an acoustic affect as well, perhaps providing a low level of background noise that could dampen other sounds coming from outside of the performance space – a kind of 'white noise' – and conceivably it was something against which actors' voices might struggle.

The awnings in 208 represent an additional expense towards the comfort of the audience. While they were less technologically developed than the later, first-century examples, Livy is referring to something: the

---

[117] Text and translation, Rouse (1975) 282–3. For the use of awnings generally, see Dodge (1999) 235.

unusual nature of the claim and the presumption that *vela* had also been used earlier make it unlikely Livy is inventing the fact. This suggests that the Comitium too could hold a theatrical audience. In itself, such a conclusion is surprising, and invites two counter-arguments. The Comitium was, formally, a *templum* ('sacred area'; see Cicero, *de Republica* 2.11) and perhaps a dramatic performance would be inappropriate for the sacredness of the place that also served as the political centre of the city. On a more practical level, even as early as Plautus it was customary to dedicate statuary within the *templum*, and this would have affected sightlines. While neither argument can be denied, the clear indication that the Comitium could be covered by *vela* diminishes their force. The theatre of Dionysus at Athens (which was a sanctuary) and the Odeion of Pericles (in which pillars affected sightlines) provide obvious counter-examples from the Greek world, and, further, the seating in a temporary wooden amphitheatre physically would have covered the Lacus Curtius, another sacred location.[118]

There is therefore evidence for many separate venues for theatrical performance at the *ludi* in republican Rome, not all of which were always employed. Locations in front of the temples of the Magna Mater and of Apollo, near the centre of the forum directly south of the Comitium, within a temporary wooden amphitheatre, and in the Comitium itself may all have been used as theatrical venues at various times during Plautus' career. They were all, in essence, 'found spaces': areas not specifically demarcated for theatre most of the year, which became theatrical venues at the appropriate time. Temple steps or places of political assembly could when needed be turned into a *cavea*, with whatever area it faced becoming the stage. While we have no details of seats in the area of the Circus Flaminius, various possibilities exist. Further, there is an idealising tradition of turf seating used in early Rome (Ovid, *Ars Amatoria* 1.107–8), which might be at the Circus Flaminius, but equally this might point to other venues again.[119]

We cannot know the precise spaces in which a play such as *Hecyra* was mounted, but the use of three different venues seems likely. The initial performance at the *ludi Megalenses* would have been before the temple of the Magna Mater on the Palatine, before the sight of a tightrope walker led to the actors being forced offstage. The second performance at the

---

[118] Welch (1994) 76 n. 41.
[119] Livy 1.35.8–9 presents a different account of earlier theatrical seating. Juvenal 3.173 suggests turf seating was still used outside Rome in imperial times.

ludi funebres in 160 may have taken place in a wooden amphitheatre, built for gladiatorial combats but used for other entertainments as well, including *ludi scaenici*. That too resulted in disaster for Turpio's troupe. A few months later, at the *ludi Romani*, the speaker of the prologue can confidently claim *nunc turba nullast* ('Now there is no mob', *Hecyra* 43). His confidence comes because the play is being performed in another venue again – the Comitium, perhaps, or the west end of the forum – where gladiators were not expected.

Taken as a whole, the importance for flexibility on the part of the performers is clear. The plays needed to be adaptable to any of a variety of venues, each of which will create its actor–audience dynamic in a different way. Barriers could be erected to direct traffic and delineate the performance area (*cancelli* are mentioned in Varro, *Res Rusticae* 3.5.4, Cicero, *pro Sestio* 124.1, and Ovid, *Amores* 3.2.64), but it would be wrong to assume either that there was a clear division between *proscaenium* and *cavea*, or that a theatre audience was ever completely removed from the rest of Rome, despite efforts to isolate the theatre space from the rest of the city. Further, in some passages Plautus has attempted to create the sense of the play being site-specific, a technique that allows the audience to believe that it is seeing something unique to themselves, which in turn reinforces its commitment to the play.

Theatre architecture encourages this commitment from the audience. There were not that many opportunities for dramatic performance in Rome, but when one arose, there was very little that would prevent an individual who wanted to see a play from getting to the theatre. A spectator made no financial commitment, and did not even need to plan to attend, since it was not necessary to claim tickets in advance. Theatrical venues were always situated centrally, in a location appropriate to the god or person honoured at the *ludi*, and so for many, attending a play would not even require any significant travel, as most in the audience would be spending some time (before or after the show) at the other celebrations. Spectators could make a day of it. The theatre space becomes a focal point, concentrating and heightening the spirit of the festival, but this mood spreads beyond the theatre infusing the surrounding area with the spirit of the comedy – as most clearly in Plautus' *Curculio*.[120]

---

[120] Bennett (1997) 126 describes how 'the milieu which surrounds a theatre is always ideologically encoded' by the presence of the theatre: restaurants are places for meals before or after a performance, etc. In Rome this encoding is bidirectional: the theatre space helps to define the surrounding area as a focal point for the day's events at the *ludi*, but the festival atmosphere contributes significantly to the otherness of the space created for the theatrical event.

SET

Against this diversity, uniformity was provided by the set.[121] The temporary stage structure, whatever its form, could be erected quickly and might serve as the backdrop for a variety of entertainments. The set requirements of Roman comedy are surprisingly minimalistic: the texts rarely provide any hints concerning set decoration, and this points to a simple backdrop. This is not to say that there was no detail on the set. When characters go house shopping in *Mostellaria*, there are references at lines 817–19 to a *vestibulum* ('forecourt'; and see fr. 146L) and *postes* ('columns'; *Asinaria* 425 has *columnis*). While these might be part of the stage set, realised either with actual columns or through a painted backdrop,[122] it is as likely that all such details were supplied by audience imagination.[123] As long as an audience member can imagine an ordinary object from everyday life, verisimilitude in the set building is not required. Similarly, there is no positive evidence for the long, thin stages that become common in the empire: they are a product of a changing dynamic between performers and the audience. Indeed, such a stage shape would not be possible in many of the venues actually used.

The set was of wood, it was temporary, and, depending on the particular venue in which the play was mounted, it may have been set up and taken down in a matter of hours.[124] Everything about the theatre context suggests that the set was generic: constructed by the magistrates for the *ludi* and not by the troupe hired to perform, a given performance area might be used by multiple troupes in a given festival (Livy 41.27.5, in 174 BC). There were three doors (which, as in life, opened inwards[125]) and a *scaenae*

---

[121] This claim will be corroborated in Chapter 3, with the discussion of role doubling.

[122] Valerius Maximus 2.4.6 indicates the first polychrome stage building was made in 99 BC: *Claudius Pulcher scaenam varietate colorum adumbravit, vacuis ante pictura tabulis extensam* ('Claudius Pulcher applied a variety of colours to the stage, which previously had consisted of unpainted boards'; text and translation, Shackleton Bailey (2000) 158–9). This is unlikely to be true. *Skēnographia* ('scene-painting') was apparently used in the Greek tradition in the fifth century (see Aristotle, *Poetics* 1449a18), and it would be surprising if it had never been employed in Rome.

[123] When I have directed Plautine comedies, the minimalism suggested by the evidence was taken to an extreme, and only empty doorframes were used to delimit the performance area with no further backdrop. This demonstrated that this limit did not in fact pose any difficulties for the actors or the audiences.

[124] On this question see also Gilula (1996) 486–9.

[125] Beare (1964) 289–90, drawing on *Curculio* 158–61.

frons, which was painted to resemble three generic attached buildings.[126] It was possible to lock a door from the outside; when it is additionally bolted from inside (as at *Mostellaria* 425–6), Plautus emphasises that no one can cross the threshold from either direction.[127]

The two side entrances of the performance area serve to polarise all outdoor offstage locations.[128] Discussions often employ the terms 'left' and 'right' without reference to whether this is from the actors' or the audience's perspective.[129] On the Roman comic stage it seems to be typical for the exit stage left to lead to the urban centre (the forum), and the exit stage right to lead to the harbour and the countryside. Characters appearing stage right come from away (*a peregre*, Vitruvius 5.6.8), as at *Menaechmi* 555–6, when Sosicles (Menaechmus II) attempts to throw off pursuers by throwing a garland stage left (*ad laevam manum*) before exiting towards the harbour stage right. Similarly, at *Amphitruo* 333, Mercurius hears the voice of Sosia to his right (*dextra*), who has returned from the harbour. It is unlikely, however, that a universal convention existed and 'it is hazardous to infer a rule'.[130] In *Andria*, the entrances are reversed. Davus says, *ego quoque hinc ab dextera | venire me assimulabo* (734–5: 'I'll pretend that I too am arriving here from the right') and soon exclaims, *quid turbaest apud forum!* (745: 'What a crowd in the forum!').[131] Confusion exists only because of the assumption that the forum must always exist stage left. It is much simpler to remove the convention entirely: the forum is in whatever direction someone exits when they say they are going to the forum, and the country is the other way, unless the play provides an alternate offstage geography. *Rudens* falls in this category. In this play, the city and harbour are thought to exist on the same side of the stage, with the shore where the shipwrecked Labrax

---

[126] On set painting see Gilula (1996) 489–92.   [127] Barton (1972) and Milnor (2002).

[128] Duckworth (1952) 85–7. See also Beare (1964) 248–55, with his summary of ancient sources and previous discussions.

[129] Since modern theatrical parlance prefers 'stage left' and 'stage right' (i.e. from the actor's position, as he faces the audience), I follow that convention here.

[130] Gratwick (1993) 191; and see *Miles Gloriosus* 1216.

[131] Text and translation, Barsby (2001) I: 134–5. Barsby's convoluted explanation, following Beare (1964) 180–81 and 248–55, requires *ab dextera* to mean 'from stage left': both suggest the actor turns to face upstage 'so that the actors' right and audience's right coincide' (134–5 n. 42, and see Beare (1964) 181 n.). Davus says *quoque* because Chremes is also coming from that direction (his house is there according to lines 355 and 361). Soon Davus wishes to confer with Mysis *ad dexteram* (line 751), which must mean that she crosses past Chremes to meet Davus near the wing he has just used. Beare is determined to demonstrate that the Romans perpetuated the Greek assignments; that claim too is dubious.

and his *meretrices* are washed up on the other. At 855–6, Plesidippus says:

> *abi sane ad litus curriculo, Trachalio,*
> *iube illos in urbem ire obviam ad portum mihi . . .*

Go then, Trachalio, run to the shore, and
tell them to go to the city and meet me at the port.

Duckworth says the shore is stage left and the city and harbour are stage
right, and argues that 'the playwright is following the normal stage setting
as closely as possible' given the remote setting of the play.[132] This is
special pleading, given that Daemones looks offstage at drowning men:
hac ad dexteram – | viden? – secundum litus (156–7: 'There they are, to the
right – do you see? – along the shore'). In the end, of course, it does not
matter for an audience seeking to understand the play in performance.
Assuming the actors have been consistent, the audience will already know
what the offstage geography is: Arcturus' prologue identifies both *villa
proxima propter mare* (34: 'a house right next to the sea') and the direction
from which the young man comes onstage, *ad portum* (65); each
comment could be reinforced with a gesture. In *Rudens*, all those not
native to Cyrene arrive shipwrecked at the shore stage right, while the
economic centre of the area is presented stage left. This distinction is
maintained consistently throughout the play, and only those expecting a
non-existent stage convention have difficulty.[133]

The Roman stage polarises local and foreign, not discriminating
whether the traveller comes by road or by ship. Most plays do not
indicate which lies in which direction, because, in performance, it is
always obvious.[134] It may be that on the Greek stage a consistent convention was employed, with the harbour and urban centre presented on
stage left and stage right leading to the country.[135] But even if a Roman
audience knew this convention, it could not be followed when the natural
distinction for the Roman mind (employed in every play except *Rudens*)
was between harbour and city centre. At times the playwright would have

---

[132] Duckworth (1952) 86, and see p. 83 for the setting of *Rudens* generally (which also applies to
Vidularia).
[133] The logical difficulty of having a shore in one direction and a harbour in the other, is of a different
order. If we must, we can assume the play takes place on a peninsula.
[134] In my experience, any difficulties with the offstage geography become painfully obvious in
rehearsal.
[135] See Pollux, *Onomasticon* 4.126, though there are inconsistencies in Pollux: 'On any view his
account is confused' (Beare (1964) 254).

to rearrange entrances as he adapted his model, but much more significant changes were regularly made.

In addition to the side entrances, it is possible for an actor to access the performance area through one of the doors in the *scaena* that constitutes the backdrop for every Roman comedy. The demands of the plays require variously one, two, or three doors. All doors will have been of equal size, and Beare is surely correct in suggesting the construction will always have had three doors, but at times one or more may not have been used: 'any door which was not required in a particular play was for the time being simply disregarded'.[136] The distance between one door and another was *tres unos passus* (*Bacchides* 832: 'three single steps'), assuming that these are normal-sized steps and are not comically exaggerated. The regularity of comic plots means that a door could represent one of three things: the house of a prominent male citizen, the house of a *meretrix* or *leno*, or a temple. The most common situation calls for two citizen houses: *Casina*, *Cistellaria*, *Epidicus*, *Miles Gloriosus* (where one is the house of the *miles*[137]), *Andria*, and *Eunuchus*. Another common situation has two doors, representing the house of a citizen and of the *meretrix*: *Asinaria*, *Menaechmi*, *Persa*, and *Poenulus*. Terence's *Adelphoe* finds a mid-ground between these two, depicting the houses of Micio (a prominent male citizen) and Sostrata (a female citizen, whose daughter Pamphilia is the beloved of Micio's adopted son Aeschinus). Rarely when only two doors are used one may designate a citizen's house, the other a temple (as in *Rudens*). Against these twelve instances, we may count two where only one door is used, and thirteen where three doors are used. When one door is used, it always represents a citizen's house (*Amphitruo*, *Captivi*). When three are used, two would typically represent citizen houses, and the third may equally be a third citizen (*Stichus*, *Trinummus*, *Heauton Timoroumenos*[138]), a temple (*Aulularia*, *Mercator*,[139] *Mostellaria*,[140] *Vidularia*[141]), or the house of a *meretrix* (*Pseudolus*, *Phormio*, *Hecyra*). The last possibility, where one house contains a citizen, the second a temple,

---

[136] Beare (1964) 285, and generally see 285–94, Duckworth (1952) 83.
[137] It is possible that there should be a third house representing a temple, but the reference at line 411 to an altar is as likely to be figurative.
[138] It is not clear that Phania's house is onstage. Barsby (2001) I: 194–5 n. 23 argues that it is, based on lines 168–72.
[139] Reference is made to an altar at 676.
[140] While the temple is not used, an altar is required from 1097 to at least 1145.
[141] Though fragmentary, the references in fr. IV *haec myrtus Veneris est* and fr. VIII *nescioqui servos e myrteta prosiluit* demonstrate that there is a 'myrtle grove' of Venus on stage which could be represented simply as a temple with altar.

the third a *meretrix*, is found in *Bacchides*,[142] *Curculio*, and *Truculentus*.[143] One door always leads to the house of a citizen; there are never two houses of *meretrices* or two temples; every other permutation is represented in the extant plays.[144] Wiles suggests that 'no play requires more than two domestic doorways'[145] and in a sense this is correct: there is no play which contains entering characters talking back into three different houses as they emerge (and this is the only means of determining when a door is 'required'). Nevertheless, so many *palliatae* plots naturally presume three doors, that we should assume three doors were always available.

Some plays require an altar in the performance area.[146] Seven plays use three doors and have one designated as the entrance to a temple; six plays use three doors and do not have a temple. It follows that there must have been a means to identify a temple that was separate from the set, and which could be introduced by the troupe. I suggest that in these cases a generic stage altar is positioned in front of the door representing a temple;[147] convention and audience imagination would provide the rest. This is not the only solution possible (minor set dressings for temples or other distinctive houses, such as that of a *leno*, may also have been added by a troupe), but a removeable altar is the most expedient solution. There is no indication of more formal sets of any kind.[148] Altars are not required simply because a character invokes a god or utters a prayer: indeed, I suggested above that prayers to Apollo make best sense in terms of production at the *ludi Apollinares*. The stage altar has no presumed association for the audience with a god until it is provided one during the performance of the play. As with the wing entrances, it remains unmarked until labelled by an actor's speech.

Occasionally, the altar is used as more than an iconographic shorthand for a temple location, and is incorporated into the action of the play.

---

[142] Reference is made to an altar at 172–3.

[143] Reference is made to an altar at 476. This is an unusual scene, however, blurring the indoor/outdoor distinction (see Duckworth (1952) 127).

[144] This is not to say other combinations were inconceivable. What, for example, was the disposition of houses in Plautus' lost *Lenones Gemini* ('The Pimp Twins')? Perhaps in this play two houses lead to the house of a *leno* (played by the same actor in the same mask?), and therefore each contained a *meretrix*. We cannot know.

[145] Wiles (1991) 55. The only source cited in support is Beare, who believes there were three doors. Indeed, his discussion of *Curculio* (Wiles (1991) 58) requires two (side) doors and an altar to Aesculapius in the centre. Such an altar is thought to be in front of a temple of Aesculapius, from which Cappadox emerges at 216.

[146] See Duckworth (1952) 83–4, Hanson (1959) 86–90, and Saunders (1911).

[147] Duckworth (1952) 83–4.   [148] Wiles (1991) 56.

At *Mostellaria* 1094–1180, the slave Tranio seeks refuge at an altar onstage and is joined by Callidamates. Similarly, at *Rudens* 691–885, Palaestra and Ampelisca seek sanctuary at the altar of Venus. Such sanctuary is inviolable, based on a religious tenet that had been exploited as a dramatic trope since fifth-century Greek tragedy. Nevertheless, a loophole existed: when the girls seek sanctuary at an altar of Venus, Labrax threatens, *Volcanum adducam, is Venerist adversarius* (*Rudens* 761: 'I'll bring Vulcan; he's Venus' opposite'). With an allusion to the divine marriage and Venus' famous adultery, Labrax intends to smoke his quarry away from their refuge. If they leave by choice (because of the heat or smoke), it would seem he has not technically violated their sanctuary (the threat is also made at *Heauton Timoroumenos* 975). Rather than seek to explain this behaviour in religious terms, it is better to see it too as a stock solution to a recurrent problem in New Comedy, one that was well known to Menander as well. In an extant fragment of *Perinthia* ('The Girl from Perinthus'), the servant Daos finds himself being smoked off an altar by his fellow slaves.[149]

There is an ordinariness in the regularity of the set. However exotic or contrived the offstage settings, and whatever name the play happens to give to the town, the setting of the *fabulae palliatae* is, essentially, always the same street. What happens on a stage street goes well beyond real-world practice. Banquet scenes (*Asinaria* 828–914, *Persa* 757–858, *Stichus* 683–775, *Mostellaria* 308–91) and *toilette/boudoir* scenes (*Mostellaria* 157–292, *Truculentus* 449–642) were occasionally taken out-of-doors to comic effect.[150] These were indoor activities for the Greeks and the Romans, yet the inherent artificiality in the stage world of the *palliatae* allows such immodest behaviour. At no point does the audience stop to wonder why Philematium in *Mostellaria* is getting dressed in public (though in performance the fact that she is invites many possibilities for comic business). It is, indeed, symptomatic of the comic exuberance of the Plautine stage world. It would be unnecessarily restricting and no less unrealistic to assume that such scenes must be performed in the *vestibulum* (assuming doors were recessed, which we have seen is unnecessary). While the setting is ordinary, it is not naturalistic.

Equally artificial is how little neighbours seem to know about each other before a play begins, even though neighbours are always thought to share a common wall (this is key to the plot of *Miles Gloriosus*, for example). There is no alley between houses that may provide locations

---

[149] Arnott (1996a) 472–501.   [150] Duckworth (1952) 126–7, Lowe (1995).

from which one may eavesdrop, as is sometimes suggested.[151] The word used in Roman comedy for the street can be *platea* (e.g. *Adelphoe* 574), *via* (e.g. *Mercator* 798), or *angiportum* (*Pseudolus* 960–61), though more usually *angiportus/-um* refers to 'a street in the rear and parallel to the stage, from which a character can reach his house through a garden'.[152] *Angiportus/-um* is never used for a route perpendicular to the stage, though this old idea is perpetuated in the *Oxford Latin Dictionary*, which defines it as 'a narrow passage, alley, lane'. The *angiportum* is most often used in Roman comedy to explain why a given character does not return to the stage by the same means that he had left it. At *Persa* 444–6, for example, Toxilus tells the *leno* Dordalus,

> *abi istac travorsis angiportis ad forum;*
> *eadem istaec facito mulier ad me transeat*
> *per hortum.*

> Go that way to the forum, using the next street.
> (*Toxilus points away from the forum.*)
> Let my woman come to me that same way,
> through the garden.

However we choose to rationalise Toxilus making Dordalus go to the forum 'the long way' (perhaps it is it to avoid the chance of meeting Sagaristio and Saturio's daughter in their Persian costumes, or perhaps it is to provide a petty annoyance for the pimp), Toxilus' instructions mean that the character of Lemniselenis does not appear on stage until line 763, a dramatic revelation at the end of the play. Later, Toxilus tells the disguised Sagaristio, *per angiportum rursum te ad me recipito | illac per hortum* ('come back to my house by the next street, through the garden that way,' lines 678–9). Sagaristio exits by means of a wing at line 710, and when he re-appears (following on the heels of Lemniselenis), he does so from the house of Toxilus' master. The *angiportum* may have been a conventional device playwrights used to help smooth the adaptation of Greek New Comedy, or it may have been a means to create stronger entrances for key characters. In either case, it too is part of the stage world defined by the set.

These examples demonstrate that backstage communication existed between all the points on stage. Not only could actors leave by one route

---

[151] Wiles (1991) 55–6 believes alleyways could exist, but does not consider the requirements of *Miles Gloriosus*.

[152] Harsh (1937), Duckworth (1952) 87, and see 87–8, Beare (1964) 256–63, and Beacham (1991) 61–2.

and return by another, but characters could as well, when the text provided an appropriate explanation. This is what we would expect, but it should be stated since not every possible stage structure would allow this.[153] Given that a Roman troupe could be using any of a number of performance spaces, a uniform set is needed: uniform both as it appears to the audience, but, more importantly, how it functions backstage. The architecturally simplest design (a flat wall with three doors placed in it) is in fact the most flexible set building from the perspective of the actors, and the most versatile for the comic narratives. Its use by Roman performers means it should be possible to discern the mechanics of the stage action even for those plays about which didascalic information (and consequently the precise performance venue) does not survive.

COSTUME

In fact costume is relatively unimportant in New Comedy.

W. Beare[154]

The genre of *fabula palliata* is defined by its costume.[155] All characters wear a *tunica* ('tunic', Greek *chitôn*) over which men typically place a *pallium* ('cloak', Greek *himation*), women a *palla*. There are of course exceptions to this, and comedy did provide opportunity for outlandish get-ups that would contribute to the humour of a play. The question is whether costuming practices represented custom (and so were flexible in their application) or convention (and thus provided rigid codification). The data concerning comic costume are mostly late, and almost certainly do not refer to second-century performance. Thus, however informative Donatus, *de Comoedia* 8.6–7, and Pollux, *Onomasticon* 4.118–20, may seem to be, and however beautiful the miniature illustrations in Ter-entian manuscripts may appear, 'all of this material is of doubtful

---

[153] Indeed, Tanner (1969) suggests that the earliest stages were built on streets of Rome and actually used real house doors for the left and right doors, while the central door was 'false' – that it just led to the alley that was perpendicular to the street with the stage. Such a stage would severely limit an actor's possibilities: because any move from a wing to a door would require travelling at least the equivalent of three city blocks (and possibly moving through buildings), many doubling options and narrative options would become impossible.

[154] Beare (1964) 187.

[155] Beare (1964) 264–6. See also Saunders (1909), Duckworth (1952) 88–92, and Beare (1964) 185–92.

value'.[156] While there is no doubt these sources present an account of comic costume, we cannot know if they refer to *palliatae* as originally performed. Pollux seems to be thinking of Greek sources, and Donatus and the Terentian miniatures reflect, if anything, later Roman stage practice. Even if these were found to be applicable to Plautus and Terence, they represent a codification that is unduly rigorous and is not likely to be applicable universally on the comic stage. While *senes* may often have worn white and carried sticks, and *lenones* may have often worn garish, multi-coloured *pallia*, it does not make sense for this to be required, when one of the chief purposes of theatrical costume was to distinguish individuals from each other. When there were two *senes*, one may have had a stick and another not had one.

Some general tendencies may be observed. For the most part, costume coincided with a generic representation of contemporary real-world clothing. The combination of *tunica* and *pallium/palla* is standard: even the shipwrecked, shivering Labrax washes ashore with both items (*Rudens* 549–50; the diminutives *tuniculam et* ... *misellum pallium* may imply they have been shrunk by the seawater, with the actor wearing clothes that are too small for him). The *pallium* indicated the genre of the play, but otherwise the plays refer to standard items of Roman clothing. Young men and particularly soldiers could wear a *chlamys*, a shorter Greek cloak fastened at the shoulder: Pseudolus declares *etiam opust chlamyde et machaera et petaso* (*Pseudolus* 735: 'I also need a military cloak, sabre, and broad-brimmed hat') for the costume of a soldier's attendant; at the end of *Miles Gloriosus*, Pyrgopolynices has been stripped *de tunica et chlamyde et machaera* (1423: 'of [his] tunic, military cloak, and sabre'); for Sagaristio's costume, Toxilus orders *tunicam atque zonam, et chlamydem* ... *et causeam* (*Persa* 155: 'tunic and belt, military cloak and Macedonian broad-brimmed hat')[157] the use of Greek names for articles of clothing reflects an interesting transference, as Roman attitudes to Greek costume items (which characterise individuals as foreign, military, and perhaps eastern)

---

[156] Beare (1964) 184. Compare Jory (1967) 21–2: 'The accounts of comic costume by the Greek Pollux (4.118–20) and the Roman Donatus (*de Comoedia* 8.6) do not tally and may reflect real differences between Greek and Roman stage practice.' For a more favourable account of the value of these passages, see Wiles (1991) 188–92: 'while Pollux is more concerned with isolating a technical vocabulary, Donatus is concerned with what the costumes mean' (189).

[157] The *machaera* was a single-bladed sword (therefore 'sabre') that had recently been introduced to Rome by soldiers fighting in Greece (Ketterer (1986a) 212 n. 13). The combination of *chlamys* and *machaera* (as well as *zona/sona*, 'belt') is adopted by Charinus in *Mercator* 910–27. The *petasus* had a strap so that it could be removed from the head and could hang down one's back, leaving one's hands free. The *causea* was a Macedonian version of the broad-brimmed hat, and therefore also associated particularly with soldiers.

function in the notionally Greek world as symbols for Persia, another foreign, eastern, military power.[158] Here and elsewhere, there are indications that a slave's costume would essentially be like that of his or her master,[159] though Epidicus needs to be given *soccos, tunicam, pallium* (*Epidicus* 725: 'shoes, a tunic, and a cloak') when he is freed.[160] Harpax in *Pseudolus* (and Simia disguised as him) wears the same costume as a soldier. Domestic slaves wore the *pallium*, but on the stage at least it may have appeared more like a modern winter scarf, and consequently was more easily thrown over the shoulder, as in the traditional gesture of the *servus currens* ('running slave'), a stock routine in Greek and Roman New Comedy (*Captivi* 778–9, *Epidicus* 194–5, fr. 178L, *Phormio* 844–5). Varro's claim that men who worked in the countryside wore goatskins (*Res Rusticae* 2.2) may also have been reflected in stage practice.

While costume was not used in specific ways to identify characters (beyond the general practices described above), there were ways items of costume could create specific associations for the audience. The use of the *petasus* funtioned as a shorthand within the stage world to indicate that a character had travelled (or was about to travel) a great distance: it was an iconographic signifier of Hermes the Greek messenger god, who corresponds in many respects to the Roman Mercurius.[161] In *Amphitruo*, Sosia, Mercurius, Amphitruo, and Jupiter all wear a *petasus* with Mercurius and Jupiter disguised as Sosia and Amphitruo respectively. Mercurius addresses the audience (142–7):

> nunc internosse ut nos possitis facilius,
> ego has habebo usque in petaso pinnulas,
> tum meo patri autem torulus inerit aureus
> sub petaso: id signum Amphitruoni non erit.
> ea signa nemo horum familiarium
> videre poterit: verum vos videbitis.

> Now, so that you can identify us easier,
> I shall always have this little feather in my hat,

---

[158] Similarly, Saturio's daughter will wear *crepidula* ('Greek slippers', *Persa* 464) as part of her Persian disguise.

[159] When Mercurius complains about *hunc ornatum* ('this costume', *Amphitruo* 116) and his *servili schema* (117: 'appearance as a slave'), he is contrasting it with the special appearance normally reserved for divine characters. There is some distinction between the appearance of slaves and free, however, as discussed in Chapter 3.

[160] Comic footwear generally is either the *soccus* ('slipper': *Cistellaria* 697, *Bacchides* 332, *Trinummus* 720, *Persa* 124) or the *solea* ('sandal': *Casina* 709, *Mostellaria* 384, *Truculentus* 363, 367, 479, 631).

[161] A South Italian comic vase (Oxford 1928.12, *PhV*² 50 (Trendall (1967) 40) shows Dionysus and an actor dressed as Hermes, wearing a *petasus*.

but there will be a little gold knot in my father's
hat. This token will not be on Amphitruo's.
No one in the household can see
these tokens, but you shall see them.

A passage like this demands speculation concerning the nature of comic description.[162] Precise details distinguish two pairs of characters which might enable the audience to tell them apart. But since each role is played by a different actor, this is not a challenge in any case. What then is the purpose of the tokens? Both are presented with diminutives (*pinnulas, torulus*) but they are, of necessity, able to be seen easily by members of a large audience. To serve the narrative function, the tokens must be visible and consequently they cannot actually have been small. The joke lies rather in the tokens' invisibility to the human characters in the play. If Mercurius wore a large ostrich feather in his broad-brimmed hat ('this little feather') and Jupiter's hat had dangling from it a long garish braid ('a little golden knot'), comic benefits emerge: Mercurius gets a laugh with the inappropriate description of his feather; Jupiter gets a laugh when the audience eventually sees his *torulus*; both divine characters wear a silly costume throughout the play that doesn't alter the way they are treated in the stage world, reducing their status, and could increase audience identification with the human characters. Further, the supposedly identical characters are probably distinguishable in any case. This example points to many of the difficulties involved in examining comic narrative for evidence of stage practice. When Curculio complains of *Graeci palliati* (*Curculio* 288: 'cloaked Greeks'), the Roman audience is aware not only that the character is a Greek himself (the play is set in Epidaurus, though Curculio's complaint and prejudices are clearly Roman), but that he, though a parasite, is performing the stock routine of the 'running slave' as the line is delivered; his *pallium* was no doubt distinctively hitched over his shoulder as he says this. Such comments cannot be taken at face value.

As these examples show, many plots of *fabulae palliatae* involve impersonation and disguise.[163] In *Asinaria*, Leonida's impersonation of the household slave Saurea does not require any change of costume, since

---

[162] Christenson (2000) 164 believes 'apart from the unusually high number of (legitimate) hiatuses in 142–7, there is no certain indication of interpolation'; even if this passage were interpolated, the issues discussed here would still hold true for the performance of the play. See also Beare (1964) 189.

[163] See Muecke (1986).

the merchant deceived has met neither. Within the world of the play, Saurea exists, but he does not appear on stage except through the impersonation. Similarly, Casina does not appear on stage in *Casina* except as played by Chalinus: there, however, Casina is a known quantity and consequently Chalinus is disguised with wedding veils. In practice, a disguise need not be convincing: the audience knows when one character is impersonating another, and so the disguise functions only within the play. In *Casina*, part of the humour stems from Lysidamus being fooled by what is clearly a poor disguise. We know that Chalinus continues to behave in a masculine way (see 840–54) and the humour is maximised if, through the audience's discrepant knowledge, it can see the dual identity that Lysidamus cannot.[164] Perhaps the wedding veils insufficiently cover the slave's beard. It follows that the nature of the plots of Roman comedy will favour a disguise that emphasises the disparity between what the audience sees and what deceived characters perceive.

An eye patch seems to have been a sufficient means to conceal one's identity. Curculio adopts this disguise in his encounter with Lyco, who calls him *Unoculus* ('One-eye'; see 392–400, 543, and 582). This and the name Summanus, who is not a real person in the dramatic world (543–7), permit the deception to last long enough. Because the disguise is particularly ineffective in real terms, it is something that Curculio can hastily don, while delivering 391:

> *simulabo quasi non noverim. heus tu, te volo.*

> (*to audience*) I'll pretend I don't know him.
>   (*He puts on an eyepatch.*)
> (*to Lyco*)   Hey you, I want you.

That the costume is assumed mid-line suggests that it takes only a fraction of a second, which further reinforces its comic success. Similarly, when in *Miles Gloriosus* Pleusicles disguises himself as a sailor, within the play the disguise is perfect: Pyrgopolynices says *nescio quis eccum incedit | ornatu quidem thalassico* (1281–2: 'I don't know this guy coming rigged like a seaman'; Pleusicles repeats the word *ornatu* in his soliloquy, line 1286). Part of this disguise involves an eye patch: *nam ille qui lanam ob oculum habebat laevom, nauta non erat!* (1430: 'Hey, that guy with the wool on his

---

[164] This does not mean that the male actor playing a male character disguised as a female character cannot attempt female mannerisms to comic effect, as long as the gesture is always affected in a way intended to fool only the character being duped.

left eye – he was no sailor!'; see 1306–10). So common is this deception that it can be alluded to in passing: Demaenetus recollects that in his youth, his father dressed as a sea-captain to help him (*Asinaria* 68–70). By identifying the *senex* as a former *adulescens*, the audience is led to believe he will not function as a blocking character to Argyrippus' schemes, though eventually he does (from 830–941). The passage unusually raises questions that consider the lives of the characters outside of the dramatic narrative. The passage forces at least some in the audience to ask if the woman whom Demaenetus loved is the shrewish wife Artemona he now seeks to undermine. Whether she is or not (it would take the convoluted plot of a *palliata* to explain Artemona's financial position if she began as a *meretrix*), the passage raises questions about the nature of dramatic love that are never answered, but which are intriguing to contemplate.

There was also a political and an economic dimension to costumes on the Roman stage. What degree of ostentation was used in the costumes? The *lex Oppia*, carried in 215, imposed restrictions on women's dress as part of a conservative sumptuary programme, *ne qua mulier plus semunciam auri haberet neu vestimento versicolori uteretur* (Livy 34.1.3: 'that no woman should have more than a half-ounce of gold, nor multicoloured clothing').[165] In particular, women wearing purple were seen as extravagant (Livy 34.7.1–10). The law was repealed in 195 (Livy 34.1–8), which means that it was in effect for all but the last decade of Plautus' career. What was its effect on performance? We do not know how the audience would respond to ostentatious costumes in the fictional Greek world that were forbidden to them in the real world, and it is possible that costumes of female characters observed the same restrictions as Roman women's dress. It might equally be that characters partake of a liberty no longer enjoyed by the Romans: when Sagaristio tries to add 10 minas to the sale price of a supposedly Persian girl *pro vestimentis* (*Persa* 669: 'for her clothes'), at least part of the cost is due to their exotic nature – she is *ornatam . . . lepide in peregrinum modum* (158: 'dressed charmingly in foreign style').[166] In favour of this possibility is the repeated emphasis on the *aurum atque ornamenta* (*Miles Gloriosus* 981: 'gold and trinkets'; see 1127, 1147, and 1302) of Philocomasium. Since the character appears both before and after these

---

[165] See Johnston (1980).

[166] The passage in which the price for Saturio's daughter is negotiated (*Persa* 661–85) is odd. Once the price of 60 minas is agreed upon (665–7), Sagaristio attempts to negotiate for more money for her wardrobe (669), with no clear resolution, and Dordalus only pays 60 minas (683), and removes the price of the bag that holds his payment (684–5; see also *Epidicus* 632 and Ketterer (1986b) 97–8). The *leno* Dordalus' petty gain is successful, but Toxilus' scheme is not. It is possible that *Persa* 668a–671a are intrusive, reflecting an alternative performed tradition.

four passages, it is unlikely her jewellery was never seen or that all four passages were ironic. Further, the play is generally thought to be early, and, though this should not be pressed, it was probably written while the *lex Oppia* was in effect. The function of the *choragus* may be related to this. Most references in the plays to getting clothing are necessarily understood in a metatheatrical context (*Curculio* 464–6, *Persa* 157–60, *Trinummus* 857–8) or may be so understood (*Pseudolus* 1184–6). We do not know if troupes owned their own costumes, or if they rented some or all of them from the *choragus*, but there does seem to be a mechanism for itinerant troupes to have access to elaborate theatrical resources.[167]

One issue not usually considered is what the Romans wore under this costume. In the Greek tradition, of course, padded body suits simulated the nudity of a grotesque human form: men appeared with a distended belly, padded buttocks, and an oversized phallus. This Greek costume was distinctive, and a key part of the Greek tradition.[168] Over the course of the fourth century, however, the grotesqueness of the form was reduced: the phallus gets increasingly shortened until, by the time of Menander, it is no longer on display beneath the next layer of the character's costume.[169] Since we lack contemporary illustrations, the evidence comes only from the text.

There are hints that in some form, the phallus was preserved as the Greek plays were adapted for the Roman audience. In *Rudens*, the slave Sceparnio has seized and released the *meretrix* Ampelisca (see 424–5), who has appeared from the temple of Venus where she has been taking refuge with a water pitcher (428–9):[170]

> SCEP.   *quid nunc vis?*
>
> AMP.   *sapienti ornatus quid velim indicium facit.*
>
> SCEP.   *meus quoque hic sapienti ornatus quid velim indicium facit.*
>
> SCEPAR. What do you want?
>
> AMPEL.   (*pointing to her pitcher*) To a person of sense,
>   This piece of equipment reveals what I want.
>
> SCEPAR. To a person of sense, this piece of equipment
>   Of mine reveals what I want, too.   (tr. Smith)

---

[167] In an epigram of Lucillius dating from the time of Nero, a tragic actor sells his props to relieve his poverty, which suggests they are his possessions (*Palatine Anthology* 11.189).

[168] Beare (1964) 356–8 n. 2 argues against the phallus in Aristophanes, but without success. *Clouds* 537–9 is funny precisely because the padded bodysuit was a standard component of comedy. See also *Clouds* 731–4, *Acharnians* 590–92, 784–7, and 1118–21, about which see Porter (2004).

[169] Green (2006).   [170] Ketterer (1986c) 38–9.

If the actor has a visible phallus, the *double entendre* is reinforced, as the repeated *ornatus* evokes the *ornamenta* of the costume and properites. More oblique is the exchange between the drunk Callidamates and his patient *meretrix* Delphium at *Mostellaria* 324–31:

CALL.   *duce me, amabo.*

DEL.   *cave ne cadas, asta.*

CALL.   *o . . . o . . . ocellus es meus;*
        tuus sum alumnus, mel meum.

DEL.   *cave modo ne prius in via accumbas*
        quam illi, ubi lectus est stratus, concumbimus.

CALL.   *sine, sine cadere me.*

DEL.   *sino, sed hoc, quod mi in manu est:*
        si cades, non cades quin cadam tecum.

CALL.   *iacentis tollet postea nos ambos aliquis.*

DEL.   *madet homo.*

CALL.   Lead me, please.

DEL.   See you don't fall. Stand up.

CALL.   (*snuggling into her breast*)
        You're my-eye-eye darling; I'm your baby, honey.

DEL.   Only see you don't first lie down in the street,
        Till we sleep together there where the bed is all spread.

CALL.   Let . . . let me fall.

DEL.   I will, but this, here in my hand . . .
        If you fall, you won't fall unless I tumble with you.

CALL.   Then someone'll lift up the two of us lying there.

DEL.   (*to the audience*) The man is drunk.

The passage contains unusually frank references to sex. Questa accepts Leo's *comcumbimus* ('sleep together') for the *coimus* ('have sex') of the manuscripts (this would be the only use of *coeo* before Lucretius). *Hoc* in 328 refers to Callidamates' penis: Nixon avoids the innuendo in his translation, but like Questa is satisfied to assign the end of 328 to Delphium, so that *hoc* is in her hand; in contrast, Lindsay assigns only *sino* to her, with Callidamates completing the rest of the line. *Cadere* is being used in multiple senses: Callidamates falls to the ground literally in lines 324 and 328; in 329, though, two other meanings are introduced: Callidamates' penis will fall once it loses its erection (*cades . . . cades*; see

Martial 7.18.12), after they have had sex (*cadam*, 'tumble').[171] Neither *hic ... ornatus* nor *hoc* require the actor to be wearing a costume phallus of any size: a well-placed gesture is sufficient for comic effect. But the possibility cannot be ruled out, and it is not acceptable to suggest the joke is an accidental holdover from the Greek original of these plays: we should always assume Plautus recognises the potential for humour in his own plays.

The most explicit *double entendres* occur at *Casina* 902–15, but (since the confusion is being described after the fact) there are no necessary costume requirements. Granting that a phallus may be part of a character's costume, potential references multiply: when Paegnium assaults Dordalus with the phrase *restim tu tibi cape crassam ac suspende te* (*Persa* 815: 'take a thick rope and hang yourself'), it should not surprise that an actor in performance would naturally add a genital gesture; in my experience actors need very little to motivate taking an easy laugh based on bawdy humour. The nature of *double entendre* means that there is no need for a physical phallus as part of the actor's costume, but if it existed, such an accessory would be able to be put to use.[172] A papyrus fragment, *P. Berol.* inv. 13927,[173] lists a mime requiring two prop phalluses. In a fifth-century AD mime, at least, they were not standard equipment and needed to be placed on the prop list for a particular narrative.

Further, the regular description of slaves, old men, and *lenones* as 'potbellied' (*ventriosus*, as at *Mercator* 639, *Pseudolus* 1218, *Rudens* 317), corroborated by visual evidence such as terracotta statuettes, also argues for some form of padding beneath the costume of certain character types. In some cases, artificial padding seems assured: Cappadox in *Curculio* has a belly so grossly distended that *geminos in ventre habere videor filios* (221: 'I seem to have twin sons inside my gut') and Alcumena in *Amphitruo* is actually pregnant with twins, which Phillips argues was represented with exaggerated comic padding.[174] Other padding for female characters may have been common. Antamonides' claims he does not want the company of a *tibicina* ('pipe-girl') because *nescias utrum ei maiores buccaene an mammae sient* (*Poenulus* 1416: 'you don't know which are bigger – her cheeks or her breasts'). Since the distended cheeks of pipers were thought

---

[171] Adams (1982) 194 gives *Persa* 656 as the only sexual use of *cado*: the *leno* Dordalus sympathises with the maiden pretending to be a *meretrix*, promising her freedom *si crebro cades* ('once you tumble a few times'). In *Mostellaria*, as Delphium switches from the second to the first person, the sense of the repeated verb needs to assume a different meaning.

[172] This question is also discussed at Prehn (1916) 71–81.

[173] See Cunningham in Rusten and Cunningham (2002) 418–21, who present a normalised text.

[174] Phillips (1985).

to be ugly,[175] the humour of this line depends on both cheeks and breasts being large (and both being ugly), and this in turn suggests that comic women would have large breasts.[176] In *Casina*, Olympio uses a diminutive to describe the disguised Chalinus' breast: *edepol papillam bellulam* (848: 'Pollux, what a nice little breast'). He is probably being ironic, or is describing what he expects to see (if this were really Casina) and not the chest evident before him.[177] Chalinus metatheatrically manipulates the same variables usually employed by an actor. Such padding was not universal: there is no indication of padding on *adulescentes*, for example.

One piece of evidence that seems not to have been adduced in this context is Cicero, *de Officiis* 1.129:

scaenicorum quidem mos tantam habet vetere disciplina verecundiam, ut in scaenam sine subligaculo prodeat nemo; verentur enim, ne, si quo casu evenerit, ut corporis partes quaedam aperiantur aspiciantur non decore.

As for stage people, their custom, because of its traditional discipline, carries modesty to such a point that no actor would ever step out upon the stage without a *subligaculum* on, for fear he might make an improper exhibition, if by some accident certain parts of his person should happen to become exposed.[178]

The use of *scaenicorum* demonstrates stage actors are being described. These actors display modesty, despite the loss of political rights associated with being *infamis*. The *subligaculum* provides protection against

---

[175] This is the traditional reason given for why Athena discarded the *auloi* when she invented them, e.g. Telestes fr. 805a *Poetae Melici Graeci* (Page), Apollodorus, *Library* 1.4.2, Ovid, *Fasti* 6.697–702, Hyginus, *Fabulae* 165, and Plutarch, *Alcibiades* 2.5.

[176] Brown (1993) explores related issues in his discussion of *Eunuchus* 313–17. On the Greek stage, female padding was identical to that of the men: same belly, same buttocks, same sagging breasts: 'to create a female role the actors wore a female mask and female clothing over the top of the standard costume' (Green (1997) 135); such characters 'are not pregnant, but just have the conventional padding'. This means that on the Greek comic stage, it was conceivably customary that the body suits of comic women also would have a phallus, though it was notionally absent and was covered by the more modest female clothing (this has implications for the 'unmasking scene' in Aristophanes' *Thesmophoriazusae*). For a Greek actor doubling roles, however, the process of changing costumes between sexes does not entail also changing the body suit. While the Roman stage did use padding, there is no indication that the use of the body suit persisted, and consequently a change of roles between sexes may have required more time for the actor to complete. Nevertheless, at least in the case of *Casina*, a good joke exists when a male character disguised as a woman is discovered to have male genitalia beneath the bridal costume (lines 904–13).

[177] At *Miles Gloriosus* 989 and *Poenulus* 347 *bellula* is used to describe an attractive young woman.

[178] Olson (2003) 206, and see 206–7, and see Wilson (1938). See Nonius 42L (29M): *subligaculum est quo pudendae partes corporis teguntur: dictum quod subtus ligetur* ('the *subligaculum* is that by which the shameful parts of the body are covered, so-called because it was "girded from below"').

accidental exposure of the actor's real genitalia.[179] In Cicero's day, at any rate, Roman actors did not wear a padded bodysuit (the leggings of which extend to the ankles). Padding is part of the costume, not a base upon which all other costumes are placed. This does not rule out the possibility of an artificial phallus, but if it existed, it was not represented in the Greek manner. It is more likely, that it was something worn over the *subligaculum* but below the (costume) tunic, perhaps hanging from a leather cord tied around the waist. This is the most likely construction for the two phalluses needed for the mime in *P. Berol.* inv. 13927. This would then explain the implied costume of the title character of Naevius' *Triphallus* ('The Guy with Three Penises').[180] No special construction would be needed; the actor would wear three cords beneath his costume, each with a hanging phallus extending beyond the length of the tunic.

Costume in Roman comedy apparently broke with Greek tradition and did not use padded bodysuits. Additional padding was used for certain roles, typically stock characters such as old men (*senes*), pimps (*lenones*), and slaves (*servi*). In some of these circumstances, an artificial phallus may also have been added, but it was not part of the standard costume for male comic characters. This technique would have been adopted from a local performance convention. Such padding has a necessary consequence for acting styles: 'one could say that padded costume almost invites violent or unsubtle activity: beating, kicking and so on seem to have been commonplace'.[181] The discussion has begun to blur the difference between costume and property, however, and it is worth having a clear understanding of how these terms can helpfully be differentiated.

STAGE PROPERTIES

The term 'prop' or 'stage property' is variously applied to various things. To understand best how properties function within a play, we can distinguish three levels at which a physical object can be used during a performance: as costume, as set, or as a property. The way these terms are used in everyday parlance (in antiquity as today) is blurred, and in particular the application of 'property' can blend into both 'costume' and 'set'.[182] The costume includes all the physical objects that go into

---

[179] It cannot be an 'apron', as Wilson (1938) 72 notes.

[180] Other titles of comedies by Naevius suggest the use of the phallus: *Testicularia* ('The Testicle Play') and *Appella* ('The Circumcised').

[181] Green (1997) 134, describing Greek padding.   [182] For this distinction, see Ketterer (1986a) 193.

identifying a given character (and in Greek and Roman drama this includes the mask). A staff carried by a *senex*, since its primary signifying function on the Roman stage is to define aspects of his character (that he is old and weak), is better thought of as part of the actor's costume than as a (separable) stage property. As costume relates to character, so set relates to space. The performance space is defined by words, the movements of actors, perhaps in some contexts by painted scenery, and by physical objects that can be labelled stage properties – the altar before the shrines in Roman comedy and its models, while it may physically be touched by actors and indicated by their words, nevertheless constitutes an immobile fixture on stage at least for the duration of the play. Its presence defines an aspect of the play's setting and is part of its set, even though it is not a permanent element of the performance space. Given this, it seems worth reserving the term 'property' for those particular physical objects in a drama that create relationships: objects that are separable from their characters, the movement or transfer of which will be reflected in the dramatic action of the play. The paraphernalia worn by the cook at *Curculio* 251–73 is part of his costume, since it does not relate to the play's action; its purpose is exclusively to identify the character as a cook. This is not true of the supplies brought by the cooks in *Aulularia*, where the lamb is the object of comic business (327–34).[183] Similarly, the writing tablets Calidorus hands to Pseudolus at *Pseudolus* 20 are physical objects that move between characters and, at lines 41–59, give voice to a third.

Properties are necessarily involved in stage action: 'Any time an object must be moved, handed from one person to another, or acted on in any way, the action required will dictate the way the stage picture looks, and the movement attracts audience attention.'[184] What the audience sees, though, is an object that may stand for many things simultaneously. This polyvalence has been examined in detail by Ketterer, who develops an elaborate semiological typology for Plautine props:[185]

---

[183] This routine was drawn from Greek comedy, where it seems to have been standard, e.g. Menander, *Dyskolos* 393–4.

[184] Ketterer (1986a) 198.

[185] See Ketterer (1986a), (1986b), and (1986c) for this whole paragraph, especially (1986a) 207–10 and (1986c) 61–6. His analysis examines props on a play-by-play basis: *Curculio* (Ketterer (1986a)), *Epidicus* ((1986b) 94–102), *Bacchides* ((1986b) 102–11), *Captivi* ((1986b) 111–18), *Aulularia* ((1986b) 118–28), *Cistellaria* ((1986c) 30–36), *Rudens* ((1986c) 36–44), *Amphitruo* ((1986c) 45–51), and *Menaechmi* ((1986c) 51–61).

I. Individual props

   A. Mechanical ('denotative') functions
      1. Scenic
      2. Causative
         a. Direct
         b. Indirect

   B. Signifying ('connotative') functions

      1. Labelling
         a. To generalise an individual
         b. To specify an individual

      2. Symbolic
         a. Brief appearance
         b. Appearing throughout the play

II. Groups of props

This typology understands stage properties in a wider sense than I do, but it is easy to see where the differences lie. When a property's mechanical function (operating at the level of the actors) is scenic, it is part of the set as I have defined it: the object's purpose is to identify an aspect of the locale. Further, when its signifying function (operating at the level of the dramatic narrative) is labelling, it may be part of the character's costume, as I have defined it: props that label a character may possess no narrative function, and when this is the case, they are an extension of the costume. Ketterer's analysis remains applicable in these cases. The most interesting stage properties are those where the mechanical function is causative, involved in actions and relationships between characters, and where the signifying function is symbolic. The function of a given property may change over time. For Ketterer, the stage altar in *Mostellaria* serves a mechanical function that is scenic, and it serves a signifying function that labels the doorway as a sacred area. At 1094–1180, when Tranio seeks refuge at the altar, its mechanical function is now causative (with the actor on the altar, he is inviolate within the world of the play) and its symbolic function, while still labelling the precinct as a temple, also symbolises sanctuary for Tranio, and an obstacle to be overcome by Theopropides. This example, though applied to a piece of the set, demonstrates three important aspects of any physical object on stage. First, the object's function(s) may change over the course of the play; its meaning is not static. Second, every stage object must have at least a mechanical function; it may further possess one or more signifying function at any given time. Third, stage objects may have different meanings for different characters simultaneously, and they may mean something else again for the audience. Comedy develops out of this discrepant awareness. There is however a practical distinction that Ketterer does not make, which has an impact on stage performance.

In the same way that the comic mask presents a distorted version of the real human face, there is no need for properties to look exactly like the objects they represent. This is particularly true when, as with the writing tablets in *Pseudolus*, their dramatic import greatly outweighs their real-world size. Exaggerating the size of a physical object can yield comic results. For example, *Miles Gloriosus* 1–78 is an exercise in character drawing: the scene introduces Pyrgopolynices, who will not return until 947, and Artotrogus, his parasite who never returns. The scene's purpose is to instil an idea about the play's chief foil in order to create audience expectation for his return. Much of the humour comes from Artotrogus' imperfect addition (42–7) and the elaborate names that trip from the characters' tongues (such as the general Bumbomachides Clutomistaridysarchides in 14).[186] Like any stage soldier, Pyrgopolynices has a *machaera* (1423), but it is worth considering whether for the actors it is actually a real sword. Certainly it is real within the narrative: Cario might even be holding it when he threatens to cut the soldier in line 1406 (with the threat of castration at 1420–22).[187] But what do the actors hold? There are four possibilities of what it could be, any of which could be true: a real sabre; a prop designed to look like a real sabre; a prop sabre of comically diminished size; or a prop sabre of comically expanded size. For the audience, the first two are the same – it looks like a normal sabre, and is therefore functionally neutral.[188] There are humorous benefits with the

---

[186] In addition to these two, compare Polymachaeroplagides (*Pseudolus* 988), Therapontigonus Platagidorus (*Curculio* 430), and Thesaurochrysonicochrysides (*Captivi* 285).

[187] He need not hold it, however. Part of the appearance of the cook is a sacrificial knife (*culter*) – *coquom decet* (*Aulularia* 417: 'it suits a cook') – and it might equally be used; see Ketterer (1986a) 208, (1986b) 125, and 134 n. 51.

[188] This is not always the case. At *Aulularia* 327–34, it does matter whether the lamb is real or not. In either case, humour arises for metatheatrical reasons: the audience sees the object both as a thing being manipulated by actors and as an object functioning within the narrative. In performance, problems can arise in a comedy when this distinction collapses. In a scene with a sword, all sorts of flourishes are possible, but if at any time the audience genuinely fears for an actor's safety, enjoyment is likely to change. This provides a reason, especially in the raw theatrical context of Plautus, for props always to be artificial: the audience is trained never to expect genuine risks for the actors.

latter two possibilities, particularly for a blowhard soldier.[189] As with Therapontigonus Platagidorus' sabre in *Curculio*, the *machaera* 'becomes a symbol of the soldier's inability to force his will on anyone'.[190] At times, large props serve a practical function for the actors. When Demaenetus throws dice at *Asinaria* 904–6, it is unlikely that most people sitting in the audience would be able to see the physical objects. For the actors, then, it makes sense either to have oversize dice (producing an easy property to manipulate, which the audience can see) or to mime the dice completely (simplifying what is needed on stage, and producing the same result from the audience's perspective). There are indications that this sort of humour was known in antiquity. While some properties depicted on the comic vases of South Italy are standard in size (ladders, spears, musical instruments, etc.), there are also some props that appear to be oversize for comic effect, such as the enormous writing tablets and stylus on a vase in Leningrad.[191]

Any physical object used in a stage performance creates relationships with the characters and affects relationships between characters. As physical objects, *cruminae* ('moneybags'), pouches worn around the neck and filled (supposedly) with coins,[192] are essentially neutral: they need not have any distinctive size or appearance, since their connotative functions are already overdetermined. Plots of Roman comedy, so often concerning true love, depend on financial transactions. Plots create a 'circuit of exchange', whereby a payment cements relationships, or prevent them from happening.[193] The contents of a moneybag may represent the purchase price for a slave's freedom (e.g. Lemniselenis in *Persa*), or at least the means for a young man to have access to the company of a *meretrix* (e.g. Philaenium in *Asinaria*). Consequently a slave with a *crumina* will be treated with a disproportionate respect, even by his own master (as at *Asinaria* 545–745).

Some properties possess a cash value that is central to the resolution of the plot: unless the object enters into the cycle of exchange, the narrative

---

[189] In my production of *Miles Gloriosus*, the soldier wielded a small plastic toy sword, but an oversize blade would have made him appear equally preposterous.

[190] Ketterer (1986a) 203.

[191] The egg is on Bari 3899, *PhV*[2] 18 (Trendall (1967) 27–78). The writing tablets are on Leningrad inv. 1661 (St. 1779; W. 1120), *PhV*[2] 33 (Trendall (1967) 34).

[192] In reality, they were not filled with coins, but with lupines (Allen (1959)): actual coins need to be seen by the audience (or mimed?) only at *Menaechmi* 219.

[193] Ketterer (1986b) 120, and see the important discussion of Lowe (2000) 188–221.

cannot progress. In these cases, discrepant understanding of an object's value by characters creates dramatic tension. Nowhere is this more clear than with recognition tokens. A recognition token provides the means to identify a character's true nature – typically the circumstances of the birth of the *meretrix*, which can convey with it citizenship and marriage rights. In *Curculio*, Philaenium's ring serves to identify her as a marriageable citizen, to disenfranchise the claim of the soldier on her hand (since he is the long-lost brother who gave her the ring as a child), and to indict the *leno* Cappadox for trafficking in citizen girls.[194] When the recognition token is held openly, as here, the plot must keep apart characters capable of making the identification. One way around this narrative difficulty is to keep the tokens in a container, such as a *vidulus* ('bag') or *cistella* ('little box'), as happens in *Rudens, Cistellaria, Vidularia*, Menander's *Epitrepontes*, etc.[195] Some characters know the contents and their value, while others, such as Gripus in *Rudens* or Cacistus in *Vidularia*, can only guess at their prize's worth. Such instances also raise the issue of discrepant value to different characters, particularly when relatively valueless objects provide the means of identification of a character as freeborn. A stage property's symbolic value therefore exists only in relationship to something or someone else. In *Aulularia*, Euclio's pot of gold possesses a symbolic value that exists because he treasures it disproportionately over his pregnant daughter, Phaedria. In what survives of the play, she does not appear on stage, but is heard giving birth at 691–2. However, when the pot appears at 449, 'the effect is like the first appearance of an important character which we have been waiting to see'.[196] Euclio is shrouding the pot with his cloak, and consequently embodies a pregnant image of his unseen daughter.

Props become a site for the development of comedy. An audience sees objects on stage and invests them with symbolic values that create networks of meaning among the characters that change during the play. These complex interactions help the audience to understand the narrative by emphasising some of what is important, for nothing appears onstage unless someone has decided to bring it onstage. Such decisions are made for a variety of reasons. At one end of the scale might be the clutter associated with a dinner party, which helps characterise the feel of celebration (as at *Asinaria* 830–941 and *Persa* 758–857). At the other end are recognition tokens central to the unfolding of the plot. Sometimes the

---

[194] In my production, oversize rings were used so that they remained clearly visible to the audience.
[195] See Ketterer (1986b) 128–9 n. 3, (1986c) 40 and 67 n. 8.   [196] Ketterer (1986b) 125.

humour of properties is prepared in advance (as with comically oversize objects), and sometimes the humour rests entirely in the situation depicted (as when Leaena serenades the wine jug at *Curculio* 96–109). The process of putting a play on stage means that a decision needs to be made about every costume and property on stage. While this reality easily slides from the mind as one reads a play, their physical existence means that properties exert a constant influence on the fictional world created.

Finally, though it refers to the performance of a mime, *P. Berol.* inv. 13927 provides important testimony of the role of properties backstage. It preserves information that must be available to every theatrical troupe – a guide for stagehands and actors, so that they might know the order of performances (compare *P. Oxy.* 2707 for the circus), and the resources each scene requires. The document as it survives falls into three parts: a list of seven titles of mimic entertainments; a list of stage properties from a work called *Leucippe* (to which reference is surely lost before the fragmentary text begins); and a list of props from the seven scenes listed at the beginning. *Leucippe* was evidently the main entertainment, and the numbered entertainments were *exodia*. The two lists of properties, called τὸ ὑπομνηστικὸν χορηγίας ('the reminder of the stage apparatus'), can only hint at what was in store for the audience. One of the mimes required φαλητάρια β' ('two phalluses'), as well as κώπας ('oars') and χόρτον ('grass'). Titles for the afterpieces include οὐ χρεία ῥημάτων ('No Need for Words', a mime that required a cithara, a little pig, a little dog, and soup ladles), τὸ τοῦ ἡλίου ('The One with the Sun', which had as its only prop ἀκτῖνας 'rays'), and τὸ τῶν Γόθθων ('The One with the Goths',[197] which required male and female Goth costumes and apparently a costume for an anthropomorphised green river). Between these last two came *tibia* music accompanied by a maiden, which required no props. The papyrus shows that there was some planning and structure to mimic presentation, and troupes could produce aides-mémoire for backstage. Props, because they are transferable, require particularly careful backstage organisation. Comparable documents must have existed for hundreds of years for all performance genres, never written with an eye to posterity, but intended to ensure the smooth running of a performance.

---

[197] The papyrus gives two versions of the title: τά τῶν Γόθθων ('The Ones with the Goths') in the initial list, but the singular title given above in the properties list. Almost certainly the first instance should be emended to a neuter singular article. This format ('The One with the ... ') is the pattern for other titles in this programme and the mistake is an easy one for a scribe with no expectation that the document will survive beyond the evening's festivities.

AUDIENCE

The theatre follows the path of least resistance to its audience...

Richard Schechner[198]

One final component is essential to the experience of a *palliata* – the audience, without which theatrical experience is impossible.[199] The audience takes an active part in the performance and it is necessary to consider the nature of its contribution: 'Any artistic form depends upon some readiness in the receiver to cooperate with its aims and conventions.'[200] The theatre audience is unlike an audience at the cinema, which is only reactive.[201] Nothing the cinema audience does can have any effect on the performance itself, though audience reaction will have an effect on the experience of the film by other spectators: one is more likely to laugh if others are laughing, and one is more likely to become uninterested if others are walking out. This same passive dynamic exists for the theatrical audience, but with it is the added dimension that the audience's response does affect the actors' performance. An enthusiastic, active, laughing audience can encourage, nourish, and inspire the stage performers.[202] Actors talk about their relationship with the audience, and thinking in terms of a relationship rightly emphasises the sense of mutual dependency that theatre creates. An audience's effect is psychological (actors feel emotions separate from their characters during the performance, and they are aware intellectually that the response is to their performance) as well as physiological (adrenaline is released, accelerating breathing and heart rate, increasing the blood flow to the muscles and brain, and contributing chemically to a sense of exhilaration for the actor).[203] Actors adjust the length and timing of their pauses based upon their perceptions of audience attention and involvement, and feel the resulting rush. And so Palaestrio warns away the unwilling (*Miles Gloriosus* 81–2):

> *qui autem auscultare nolet, exsurgat foras,*
> *ut sit ubi sedeat ille qui auscultare volt.*

---

[198] Schechner (1969) 35.
[199] See Beare (1964) 173–5, Chalmers (1965), Handley (1975), and Csapo and Slater (1995) 306–17.
[200] Sinfield (1983) 185.   [201] Bennett (1997) 75–6.   [202] Bennett (1997) 9.
[203] Plutarch, *Moralia* 45 e–f, recognises this in his metaphor describing the role of the ideal listener: ὥσπερ ἐν τῷ σφαιρίζειν τῷ βάλλοντι δεῖ συγκινούμενον εὐρύθμως φέρεσθαι τὸν δεχόμενον, οὕτως ἐπὶ τῶν λόγων ἔστι τις εὐρυθμία καὶ περὶ τὸν λέγοντα καὶ περὶ τὸν ἀκροώμενον, ἂν ἑκάτερος τὸ προσῆκον αὑτῷ φυλάττῃ ('just as in playing ball it is necessary for the catcher to adapt his movements to those of the thrower and to be actively in accord with him, so with discourses, there is a certain accord between the speaker and the hearer, if each is heedful of his obligation': text and translation, Babbitt (1927) 244–5).

> He who doesn't want to listen should get up and leave
> So that he who wants to listen can sit in that place.

It is rare that Plautus has an actor doubt the success of the theatrical enterprise,[204] but the challenge comes early in a long play, immediately following a very funny exchange (lines 1–78). No spectator is likely to leave after such a challenge, and so the actor may continue on the assumption that the entire audience is on his side. Even if one or two individuals should decide to depart at this point, they leave themselves open for comic attacks, and the result is again an audience purged of potentially disruptive elements; again the audience is consolidated.

Audience members are both the consumers of the artistic product, but they also contribute in a very real sense to its success. Bennett describes 'the production–reception contract' that exists between actors and spectators: each side has an obligation to the other, but what unifies the two is not always finances. In fact, the economic basis for Roman comedy, funded through the magistrates, explicitly removes money from the performers' contract with the audience. The obligation of the spectators is to enjoy the show in a sufficiently public way so that the magistrates will offer future contracts to the troupe.

The process of determining the size and composition of a typical theatre audience in an historical context is particularly difficult. A lack of clear, meaningful data and various assumptions lying beneath given estimates (when such assumptions are elaborated) further complicate matters. Academic trends also play a part. When scholarship downplays the size of theatre audiences, this serves as a corrective to previous tendencies to exaggerate audience size in order to magnify the significance of the cultural event.[205] There are similar questions about the composition of the audience. Even the usual claim that Athenian New Comedy

---

[204] The nature of the joke is very different when Acanthio asks *dormientis spectatores metuis ne ex somno excites?* ('Are you afraid you will wake the resting spectators from their sleep?', *Mercator* 160). Here, the accusation is not directed at an individual, and is funny regardless of audience tiredness, since the joke is motivated from within the play, since Charinus wishes to speak *placide* (159: 'gently').

[205] Dawson (1997), esp. 7–8, argues that the Periclean theatre of Dionysus may have held as few as 3,700 spectators, less than a third of the number normally assumed. Schumacher (2000) develops several arguments which suggest that ticket sales at the Comédie-Française in seventeenth-century Paris present a misleadingly high estimate of actual theatregoers because of repeat attendance.

catered to more refined tastes and privileged a more affluent fraction of the potential audience has encountered reasoned resistance: 'There is no reason ... to doubt that New Comedy remained mass entertainment, with admission either free or at a modest fee of two obols, hardly enough to keep all but the poorest Athenians from attending.'[206]

The audience of Plautine comedy was composed of individuals from every social station in Rome. Metatheatrical reference by stage characters to the audience provides a reliable gauge: one prologue of *Captivi* addresses *vos qui potestis ope vestra censerier* (*Captivi* 15: 'you who with your wealth are able to be taxed'), which means some spectators were on the citizen rolls. This group is later subdivided (*Captivi* 67–8):

> *valete, iudices iustissimi*
> *domi duellique duellatores optumi.*
>
> Farewell, most just justices
> Here at home, and the best warriors of war.[207]

Amphitruo 1–7 assumes that some in the audience have business dealings that are both local and foreign (5: *peregrique et domi*) and *Menaechmi* 51–2 implies that these financial concerns might extend as far as Greece.[208] The call for applause at *Mercator* 1025 isolates the *adulescentes* in the audience. Ballio implies that boys in the audience are particularly interested in *nugas theatri, verba quae in comoediis | solent lenoni dici, quae pueri sciunt* (*Pseudolus* 1081–82: 'theatrical trifles, words which are usually said by the pimp in comedies, as boys know').[209] Cicero, *de Finibus* 5.48, emphasises the rightful place of children at spectacles. A particularly rich source for audience composition is the prologue of *Poenulus*, which addresses prohibitions to prostitutes (17: *scortum exoletum*, 'whoring rent boy'[210]),

---

[206] Rosivach (2000) 170. He cites a *scholion* to Demosthenes 1.1 which ties the entrance fee particularly to the use of temporary wooden seats: 'the admission fee was intended to cover the expenses of the contractor (*arkhitektôn*) who maintained the wooden bleachers' (170), and might not be in effect when there was an established stone theatre. While some performance venues in Rome would have had wooden bleachers, there is no indication that any in the audience paid an admission fee.

[207] The military metaphors at *Cistellaria* 197–202 and the reference at *Bacchides* 1074 do not require soldiers in the audience to understand them.

[208] The point of the joke involves wordplay with the (supposed) etymology of Epidamnus (see Gratwick (1993) 139–40), not with the exaggerated remoteness of the location.

[209] Kiessling, followed by Leo, deleted lines 1079–86. Though I believe the lines authentic, even if they are an interpolation from later in the second century, they attest to boys in the republican audience. See also Zwierlein (1991b) 49.

[210] The phrase is also found at *Curculio* 473.

lictors (and the magistrates they accompany, presumably: 18[211]), slaves and freedmen (23–4), nurses with infants (28–31), married women[212] and their husbands (32–5).[213] The wording of each warning implies that normally each of these groups would be present to some degree.[214] All levels of society were present at Roman comedy, with no apparent restrictions based on finances, sex, age, or social position. Indeed, so complete is the representation that any omissions (such as female infants and female prostitutes) should be seen as accident rather than exclusion. Yet we must be wary of importing modern demographic distributions to this set. Less than 20 per cent of the population reached age sixty, and three-generation families headed by a grandfather were rare.[215]

We do not hear of foreigners in Plautus' audience directly, and consequently the absence of any positive indications of their presence serves to reinforce the cultural unity of the audience. There are no known restrictions banning them from the *ludi*, and I suspect that they must have been in attendance. This adds a fascinating reflexivity to Curculio's initial entrance, when he pushes his way through the crowd and rails against *isti Graeci palliati* (*Curculio* 288: 'these cloaked Greeks', continuing his deprecations at lines 288–95). On one level Curculio refers to Phaedromus and Palinurus, the two characters in a *fabula palliata* standing on the stage; and an appropriate gesture could make this clear. On another level, though, Curculio could refer to the actual Greeks in the audience wearing *pallia*; this too could be clarified with an appropriate gesture. The detail of Curculio's harangue goes well beyond what the play has established for the stage characters, and this encourages the latter interpretation: the Curculio actor is physically making his way through the audience during this speech, and, on finding a cluster of Greeks, or a single individual who happens to be carrying a book satchel (289: *suffarcinati cum libris*, 'bulging with books'), focuses the character's venom on a single spectator. A clear gesture could exclude either interpretation, but an imprecise movement could equally allow for both

---

[211] The word order is unusual and perhaps conceals a subtle joke. The prologue fears the *virgae* will produce not *verba* ('words') but *verbera* ('blows'); compare *Epidicus* 25–8, but the humour seems very compressed.

[212] The *clamor mulierum* ('racket of women') is also identified at *Hecyra* 35.

[213] Zwierlein (1990) 206–24 provides the most recent discussion of the textual issues surrounding the prologue. Maurach (1988) does not impugn any of the lines mentioned here. The passage remains valuable even if it is interpolated, since it would still describe second-century practice.

[214] Slater (2000) 155: 'The message of order is made palatable by being directed ostensibly at everyone except the majority of the audience.'

[215] Hansen, in Potter and Mattingly (1999) 27.

interpretations simultaneously. Plautus blends the stage world with the world of the audience, creating the rapport that Moore has thoroughly documented.[216]

Plautus sought to take the diverse individuals in the audience and treat them as a corporate whole, perhaps at the expense of a scapegoat or two, such as a reluctant spectator (*Miles Gloriosus* 81–2), a Greek slave or tourist (*Curculio* 288), or the *praeco* (*Asinaria* 4–5, *Poenulus* 11–15). The magistrates in charge of the festivals had different motivations. They wished to emphasise Roman social stratigraphy. In 194, they deliberately introduced segregation, separating the audience between the senatorial orders and others. Livy 34.54.3–4, 6–8 is passionate about the change:

Megalesia ludos scaenicos A. Atilius Serranus, L. Scribonius Libo aediles curules primi fecerunt. horum aedilium ludos Romanos primum senatus a populo secretus spectavit praebuitque sermones, sicut omnis novitas solet ... ad quingentesimum quinquagesimum octavum annum in promiscuo spectatum esse; quid repente factum cur immisceri sibi in cavea patres plebem nollent? cur dives pauperem consessorem fastidiret? novam, superbam libidinem, ab nullius ante gentis senatu neque desideratam neque institutam. postremo ipsum quoque Africanum, quod consul auctor eius rei fuisset, paenituisse ferunt. adeo nihil motum ex antiquo probabile est; veteribus, nisi quae usus evidenter arguit, stari malunt.

At the Megalesian Games dramatic performances were for the first time introduced by the curule aediles Aulus Atilius Serranus and Lucius Scribonius Libo [in 195 BC]. At the Roman Games given by these same aediles, the senate for the first time looked on segregated from the common people, and this caused gossip, as every novelty usually does ... For 558 years, they said, people had looked on from seats chosen at random; what had suddenly happened to make the Fathers unwilling to have the plebians mingle with them in the crowd, or the rich man scorn the poor man as his neighbour at the show? This was a novel and arrogant caprice, never desired nor practised by the senate of any other people. It is reported that in the end even [Scipio] Africanus had repented that in his consulship he had suggested this innovation. So difficult it is to prove the need of any variation from ancient custom; people always prefer to stand by the old ways, unless experience convincingly proves them bad.[217]

---

[216] Moore (1998b). Here is a representative citation: 'Through monologues and other elements, Plautus encourages in his plays a hierarchy of rapport, as some characters are more successful than others in their attempts to form a bond with the spectators' (p. 33).

[217] Text and translation, Sage (1935) 555–7. See also Valerius Maximus 2.4.3 and 4.5.1. For discrepancies between this and other sources, see Lenaghan (1969) 121–23. Gruen (1992) 204 suggests that the discontent is invented by the later historians. Vitruvius 5.6.2 attests to separate seats for senators in later theatres.

The change came three years before the inauguration of the temple of the Magna Mater and the performance of *Pseudolus*, a time when Plautus was evidently at the peak of his career. The effect of such a division is not slight, but the way Plautus has his actors relate to the audience draws attention away from any such divisions. Plautus reminds them that all may sit – even, at times, the slaves (*Poenulus* 23–4).[218] Plautus encourages the audience to put aside differences and unite behind the action of the play.

There were, to be sure, other ways individuals sought the best seats for themselves. Apart from the reservation of senatorial seats after 194, spectators took their places on a first-come, first-served basis,[219] though Moore may be correct that there were some self-regulating mechanisms prior to this whereby slaves and social inferiors would normally not take seats at the front.[220] The front seats were the most desirable, in part because of audibility (*Captivi* 11–14 are addressed to a spectator in the back row who cannot hear).[221] There exists a tension between the solidarity created when a group of spectators become an audience and the genuine diversity of experience that the spectators possess. While Plautus treats the audience as a unit, he knows that spectators possess an intellectual diversity that makes them crave different types of humour. He caters to this diversity by producing comedy which itself is pluralistic in its humour. Heterogeneous appreciation characterises the audience's engagement and arises directly from its diversity.[222]

Rome produced many audiences, and while the Roman playwright clearly aimed at drawing a diverse crowd, the experience of *Hecyra* demonstrates that the audience for Terentian comedy was different from the audience for gladiatorial fights. Contrary pressures also inform

---

[218] Despite many of the passages cited above, it remained a question for some time as to whether the second-century Roman audiences stood or sat. The matter is settled by Beare (1964) 171–2, 241–7, and see *Poenulus* 1224: *sitiunt qui sedent* ('those sitting [i.e. the audience] are thirsty'), *Pseudolus* 1–2, *Epidicus* 733, etc. The audience sat in the *cavea* (Livy 34.54.6, Cicero, *Laws* 2.38) on *subsellia* ('benches'; see *Amphitruo* 64–8).

[219] Beare (1964) 174.

[220] Moore (1994) 122, arguing generally for an intense competition for available seating.

[221] Other prestige locations apart from the senatorial seats had been used since the fourth century, but these were for the *ludi* generally and not specifically for theatre: 'Festus, *s.v.* Maeniana, describes the galleries which were first built by Maenius, the censor (318 B.C.), over the shops in the forum, that from them the spectacles of the market-place might be witnessed' (Saunders (1913) 94). Vitruvius 5.1.1–2 describes balconies (*maeniana superiora*) rented out for views; Ps. Asconius, *ad Cicero, Divinatio in Q. Caecilium* 16–50 ties their construction to the Basilica Porcia, built in 184. Such balconies would not be available for every performance venue.

[222] Wilson (1998) 18–54, who engages with Chalmers (1965) and his emphasis of a unified, collective response. See also Bennett (1997) 153–6.

audience composition. It is misleading to think of a theatre audience as a cross-section of the population: the ratios are necessarily wrong. 'There is always a diversity of publics',[223] and that of the *palliata* was for the most part urban, with the level of sophistication that entailed. There was a worldview and ideology defined by class, material situation, education, levels of culture, age, sex, attitude to the arts, previous experience with the theatre, etc., which pre-existed whatever happened on stage.[224] All of these factors help to unify an audience, and necessarily temper claims of heterogeneous appreciation. The Roman audience brings to the performance common interpretative strategies, some of which are created by the experience of comedy itself:

[A play] promises the audience two performances: one of the show itself and the other is the experience of being in the theatre. To both performances is attached the expectation of pleasure.[225]

Both of these are at work in the imaginations of each spectator. The distinction is important, because one can enjoy the experience of attending the theatre without necessarily liking the play. Ovid hints at these dual motivations (allusively and in an erotic context) when he describes the women at the theatre: *spectatum veniunt, veniunt spectentur ut ipsae* (*Ars Amatoria* 1.99: 'They come to watch, they come to be watched themselves').

The size of an audience is difficult to determine. Goldberg calculated that the seating at the *ludi Megalenses* allowed for fewer than two thousand spectators, leading him to ask, 'Is it possible that the audience was in fact so small?'[226] For almost any live performance tradition other than Athenian drama, an audience of one or two thousand would be considered substantial. Larger audiences attended Roman circus events (as they do at modern rock concerts and sporting events), but there is no reason to deprecate a crowd size of one or two thousand spectators, and modern notions of 'mass entertainment' (conditioned particularly in a world of cinema and television broadcasts) must be put aside. Roman comedy makes claim to elite cultural values, and, whatever the truth of the claim, it did not appeal to everyone, despite the playwright's best

---

[223] Bennett (1997) 94.   [224] Naumann (1976) 121.
[225] Bennett (1997) 118, and see 82–3, where she cites Ellis (1982) 26, who distinguishes going to the cinema (the whole experience) and seeing a film (the projected narrative).
[226] Goldberg (1998) 14.

efforts. The weather also is a factor, and the lack of a regularised calendar means that many festivals occur at colder parts of the year.[227]

Since venues were temporary, it is difficult to get a clear sense of their sizes. Previously we saw that Welch believes a temporary wooden amphitheatre built in the forum could hold 10,000 spectators,[228] and I suggested less than a third of this space would probably be available for a theatrical performance, yielding a maximum audience of c. 3,400 in the largest of the temporary performance venues available to republican Rome.[229] In comparison, the roughly contemporary stone theatre at Pompeii seats 5,000.[230] Any calculation assumes ideal seating arrangements, without regard for varying concerns for personal space, individuals holding seats for friends who may or may not appear, the gradual influx of spectators to a partially filled venue, etc. Seats were not assigned (it would be difficult to do so without entry tickets), and I suspect that these factors would further diminish the seated audience size by more than 10 per cent, and it is unlikely those standing would recover this amount. Different performance spaces would have different seating capacities and conventions. While all elements of society were represented in the audience, attendance was not universal, and an audience of a few thousand spectators probably represents an extreme upper limit range.

This was not the total size of the audience, however, because games had more than one day of *ludi scaenici*, and this means Roman plays were presented with a limited run. Leaving aside the issue of *instauratio* (which for example affected *Stichus* in 200; see Livy 31.50.3), we know that troupes would perform on more than one of the days available for performance. The *envoi* at the end of *Pseudolus* tells the audience, *verum si voltis adplaudere atque adprobare hunc gregem | et fabulam in crastinum vos vocabo* (*Pseudolus* 1334–5: 'Still, if you applaud and cheer this troupe, I'll even invite you to tomorrow's play'). It is inconceivable that such an invitation would be offered unless the same troupe were performing the next day. We know *Pseudolus* was performed at the *ludi Megalenses*, which was the festival that placed the greatest restrictions on rehearsal time for the troupe. The natural inference, when we consider the enjoyment of the audience, the practical demands upon the theatrical troupe, and the

---

[227] Goldberg (1998) 15. Vitruvius 5.9 discusses the effects of adverse weather; Ovid, *Fasti* 4.385–6, mentions rain during the *ludi Megalenses*; Martial 4.2 envisages snow covering spectators.
[228] Welch (1994) 76.
[229] The Circus Maximus was of course larger, but there were no indications that it was used as a theatrical venue in the early second century.
[230] Beacham (1991) 59.

economic limits of the magistrates funding the *ludi scaenici*, is that each troupe would present a single play at a festival, and the same play would run for its length, which at times could be extended by *instauratio*. Terence provides the only known exception, when *Hecyra*, the previously unsuccessful play, was remounted with *Adelphoe* at the privately funded *ludi funebres* of L. Aemilius Paullus in 160.[231]

Audience psychology is difficult to fathom, and individuals at *ludi* probably behaved differently than they otherwise would. While we may be able to get some sense of the audience, in the end we only know that there were individuals who enjoyed Plautus' plays, then as now. Staging Roman comedy in modern performance contexts can reveal questions that otherwise would never occur. Often, these concern the play, and how it creates its theatrical effects. At times, though, the practice can also yield new understandings for how an audience might respond. As I discovered from my productions, there is an unexpected consequence when plays are presented in a run and admission is free and largely unregulated: the plays attract repeat attendees. Spectators come on multiple days, bringing different people with them as they do. Others come late to one performance, stay to the end, and then watch the beginning of the play on the next day, or on the day after that. When we consider the experience of Roman comedy, in all its dimensions, this seems to be a natural result, and has implications for the actors and for the playwright. For the actors, their job is clear: whatever the venue, their obligation is to attract and keep as substantial a crowd as they can. The troupe's economic relationship with the magistrates and its chance for future contracts depends on this success. Any means to secure repeat viewers, even those as obvious as *Pseudolus* 1334–5, work towards this end. For the playwright, the structure of the plays must make some allowances for these drifting spectators. This impacts upon characterisation, narrative development, and emotional engagement with the play, and constitutes another way in which the troupe depends on the active cooperation of the audience at all times.

The plays of Plautus have had many audiences over the years. Cicero watching Roscius act Ballio in *Pseudolus* in the first century BC experienced theatre differently from how spectators did in 191, and, differently from how we experience it today, whether reading it or seeing it in

---

[231] Goldberg (1998) 15–16 and 16 n. 53 understands the second performance of *Eunuchus* in 161 to be an encore. I suspect rather that this is additional evidence that in the early second century there were only two *ludi scaenici* at the *Megalenses*.

performance. We lack the necessary 'levels of cultural competence'[232] to appreciate all that transpired on the stage. We have the words (or many of them, allowing for issues of textual transmission), but we have lost all traces of vocal inflection, mask, gesture, body movement, posture, costume properties, stage design, the effects of natural light, music, the use of noise and silence, etc. Reading the play, we miss the experience of being in an audience, being pressed on the sides, hearing laughs, smelling the odours of food and people, and observing the stage from a fixed point in the *cavea* with perhaps a limited field of vision.[233] We have not walked through the festival crowd, arrived early in hopes of a good seat (close to the stage or near to our friends), waited in expectation for our favourite actor to appear, looked at the other spectators assembled, or selected this from among other festival entertainments. All of these factors also contributed to the original experience of Roman comedy, and were part of what it meant to be part of Plautus' audience.

---

[232] Bennett (1997) 68.   [233] Bennett (1997) 65.

CHAPTER 2

Actors and Roles

THE *GREX* ECONOMY

Ultimately theatre is an economic commodity.

Susan Bennett[1]

At each opportunity for dramatic performance in the Roman republic[2] there were magistrates – either aediles or praetors – who were responsible for hiring troupes.[3] One can conceive of the theatrical economy in terms of magistrates hiring a troupe as a gift (*munus*) to the audience – one of the expected components of religious ritual and celebration. This is a straightforward view: the state or rich individuals hire a troupe to present entertainments for an audience. It lies behind the analysis of Beare: 'Between the impecunious dramatist who wanted to sell his play, the general public who wanted to be amused at some one else's expense, and the ambitious magistrate who was willing to supplement the State grant (*lucar*) out of his own resources, an essential link was the producer and actor–manager.'[4] Beare's summary recognises that other parties benefit in this transaction. For the audience returns its support to the magistrates and all they represent as the price for the entertainment. In this view, the troupe and its plays are the product being sold to the Roman audience, in hopes of non-financial but nevertheless very real benefits in return. Seeing the troupe as a commodity does not take us far in terms of understanding what its role in the process actually is.

A better way to think of the Roman theatrical economy is this: the troupe sells an audience to the magistrates for a price. The financial relationship exists between the troupe (*grex*, 'flock', or *caterva*, 'band'),

---

[1] Bennett (1997) 118.

[2] For other discussions of Roman actors, see Beare (1964) 164–70, Duckworth (1952) 73–6, Brown (2002), and Garton (1972) 231–65, 'A Register of Republican Actors'.

[3] *Eunuchus* 20: *aediles emerunt*. Normally the magistrates were aediles, but it was a praetor at the *ludi Apollinares*; see Barsby (1999) 7.

[4] Beare (1964) 164. For actor–managers generally, see Garton (1972) 60–65.

and more particularly the actor–manager (*actor*),[5] and the state, which is represented by the magistrates. The return on investment is a satisfied audience, and it is the troupe's responsibility to ensure the audience is pleased. If it is not satisfied with the performance, there may be complaints and dissatisfaction with the state, and future contracts for the troupe are endangered. Fundamentally, the magistrates do not care how they get a satisfied audience: if it can be accomplished by dancing bears, tightrope walkers, gladiators, or mimes, that is equally acceptable.[6] We can imagine that there were expectations on all sides – concerning the length of a play, its structure, and the morality depicted within it – and violation of these expectations could reduce an audience's satisfaction, and thereby reduce satisfaction among the magistrates.[7] This provides a mechanism that ensures a relatively stable notion of what a play is. The play put on is meant to entertain, and to hold an audience for a long period of time. The network of economic ties is seen in *Asinaria* 1–3, where the troupe (*grex*), audience (*spectatores*), and magistrates (designated as 'contractors', *conductores*) are all invested in the play in one way or another. So too are the *domini* ('masters'), which might refer to the (free) principal actors in the troupe (the usual word for 'actor' is *histrio* or *cantor*), the owners of the slave performers, or perhaps to other financial backers of the production.[8]

Furthermore, everything that the troupe does is designed to maximise its returns on the investment (Horace, *Epistles* 2.1.175–6, may refer to this). All expenses must be deducted from it, so there is a real incentive for the troupe to keep its expenses low. From the magistrate's perspective, the presence of rival entertainments means risk is minimised – they divide their capital so as to reduce the consequences of a single poor investment; a diversified portfolio is always safer. It also means that the troupe is in direct competition with other types of entertainment hired for the *ludi*. The troupe is competing for a limited resource (contracts) and must offer a product that will generate wealth (a satisfied audience) so that future magistrates will make future purchases from the same source. Nor was this aspect hidden from the public. On the contrary, references to prizes awarded to individuals or companies suggest that, while never as formalised as the competition in Athens, there was a mechanism for publicly

[5] Brown (2002) 228–9 cites *Bacchides* 213 and *Phormio* 10 and 33.

[6] This inference is drawn from *Hecyra* 4–5, 29–42. See Gilula (1981).

[7] In theory, it could also increase audience satisfaction, but this economic model would seem to discourage experimental theatre.

[8] See Brown (2002) 235 n. 44.

recognising the best plays or performances.[9] In order to maximise its returns on the contract, the troupe needed not only to keep costs low, but also to compete with other entertainers for the greatest portion of the audience, to provide that audience with the best entertainment for the longest time, and, always, to leave them wanting more.

This perspective positions the actor–manager as the vendor, selling a product to a restricted clientele. Viewed thus, what motivates a troupe becomes clear, and all other economic activity of the troupe can be explained. Let us consider L. Ambivius Turpio, a comic actor and manager of a Roman theatre troupe c. 185–160 BC and perhaps beyond.[10] As *actor*, he seems to have been successful both with the plays of Caecilius Statius, whose style has been shown to be quite similar to Plautus,[11] and those of Terence (*Hecyra* 9–19). He claims – or Terence claims for him; it is typically presumed Turpio himself delivers this prologue for the third production of *Hecyra* in 160 BC – to have nurtured both playwrights, refining the means by which he sells an audience to the magistrates.[12] Turpio buys plays from playwrights in advance of production (*Hecyra* 57: *pretio emptas meo*, 'bought at my expense'). Some playwrights sold plays to more than one troupe (*Phormio* 35–47, a passage which also demonstrates that Turpio took the title role of Phormio). When the playwright was not a performer in the troupe, this was conceivably the extent of his involvement in the show (though an anecdote in Donatus on *Phormio* 315, cited below, suggests Terence did attend at least some rehearsals). We are told that Terence received 8,000 sesterces for *Eunuchus*,[13] whereupon (we must presume) the play belonged to Turpio and he could do with it what he wished, using performances of the play to sell audiences to as many buyers as he could manage. However, if the play was not performed, it was apparently returned to its author, as happened with *Hecyra* when it was originally written in 165.[14] This explains the emphasis in Terence's prologues on the fact that plays were new; Plautus does not make such claims.[15] New or not, what mattered was the troupe's ability to deliver a pleased audience to the magistrates. Those troupes which had a

---

[9] *Amphitruo* 69–74, *Poenulus* 37–9, Pliny, *Natural History* 21.4. See Jory (1988) 73–6 and Beare (1964) 167–8.

[10] Garton (1972) 236.   [11] Wright (1974) 87–126.

[12] On the Terentian prologues generally, see Gilula (1989), who stresses that even Turpio speaking in his own voice is a role written by Terence (p. 105).

[13] Suetonius, *de Poetis* ('Terence' 2).

[14] Carney (1963) 35, and see Brown (2002) 231, Gilula (1985–88).

[15] Beare (1964) 165 stresses the cost savings in presenting plays already owned by a troupe, and the Elizabethan theatre provides parallels for a troupe staging several plays in repertory.

resident playwright, already on the payroll, would be able to save on this preliminary expense.

There is no certain evidence that Plautus belongs in this category and performed in his plays. It is nevertheless an attractive hypothesis that has appealed to many scholars, particularly since metatheatrical references have been identified to an increased degree, and it is a hypothesis that makes good economic sense. Elements of Aulus Gellius' brief biography (*Attic Nights* 3.3.14–15) have been questioned as fictional inventions, but there is no fundamental reason to doubt that Plautus did have experience *in operis artificium scaenicorum* (3.3.14: 'in the service of theatrical artists'). That would also explain the fact that his name – Titus Maccius Plautus – is so clearly invented for the stage.[16] Livy 7.2.8 suggests Livius Andronicus *id quod omnes tum erant* ('like everyone else at that time') acted in his own plays.[17] The absence of references to buying and selling plays in the Plautine corpus may be thought to corroborate the supposition that he performed in his own work. So while we cannot know that Plautus was associated with a single troupe, it does seem likely. Even with this caveat, we can still meaningfully use the term 'Plautus' troupe' to refer to the group of performers that regularly acted the plays of Plautus, even if its composition changed over time. It is also possible that, perhaps only later in his career, Plautus was the *actor*, the principal comedian in his own plays, who himself would be responsible for negotiations with the magistrates.

The *grex*, then, is a dynamic unit whose focus is the *actor*. Different plays might make different demands on the troupe, but it makes no sense for a troupe to leave some of its resources idle. Every troupe required a *tibicen* ('piper') for example: for *Stichus*, 200 BC, the *tibicen* was Marcipor, the slave of Oppius. We cannot know how long Plautus' troupe used this musician. The answer depends on who Oppius was. It is possible that the *tibicen* was hired from Oppius for a single production or for training, as we know happened: Cicero describes a slave actor, Panurgus, owned by Fannius but trained by the actor Roscius. The training so increased the value of Panurgus that a dispute arose over ownership (Cicero, *pro Q. Roscio comoedo* 10.28). This is a possible analogue to the Plautine situation, but it is more likely that Oppius was part of the troupe, as a performer as well as the owner of the *tibicen*.[18] This too would make

---

[16] Gratwick (1973).

[17] Oakley (1998) 65–6 emphasises how little weight can be placed on this claim, though Brown (2002) 226–7 notes the parallel in Festus 333 M, which even suggests the possibility of an actor's guild in Rome.

[18] He is not however listed in the register of Garton (1972) 231–65.

economic sense since a talented *tibicen* was always required. Similarly, Flaccus, slave of Claudius, was the *tibicen* for Terence's plays. At least some in the troupe are free, but their status is always low because of this apparently interchangeable association with slaves. Though not completely reliable for this period, Livy 7.2.12 and Valerius Maximus 2.4 indicate that actors were exempted from military service, which also demonstrates that at least some were free citizens otherwise eligible. It is even possible that there was an actor's guild (*collegium*) in Rome similar to the Greek Artists of Dionysus, which also attests to the presence of free actors.[19]

To be an actor involved a reduction in one's citizen rights – *qui in scaenam prodierit infamis est* ('whoever goes on stage is *infamis*')[20] – but that does not affect the economic gains from minimising the number of free individuals in the troupe if the slaves are also owned by troupe members. It does suggest that any free men who were actors would not have come from the upper classes, as was the case later when such rules were enforced by legislation. In imperial times, entire troupes – of pantomimes (Pliny, *Letters* 7.24.4–5) or actors (Petronius, *Satyricon* 53.13: *comoedos*) – could be slaves, but this is less likely in the republic when opportunities for dramatic production were exclusively public. In Cicero's day, Roscius provides an example of a free actor who performed alongside his own slaves (*pro Q. Roscio comoedo* 27–8). Slaves could of course buy their freedom, but they would still be obliged to continue performing in the same troupe, as a ruling on a Hadrianic pantomime attests (Justinian, *Digest* 28.1.27). The troupe would always stay intact if the actor–manager so wished.

The presence of slave alongside free on the Roman stage leads to some paradoxes inherent in the performance situation. Actors play roles, and those roles need not correspond to their status offstage. In what is probably a joke, the closing lines of *Cistellaria* acknowledge that for the slaves in the troupe, there are possible repercussions that echo what has transpired within the play: *qui deliquit vapulabit, qui non deliquit bibet*

---

[19] Brown (2002) 227–8 and Gratwick (1982) 84.

[20] Ulpian, *Digest* 3.2.2.5. See Csapo and Slater (1995) 281–3, Suetonius, *Augustus* 45.3, *coercitionem in histriones magistratibus omni tempore et loco lege vetere permissam ademit praeterquam ludis et scaena* ('From the magistrates [Augustus] took the ancient law allowing them to beat actors at any time or place, restraining them to the games and stage [*scaena*]'), and Suetonius, *Tiberius* 35.2, *et ex iuventute utriusque ordinis profligatissimus quisque, quominus in opera scaenae harenaeque edenda senatus consulto teneretur, famosi iudicii notam sponte subibant* ('And the most profligate of young men from both orders willingly demoted their rank, lest the decree of the senate hold them off the stages [*scaena*] and arenas').

(785: 'he who messed up will be beaten; he who didn't will drink!').[21]
Seneca applies this paradox 'quite often' (*saepius*) to the comedy of life
(*humanae vitae mimus*) when he writes (*Letters* 80.7–8) that the actor on
stage playing a king might not have enough money to eat. Seneca
examines only slaves playing royalty because it serves his rhetorical end,
but the reverse is equally likely to occur, with free men playing slaves, as
in the possible case discussed below, with Plautus playing Chrysalus in
Bacchides. The names of actors (even though some of these are stage-
names) suggest that some performers have citizenship, but the largest
roles in Plautus all require the leading actors to play slaves. This creates
convoluted situations where (potentially) a free actor plays a slave who
during the play beats or threatens to beat a slave playing a free actor. The
social inversion inherent in so many Plautine plots[22] creates so many
hierarchies that resonate with the socially diverse audience in different
ways that it is almost impossible to appreciate the many ways social
convention might be challenged in a given play. This is especially true in
Captivi, where the plot hinges on free characters wrongly being treated as
slaves.[23]

Could the audience during a performance discern which of the performers were free and which were not (assuming they would even be
inclined to ask)? The social stratification in the audience is mirrored in
the composition of the troupe. Some audience members (senators, say)
will be higher in social status than all members of the troupe, and will
know this to be the case. Slaves will know that their social standing is no
higher than any in the troupe. A freedman might know some of the actors
are slaves (even if he does not know which ones), and so see them in a
position he had once shared, while others are of his present status or
higher. Plautus creates a situation – at the *ludi* where some argue there
was an element of topsy-turvydom already – in which the audience
identifies with different actors differently as they change their roles. This
occurs whether or not the audience is aware who is really a slave and who
is not: absence of clear information will only multiply the number of
interpretations available. Further, women in the audience will see free
actors and slaves playing various women of different status, and this too
opens up a number of possible avenues for interpretation that can be only
imagined. For the playwright working in a medium that prizes the

---

[21] The verb *delinquere* is used here for bad acting; in *Persa* 624–30 the verb is *peccare*. Brown (2002)
235 n. 41 lists some other possible references to beating slave actors, but discounts their value.

[22] This has been the particular focus of Segal (1987) and McCarthy (2000).

[23] See Moore (1998b) 181–201, 226–8, and McCarthy (2000) 167–209.

aggressive blurring of fiction, 'reality', and reality, there is a seemingly uncontrollable aspect to these nuances. Only 'seemingly' though: despite the freedom and social inversions that are exhibited, the bulk of the play is mediated through a small core of key performers who are rigorously trained in the possibilities of Roman comic theatre.

The other name sometimes associated with Plautus' troupe is T. Publilius Pellio, whom Symmachus 10.2[24] ranks as an actor alongside Roscius and Turpio. Pellio is listed as the *actor* in the production notice preceding *Stichus*. In *Bacchides* 213–15, Chrysalus refers to him by name:

> *non res, sed actor mihi cor odio sauciat.*
> *etiam Epidicum, quam ego fabulam aeque ac me ipsum amo,*
> *nullam aeque invitus specto, si agit Pellio.*
>
> It's the actor not the tale that pains my heart.
> The play I love as I love myself, *Epidicus*,
> Is the one I hate the most if Pellio's acting.   (tr. Barsby)

Another reference to *supellex Pellionis* (*Menaechmi* 404: 'Pellio's para-phernalia') seems probable.[25] The *Bacchides* passage implies *Epidicus* predates *Bacchides*. Second,

It can be taken to imply that Plautus had fallen out with Pellio after *Epidicus* and was now using another actor-manager, though there is the alternative possibility that it is simply a piece of good-humoured leg-pulling, which gains more point if Pellio was actually taking part in the play (playing Pistoclerus, perhaps, or even Chrysalus, which puts the joke in his own mouth).[26]

Putting the joke in the actor's own mouth seems an odd joke for which I can find no ancient parallel. However, that the actor speaking the 'I' is Plautus himself seems very likely, and gives the play's largest role (over 420 lines of verse, more than double the length of the next longest part, Nicobulus) to the author. It is then imaginable, though hardly necessary, that Pistoclerus was played by Pellio.[27] The alternative, that Plautus was now associated with a different troupe, leads to the speculation that

---

[24] See Frank (1932) 248–51.
[25] Mattingly (1957) and (1960), followed by Zwierlein (1992) 199–212, argue that the passage is a posthumous insertion, but this does not remove its difficulties. See Gratwick (1993) 178. Part of the argument of this book is that the genesis of the Plautine text is a knot of Gordian proportions, but there is no specific reason to exclude this passage rather than any other. What the *supellex* is remains unclear.
[26] Barsby (1986) 115–16, citing Gratwick (1982) 80 and Fraenkel (1960) 239–41, and see 431.
[27] Frank (1932) 248.

Plautus started his own company (sometime in the 190s?) after establishing himself as an actor in Pellio's troupe. If Pellio is no longer associated with Plautus, the phrase *si agit Pellio* raises another issue, that Pellio continues to perform a Plautine play even though he is no longer associated with the author (though here and with *actor* in *Bacchides* 213 a more limited sense of producer/director could be meant[28]). There is then an implied sense of copyright violation, with Plautus (still possibly playing Chrysalus) regretting the loss of authorial control over his 'favourite' play. This comment need not be directly hostile, however. Perhaps Plautus has sold the play to Pellio (after its initial performance?) and is here trying to downplay his rival's successes with it. We cannot know, but even these few tantalising hints suggest strong personalities of individual actors emerging during dramatic performances.[29]

This is also suggested by an examination of acting styles. Whatever the meaning of *Bacchides* 213–15, it is clear that the character Chrysalus speaks not in the *persona* of the slave of Nicobulus, but in the person of Plautus himself. Wiles describes this dynamic with reference to the actor in *Pseudolus*: 'the actor playing Pseudolus, for instance, was required to present three faces to the audience: (1) as an Athenian domestic slave, (2) as an actor participating in the Megalensian games, and (3) as the mouthpiece of Plautus the Roman poet'.[30] This is true, so far as it goes. In both of these examples, *Bacchides* and *Pseudolus*, we must recognise the possibility that the actor speaks as the mouthpiece of Plautus (3) precisely because the actor is Plautus, and the audience knows this to be so. This is not required, of course: the lines work differently in either case, but both can work. The middle term is also open to examination, for in speaking as a Roman performer outside of the dramatic narrative (2), the actor nevertheless continues to deliver his lines in verse. The extra-dramatic communication (here, or with the accompanied verse of the Choragus in *Curculio* 462–86, for example) continues to be scripted and rehearsed, and is not as separable from the work of the playwright as it might initially seem. Nor is it unproblematic even to think of the Pseudolus actor playing an Athenian slave (1), for this might be just one of the roles played by the actor in the play (the role of Pseudolus can be doubled with the cook, for instance). Since disguise and dissimulation are a regular part of Plautine narratives, the actor might also be playing a character who is

---

[28] Compare Brown (2002) 229.
[29] Other contemporary or political allusions are discussed at Garton (1972) 32, and it is in this context that we can best understand the reference to Naevius at *Miles Gloriosus* 211–12.
[30] Wiles (1991) 32.

adopting another role within the drama: this is seen when Curculio plays Summanus, Leonida in *Asinaria* plays Saurea, Simia in *Pseudolus* plays Harpax, or any of the many other examples the plays of Plautus provide.

There are considerably more than three levels operating, then, and there is no clear demarcation separating one from another. These levels blend together to produce a performance continuum that corresponds to the blurred dramatic space, which represents neither the Greek city described in the play nor the Rome in which it is performed, but a happy fusing of the two, creating a hybrid setting that Gratwick has felicitously called 'Plautinopolis'.[31] Each level of actor's delivery can blur into the other, and this effect will be further enhanced if, as I argue in Chapter 6, there was a substantial improvisational element to the performance. The blurring is conscious and deliberate, and it is not without risks for the actor. The audience needs to accept the composite world created, and it is exactly this that the early audiences of Terence's *Hecyra* failed to do.[32] Though risky, there are great rewards offered by this technique as well, for at each of these levels different opportunities for comedy present themselves.

Later descriptions of stage performance, particularly Quintilian's use of theatrical examples in his advice to orators centuries later, describe very precise, decorous movements and gestures, each associated with a very particular set of meanings. Quintilian urges the orator modestly to adopt the gestural language of the stage because it communicates nuances so clearly.[33] It is possible to link such discussions to the illustrations of Terentian manuscripts,[34] and it would be a great gain for production criticism if we could know how such gestures relate to the Plautine stage. There is good reason, however, to believe that they do not. Such a gestural language exists as one component of a much larger field of semiological content, and accomplishes its goal by fitting into all of the other variables like a piece in a puzzle. Quintilian is able to transfer theatrical gestures to the assembly because he sees both spaces as analogous: the use of permanent stone buildings with a semicircular orchestra, with a speaker positioned before an seated audience that intends to stay for the entire performance allows for controlled, precise gestures, in the same way that Noh drama does in Japan for its audience. Attending the

---

[31] Gratwick (1982) 104 n. 1; 'Plautinopolis' at (1993) 34.
[32] Garton (1972) 25–6. On the blurring of Greece and Rome, see Moore (1998b) 53–61 and Wiles (1991) 33–4, who discusses the end of *Stichus*.
[33] See Fantham (1982), (2002), Graf (1991), and Wiles (1991) 198.
[34] See Jones and Morey (1930–31) and Dodwell (2000).

theatre in the early empire was a very different experience from attending it in Plautus' day. Certainly it is possible that some of the gestures Quintilian describes were employed on the earlier stage, but we cannot know that they are the same; indeed I rather expect that the set of signs Quintilian outlines developed after the establishment of a permanent theatre in Rome in 55 BC, accumulating rapidly as actors worked to create anew the relationship between performer, space, and audience. Some of these may have been taken from earlier comic theatre, but there are many other possible sources. Theatre always represents a fluid space, in which the change of one element in the equation necessitates a series of further changes to the other elements so that harmony can be restored.

Such a balance will be unique for each performer. Ironically, our ancient authority for this is Quintilian, who argues *saepe aliud alios decere* (11.3.177: 'different things become different speakers'). His illustration must be cited at length (11.3.178–80):

maximos actores comoediarum, Demetrium et Stratoclea, placere diversis virtutibus vidimus. sed illud minus mirum, quod alter deos et iuvenes et bonos patres servosque et matronas et graves anus optime, alter acres senes, callidos servos, parasitos, lenones et omnia agitatiora melius – fuit enim natura diversa: nam vox quoque Demetri iucundior, illius acrior erat; adnotandae magis proprietates, quae transferri non poterant. manus iactare et dulces exclamationes theatri causa producere et ingrediendo ventum concipere veste et nonnumquam dextro latere facere gestus, quod neminem alium, Demetrium decuit (namque in haec omnia statura et mira specie adiuvabatur): illum cursus et agilitas et vel parum conveniens personae risus, quem non ignarus rationis populo dabat, et contracta etiam cervicula. quidquid horum alter fecisset, foedissimum videretur. quare norit se quisque, nec tantum ex communibus praeceptis sed etiam ex natura sua capiat consilium formandae actionis.

We have seen those great comic actors, Demetrius and Stratocles, give pleasure by very different qualities. This is the less surprising, because one of them was very good at acting gods, young men, good fathers and good slaves, married ladies, and respectable old women; the other did better with angry old men, shifty slaves, parasites, pimps, and all the livelier characters. Their natural gifts in fact differed. Demetrius had the pleasanter voice, Stratocles the more penetrating. Even more noteworthy were the peculiar, and non-transferable, features of each. The hand-waving, the lovely long cries meant for the audience, the way of catching the wind in his clothes as he came on, the occasional expressive movement of his right side – all this became Demetrius and no one else; his height and his good looks helped him in it all. What became Stratocles, on the other hand, was his speed and agility, his laugh (not always in keeping with the character, but a conscious concession to the audience), and even his hunched-up neck. If the other had done any of these things, it would have seemed a disgusting performance. So let everyone 'know himself', and take counsel in forming his delivery not only from general rules, but from his own nature.[35]

Each actor's style of performance is tailored to particular types of characters, and their acting styles are very different. There is much that Quintilian assumes. The two actors perform complementary roles, and they may belong to the same *grex*: Juvenal 3.99 also associates the two. Both names are Greek, perhaps attesting to multicultural influences on their comic styles. Both men have techniques that establish a rapport with the audience – Demetrius his *dulces exclamationes*, and Stratocles his *risus*, even when (significantly!) the laugh was not appropriate to his character. Quintilian provides evidence for the blurring of levels of delivery isolated above. This is testimony for a later period, but its applicability is not governed by the performance context: two actors in the same space with the same audience do different things, and both are appropriate, and this is equally likely in the less formal theatre of Plautus.

Donatus provides another example, where the actor's personal habits inform the choices made for his character (*ad Phormio* 315):

adhuc narratur fabula de Terentio et Ambivio ebrio, qui acturus hanc fabulam oscitans et temulentus atque aurem minimo inscalpens digitulo hos Terentii pronuntiavit versus. quibus auditis exclamavit poeta se talem eum scriberet cogitasse parasitum, et ex indignatione, qua eum saturum potumque deprehenderat, delinitus <est> statim.

The story is still told about Terence and the drunken Ambivius who, when he was going to perform this play, delivered these lines by Terence yawning, drunk, and scratching at his ear with his little finger; whereupon the author exclaimed that that was how he had thought of the parasite when he wrote it – and he was immediately calmed down, having been angry because he had caught him full of food and drink.[36]

There are some problems in accepting this story at face value, for the naturalism implied suggests Turpio is not here wearing a mask. To act yawning and drunk in a mask requires a very different set of actions than to yawn and behave drunk without one. Perhaps this is evidence for

---

[35] Text and translation, Russell (2001) 178–81.
[36] Text, Wessner (1902–8) II: 426; translation, Brown (2002) 232.

unmasked rehearsals, though if so they were probably early in the preparation process;[37] it also suggests that the playwright does not normally contribute to the interpretation of a part. In any case, one point of the anecdote is that the rehearsal process necessarily obscures an easy distinction between actor and role.

Very little can be known about actors and the troupes in which they performed. We can speculate on some of the relationships that existed within the troupe and outside of it, as the troupe creates an economic base by which it can survive. The few indications about performance styles suggest only that there was a great degree of variation. We know that actors were male, and they regularly played both male and female parts, which was not the case when Donatus wrote in the fourth century AD.[38] While the Hellenistic theatre does afford some evidence for the use of adolescent (boy) actors,[39] there is no direct evidence in Plautus and Terence. Perhaps we might imagine the *puer* in *Pseudolus* 767–89 or the *puer* that leads Ballio to market (170, 241, 249) to be adolescents, but we cannot be certain: *puer* is the standard designation for a slave on stage, and regularly represents a bearded adult male.[40] Perhaps the strongest indication is the description of Paegnium in *Persa*, who is designated not only as a *puer* (line 192), but also as weighing barely eighty pounds (lines 229–31). Assuming that such claims are to be accepted at face value, we can tentatively conclude that at least one of the members of Plautus' troupe was physically small. While this is not much, it is possible to apply this information to begin to develop an understanding of how roles were divided in Roman comedy, and what implications this has for the size of Plautus' troupe.

DOUBLING AND THE SIZE OF PLAUTUS' TROUPE

In the Greek theatre, beginning with tragedy in fifth-century Athens and evidently extending into the Hellenistic times of Menander, there was in

---

[37] When masked plays are rehearsed today, it is usual for the early rehearsals to be conducted without masks, and, only once the actors are 'off book' and the initial blocking is established are masks worn. This may have been so in antiquity. For a discussion of the scripts used in a Roman rehearsal for a play by Euripides, see Marshall (2004).

[38] Donatus, *ad Andria* 4.3.1, line 716: *hoc est personae femineae, sive haec personatis viris agitur, ut apud veteres, sive per mulierem, ut nunc videmus* ('this [Mysis] is a female character, and either this character is played by a male, as in the time of our ancestors, or by a woman, as we see now').

[39] Sifakis (1979).

[40] In the most recent examination of this passage, Jocelyn (2000) 435 n. 18, assumes that the slave is young, but notes the meaning of *puer* 'extends a long way either side of puberty'.

operation, at least in some form, a Rule of Three Actors. Dramatists were 'granted a chorus', and were provided with three actors, among whom all the speaking roles needed to be assigned. Rather than being an arbitrary limit imposed on the dramatist for financial or for other reasons, the purpose of such a rule was to establish a common ground for the competetive aspect of the festival: playwrights, having been allotted at least nominally identical resources, demonstrated their creativity at least partly through their use of these resources – by having actors play multiple roles, perhaps of considerable variety. That the audience would be aware of such effects is shown by the fact that, in Athenian competition, prizes were awarded to the best actor (and not to the best performance or role). On the Athenian stage, any number of unspeaking performers was permitted, so long as the rule was observed. While this has been doubted in some particular instances, as a general principle it seems to hold true, and this was the principle that Horace espoused as a dramatic ideal in *Ars Poetica* 192.[41]

In Rome, the situation was different, and the situation changes in a way that has not been generally recognised. A dramatist was contracted to present shows at *ludi*, and did so for a fee. While the Greek original operated with a Rule of Three Actors and a Chorus, the Roman dramatist was not so restricted. One must not, therefore, create a false analogy with the performance conditions of the Greek theatre. Critics are all but agreed that there is some degree of economy in the allocation of acting resources. Most scholarly views vary between assuming the minimum number of performers for a play (advocated for example by Kurrelmeyer), to assuming a small troupe of five or six actors who divided roles between them, regardless of the needs of the play (this is found in Duckworth, for example); one actor per role is maintained in most modern productions of Plautus.[42] There is no *a priori* reason why roles would be shared with divisions similar to the Greek source play, even when the adapted script will permit it. Rather, as opposed to the limits for the plays which formed Plautus' models, the limits that constrict Plautus are in the first instance financial: every performer who appears on the Plautine stage is in one way or another on the pay-roll, whether he speaks a line or not. The Greek distinction between speaking 'actors' and non-speaking performers

---

[41] For general discussions on how the rule operates, see Pickard-Cambridge (1968) 135–56, Damen (1989), Marshall (1994), Cohen (1999). Some further specific examples: over a tetralogy, Marshall (2003); in Aristophanes, Marshall (1997a) (though this has not met with general acceptance) answering MacDowell (1994); in Menander, Handley (1965) 25–30 and see Marshall (2002) 6 n. 12; for the lack of applicability to Senecan drama, Marshall (1998).

[42] Schanz and Hosius (1927) I: 146.

(κωφὰ πρόσωπα, 'mute masks') is therefore not applicable. The size of Plautus' troupe becomes relevant, as it is from this number (fixed at least for a given performance) that all those who appear on stage must be drawn, speaking and unspeaking characters alike.

Doubling was standard in all ancient stage genres, and Plautus is no exception, as can be seen from the prologue of *Poenulus*.[43] Unfortunately, the reference is not as helpful as it might be. The unnamed speaker concludes saying *ego ibo, ornabor* (123: 'I must go and get into my costume'; tr. Nixon) and at 126 he repeats, *ibo, alius nunc fieri volo* ('I am going, I must become another man'; tr. Nixon).[44] Here are two explicit statements of role sharing. The prologue will take some other role in the drama, but (unhelpfully) there is no indication which role he will take: *alius* is not specific. The *Poenulus* prologue is replete with references to the theatricality and metatheatricality of the play but for this particular aspect of performance, details are slight.[45] Nor should we think that only prologues doubled: the prologue speaks about as many lines in the play as the *advocati*, slightly fewer than Hanno and Lycus, and considerably fewer than Agorastocles and Milphio. There are eight other characters in the play, with parts ranging from part of less than one line (the *ancilla* at line 332 and the Carthaginain *puer* at line 1141) to 108 lines (Adelphasium), all of whom are likely to be doubled with other parts. The impermanence of the actor-role association is also suggested in *Menaechmi* 72–6, where the neutral stage space is capable of accommodating any narrative setting provided by Greek New Comedy.

There are even hints within the plays themselves – lines that acquire resonance when heard not as something spoken by the character, but by the actor. There is a surprising number of such references, which actors today often are able to discover for themselves. For example, in *Mostellaria* 1123–7, Callidamates says to the audience,

> *Philolaches venisse dixit mihi suom peregre huc patrem*
> *quoque modo hominem ad venientem servos ludificatus sit,*
> *ait se metuere in conspectu sui patris procedere.*
> *nunc ego de sodalitate solus sum orator datus*
> *qui a patre eius conciliarem pacem.*

---

[43] The following has been informed by the methodologies of the many excellent studies of doubling in Elizabethan theatre, including Smith (1967), Ringler (1968), King (1992), Bradley (1992) 40–57, and McMillin and MacLean (1998) 97–120.

[44] Textual issues concerning this passage will be discussed in Chapter 6.

[45] Similarly, Slater (2000) 149–62 does not draw any conclusions about this in his discussion of the prologue; see Beare (1964) 308.

Philolaches told me that his father's back from overseas,
Also how the slave had fooled the father as he just arrived.
Philo's too ashamed right now to step into his father's sight.
So our little social circle chose me as the ambassador to
Seek the sire and sue for peace. (tr. Segal)

This awkwardly prevents the father–son reunion that one might reasonably expect given the father's long absence. Why does Plautus avoid such a scene? It is obviously insufficient to say 'because his Greek model avoided it'; *Bacchides* proves Plautus is capable of large-scale revision if he wishes it, and it is natural to think of such a scene as having the potential for high emotions expressed through song, or whatever. I suspect rather that Theopropides and Philolaches were played by the same actor (a division accepted by both Kurrelmeyer and Llarena i Xibillé[46]). He, with the Tranio actor, then becomes one of two star performers in the play, sharing over 65 per cent of the play between them.[47] Such jokes are never central to the plot, but they may reinforce larger themes. The audience is not required to interpret what they see in this way, but it remains

---

[46] Kurrelmeyer (1932) 70–72, Llarena i Xibillé (1994) 141–51.

[47] This has consequences for the ghost scene: *heus, Tranio!* (515: 'Hey Tranio') is usually understood to be spoken by Philolaches, within the house and mistaken for a ghost. If I am right about the role doubling here, either another actor within the house is impersonating Philolaches, or, conceivably, the actor who is on stage as Theopropides delivers the line using his Philolaches' voice (in effect, a type of ventriloquism, with the speaking actor 'throwing' his voice inside the house). Marshall (1997a) 77–9 suggests that ventriloquism of this sort was possible in Aristophanic comedy. For ventriloquism in antiquity generally, see Davis (2003). Damen (1985) 374 attributes the line to an actor other than the one playing Tranio or Theopropides.

There are of course other ways to read the humour in the scene. The voice from within (the manuscripts write *intus*) calls out *heus Tranio* (515), and *quaeso* (517: 'please … '), and is cut off both times by Tranio. We don't know what the voice wants – more wine? Someone to clean up after Callidamates? Information as to whether Theopropides has been duped? – whatever it is, it endangers Tranio's ruse. It is clearly inappropriate for one of the slaves to make a request of Tranio at this time: for comic effect, the danger must come from one of the people Tranio is attempting to help. There are four free characters inside: Philolaches the son, Callidamates the son's friend, Philematium the son's girlfriend, and Delphium, the son's friend's girlfriend. While all four characters have appeared on stage, and any could be speaking within the house, comedy arises if the voice is recognisable as one of these four. Callidamates had been the first to leave the stage at 386, and after that Philematium did not deliver any lines. The prominence given to Delphium in the lines immediately following that (whatever character corresponded to her in the Greek original, we may be confident that it was not a speaking part; Gaiser (1972) 1074–5, Barsby (1982) 84–6) perhaps provides reason to think the voice is hers – it will at least be recognisable to the audience. Similarly, Philolaches as the son represents the character closest to Theopropides, and so can be seen as the least appropriate (and therefore most appropriate) individual to threaten the deception. Matters of doubling point to a metatheatrical interpretaion if the lines are delivered by Philolaches, but that is irrelevant to the present argument (it is a result of the staging choice, not a reason for it). Delphium, who is the individual most removed from the affairs of the house, and whose prominence in previous scenes suggests such shouts might be within her character, is equally possible, though.

available for those in the audience who are inclined to identify these metatheatrical levels.

To maintain any position on role doubling it is necessary to provide some explanation for how and why the practice comes into use, and here lies the start of the problem. Any answer given on false analogy with Greek drama will be found to be lacking. Certainly, Plautus' Greek originals were written with a prescribed actor limit, but unless we posit a philhellenic and sentimental Plautus, there is no reason for him to maintain the low limit, since Roman theatrical festivals were not competitions, but were 'entertainments', *ludi*.[48] For this reason that I do not consider part-splitting – assigning the same role to multiple actors at different points of the play, which was a feature of the Menandrean use of the Rule of Three Actors[49] – relevant for Plautus and Terence, except to accomplish a specific special effect, as in *Menaechmi* (discussed below). The benefits of such part-splitting derive primarily from a system that operates within an actor limit.

Previous studies of doubling in Plautus are typically concerned with the three-actor structure of the Greek original that lies behind Plautus' play. This has no necessary impact on how Plautus used his actors. In *Mostellaria*, the doubling of father and son is likely in both plays, but we cannot know that this is the case. It is possible at times to identify the underlying three-actor structure from Plautine drama, but this has no necessary bearing on a Roman performance. By including all performers in my reckonings of troupe size, I am fundamentally changing the question from what has been asked by Kurrelmeyer, Barsby, Damen, Lowe, and Franko.[50] While there is much of value in these studies, it lies principally in what they reveal about the Greek models of the plays. Llarena i Xibillé's concerns are closer to mine, but differing assumptions lead to very different conclusions.[51] When the text refers to attendants in the plural, I assume there are only two, though of course more are possible. Similarly, I believe 'lightning changes' (an actor changing characters in a very short time – zero to five lines) were possible on the ancient stage, and shall note where my argument depends on their use.

---

[48] As Jory (1967) 21 claims, 'There is no clear evidence for poetic competitions during republican times' (citing *Casina* 17 and *Phormio* 16–17 in his n. 5 as metaphorical; see Volcacius Sedigitus in Aulus Gellius, *Attic Nights* 15.24, and Horace, *Epistles* 2.1.181); 'There were however acting competitions': Jory (1967) 22, citing *Trinummus* 706, *Amphitruo* 69, and *Poenulus* 37.
[49] See Goold (1959) 144–50 and Handley (1965) 25–30.
[50] Kurrelmeyer (1932), Barsby (1982), Damen (1985) 127–97, 307–17, 333 nn. 46–9, 373–6, 393 nn. 26–8, (1992), (1995), Lowe (1997), Franko (2004).
[51] Llarena i Xibillé (1994).

Different assumptions might increase the troupe size again, taking us even further from the standard interpretation. Reasons why there might exist actor limits in Roman comedy may be artistic or they may be financial. For a travelling troupe, fewer performers reduce overheads, and this must be a factor, at least to some extent, because of the economy of the *ludi*. Fewer personnel increase returns. This will always be the bottom line for Plautus.

An example will clarify the situation. In Plautus' *Pseudolus* there is only one scene that uses more than three speaking actors. The *servus callidus* Pseudolus and his master's son Calidorus are onstage when the *leno* Ballio appears with his silent slaves, whereupon one of them[52] talks back to his master (159: *at haec retunsast*, 'but this [axe] is dull') – a fourth speaking actor onstage. The standard response sees this as evidence of Plautine adaptation; in the Greek original, the slave would have remained silent. Previous considerations of role doubling extend this solution to the play as a whole, dividing the roles between three-and-sometimes-four actors: they note the thematic unity achieved where one actor, perhaps Plautus himself, would play Pseudolus and the Cook; a second would play Ballio, Charinus, and Callipho (the *leno* and the two friends of the central father/son pair); the third would play Calidorus, his father Simo, and Simia the other *servus callidus*; and the fourth would play the slave and Harpax, servant to the *miles* Polymachaeroplagides (who is not a character in the play). Even allowing for 'translation' to the Roman theatre, a division of this type is predicated on an understanding of the Rule of Three Actors as practised by the Greeks. It assumes that the parts are being assigned to limit the number of speaking actors on stage, as if in an effort to create a level playing field for competition. The elimination of the demands of competition means that the criteria governing the economic use of resources must include the full company: one way or another, *mutae personae* are also on the company pay-roll, which is not the case in competition at the Athenian Dionysia.[53] This problem becomes particularly acute in *Pseudolus*, when Ballio is assigning duties to five slaves (157–62), and instructs four slave girls on the type of clientele they are to pursue (185–229).

---

[52] While the manuscripts identify this character as a *lorarius*, he is not a strap-bearing thug usually associated with the title. I therefore follow Usener and think of him as a *servus* – so Willcock (1987) 103.

[53] It was, however, probably part of the economy of theatrical production when successful shows were exported to other *poleis* and South Italy. In these cases, it is possible that variations in the performance scripts were introduced.

Characters like Ballio's axe-wielding slave can be found throughout the Plautine corpus. The joke made by the *ancilla* in her only line at *Poenulus* 332 is funny, but it is surely disposable: its presence demonstrates that Plautus was not operating within the framework provided by the Athenian rule. This is even more so for the Punic *puer* at 1141. There are a number of characters that can be similarly identified as 'walk-on' parts. If we somewhat arbitrarily designate five lines of verse (adding together partial lines) or less as the measure of a small part, we have the fourteen roles.[54] Extending the range to ten lines adds six more characters, all of whom are more substantial stage presences than the first list.[55] In Aulularia, Pythodicus speaks a monologue, and it is likely that this provides a buffer for the actor to double the roles of Strobilus and Euclio (compare this with Staphyla's speech at 274–9 which allows the initial change).[56] Similarly, the absence of Palaestrio from the final scene of *Miles Gloriosus* seems odd until it is recognised that the actor has come onstage as the knife-wielding cook Cario. In both *Miles* and *Pseudolus* the actor playing the largest role in the play may double that part with the cook so as to have the opportunity to partake in a standard set of comic routines associated with the cook that continue from Greek New Comedy. Nine more characters would be added if the range were extended to fifteen lines.[57] Two further characters are added if it extends to twenty lines.[58] Wherever we draw this line, there can be no doubt that Plautus could easily have made all of these roles non-speaking parts or assigned the lines or their content to different characters if he had wished to do so (though

---

[54] In addition to the *lorarius* in *Pseudolus* and the two roles in *Poenulus*, there are Blepharo in *Amphitruo* 1035–7 (though the character may have spoken in the fragmentary scene that precedes this), Phaedria in *Aulularia* 691–2, Chytrio in *Casina* 720–23, the *captivi* in *Captivi* 200, the *servus* in *Epidicus* 400, the *danista* in *Epidicus* 629–33 and 647, Telestis in *Epidicus* 637–49, the *lorarii* in *Menaechmi* 1015–16, the *lorarius* in *Miles Gloriosus* 1424, the *puer* in *Mostellaria* 420–22, and Inopia in *Trinummus* 2. This does not include the two-line prologue to *Pseudolus*, and the lines designated as *caterva* or *grex*, which frame the narrative and are not tied to a dramatic identity.

[55] Pythodicus in *Aulularia* 363–70 (a monologue), Philopolemus in *Captivi* 928–53, Demipho in *Cistellaria* 774–81, Cario in *Miles Gloriosus* 1398–1423, the *lorarii* in *Rudens* 764, 826–36, and 879–81 (unlike the other characters being considered, these *lorarii* speak in more than one scene), and Syra in *Truculentus* 791–805.

[56] Lindsay suggests that lines 363–70 are delivered not by Pythodicus but by Strobilus. If so, then the doubling suggested would require a lightning change following line 370. This is possible, but not needed. The uncertainty of line assignments prevents this example from being pushed too far: Leo gives Pythodicus more lines in the previous scene so as to fill out his character.

[57] The *puer* in *Captivi* 909–21 (a monologue), the *cocus* in *Curculio* 251–73, Chaeribulus in *Epidicus* 106–57 and 323–79, the *fidicina* in *Epidicus* 496–516, Acropolistis in *Epidicus* 570–95, the *ancilla* in *Menaechmi* 524–48, the *puer* in *Miles Gloriosus* 1378–93, Delphium in *Mostellaria* 320–98, and Lemniselenis in *Persa* 763–851. This excludes the prologue of *Asinaria*, lines 1–15.

[58] Cleomachus in *Bacchides* 842–904 and the *lorarius* in *Captivi* 119–23 and 195–215.

in some cases, such as Philopolemus in *Captivi*, this would have an impact on the narrative).

Rather than attempt to interpret the decision to give these characters voice in terms of an opportunity to give amateur actors or new members of the company a chance to get stage time (an unlikely motivation), we need to recognise that the existence of these parts marks a different understanding of how a theatre troupe operates. Because all actors receive a portion of the fee paid to the troupe to perform (even slaves will need to be fed), Plautus has no motivation to keep his total number of characters to a minimum, or to keep an onstage character silent, except as mandated by his artistic sense. Further, we can see that in at least some cases, this artistic motivation is likely to be driven by the audience's perceptions not of the characters in the play, but of the actors, as individuals are recognised behind the masks of the roles that they play.

To understand the functioning of the Plautine theatre better, it is necessary to consider what happens with role division when we go backstage with Plautus. What types of movements are, or can be, expected of the actors backstage, given a particular division of roles? When Ballio and his slave exit stage left to the forum at line 380, and minutes later at line 415 Callipho and Simo appear stage left from the forum, it does not require a great imaginative leap to see the characters as being played by the same actors (note that this differs from the initial suggestion reached earlier when considering only the onstage action). Pseudolus' monologue (lines 394–414) can be seen as a dramatic device to allow time for the required mask and costume change.[59]

We can designate this as an 'easy' costume change: an actor exits as one character, changes costume while another actor speaks (often in soliloquy), and then enters from the same location as a different character. Within *Pseudolus*, it is possible to assign parts based purely on this criterion: giving an actor only 'easy' costume changes. For example, the actor playing Calidorus is onstage from 3 to 393, when he exits stage right. At 595, Harpax enters stage right, where he exits at 665. Pseudolus has a monologue (667–93) and then Calidorus enters stage right, at 694. He exits to the forum, stage left, at 758. The character is not to be seen again,

---

[59] A summary of the main arguments concerning *puer*-scenes can be found in Duckworth (1952) 96–97, 101, though see Prescott (1910), (1923), (1932), (1934), (1937), and Kurrelmeyer (1932) 17–44. Prescott's arguments are a helpful complement to my discussion, since they examine onstage activity that can be used to 'cover' backstage costume changes. Plautus however is manipulating a number of variables as he writes. In addition to doubling possibilities, the influence of the Greek model(s) and the effects of metre, music, and stock comedic routines will all impact upon the size, scope, and frequency of speeches that might appear as 'transition monologues'.

though the actor returns as Simia, from stage left, at 913. Simia exits stage right at 1051.[60] At 1103, Harpax returns from stage right. Finally, he exits with Ballio, not to return, at 1237, stage left. If this division of roles – giving one actor the parts of Calidorus, Harpax, and Simia – could be shown to be correct, there would exist a situation where the actor makes four 'easy' costume changes. Nothing unnatural or disjunctive is expected of the performer backstage. I am not certain, however, that this is the most desirable aesthetic: it does possess a simple elegance, but it is not possible to perform such feats for all of Plautus' character/actor divisions while maintaining a strict economy.

To give another example, it has often been supposed that the role of Pseudolus, the single most demanding part in Plautus, was doubled with the unnamed cook. Evidence for this position is in the *puer*-scene that immediately precedes the Cook scene.[61] Pseudolus exits the stage at 766; there is a monlogue by one of Ballio's slaves that is thought to allow time for a costume change (767–89), and the cook enters. The cook leaves the stage at 892. Ballio closes the scene with a monologue (892–904), whereupon Pseudolus returns. But, while the cook enters from the forum stage left (an 'easy' costume change), the cook exits into Ballio's house (see 890). This matters because Pseudolus returns from stage left. The extent to which this may be significant depends on how much backstage movement is thought to be possible during Ballio's thirteen lines. If the Pseudolus actor also plays the cook, it becomes necessary to assume some degree of rapid backstage communication between doors and side entrances. This may not be much to assume, especially since Ballio's is the leftmost door on the stage, but it does represent a significant claim for stage architecture and in the practical requirements for mounting the play. The flexible performance space for which I argued in Chapter 1 presents no obstacles to a backstage move of this type. Moves from a wing to a door, or even from one wing to the other, are regularly expected of actors in Greek theatre within a relatively short stage time, in both comedy and tragedy, and in both the fifth and fourth centuries. But, since the exigencies of the Rule of Three Actors are not functioning on the Roman stage within the same parameters that they had on the Greek

---

[60] To be fair, I should say that this destination is not certainly clear in the text – they are going to a safe house, somewhere. Willcock (1987), followed by Smith (1991), argues that it is Charinus' house, somewhere offstage right. The present argument could perhaps be used to strengthen this claim.

[61] See Jocelyn (2000). Prescott (1910) 39–45 and (1923) 29–30 discuss this speech as a means of facilitating this doubling.

stage, backstage movement of this type cannot be assumed: we have no external evidence that it is a necessary part of the Roman theatrical aesthetic, and this dramatic situation cannot be taken as proof that such a move was physically possible on the Roman stage.[62]

To return to the first role division suggested for *Pseudolus*, if the same actor plays Ballio, Charinus, and Callipho (which was desirable in terms of onstage thematic unity), the actor is expected to make two 'easy' costume changes: first, from Ballio to Callipho (exit 380, enter 415; thirty-four lines for the change); second, from Charinus to Ballio (exit 758, enter 790; thirty-one lines). To accomplish the change from Callipho to Charinus, however, the actor enters Callipho's house (the rightmost door on the stage) at 560, and enters as Charinus from stage right at line 693. That is 133 lines for the actor to move from the door backstage to the wing where he will enter: demands considerably easier than the thirteen lines the Pseudolus actor is given to make the move on the other side of the stage if he plays the cook. Other permutations of the roles are possible, but these seem to be the most efficient ones in terms of minimising the amount of movement that is expected backstage.

None of this changes the fact that *Pseudolus* requires nine performers onstage at one time. Pseudolus and Callidorus are onstage preparing to eavesdrop when Ballio emerges at 132, driving his slaves (*ignavi*, 'fools'). How many slaves there are can be seen in his instructions to them at 157–62, where five sentences begin with a second person pronoun, which, with the absence of any connecting particles, indicates that five separate slaves receive instructions (in the final instance two tasks are given to the same slave). Finally, Ballio is led by a slave boy (addressed at 170 and 241), which means there are nine actors on stage, plus the *tibicen*. All of these will have been in the troupe. Later in the scene, Ballio sings to four of his *meretrices* individually (188–229). Usener and others have deleted lines 218–24 as a doublet of 209–17.[63] Since the scene represents a maximum demand on troupe size for extant Plautus, it seems certain that we should see the *meretrices* being played by the same actors who had played the *servi*

---

[62] I suspect that most readers would consider this a trivial point to establish, but many contemporary theatre spaces (particularly black box theatres) do not possess this degree of flexibility. The lack of easy communication of a wing with the central door meant that an actor had to run outside the equivalent of two city blocks in my 1990 production of Sophocles' *Electra*.

[63] It is possible that at some point in the history of the text a fifth *meretrix* was addressed at this point, and her 'speaking' name has either been replaced by or corrupted to *excetra tu* ('you watersnake') in line 218, though in Chapter 6 I suggest this is a doublet arising from the performance tradition. The same phrase has been restored to the text of *Casina* 644, and Plautus uses the word also at *Persa* 3.

(i.e. that the troupe had nine actors and not thirteen). If, therefore, we are going to argue for almost any other doubling in the cast – e.g. of Pseudolus and the Cook – we may not do so based on necessity, because no particular doubling of speaking parts is necessary when the cast has nine actors. We must instead argue that a particular doubling creates a desirable, Roman aesthetic. When the *puer* emerges and speaks 767–89, it will be one of these male slaves: is it the back-talking axe-wielder? Also, which actor plays Phoenicium, Calidorus' beloved? One of them will, and one can even start to see how a string of these small parts (Phoenicium does not speak but is a key figure in the plot and will appear later in the play) can begin to constitute something desirable for an actor. In *Mostellaria*, there were narrative implications with stock characters being doubled, when the same actor played both *senex* and *adulescens*. With a cast of nine in *Pseudolus*, the minimum required by the play, the only certain doubling is between Ballio's (male) slaves and the girls he rents or sells.

The stage space was designed to be particularly adaptable to the needs of a variety of performances. If backstage communication is permitted in one play, we should assume that the same move is permitted in any play, unless there are reasons to believe the contrary. The architecture of Plautus' theatre buildings is not known, but given that multiple spaces were used, and some of them were conceivably constructed *ad hoc*, it should be possible to discern the mechanics of the stage even for those plays about which didascalic information does not survive. What assumptions are being made about backstage actor movement when role division in Plautus is discussed? There are many variables of unknown significance that face us: what type of stage was used; how many people were available for the performance; what was the extent of metatheatrical awareness on the part of the audience; even, was there a tradition for role sharing within the *Atellanae* that has carried over into Plautus? What must be avoided is importing assumptions about these conventions from the Greek stage. The extant comedies suggest that backstage movement in Plautus need not have been as extensive as it had been in the Greek theatre. Consequently any reckoning of the size of Plautus' troupe must include all non-speaking parts in the calculations.

There is one certain example of backstage communication. In *Miles Gloriosus*, a ruse is created whereby Philocomasium appears to be twins by entering one door and exiting another. Whereas under normal circumstances this would only happen when an actor also changes masks, such a move is permitted in this play because the plot establishes that there is a hole in an interior wall through which she can crawl. Of course, for the actors there is no interior wall: it is only a feature of the offstage dramatic world of the play. Palaestrio takes great pains to make this distinction clear to the audience in the play's delayed prologue (*Miles Gloriosus* 138–53, esp. 150–52):

> *et mox ne erretis, haec duarum hodie vicem*
> *suam et hinc et illinc mulier feret imaginem,*
> *atque eadem erit, verum alia esse adsimulabitur.*

> Don't you be fooled: today this woman will bring
> Her form both here and there in the place of two.
> She will be the same, but will pretend to be another.

This is one of the rare times in Roman comedy where the audience needs a particular piece of information to understand a scene correctly, and Palaestrio's emphasis gives positive evidence of backstage communication between at least two doors. Plautus needs to emphasize that, uniquely in this play, an actor can enter one door and emerge from another and not change roles.

The reason for Palaestrio's insistence, I suggest, is because Plautus is appropriating and varying a technique regularly used in twin comedies, and that in other twin comedies, such as Plautus' lost *Lenones Gemini* ('Twin Pimps'), the same actor would play both siblings. Moorehead independently suggests this for *Menaechmi*:[64] Plautus has carefully organised stage movement so that a single actor can play both Menaechmus (of Epidamnus) and Sosicles (Menaechmus II, of Syracuse). To help the audience distinguish the roles, Rambo[65] suggested that each brother used a separate wing, and Beare noted that the *palla* served as a valuable identifying stage property.[66] Further, Moore notes music always accompanies the entrances of Menaechmus of Epidamnus.[67] Only in the final scene, where the brothers finally meet, would a substitute actor be used for Sosicles. Plautus even points to this substitution within the play: Messenio says, *illic homo aut sycophanta aut geminus est frater tuos* (1087: 'That man is either a fraud or he's your twin brother');[68] as it happens, both are true. This same convention allows Sagaristio (disguised as a Persian) in *Persa* 692–9 to claim he has a twin brother in town – his

---

[64] Moorehead (1953–4). [65] Rambo (1915) 421.
[66] Damen (1988) 412–19 teases out the implications of this casting decision.
[67] Moore (1999) 136–41. [68] This is the only use of *sycophanta* in the play.

undisguised self! – completely within the expectations of the audience for twins.

If twin comedies in Rome habitually used the same actor, there is an inherent 'challenge' to any such stock situation – how aggressively can the playwright maintain the doubling? By reserving the use of a substitute Sosicles until the very end of the play, Plautus maintains the comic suspense for the longest time possible.[69] Recognising this removes some of the apparent novelty from *Menaechmi*; rather, *Amphitruo*, where each of the two sets of identical characters (Jupiter and Amphitruo, Mercurius and Sosia) must be played by a different actor, is more innovative.[70] Uncertainties remain: what happened, for example, in (pseudo-)Plautus' lost *Trigemini* ('Triplets') or Naevius' *Quadrigemini* ('Quadruplets')? Whatever the answer, there is a clear sense of a recurring joke being magnified for comic effect.

If this is so for *Menaechmi*, then we have a gauge for the amount of time the playwright will allow for backstage moves. If one actor plays both Menaechmi – a 'star part' if ever there was one – then it must be possible for an actor to move from one wing to another in just over ten performed lines: such a move is required twice in the play (216–25 and 558–70).[71] This may be contrasted with the 20–25 pentameters that Shakespeare scholars typically give their actors to change characters (with or without a move). An even tighter transition is required at 701, where the actor must make an immediate wing-to-door move. For some, this will be thought to be an insurmountable obstacle, and constitute sufficient evidence to suggest that the roles of the twins would not be doubled. But, in a non-naturalistic theatre, such assumptions are not safe.[72]

---

[69] In this respect he may be compared to a later emulator. When Carlo Goldoni wrote *The Venetian Twins* in 1748, he too had the same actor play both brothers, but he instead killed one of the twins to prevent them ever meeting each other. I suspect that this offers much less satisfaction for an audience.

[70] The sisters in *Bacchides* are not twins (Braun (1970) 52), and need not appear identical, though they doubtless were similar to each other. As it is, the characters are central to the plot, but appear onstage only in the opening and closing scenes. The actors probably double in other parts (Lydus, Chrysalus, Mnesilochus, Cleomachus, and the parasite are all possible roles for these actors).

[71] Arnott (1989) argues a change in just less than ten lines was required at Menander, *Dyskolos* 381–92.

[72] I believe a costume change is possible in fewer than five lines, and this can be suggested in brief by an anecdote from my production of *Curculio*. Roles were shared, and, at one point, an actor exited stage right speaking a line as one character (Phaedromus the *adulescens*), changed costumes, and returned as another character (Lyco the *banker*), from the other side of the stage, speaking the following line. This was deliberately contrived as a 'most difficult case': could unscripted slapstick 'cover' a costume change represented in the script by a gap of no lines at all? The answer, in all six of the outdoor performances, was yes. The change was effected without the audience being made aware of the *coup-de-theatre* at work, and Palinurus' improvisations during the change and the run

The audience knows that the two brothers are doubled, and it consequently supports the actor's efforts to meet the challenges posed by the playwright. Comic success in this context is achieved not by maintaining a seamless illusion about the separate identity of the characters, but by calling attention to the theatrical convention. The addition of comic routines, the use of the *tibicen,* and the humorously artificial representation of time on the Plautine stage further serve to mitigate any difficulties. Indications of Plautus manipulating time on stage can be found a little later in *Menaechmi.* At 875, the *senex* goes to get a doctor: *ibo atque accersam medicum iam quantum potest* ('I'll go and fetch a doctor as quickly as I can'). He returns seven lines later, complaining about the long wait (882–4). The slower the old man's entry here, the clearer the time dilation will appear to the audience and humour achieved.[73]

Mostellaria gives a similar indication for backstage communication between a door and the wings, though this involves reference to the *angiportum,* which gives access to the (imagined) back door of the house. References to the *angiportum* typically indicate a back street parallel with the street represented by the stage, and are employed by the playwright to motivate entrances of a character from locations other than the one in which they were last seen heading. In *Mostellaria,* Tranio is sent to the country in search of Philolaches at 931–2. As Tranio knows, the young master is actually inside the supposedly haunted house – more specifically, the character of the young master is inside the house; the actor who played Philolaches is almost certainly onstage playing the character of Theopropides. Rather than exit down some alley between the houses, I believe Tranio exits 'normally' to one of the wings. This allows the focus to change smoothly to the door-knocking routine that is already taking place. When Tranio next appears, he emerges from within the house – a strong entrance for the triumphant *callidus.* He justifies the unusual entry with reference to the *angiportum* and the house's back garden, in what amounts to a theatrical in-joke (*Mostellaria* 1044–6):

> *abii illac per angiportum ad hortum nostrum clanculum*
> *ostium quod in angiportu est horti, patefeci fores.*

> I went away from there secretly through the back street to our garden,
> I opened the door of the garden gate, which is in the back street.

from one wing to the other became funnier with each subsequent performance. Marshall (2003) 267–9 argues for a similar move in Aeschylus' *Eumenides.*

[73] There is an empty stage at this point, but this does not require a pause (or 'act-break'): see Conrad (1915), Duckworth (1952) 98–101, and the discussion in Chapter 4.

For our purposes, this demonstrates the existence of backstage communication between a wing and a door. It also suggests that maintaining a consistent onstage geography was important to Plautus.

As with any attempt to understand a foreign performance practice, there is a danger in importing one's own presuppositions about what is aesthetic or desirable. How quickly a character might change mask and costume to become a new character, is a case in point. Prescott, for example, believes it is 'obvious and necessary'[74] that no actor will leave as one character and re-appear immediately as another, though he is willing to accept a change in as few as five lines (at *Miles Gloriosus* 813–17), which 'is much shorter than those [passages] which usually provide for a change of rôles'.[75] I would suggest that his attitude reflects a particularly modern, naturalistic bias common in western theatre, and that we should acknowledge the possibility that a different aesthetic operated in Rome, particularly since we know that metatheatrical reference was intrinsic to the theatrical form. For example, in Japanese Kabuki theatre, rapid costume change is deliberately introduced because of the artistic challenge that it poses to the actor: 'an actor may make a complete [costume] change between two scenes in which in point of time the action is continuous. The reasons for this are purely decorative, being conditioned by considerations of colour and pattern.'[76] Through these *hayagawari*,[77] the actor could demonstrate a particular kind of virtuosity that was particularly appreciated in the Bunka-Bunsei eras (1804–30), and in the performances of Onoe Kikugoro III (1784–1849). This is, in essence, what I believe the play construction indicates for comedy in the Roman republic. In Kabuki, the art of the costume change has been taken a degree further:

There is a further and more dramatic form of change which calls for a complete transformation in a matter of seconds and, before the public, on the stage . . . Such changes are achieved by the technique known as *hikinuki*. The outer garment is kept in place during the first part of the scene by threads. At the right point the actor's dresser, or a *kurogo* [an onstage stagehand dressed in black], rips out these threads and the outer kimono either falls to the ground or is neatly turned inside out to reveal a new (and usually more splendid) costume.[78]

The assumptions about what might be perceived as an 'obvious' stage practice are culturally determined. Every audience member reads a performance work within his or her personal set of familiar performance

[74] Prescott (1923) 28.   [75] Prescott (1923) 33 n. 1.   [76] Halford and Halford (1956) 426.
[77] Brandon (1992) 165.   [78] Halford and Halford (1956) 426–7.

codes. For Rome such codes are unlikely even to include knowledge of the play which the playwright claims as his source for the present entertainment.

If Greek models are insufficient for consideration of the size of Plautus' troupe, then the overall financial implications must be borne in mind by asking how many are on the pay-roll. The result is a situation not par-allelled in Greek drama, but one which is similar to Elizabethan theatre companies, where the size of the troupe can be discerned by the dis-position of performers in the plays.[79] Since it seems that Roman comedy can expect 'lightning changes' of its actors, the clearest indication of troupe size generally is dictated by the scene with the greatest number of people onstage. I have tabulated such scenes and the size of the troupe that they imply (always excepting the *tibicen*).

FOUR PERFORMERS:

Cistellaria 639–52: Alcesimarchus, Melaenis, Selenium, Halisca
(*muta*; speaks after re-entry at 671)

Epidicus 475–92: Periphanes, *miles*, *fidicina*, *servus* (*muta*; imperative at 437; are additional slaves required at 472–5?)

621–47: Epidicus, Stratippocles, *danista*, Telestis

FIVE PERFORMERS:

Amphitruo: see note[80]

Curculio 679–729: Phaedromus, Planesium, Therapontigonus, Cappadox, Curculio (silent here, but he has spoken at 677[81])

Mercator 741–82: Lysimachus, Dorippa, *cocus*, two slaves (*mutae*; plural imperatives at 741, 782)[82]

---

[79] On this point, I have been particularly challenged by studies such as McMillin and MacLean (1998) 99–102, which presents clear evidence correlating troupe size with production dates in an Elizabethan troupe. No comparatively impressive results are possible for Roman comedy.

[80] One scene requires four actors: at 770–79, Amphitruo, Alcumena, Sosia, and Thalassa (*muta*) are on stage together. Across the play, however, separate actors are required for Mercurius, Sosia, Jupiter, Alcumena, and Amphitruo, and five actors become necessary. In this context, it may be relevant to note that in the lacuna following 1034 Amphitruo, Alcumena, Mercurius, Jupiter, and Blepharo all apparently speak.

[81] While it is possible for Curculio to leave at line 678, this does not avoid the use of a fifth actor without part-splitting, since Cappadox and Curculio have appeared together on stage earlier. There is consequently no reason for Curculio to leave, and we may follow Ernout, who accepts the reading of manuscript B, and tentatively assign 712 (to *tarpezita*) and 713–14 (to *factum est*) to Curculio, perhaps even adding 693 (from *collum*; see Wright (1993) 81–3).

[82] There are fewer than five lines for the cook (or one of his slaves) to become Syra.

Stichus 347–360:   Gelasimus, Pinacium, Panegyris, two slaves
(plurals at 347, 357)[83]

Trinummus: see note[84]

SIX PERFORMERS:

Bacchides 842–904:   Cleomachus, Chrysalus, Nicobulus, Artamo, two
slaves (mutae; plural imperative at 862)

Captivi 195–215:   Philocrates, Tyndarus, two lorarii (one muta) two
other captives

950–53:   Philocrates, Hegio, Philopolemus,[85] Stalagmus, two
lorarii (mutae; plural imperative at 950)

Casina 960–1018:   Lysidamus, Olympio, Chalinus, Pardalisca, Cleostrata,
Myrrhina (and see 815–37, with plural imperative
at 837)

Menaechmi 351–445:   Sosicles, Messenio, Erotium, Cylindrus,[86] two slaves
(plural imperative at 445)

Miles 1338–53:   Palaestrio, Philocomasium, Pyrgopolynices,
Pleusicles, two slaves (mutae; plurals at 1340–41)[87]

Persa 778–857:   Toxilus, Lemniselenis, Sagaristio, Dordalus,
Paegnium and another slave (plural imperatives in
769)

Poenulus: see note[88]

---

[83] I assume that the additional plurals at 358–60 are not directed at individuals seen by the audience; Pinacium is caught up in his own verbiage, and is barking orders to *alii ... alii* even when there are no *alii* left. Otherwise, we would require at least nine performers here.

[84] The play has one four-person scene, 1176–88, with Lysiteles, Charmides, Callicles, and Lesbonicus. From 627–716, however, Lysiteles, Lesbonicus, and Stasimus are onstage, and from 1094–1109 Charmides, Calicles, and Stasimus are onstage. Five actors are therefore needed if part-splitting is to be avoided.

[85] This requires doubling Tyndarus and Philopolemus, i.e. both sons of Hegio.

[86] This requires doubling Cylindrus and Peniculus, i.e. the cook and the parasite.

[87] Does the *puer* leave the stage at line 1393? I presume so (*nunc in tumultum ibo*) but some may prefer to keep him onstage, with Periplectomenus' entrance at line 1394 interrupting the *puer*'s departure (this would avoid an momentarily empty stage, though I believe this could easily be covered by sound effects from behind the *scaena*). If he remains, there will be six characters on stage at lines 1394–1437, including two mute slaves who enter the house at 1427 and then re-appear at a wing that same line. So a quick run is necessary to avoid having seven or (if the *puer* remains on stage) eight performers for this play, which remains possible. See also Prescott (1923) 32–3.

[88] The play has several six-person scenes. At 1120–54, Hanno, Milphio, Agorastocles, Giddenis, *puer*, and another slave (*homines* at 979) are on stage. At 1338–1422, Hanno, Agorastocles, Adelphasium, Anterastilis, Antamonides, and Lycus are on stage. The scenes with the *advocati* are discussed below, but I believe they too involve six actors. Leo has deleted many lines from the end of the play, and these emendations are generally accepted (see also Franko (2004) 53–4). A different view is offered by Zwierlein (1990) 56–101, about which see Jocelyn (1993) 133–4. This does not affect the cast totals.

SEVEN PERFORMERS:

Asinaria 851–941:	Argyrippus, Philaenium, Demaenetus, Artemona, Parasitus, two slaves (*mutae*; 891 *puere*, 906 *pueri*)
Aulularia 280–334:	Pythodicus, Anthrax, Congrio, Phrygia and Eleusium (*mutae*), two attendants (*mutae*; 330 *vos ceteri*)
Truculentus 551–630:	Phronesium, Astaphum, Stratophanes, Cyamus, two slaves of Cyamus (plurals in 551–52),[89] slave to Stratophanes (535 *tu*)

EIGHT PERFORMERS:

Mostellaria 348–91:	Philolaches, Philematium, Callidamates, Delphium, Tranio, two slaves (*mutae*; plurals at 391)
Rudens 706–891:	Trachalio,[90] Ampelisca, Palaestra, Daemones, Labrax, Turbalio, Sparax, Plesidippus[91]

NINE PERFORMERS:

Pseudolus 133–69:	Pseudolus, Calidorus, Ballio, slave (*muta*; *puere* at 170), five other slaves (addressed individually at 157–62; see above)

When the presuppositions about actors that were imported from the Hellenistic Greek theatre are removed, we discover that the plays of Plautus require many more performers than has been generally thought, from as few as four to as many as nine. The upper end of this range is significantly greater than the 'five or six actors'[92] normally reckoned to be in the troupe. Even if some of the assumptions I am making are rejected, or if we relax the tightness of the troupe's cohesion and allow an extra performer in plays at the lower end of this range, the variation does suggest that troupe size was not a constant, and that Plautus' core group could at times be enlarged. The numbers provided when examining the

---

[89] This requires doubling the slaves with the two Syrian maids (530–34), who were onstage from 482 to 541.

[90] This requires doubling Trachalio with Charmides; the alternative, if we are to preserve the minimum cast size, would double Daemones with Charmides, which would require two instant changes from one character to another, at 592/593 and 891/892.

[91] This requires doubling Plesidippus and Gripus. Plesidippus and Daemones do not appear on stage together here, but they do at lines 97–159.

[92] Duckworth (1952) 76.

scenes involving the largest number of performers on stage can serve as a minimum size of the troupe. This notion of the troupe is very different from what was inherited from his Greek models.

Further insight into the playwright's design can be seen in the 'collective characters' introduced in both *Rudens* and *Poenulus*. It has been assumed that Plautus is adapting the choruses in his Greek original.[93] In *Rudens* a group of fishermen (*piscatores*) occupy the stage from lines 290 to 324, and help to establish the setting of a remote African fishing village (albeit one with a forum; lines 974, 988), a setting paralleled only in *Vidularia*. In *Poenulus*, a group of hired witnesses (*advocati*[94]) interact with the other characters to a much greater extent than do the fishermen. Lowe has refuted this possibility: 'both *advocati* and fishermen are very largely the creation of Plautus, ... the *advocati* have no direct connection with Greek choruses and the fishermen a minimal one'.[95] Lowe's conclusion has no impact on the staging of the plays by Plautus, however. More relevant for our concerns is the fact that in neither play is the scene with the so-called chorus also the most taxing scene in allocating performers. *Poenulus* has six performers onstage at 1120–54 and 1338–1422. This means that there are always at least three actors available to play the *advocati* during their scenes from *Poenulus* 504–816, as long as Milphio doubles as Lycus. *Rudens* has eight onstage at 706–891, and this means that there are always three or four performers available to play the *piscatores*, as there are to play Plesidippus' friends at 89–184 (who are armed with cloaks and swords; see 315). In the Roman performance spaces, three individuals can easily be thought to represent a crowd.[96]

As often in Plautus, the closing scenes in *Poenulus* bring onstage a large number of performers. When six are onstage beginning at 1174, it is worth considering whether this represents 'the company': whether Plautus brought all of his actors onstage in the final scenes in the same way that a modern performance might use a curtain call. I suspect that, at least in this instance, this is so. We even see Plautus recognising this limit. Six performers are on stage as Agorastocles calls for slaves with clubs (line 1319). Either the troupe numbers at least eight performers, and this scene

[93] Maidment (1935) 23, Beare (1964) 209, Hunter (1979) 37–8.
[94] *Advocati*: lines 506, 526, 531, 546, 568, 767, and 806. They are also called *testes* ('witnesses'; lines 531, 565, 582, 711, 765) and *amici* ('friends'; lines 504, 508, 512, 573). For their identity, see Rosivach (1983) 83–90.
[95] Lowe (1990) 277.
[96] Calder (1975) argues this for Roman tragedy, and indeed Lowe (1990) 297 believes that Plautus found his model for these collective characters in Roman tragedy. It is also possible *Poenulus* 619 is sarcastic or ironic.

exceeds the minimum size needed elsewhere in the play by two (compare *Pseudolus*), or the slaves never appear, which I believe to be more likely. This follows Nixon's stage direction: 'Agorastocles halts the slaves at the doorway.' Antamonides' backtracking (1320–21: *si quid per iocum | dixi, nolito in serium convertere*, 'if I said something as a joke, don't make it something serious') means that *lorarii* are not needed on stage. Eight of Plautus' twenty plays create this 'curtain call' effect, with the maximum of onstage characters appearing in what the manuscripts label as the final act: *Epidicus* with 4, *Curculio* with 5, *Casina*, *Captivi*, *Miles*, and *Poenulus* with 6, *Asinaria* and *Persa* with 7. *Bacchides*, *Trinummus*, and *Menaechmi* use all but one of the actors available (though an extra attendant could bring the remainder onstage but in the background at this point too).

Several conclusions emerge from this discussion. There is no reason to doubt that the playwrights used their performers efficiently. This is seen in the way that the number of performers in the largest scene is in all cases but *Trinummus* equal to the minimum number of performers required without part-splitting. It also seems likely that many plays engineered a 'curtain call' effect, bringing all or most of the cast on stage near the end of the play. Further, the number of performers available to Plautus varied from play to play. While a large group of plays do require six performers (plus the *tibicen* who provides musical accompaniment, to whom reference is made, e.g., at *Casina* 797, *Pseudolus* 573a, *Epidicus* 394, and *Stichus* 683–775), six plays require seven, eight, or nine performers, and seven plays can be performed with four or five actors. Plautine chronology is notoriously uncertain, and none of the proposed chronologies for Plautus easily accounts for a development towards a larger or smaller cast. We can see this by looking at the two plays for which there are production dates. *Stichus* in 200 requires five actors, and *Cistellaria*, requiring four, is thought to be slightly earlier by Enk, Buck, Sedgewick, and Schutter. These scholars consider *Asinaria* (requiring seven) and *Mercator* (requiring five) earlier still. Enk, Sedgewick, and Schutter place *Epidicus* (which also requires four) soon after 200. Similarly, *Pseudolus* in 191 requires nine performers in Plautus' troupe. Only De Lorenzi believes that *Mostellaria* and *Rudens* (which both require eight) are from this period (he believes they precede *Pseudolus*), along with *Truculentus* and *Aulularia*, which require seven.[97] This is not the neat chronological solution that we might wish.

Perhaps we do best to imagine a core troupe of four or five performers, plus the *tibicen*, who were in the habit of hiring one or two others for

---

[97] For all of these dates, see De Lorenzi (1952) 220–21.

most performances. When finances were tight (if a play was touring outside of Rome, for instance) it was possible to economise by not having these additional actors and adjusting the play accordingly. With more lavish bookings – *Pseudolus* at the Megalensian Games of 191 being the most extreme case – even more extra performers could be hired. For through all of this, there are indications, suggested in *Mostellaria* and perhaps in *Pseudolus*, of role division being used to craft a star part in Plautus' troupe: in this troupe, not all actors were created equal.

STAR PARTS

The size of Plautus' troupe was larger than has been usually accepted, but, as has been seen in the foregoing section, it was usual that all the members of the cast appeared onstage together only once. Further, the troupe size discussed in each case reflects a minimum, and many plays could easily have made use of an additional body or two. This has implications both backstage and within the performance. Within the performance, it is not certain what aesthetics were at work. Role doubling presents a director with many opportunities for interesting, subtle, nuanced effects, but, without a fixed limit on cast size, we cannot know that a particular aesthetic is operating and available for the ancient audience. There is also a much greater degree of flexibility in casting, so that subsequent productions (remountings by the same or another troupe) will not be obliged to reproduce the original casting of parts, if indeed they were even interested in doing so. Different productions may double parts differently, for diverse effects. The actor–manager may choose to try to allocate roles evenly among the troupe. The supposed benefits of such an approach, however (it saves actors from being 'distracted' from large parts; it is more 'fair') are offset by the assumptions which lie behind it: that there is no premium placed by the audience on (creative) role doubling, and that the audience is not interested in seeing a leading actor's flexibility as he creates different parts in the same performance. Such an approach also carries with it an assumption that leading actors want to identify with one part alone, an understanding of acting conditioned largely by experiences with twentieth-century western theatre. Alternately, one can give a few players the vast majority of the lines. For Roman comedy, I think this is more likely. It assumes that the audience is interested in the multiple levels of delivery that we have seen to be an essential part of Plautine presentation of character, that it will acknowledge and reward challenges accepted by an actor, that it wants to see an actor exhibit dramatic range, and that it wants to identify star actors beneath their masks.

The plays of Plautus contain twelve roles longer than three hundred lines, listed here in order of total length of the part:[98]

Role	Play	Length	Percentage of Total
Epidicus	*Epidicus*	305	42%
Hegio	*Captivi*	312	30%
Lysidamus	*Casina*	313	31%
Toxillus	*Persa*	318	36%
Euclio	*Aulularia*	320	38%
Mercurius	*Amphitruo*	321	28%
Sosia	*Amphitruo*	331	29%
Charinus	*Mercator*	382	37%
Tranio	*Mostellaria*	404	34%
Chrysalus	*Bacchides*	421	35%
Pseudolus	*Pseudolus*	500	37%
Palaestrio	*Miles*	532	37%

The length of the part is one measure of how much work the actor is doing. It is not the only measure, and it is not a completely balanced assessment: different results would be obtained if one measured how much stage time each character had, for example. Percentage of the total length of the play is a measure of the audience's perceptions, what portion of the play the character's lines occupy. Epidicus is not the largest role in Plautus, but it is the part that occupies the greatest percentage of stage time, and we can remember in this context Plautus' fondness for this play as expressed in *Bacchides* 213–15. Only *Amphitruo* has more than one large part. Apart from *Amphitruo*, where the work is clearly being shouldered

---

[98] While here and in what follows I give precise line totals, it is necessary to stress the presence of a considerable margin of error. Totals were achieved by adding (complete lines) + (half lines/2) + (partial lines/3), as found in Lindsay's OCT. Obviously, there exist interpolations and lacunae that affect these totals. It can also be argued that half and partial lines may each have a cue that needs to be learned, and for the actor do not represent half or a third of the mental effort required to deliver a full line of verse; in fact, they may require more. Also, no effort has been made to distinguish metre in these raw totals, or to identify the number of cue lines that need to be memorised. These, and whether delivery is accompanied by the *tibicen*, certainly affect the overall impression of the actor's work that an audience will take away from a performance, but are ultimately not quantifiable. All of these are important factors in understanding what is required of an actor in a play. For my present purposes, approximate totals are sufficient to make my point. Fractions have all been rounded up to the nearest whole number.

between two actors, each of these large roles represents at least 30 per cent of the total length of the play. While it is not surprising that the largest roles are found in the longest plays, the ratio of the lengths of the two longest roles, Pseudolus and Palaestrio, to the rest of their plays is not disproportionate when compared to other large roles.[99] To the items on this list we may compare the largest role in the other plays (each totalling fewer than 300 lines):

Role	Play	Length	Percentage of Total
Lampadio	*Cistellaria*	104	13%
Curculio	*Curculio*	172	24%
Stasimus	*Trinummus*	195	16%
Libanus	*Asinaria*	210	22%
Gelasimus	*Stichus*	212	27%
Menaehmus	*Menaechmi*	239	21%
Daemones	*Rudens*	262	18%
Diniarchus	*Truculentus*	275	28%
Agorastocles	*Poenulus*	294	21%

Cistellaria is so fragmentary that the size of its roles cannot be properly assessed. It may be felt that the roles of Gelasimus and Diniarchus are close enough to the earlier ratios that they should be included in the list of large roles. Similarly, Agorastocles is just shy of the arbitrary figure of 300, but he represents a considerably smaller percentage of that play.

What are these tables telling us? Let us consider the examples of doubling suggested in the previous two sections. With *Menaechmi* I argued that the Menaechmus actor (239 lines) also plays his twin brother Sosicles until line 1050 (187 lines of the character's total of 221 lines). If so, this is 36 per cent of the play. Other possible doublings in this play include Peniculus (146 lines) with the *senex* (97 lines) and Messenio (171 lines) with the *matrona* (73 lines). A Peniculus–*senex* doubling would also allow for this actor to take Sosicles from 1055 to the end. Any of these three actors may speak the prologue (33 lines). If this were the case, then these three actors would share among them 84 per cent of the play. For

[99] Shakespeare provides a helpful comparison. The three largest roles are Hamlet (in *Hamlet*), Iago (in *Othello*), and Richard III (in *Richard III*). Hamlet in the First Quarto (Q1) speaks 819/2129 lines (38.4%), in Q2 1338/3680 lines (36.4%), and in the Folio (F) 1240/3593 lines (34.5%). Iago in Q1 speaks 1032/3238 lines (31.9%), and in F 1098/3593 lines (30.7%). Richard in Q1 speaks 1062/3419 lines (31.0%) and in F 1116/3731 (29.2%). Data are from King (1992).

Mostellaria, I suggested Theopropides (215 lines) and Philolaches (155) were doubled. These 370 lines represent 31 per cent of the play, slightly less than the 404 lines spoken by the Tranio actor. If we wished, we could build the Tranio assignment to almost 40 per cent of the play by giving this actor the part of Scapha (63 lines). Even without this, though, in a play that requires a troupe of at least eight performers, two of them share between them two-thirds of the lines. In *Captivi*, Tyndarus (243 lines) needed to be doubled with Philopolemus (7 lines) if the minimum cast size was to be maintained.[100] This example tells against the suggestion that actors playing the larger roles were unwilling or unable to play smaller ones as well. The 250 lines assigned to this actor represent 24 per cent of the play. If we allow a lightning change at lines 191–4, it is also possible to double Ergasilus (211 lines) and Philocrates (93 lines), to create a role that fills 29 per cent of the play. With the Hegio actor (312 lines), these three actors would speak 84 per cent of the play. If one of them additionally spoke the prologue (68 lines; this is likely, given that Turpio spoke at least some of Terence's prologues) the total is 90 per cent of the play; 92 per cent if the Tyndarus–Philopolemus actor also plays the *puer* (14 lines).

The Pseudolus actor (500 lines) might have played the cook (58 lines) in his play – an additional role for an already hardworking actor. Similarly, in *Miles Gloriosus*, Palastrio (532) might have been doubled with Cario the cook (9 lines) in the final scene. Even with these doublings, the proportion of stage time does not exceed the role of Epidicus – and the Epidicus actor's assignment could be bolstered further by adding the *miles* (25 lines) and/or Philippa (32 lines). Was it the case then that the actor playing the largest part regularly also played the cook, if there was one? In *Mercator* the Charinus actor (382 lines) can play the cook (27 lines), giving him 40 per cent of the play. With a lightning change at line 397, the Euclio actor in *Aulularia* (320 lines) can also play Anthrax, the cook at Megadorus' house (30 lines) but not his own cook, Congrio (42 lines). The Phaedromus actor in *Curculio* (140 lines) can play Lyco (61 lines), and Palinurus (107 lines) can play Therapontigonus (67 lines). The Curculio actor (172 lines) can play the cook (12 lines), and also Leaena (31 lines) if that actor also wanted the play's most musical passage.[101] This would give that actor almost 30 per cent of the play, a total in accord with

[100] Above, n. 85.
[101] If we follow the manuscript assignments and take lines 274–5 and 277–9 as spoken by the cook (rather than Palinurus), the entry assumes a funny metatheatrical dimension as the actor playing the cook sees 'himself' coming! I am grateful to Fred Franko for this observation.

the ratios found in the twelve largest parts in Plautus. If this were the division, these three actors would share 81 per cent of the play. Not every cook can be assigned to the lead player however. The two short speeches of Chytrio barely constitute one line, but neither of the major players in *Casina* can play this cook. Similarly, if Menaechmus doubles with Sosicles for most of *Menaechmi*, this actor cannot play Cylindrus (38 lines), nor indeed can any of the three principal actors in what was suggested above for this play. These possibilities can only suggest the impact of a consciously constructed doubling on an audience in performance. But it does indicate that there is nothing preventing a director from giving a small additional role to the Pseudolus or Palaestrio actor, especially when it offers such strong comic opportunities for the performer. Even a much smaller role by comparison, such as Gelasimus (212 lines) in *Stichus*, could be supplemented with Sagarinus (56 lines), yielding a combination of parts that gives the actor 35 per cent of the play. Doublings of this sort were clearly possible on the Roman comic stage.

In *Poenulus*, it was necessary to double Antamonides (74 lines) with Collybiscus (35 lines). As it happens, this does not involve a major actor, although this actor could conceivably take Syncerastus (55 lines) and the Prologue (128 lines) for a meaty assembly of parts that is about the length of the Agorastocles part. *Poenulus* also requires doubling Milphio (260 lines) and Lycus (149 lines) if the minimum cast of six is to be maintained, and this pairing constitutes 29 per cent of the play. If this actor or the Agorastocles actor also delivered the prologue, the two actors would share 58 per cent of the play. The Hanno actor (148 lines; he also plays one of the *advocati*, though we cannot specify how many of their 125 lines he speaks) has not figured in this sum. He evidently is not one of the star actors, though he is certainly a scene-stealer when he does appear. Cappadox (85 lines) in *Curculio* is another role that fits this category, as perhaps is Cylindrus (38 lines) in *Menaechmi*. In *Truculentus*, the largest role, Diniarchus (275 lines), can be doubled either with Truculentus (64 lines) or Stratophanes (100 lines). Either of these pairings would give this actor a substantial role equal to 35 per cent or 38 per cent of the play.

Not every play exhibits this tendency to favour only two or three actors. *Rudens* needs to double Trachalio (248 lines) and Charmides (47 lines) for a role speaking 21 per cent of the play, and Gripus (210 lines) and Plesidippus (55 lines) for a role speaking 19 per cent of the play. Along with Daemones (262 lines), these three actors speak 58 per cent of the play. A lightning change at 485 would allow the Sceparnio actor

(89 lines) to play Labrax (156 lines) and speak 17 per cent of the play. Compared to the plays discussed above, this is a remarkably even division of labour. *Amphitruo* favours two actors, playing Sosia (331 lines; to him we should also give the 4 lines of Blepharo since Sosia does not seem to appear in the fragmentary portions of the play) and Mercurius (321 lines). Unlike most of Plautus' plays, however, there are no very small assignments: Jupiter (125 lines), Alcumena (143 lines), and Amphitruo (181 lines) are all substantial parts. The character Bromia (53 lines) appears only with Amphitruo, and it is not clear that any one actor should be assigned that part over another. The greatest possible range between casting assignments (if the Sosia actor also played Bromia) is 388:125 (34 per cent:13 per cent); the smallest range (if the Jupiter actor plays Bromia) is 335:143 (29 per cent:12 per cent). The difference between these is slight; no actor should feel underappreciated.

In some plays, while it is certain that two or three actors are being favoured by the construction of the play, some plays have so many different ways to divide roles that we cannot be certain who were the leads. *Trinummus* is such a play, requiring at least five actors, but Luxuria, Megaronides, the *sycophanta*, and Philto remain unassigned:

Lesbonicus 77 (+ Lux. 21?) (+ Meg. 175?) (+ *syc.* 93?)
Callicles 146 (+ Lux. 21?) (+ *syc.* 93?) (+ Philto 141?)
Charmides 164 (+ Lux. 21?) (+ Meg. 175?) (+ Philto 141?)
Lysiteles 167 (+ Lux. 21?) (+ Meg. 175?) (+ *syc.* 93?)
Stasimus 195 (+ Lux. 21?) (+ Meg. 175?) (+ *syc.* 93?)

Roles could be concentrated on the Stasimus and Charmides actors, for instance, which would give these two up to 66 per cent of the play; but many permutations are possible, depending on the desirability for quick changes and similar or contrasting role types. Similarly, one possible division of roles in *Asinaria* had one actor doubling Libanus (210 lines) and Artemona (38 lines), another doubling Leonida (178 lines), and Demaenetus (84 lines), and a third doubling Argyrippus (134 lines), and the *mercator* (36 lines). Any of these actors could take Diabolus (34 lines). These parts concentrate 75 per cent of the play's lines with three actors, leaving a fourth actor Clearata (74 lines), and the *parasitus* (84 lines).[102]

---

[102] This was the division of roles I used in my *Asinaria* production. Diabolus was played by the Libanus actor.

A similarly great degree of variation is possible in *Pseudolus*, especially since the play requires so many actors to perform. While it is not possible to produce a grouping of roles that will match Pseudolus (or Pseudolus and the cook) for size, almost any allotment of roles concentrates the bulk of the play on two or three performers. Finally, we may consider *Bacchides*, in which we saw there was a joke (lines 213–15) that could work well if Plautus himself were playing Chrysalus (421 lines) and Pellio were playing Pistoclerus (134 lines). It is possible to double Chrysalus with Philoxenus (51 lines) and Pistoclerus with Nicobulus (204 lines) without difficulty. Such a hypothetical casting would give these two actors, whoever they were, 67 per cent of the play.

All of these figures express possible allocations of actors for the Plautine plays. They assume a few minimum principles at work, to which more could be added. An actor might specialise in women's parts, for example, or perhaps Plautus concentrated *cantica* in the mouths of only a few actors. None of these doublings need to have been used by Plautus' troupe, and it is always possible the minimum number of actors required was not used. Even saying that, though, it is striking that when the minimum is preserved, most plays produce castings that give one actor at least 30–42 per cent of the play, and three actors 66 per cent or more. It does not require a great imaginative leap to see these star actors as constituting the core of the company. In addition to these two or three actors, a fourth actor was apparently employed for roles in which he would have the opportunity to create a particularly memorable interpretation: Cappadox, Hanno, perhaps Ballio, and conceivably Alcumena. It is this sort of actor that Cicero might have in mind when he wrote *neque enim histrioni, ut placeat, peragenda fabula est, modo in quocumque fuerit actu probetur* (*de Senectute* 70: 'for it is certainly not necessary for the actor to perform to the end of the play in order to please, but only to prove himself in whichever acts he may be in') – the ancient equivalent of the modern theatrical dictum, 'there are no small roles, only small actors'.

TERENCE

For comparison, we may consider the plays of Terence, and the implications for the composition of Terence's troupe. The data are not as straightforward, and this would seem to indicate a different conception behind the creation and adaptation of plays. As with Plautus, assumptions are important. It is generally believed that Terence was more faithful in his adaptations of his Greek originals, and that it is possible to diagnose occurrences of *contaminatio*, from the author's own explicit statement or through the commentary of Donatus. This is not a problem-free enterprise however, and though advances can be made[103] there are reasons to remain agnostic about the shape of any Greek play lying behind a Roman comedy. Even if Terence is more 'faithful' (whatever that should prove to mean), there will still be considerable changes as a play is translated from one context to another. The results are broadly similar to Plautus in terms of troupe size, but the road to that conclusion is more arduous.

The smallest suggested troupe sizes are required for *Adelphoe* and *Hecyra*, both of which were produced in 160. There are several four-actor scenes in Adelphoe.[104]

Adelphoe 155–75	Sannio, Parmeno, Micio, Bacchis
265–80	Sannio, Aeschinus, Ctesipho, Syrus
485–6	Demea, Hegio, Geta, Pamphila (inside)
899–919	Demea, Aeschinus, Geta, Syrus
958–97	Demea, Aeschinus, Micio, Syrus

If only four actors were used in *Adelphoe*, then a number of doublings are required: Demea and Sannio; Aeschinus and Hegio; Syrus and the voice of Pamphila; Micio, Geta; and Ctesipho. The doubling of Aeschinus and Hegio does require a lightning change at lines 609/10 and a backstage run for the actor from a door to a wing. This is possible, but it may be thought enough to require the use of a fifth actor. Similarly, Gratwick believes that at line 155 Sannio is restrained 'by three or four of Micio's staff';[105] this is however unsupported by the text, and can be thought to involve an unnecessary degree of naturalism. It is perhaps also significant that the original of this scene comes not from Menander's *Adelphoe B*, but has been added from Diphilus' *Synapothnescontes* and was patched into the play for the expressed reason that in Plautus' version, it had been omitted (*Adephoe* 6–11). One reason for its omission in the (lost) Plautine version may have been the demand on the troupe for casting. *Hecyra* 767–9 is similar, where Bacchis, Laches, Phidippus, and the Nurse (*muta*) appear on stage together. This requires doubling the nurse with the slave who fetches Bacchis at 719. While it is not clear when the slave leaves the stage, he is last referred to at 733, which leaves plenty of time to change costume

---

[103] See Gratwick (1999) for a notable example.   [104] Lowe (1997) 167–8.
[105] Gratwick (1999) 73.

and mask. This also presumes the lack of a demonstrative pronoun means that the maids referred to at 773 (*ancillas*) are not on stage. If they are, then six actors are required.[106]

We know *Hecyra* was was not produced when it was originally sold for the *ludi Megalenses* in 165, but it was produced later at the *ludi funerales* of Aemilius Paullus in 160 and the *ludi Romani* in 160. It is not clear how much revision occurred between initial purchase and production. It is possibly of great significance that the two plays not written for public games but for the funeral games of L. Aemilius Paullus, *Adelphoe* and *Hecyra*, make the smallest demands on troupe size. This would assume some revision after the initial failure in 165 ('streamlining' the play for a smaller troupe), but no revision before the *ludi Romani* in 160. Even to raise this issue suggests many more possibilities for the troubled history of a Roman comedy. Once streamlining (or its opposite, 'filling out') is raised as a possibility, our understanding of the relationship between text and performance in Plautus is further complicated. *Pseudolus*, for example, with a required cast of nine, could easily have been streamlined to need seven or fewer performers (indeed, *Pseudolus'* cast demands might be tied to its later production history, when it became a staple in Roscius' repertoire[107]).

At the other end of the scale, *Eunuchus* 771–816 requires eight performers: Thraso, Gnatho, Thais, Chremes, Sanga, Simalio (*muta*), Donax (*muta*), and Syriscus (*muta*).[108] Three mute servants are named as individuals (772–6) and are positioned onstage so as to evoke the three lines of a Roman battle formation: Thraso hides behind the *principia* (second line) at 781. The leader of these slaves is Sanga, who is given some dialogue (776–80). The stage property (Sanga's sponge, *peniculus*) reifies military imagery in the dialogue by being brandished like a weapon.[109] Further, it is possible to see in this passage some recognition of role division in this scene, which becomes evident in two ways. Thraso asks

[106] Carney (1963) 24 divides the roles as follows: Actor I (Turpio) Prologue, Parmeno, Phidippus; Actor II Philotis, Pamphilus; Actor III ('the specialist in female roles') Syra, Sostrata, Myrrhina, Bacchis; Actor IV Laches and Sosia.

[107] For this production, see Garton (1972) 169–88.

[108] Ludwig (1959) 24–9. Given this, it seems hard to comprehend Donatus' comment at *Eunuchus* 967, *choragi est administratio, ut opportune in proscaenium*. The passage seems to imply the *senex* is played by someone backstage (a '*choragus*') from 971–96 (the character's only appearance), but this is not needed if the cast is the size I suggest. If Donatus' comment (or that of his source) is rooted in performance rather than being an 'educated' guess, it is possible a pared-down script was used.

[109] Barsby (1999) 232: 'the pictures of the medieval MSS show Sanga brandishing a sponge as if it was a missile (Jones-Morey pls. 259–61)'.

ubi centuriost Sanga ... ? (776: 'Where is centurion Sanga?'). Such questions are standard on the Roman comic stage, but it is worth noticing that one of the four servants will be played by the actor who had recently played Pythias – if not, then a ninth actor is required for this play. Pythias had come in and out of the house more than once in the scenes immediately preceding this passage, and had last spoken at 767, when he had reappeared with the box containing recognition tokens. He next speaks at 822, six lines after the slaves depart. At 822, he is emerging from Thais' house, but it is not explicit when he enters (the most economical answer is that he departs immediately after handing over the box, so that he may return as one of the slaves at 771, or soon thereafter). We cannot know whether the Pythias actor was also given the small role of Sanga (who is probably a cook) as opposed to one of the mute servants, but the way he is singled out for attention does perhaps hint that Sanga appears later than the others, and the audience can associate this delay with the costume change and backstage run as the actor enters the house, and emerges stage right as a new character. There is also surely an element of comedy when, in the busiest scene in the play, Thraso asks Gnatho where the other slaves are (780: *ubi alii?* 'Where are the others?').[110] This effect is enhanced if the audience has the means to realise that there are no others backstage to play the *alii* requested. Gnatho's response (which the scholiast assigns to Sanga) suggests that there is only one slave left, and he's at home. For a moment, a question within the dramatic narrative is governed by the physical restrictions of the troupe.

The situation in *Heauton Timoroumenos* is less straightforward. At line 743 there are four actors on stage, those playing Syrus, Clinia, Bacchis, and Phrygia, whereupon Dromo comes onstage. Syrus gives him the following instruction: *ancillas omnis Bacchidis transduce huc ad vos propere* (744: 'Hurry and bring all Bacchis' maids over here to your place'). Dromo enters Chremes' house (probably at the end of 745) and emerges with 'all Bacchis' maids' (probably at the end of 747) whom he leads into Mendemus' house (at the end of 748) along with Clinia. While previously we have assumed that a plural referent to unspeaking characters was realised by two onstage performers, it seems hard to deny that with *omnis* more here are intended. That would again bring the total number of performers needed to eight, as in *Eunuchus*. Though there is considerable

---

[110] Barsby (1999) 232 notes that Donatus sees humour operating on one level here, complementary to my hypothesis: *non reliquos dixit sed alios, quasi multi sint* ('he doesn't say "the rest" but "the others", as if there were many').

stage business going on at this point, the actor playing Clinia or one of the maids re-appears immediately as Chremes to speak the next line in the play (749). Avoiding this lightning change would increase the number of actors to nine.[111] To my mind, Lowe misplaces the emphasis when he observes that 'the transfer of Bacchis' entourage from the house of Chremes to that of Mandemus in 744–748 involves drastic telescoping of off-stage action'.[112] The number of maids appearing at *Heauton* 747–8 affects an earlier scene, too, for when Bacchis and Antiphila arrive at lines 381–409, they should have their slaves. This yields a seven-actor scene: Bacchis, Antiphila, Clinia, Syrus, and three maids (*mutae*, 744). Without the maids, the play would require only five actors.

Six performers are required in *Phormio* and *Andria*. In *Phormio*, this is straightforward: at lines 348–440, Phormio, Geta, Demipho, Hegio, Cratinus, and Crito appear together. In *Andria*, there are a number of four-person scenes,[113] but the play requires six actors, as is evident when we consider five scenes:

	1	2	3	4	5	6	(unassigned)
459–67	Mysis	Davus	Simo				Lesbia[114]
684–708	Mysis	Davus		Pamph			Charinus
740–89	Mysis	Davus			Chremes		
796–819	Mysis	Davus				Crito	
904–52			Simo	Pamph	Chremes	Crito	

The fifth of these scenes, which brings onstage four individuals each of whom have appeared in a scene with Mysis and Davus, means that the play cannot be staged with fewer than six actors if part-splitting is to be avoided. This is easily the most sophisticated disposition of actors

[111] It is possible on a modern stage to reduce the number of performers needed in a scene like this: one actor could play all the maids, and simply move in circles around the doors, emerging from Chremes' house, walking across the stage, entering Menedemus' house, dropping the stage property baggage, moving backstage to the Chremes door, picking up a different piece of baggage, and emerging from Chremes' door again. This process could indeed be repeated for comic effect easily. It was used in my production of *Miles Gloriosus* at 1338–53, so that only five performers would be needed for the play (not the six for which I argued above). While it would have been possible on the ancient stage, we cannot know that such a technique would appeal to a Roman sensibility, or be perceived as coherent, especially in a play that is already calling attention to an unusual use of backstage moves by actors by means of the twin-deception.

[112] Lowe (1997) 163.

[113] Lowe (1997) 159–60.

[114] Both Mysis and Lesbia are inside the house and either actor is able to deliver Glycerium's single line 473, from within.

evident in any Roman comedy, an unexpected discovery in Terence's earliest play.

Given the tighter chronological range in which plays were originally presented, we might expect to find a greater degree of cohesion in Terence's troupe as a unit than Plautus' troupe, but this is not the case. *Andria*, produced in 166, requires a troupe of at least six actors. *Heauton Timoroumenos* (163) and *Eunuchus* (161) both require eight actors. *Phormio* (161) again requires six, and *Adelphoe* (160) requires four. If we knew more about the social conditions of troupe dynamics, it might be possible to plot a chronological development, in which case *Hecyra*, which requires four, would reflect the version performed in 160, and not the version performed in 165. As with Plautus, it also seems two or three actors were foregrounded. The didascalic notices preceding several plays indicate that they were acted/produced by L. Ambivius Turpio and Atilius of Praeneste. Donatus on *Eunuchus* and the scholiast on *Adelphoe* also give the name L. Minucius Prothymus.[115] Ultimately, such observations remain speculative. A study of troupe size, role assignment, and disposition of actors in Roman comedy cannot produce certain conclusions, but can demonstrate a set of several likely tendencies in Roman production practice.

[115] Barsby (1999) 78.

CHAPTER 3

Masks

GREEK MASKS AND THE ROMAN STAGE

Masked performance was a standard feature of Greek and Roman theatre.[1] Masks do not operate in isolation: they are necessarily only components in a larger visual system that presents a complex of relationships that extends in three directions. First, masks relate to one another structurally, as has been shown for comedy and tragedy in the fifth century[2] and later for Menander and New Comedy.[3] Second, masks coordinate with other resources the actor brings to his part: to be effective, a masked actor must use his body and voice in a way that harmonises with the mask. Finally, masks may resonate with the society that produces them, so that when an audience sees a mask, it may make associations with particular individuals (as in the case of the so-called portrait masks of Aristophanes[4]) or with representations of faces in other plays or other

---

[1] I do not believe the scant evidence that might suggest Plautus' actors would not have worn masks. Every staged performance tradition in Greece and Rome used masks, and anything else would have been inconceivable. Greek New Comedy and the *fabulae Atellanae* were masked theatre traditions, and these were Plautus' principal influences. Further, later Roman New Comedy was masked. It seems perverse to propose an intermediary unmasked stage of comic development. See Gow (1912), Duckworth (1952) 92–4, Beare (1964) 186–95, 303–9, 372–4, Jocelyn (1967) 22 n. 1, Gratwick (1982) 83–4, Wiles (1991) 129–33. The view of scholars such as Hoffer (1877) and Della Corte (1975) that Plautus was performed without masks, cannot stand: Beare (1964) 303–9 assembles much of the data. In order to assume another identity as part of a staged entertainment in antiquity, one put on a mask. When this was not the case, as with the Hellenistic–Roman mime, the difference was noted, since non-masked performance implies a different kind of *mimêsis*.

[2] Marshall (1999b), with bibliography. In my productions of Greek tragedy, I have not usually used masks. I have, however, often tried to reproduce the effect of ancient role sharing, dividing the roles other than the chorus between three actors. Quick changes do not need masks, and an audience will accept whatever the dramatic situation presents.

[3] Wiles (1991). It is not possible here to isolate all the points of contact with Wiles' detailed analysis. Broadly I agree with his semiological analysis, but believe that some refinements are necessary when the Greek New Comic tradition is transferred to Rome. While there are differences between my account of Greek masks here and Wiles, I do believe the different perspectives are largely compatible.

[4] See Marshall (1999b) 194–5.

artistic media. It is this third, societal, dimension that should make us question any direct continuity of the system of masks used from Greek New Comedy to the Roman New Comedy of Plautus a century later. Just as the script has been freely adapted into Latin, so is there a parallel transposition of the Greek masking tradition.

The mask is one tool available to Plautus' actors in their performance. Aulus Gellius (*Attic Nights* 5.7) confirms Roman masks covered the whole head, as was the case in the Greek tradition.[5] Though there are some late and conflicting sources questioning whether Plautus' actors wore masks, the word *persona* is already being used by Terence to designate a character, so it should not be surprising that sources centuries later use it to mean 'masked actor'.[6] Because many scholars writing about masks in antiquity and modern times have not had experience using masks in performance, there are a lot of assumptions about masked acting that are uncritically repeated. It is, for example, simply wrong to assume that the chief benefit of masks was to facilitate the doubling of parts, or the playing of twins: the original performance of Shakespeare's *Comedy of Errors* instantly provides an effective use of these devices without recourse to masks.[7] It is also wrong to assume that masks imposed a limitation on the actors, preventing them from representing such features as a character blushing (as at Terence, *Adelphoe* 643).[8] It is precisely the power of the

[5] Beare (1964) 186, 309.

[6] Terence, *Eunuchus* 26, 32, 35. Beare (1964) 193, 309. Diomedes, a late Roman grammarian (p. 489 Kiel), is the best evidence for no masks in the time of Plautus, though his claim that Roscius was the first to use masks to disguise his squint follows no logic, and might be derived from a misreading of Cicero, *de Oratore* 3.59.221. This fact essentially removes any other ancient objections. Relevant passages are collected by Beare (1964) 303–6.

[7] Duckworth (1952) 93, Beare (1964) 187, 192, 307–8. A few small points do need to be made, however, because often the arguments for or against masks are presented with simplistic assumptions. McLeish (1976) 28 presents such a view and is representative of the complaints often raised. For him, the benefit of masks is that quick changes are possible (in as few as six lines, he suggests), but the drawback is that expressions are fixed, and the text can only give a lame confirmation or denial of what is already obvious to the entire audience. Duckworth (1952) 93 notes the large number of 'twins' on the Plautine stage, an effect that he suggests is only possible with masks. All of these considerations are, I believe, false, and misunderstand how masks work. Second, the notion that a mask has a fixed expression is not borne out by experience. Expression from a masked actor is conveyed by body language and posture: the same mask can be made to look like a king or a slave, depending on how the actor inhabits the mask. What most surprises audiences when they first see a masked theatrical performance is in fact how expressive the masks can be. It is not, then, self-evidently true, as Duckworth (1952) 93 contends, that 'The remarks in Donatus' commentary about the expression (*vultus*) of the characters were obviously intended for readers, not for actors.' Certainly, the presentation of twins is easily effected by masked performance, and the large number of Atellan titles referring to twins show that this was often done in antiquity in what is known to have been a masked theatrical form, but there is no necessary connection.

[8] The example comes from Beare (1964) 193, and see 191 and 306–7, and Duckworth (1952) 93. It is these 'realistic' concerns that constitute Chiarini's objections to masks; see Chiarini (1989) 141–2.

mask to appear to come to life and move and convey emotion, when properly animated by a trained actor. Cicero recognised this, and it is possible to detect some surprise in his description of the counter-intuitive effect masks have on an audience: *quid potest esse tam fictum quam versus, quam scaena, quam fabulae? tamen in hoc genere saepe ipse vidi, ut ex persona mihi ardere oculi hominis histrionis viderentur spondalia illa dicentis...* (Cicero, *de Oratore* 2.46.193: 'What could be so artificial as poetry, as the stage, as drama? Nevertheless, in that medium I have myself often seen how the eyes of the man acting seemed to me to blaze through the mask, when he intoned these lines...').[9] Cicero proceeds to quote passages he has found particularly moving in the theatre, and speculates on their emotional impact on the actor.

Creating such effects is not easy: it requires physical exertion from the actor, with particular demands on the neck. Though he refers only to his trademark 'neutral mask', Jacques Lecoq describes a dynamic that is true of full masks generally: 'Beneath the neutral mask the actor's face disappears and his body becomes far more noticeable... With an actor wearing the neutral mask, you look at the whole body... Every movement is revealed as powerfully expressive.'[10] Great flexibility is required, as well as training to harmonise properly an oversize headpiece to the actor's body. But it can be done, as is clearly demonstrated by living mask traditions in Japan such as Kabuki and Noh: 'formal movement does not prevent the expression of emotion in Noh, but becomes an aid to its controlled release'.[11] Lecoq indeed reverses this dynamic, and defines a successful mask in terms of its ability to allow these effects: 'A good theatre mask must be able to change its expression according to the movements of the actor's body.'[12] The precise nature of the physical exertion depends on the type of mask being used: half-masks, as in the *commedia dell'arte*, require the actor to continue to act with his lower jaw, creating continuity between the leather of the mask and the visible portion of the actor's face. Full masks, particularly with a wig attached to create a headpiece, require a different sort of exertion. The mask is

---

[9] The word *spondalium* (or *spondaulium*) is found only here and at Diomedes, p. 472 (Kiel) *fin.* P. *spondalium canere* ('to sing the *spondalium*'): Lewis and Short's definition, 'a sacrificial hymn, accompanied with the flute', seems over-assured; the word is not in the OLD. In any case, Cicero is thinking of lines delivered with accompaniment during a play.

[10] Lecoq (2001) 38. For a series of testimonia on how masks appear to come to life when inhabited by an actor, see Barba and Savarese (1991) 118. See also Johnson (1992) 25.

[11] Johnson (1992) 24.   [12] Lecoq (2001) 53–5.

attached to the head in the same way, perhaps with linen strips.[13] The actor moves more, but need not 'act' with his face. He may instead concentrate on vocal delivery and increasing audibility, for the mask may inhibit clarity in an outdoor venue.[14]

In fifth-century Athens, theatrical masks isolated two variables, age and sex. Adults are presented as young, mature, or old and as either male or female: there are therefore six basic mask types, each of which could be clearly identified at a distance by the audience. This does not mean, for example, that every old man on the Attic stage looked identical, or that comic old men looked like tragic old men. Rather, what the audience noticed about any old man mask in tragedy or comedy was, principally, the character's age and sex. Special masks could be created, but in the late fifth century when this happened, it was the markers of age and sex only that were changed.[15] The actor had other resources available – costume, posture, voice – for the representation of other features, including social position.

The masks of Menander are different. New Comedy does not represent three adult generations on stage, but only two. Fathers are invariably old men (Greek γέροντες; Latin *senes*) and sons have invariably just come of age. For men, then, one generation would be represented with white hair and beards, and the other with dark hair[16] and no beards. The mature generation, which had previously been represented with dark hair and beards, is absent. Why this should be can be seen most clearly by examining the list of New Comic masks found in Pollux (*Onomasticon* 4.143–54), who lists forty-four New Comic mask types, which may be divided into five broad categories:[17]

old men	masks 1–9
young men	masks 10–20
male slaves	masks 21–7
old women	masks 28–30
young women	masks 31–44

---

[13] Beare (1964) 309.

[14] Before the origins of the word *persona* were recognised as coming from the Etruscan (φersu, it was sometimes held that the Latin derived from *per-sonare*, but this is recognisably false because the syllable *son* in *sonare* is short, but long in *persona* (Beare (1964) 22 and 356 n. 8).

[15] See Marshall (1999b) 194.

[16] I use 'dark' to represent any non-white hair shade. While it is sometimes claimed that slaves were red-headed in comedy, the explicit examples of this are few, and are discussed below; see also Duckworth (1952) 89.

[17] See Webster (1995) vol. I: 6–51, whose numbering I follow. Brown (1987) 185 says there are more: 'I suspect that it would be sensible to classify the surviving material into more than 44 types.' Wiles (1991) 77 and 150–77 here sees four *genera*, with the women taken as a single group.

All of the masks with dark beards (masks 22–7) are slave masks; significantly, the one mask Pollux lists in this category with white hair (mask 21) represents a freedman.[18] For male masks, the introduction of the variable of social status while maintaining the inherited iconographic markers has created a different set of associations in the audience for dark-haired, bearded masks.[19] For female masks, the representation of only two generations is in fact more easily represented than it had been previously. In the fifth century, white hair represented old women, but the only means to distinguish the young female masks from the mature at a distance was by hairstyle.[20] The generation to which a New Comic woman belonged could now be signalled to an audience by hair colour alone. It is less essential to represent social position among women particularly since many New Comic plots depend on the ambiguous representation of young (and therefore dark-haired) women, who are often in the position of slaves or *meretrices* and are later discovered to have been freeborn.[21] It is therefore beneficial to the playwright that the system of relationships represented by the masks obscures this difference. My reading of Pollux privileges these broad categories over the descriptions of individual masks, and consequently suggests that efforts to identify a given mask in the iconographic tradition with an item in Pollux's list are ultimately misplaced.

All of the characters within a Greek New Comedy can be accommodated into this five-mask scheme, which coincides to a large extent with the *genera* identified by Wiles. There is no regular indication of 'special masks' being needed outside of this *schêma*, except perhaps for a divine prologue such as Pan in *Dyskolos*. Rather, individuals are distinguished within these types by more naturalistic features including skin colour and hairstyle: we know for example, some cooks in Greek New Comedy are represented as African.[22] In Menander's *Dyskolos*, the only

---

[18] Webster (1995) vol. I, 26: ὁ μὲν πάππος μόνος τῶν θεραπόντων πολιός ἐστι, καὶ δηλοῖ ἀπελεύθερον ('The Pappos is the only servant's mask with white hair, and indicates a freedman').

[19] Occasional Plautine slaves are called *adulescentes* (and might therefore have no beard), as in *Captivi*, discussed below.

[20] Marshall (1999b) 191 and 199 n. 31.   [21] Willcock (1995) 20–24 is helpful.

[22] Sikon from Menander's *Samia* appears in a mosaic from the House of Menander, Mitylene, labeled as *mageiros* (a sacrificial butcher often identified as a 'cook') with a black (ethnographically African) mask (Webster (1995), 6D M2.2, vol. II: 469 and see vol. I: 93). Significantly, his neck and exposed left hand are not similarly coloured. The Cicada mask (Τέττιξ; see vol. I, 32) is described by Athenaeus 459a as ἔκτοπον ('foreign' more likely than 'extraordinary') and probably coincides with the mask given to Sikon (Webster (1995) vol. I, 31–2). In my production of *Miles Gloriosus*, this *mageiros* was used as the model for the mask of Cario.

characters for whom there can be any uncertainty as to which of the five mask types they wear are the *mageiros* Sikon and Chaireas, who is described in the *dramatis personae* as a parasite. These though are easily placed in terms of their relationship to other characters in the play: artistic representations of cooks show beards, and this confirms for the audience their servile status; Chaireas is Sostratos' friend and age-mate,[23] and Pollux's list appropriately presents the parasite as one of the young men's masks.[24]

My position is therefore closest to that of Poe ('the masks of New Comedy were not as stereotyped as people usually take for granted'[25]), and is therefore different from the structuralist understanding of Wiles and the detailed taxonomies of Webster, Seeberg, and Green. This is not to deny any associations between character type and the mask an audience sees, but it does deny a fixed, necessary association. A mask is a tool, and however much information it might convey to an audience, it will always be dependent on how the mask is animated by its performer.[26] A given mask may suggest particular characteristics to an actor that can have an effect on how he interprets the character, and such influences may coincide with physiognomic theory, theatrical tradition, or any of a number of codified means of interpreting character. But there is no way to guarantee that everyone in the audience will interpret it identically, parti-cularly given the spectators' varying degrees of sophistication and (more importantly) the additional variables introduced by the actor himself. Similarly, MacCary attempted to tie Menander's masks to character names.[27] Though the conclusion is demonstrably false in some cases, it remains tempting with a character name such as Daos:

Daos appears in at least eight of sixteen better-known Menander plays. No doubt he looked the same in each and the Athenian audience knew who he was without being told and how he differed in physiognomy from his fellow-slaves

---

[23] Handley (1965) 132.

[24] Webster (1995) vol. I: 22–4. Parasites in comedy were typically young men: see Arnott (1996b) 730–31, and, for parasites generally, see Brown (1992) 98–107, Handley (1965) 140–41, Arnott (1968), and Nesselrath (1985) 309–17.

[25] Poe (1996) 312, and see 311 and 324–5.

[26] In a masked production of *Rhesus* in 2001, many students who had been in the audience were surprised to discover later that each of the choristers had worn identical masks. When placed on the different bodies of the actors, with different hairlines, otherwise identical masks appeared as the faces of individuals. Euripides, *Rhesus*, directed by George Kovacs; produced by Modern Actors Staging Classics (St John's, Newfoundland; October, 2001).

[27] MacCary (1970) and see MacCary (1969), (1971), and (1972).

Parmenon, Getas and Tibeios. This, however, did *not* determine his ethos, at least in the hands of a master like Menander.[28]

This position is answered by Brown, who asks, 'if the ethos of a character can change from play to play, what do we gain by regarding him as one character making eight appearances rather than as eight different characters who happen to have the same name?'[29] Such default associations with masks are not possible in Plautus' Rome, as drama is imported and adapted for a local audience which does not possess generations of cultural experience with these characters.

To argue that the mask reveals everything about a figure on stage is fundamentally to deny that there is any meaningful contribution made by the actor to the creation of a dramatic character. If we are to see the ancient actor as anything other than an idealisation of E. Gordon Craig's *über-Marionette*, an original contribution by the person behind the mask must be possible, and that means that whatever the mask contributes, it is not the totality of the character. Beyond classifying an individual among one of the five broad categories I have described, the principal benefit to be realised from two masks from the same category is to allow easy differentiation between the two in performance.[30] Poe's conclusion, that Pollux's list derives from the masks contained by a given troupe, and that a different troupe would have a similar set of masks manipulating the same variables but not an identical set, seems virtually certain.[31]

This, then, is the masking system that Plautus inherited from Greek New Comedy. With the plays comes an understanding of characterisation that uses largely overlapping cultural codes to establish meaning. In this way, Wiles is right to use both Greek and Roman examples in his study of New Comic masks.[32] I wish to suggest, however, that in addition to these Hellenistic mask types, Plautus adapted some mask types to include elements foreign to the Greek theatrical tradition. Plautus' plays are populated with stock characters – a term that I will explore more fully below – and in many cases we can comfortably associate a given character type with one of the five Hellenistic mask types. In a play such as *Asinaria*, it is straightforward to see Argyrippus, Diabolus, the *parasitus* and the *mercator* (see line 337) as young men, Demaenetus as an old man, Philaenium as a young woman, Artemona and Clearata as old women,

---

[28] Gratwick (1982) 105.   [29] Brown (1987) 183.   [30] Poe (1996) 319.

[31] Wiles (1991) 80–83 notes that the masks on terracotta figurines from Lipari do not map onto Pollux exactly, but do manipulate the same variables. See also Bernabó-Brea (1981).

[32] Wiles (1991) 134.

and Libanus and Leonida as *servi*. Plautus can even draw attention to the artificiality of a stage world where there are no free men with dark beards by having a character ask a slave whether or not he is free, either from a position of superior knowledge (Mercury asking Sosia at *Amphitruo* 343) or ignorance (Harpax asking Pseudolus at *Pseudolus* 610).

Problems begin to develop, however, with those characters whose appearance is described most vividly. At *Pseudolus* 1218–20, the title character is described in detail:

> *rufus quidam, ventriosus, crassis suris, subniger,*
> *magno capite, acutis oculis, ore rubicundo, admodum*
> *magnis pedibus.*

> Bright red hair, protruding belly,
> Rather swarthy, chubby calves,
> With large head, ruddy face, sharp eyes,
> And utterly enormous feet.

> (tr. Smith)

Pseudolus has been on stage for much of the play, and the lines are only sensible if they coincide meaningfully with what Pseudolus looks like.[33] The interest of this description becomes clear in light of another passage in a different play. In *Asinaria*, Leonida (who has assumed the name Saurea, just as Pseudolus had adopted the pseudonym Syrus) is described, again by an out-of-towner, who has fallen into the snare laid by the slave (400–01):

> *macilentis malis, rufulus aliquantum, ventriosus,*
> *truculentis oculis, commoda statura, tristi fronte.*

> Jutting jaw and reddish hair,
>   Rather fat and flabby;
> Average height, with scowling eyes;
>   Expression grim and crabby.

> (tr. Smith)

Hair,[34] eyes, belly, and expression overlap, sometimes with identical vocabulary, and none of the details in these descriptions exclude any of the others. In fact, it is perfectly possible to assume both descriptions

---

[33] It is the mention of the large feet that sends the pimp Ballio into apoplexy, and confirms the identification with Pseudolus. Twenty-six lines later, Pseudolus returns, drunk, singing the fifth of the play's *cantica*, which in his staggering stupor is addressed to the oversized feet (*Pseudolus* 1246–8).

[34] See Duckworth (1952) 89.

are equally true for each character, and that the two slaves, Pseudolus and Leonida, were represented on stage with the same mask, the same costume, and conceivably were portrayed by the same actor.[35] Indeed, these two are the only explicitly red-headed slaves in Plautus. It is even possible that the word *truculentis* (*Asinaria* 401) suggests that the title character of *Truculentus* bore a similar appearance. Also a slave, Truculentus appears almost as a 'cameo': two short scenes of verbal gags, spotlighting this otherwise incidental character (the only one with a Latin name, too). Though this is often considered a late play, the appearance of Truculentus (foregrounded in the play's title) could indicate the return of a popular character to the stage to help draw crowds.[36]

One further feature of this slave mask can be identified. In antiquity, a waggling eyebrow could signify an omen (as at Theocritus 3.37). In *Pseudolus*, the title character announces *ita supercilium salit* (107: 'thus my eyebrow quivers'). While some might take this as evidence that masks were not worn, most would see it as an anticlimactic possibility that is not fulfilled on stage. Slater even posits, perhaps frivolously, a mechanical eyebrow that could be twitched at this point.[37] Such a device is not necessary, as long as the actor is wearing a certain type of mask. Wiles describes how a mask with an asymmetrical brow appears to offer different expressions when viewed from different angles.[38] Such masks typically present a greater range of emotions since the same face does not clearly depict any one state; it is not accidental that one of Jacques Lecoq's most successful masks is his 'Jesuit', an asymmetrical mask.[39] By wearing a mask with one eyebrow raised and shaking his

---

[35] Wiles (1991) 138 connects these descriptions to all Plautine slaves. For a good discussion on the problem of connecting masks with names or even with specific character types, see Brown (1987) 190–99.

[36] It is perhaps worth noting the suggestion that the character of Pseudolus (and therefore, by extension, Leonida and Truculentus?) was played by Plautus himself (Slater (2000) 119). The evidence for this is slight but is perhaps corroborated by the detail that so captured the pimp's attention, the big feet. Plautus' name can be rendered etymologically as 'Flatfoot' (see Duckworth (1952) 50) and it is reasonable (though by no means certain) to imagine that Plautus' name reflected this particular physical detail (when he was performing onstage, most likely), though its primary referent remains the barefootedness of the Hellenistic–Roman mime. In the prologue of *Pseudolus*, much scholarly criticism of the speech has focused on the use of Plautus' own name: *Plautina longa fabula in scaenam venit* ('A long Plautine play is coming to the stage,' *Pseudolus* 2). When he mentions himself in his prologues, Plautus sometimes calls himself Maccus (as he does in *Asinaria*, where the homophonic *macilentis* in line 400 is used in the description of the slave). In *Pseudolus*, though, it is possible that the name Plautus anticipates this detail later emphasised.

[37] Slater (2000) 99–100.   [38] See Wiles (1991) 166–7, figs. 5–6.

[39] Lecoq (2001) 56: 'The mask then becomes a sort of vehicle, drawing the whole body into an expressive use of space, determining the particular movements which make the character appear'; 'The character arises out of the form.'

head back and forth, the actor presents every section of the audience with a changing eyebrow elevation. By moving the mask only on the horizontal axis, it is possible for the actor to present to the audience what could be taken for a waggling eyebrow. This not only explains the line, but in so doing isolates another feature of the recurring mask.

Eyebrows are one of the features Pollux often identifies on his male masks.[40] Of the twenty-seven males he describes, five have their eyebrows raised,[41] and three explicitly do not have raised eyebrows.[42] As many as six of Pollux's masks have asymmetrical brows.[43] Pollux does not present a binary polarisation between symmetrical and asymmetrical eyebrows. Instead at least three permutations are isolated: neutral, raised, and asymmetrical. Internal (ethical) qualities – busibodiness or evil intentions – are made explicit only for asymmetrical eyebrows (in masks 7 and 17), where the greatest ambiguity exists. The twitching eyebrow effect would be possible with any of the asymmetrically browed masks. Of these, it is natural to associate Pseudolus and Leonida with mask 22 ('the Leading Slave'), of whom Pollux says σπεῖραν ἔχει τριχῶν πυρρῶν ('he has a roll of red hair').[44] Similarly, Quintilian 11.3.74 writes:

in comoediis ... pater ille, cuius praecipuae partes sunt, quia interim concitatus interim lenis est, altero erecto altero composito est supercilio, atque id ostendere maxime latus actoribus moris est quod cum iis quas agunt partibus congruat.

In comedy ... the father who has the principal role has one eyebrow raised and the other not, because he is sometimes angry and sometimes calm, and the actors regularly turn towards the audience that side of the mask which suits the particular part they are playing.[45]

---

[40] See Poe (1996) 320–21.

[41] Masks 5, 6, 10, 12 indicate ἀνατέταται τὰς ὀφρῦς *vel sim*; mask 23 ἐπηρμένος τὰς ὀφρῦς.

[42] Mask 4 οὐκ ἀνατέταται τὰς ὀφρῦς mask 11 καθειμένος τὰς ὀφρυς and I would include mask 1 ἡμερώτατος τὰς ὀφρῦς.

[43] Mask 3 ('The Leading Old Man') τὴν ὀφρὺν ἀνατέταται τὴν δεξιάν ('has lifted up his right eyebrow'); mask 7 ('the Lykomedian') ἀνατείνει τὴν ἑτέραν ὀφρύν, πολυπραγμοσύνην πασαδείκνυται ('lifts up the other eybrow [and] indicates busybodiness'). Webster also under stands mask 22 ('the Leading Slave') ἀνατέταται τὰς ὀφρῦς, συνάγει τὸ ἐπισκύνιον ('he raises the eyebrows [and] contracts the forehead') as a mask with an assymetrical brow, I believe rightly. If so, mask 8 ('the Brothelkeeper' or *pornoboskos*) should also be included, since συνάγει τὰς ὀφρῦς ('he contracts his eyebrows'). Mask 27 ('the Wavy-Haired Leading Slave') is similar to mask 22 except for the hair, which is ἐπίσειστος. Finally, I would include in this category mask 17 ('the Flatterer'), of which Pollux says ὁ κόλαξ, ἀνατέταται κακοηθέστερον τὰς ὀφρῦς ('the flatterer raises his eyebrows with rather evil intentions').

[44] For the *speira*, see Webster (1995) vol. I: 27. Mask 27 is also a possibility.

[45] Text and translation, Russell (2001) 122–5. See Beare (1964) 191.

Quintilian's first-century experience of performance is different from that of Plautus. While it is not possible to tie each character type to an individual mask (he is thinking of the whole appearance of the character, including costume and the use of typical props, though the immediate context is facial expression), Quintilian does isolate a mask that is not too different from 'the Leading Old Man' which possesses an asymmetric eyebrow, and he recognises that it facilitates the presentation of a range of emotion. While Russell's translation implies a static realisation of these emotions, the verb *ostendere* could include the full range of movement here described.

I have tied two Plautine characters to a particular mask, and noted the possibility that the mask corresponds (in some respect) to one in Pollux's list. This does not mean that every slave in Plautus is also to be associated with this same mask, however.[46] Pseudolus and Leonida are exceptional in their appearance, not ordinary. Despite the red hair and asymmetrical eyebrows, it is equally likely they are not to be associated with one of Pollux's slaves. For, in addition to divisions based on age, sex, and social position, characters may be representatives of stock types. This mask may be associated with one particular stock type, the *servus callidus* ('clever slave'). If we had other plays by Plautus (or by his contemporaries) it would not surprise us to find complementary descriptions of this mask. Other descriptions similarly match what is seen in the iconography for other types. *Mercator* 639–40 presents a description of a stock *senex*:

> canum, varum, ventriosum, bucculentum, breviculum,
> subnigris oculis, oblongis malis, pansam aliquantulum.

> grey-haired, bow-legged, pot-bellied, jowly, stumpy,
> rather dark eyes, with a broad jaw, and somewhat splay-footed.

What do we mean, then, by a 'stock character'? Such a term is often used in a pejorative sense. More constructively, to refer to a clever slave as a 'stock character' is to say something about the actors and something about the audience.

Actors played stock characters who 'lack subtlety and complexity, and they do not grow or develop over the course of the play'.[47] Given the mask as a constant, characters are 'put on', 'taken off', and transferred from one play to the next. Even if it could be demonstrated that

---

[46] See Brown (1987) 190–99.   [47] Duckworth (1952) 270.

masks were not used in Plautine performance, the point remains: a mask can be anything concealing the actor from the audience. A clown's make-up similarly can transform an actor.[48] Other masked theatre traditions confirm this experience. Since antiquity the only living masked theatrical tradition in the West has been the *commedia dell'arte*, thriving in Italy, France, and Spain from the sixteenth to the eighteenth centuries. Stock character types (e.g. *harlequino, brighella, capitano*) perform simple narratives in a style that is very evocative of Plautus: standard gags and predictable plots combine with *lazzi* (stock physical routines that can be expanded or contracted by the actors according to audience response, like the running slave so popular in Plautus) to yield an entertaining outdoor masked theatrical form. Some of the stock characters in the *commedia*, such as the Lovers, were performed without any physical mask on the face of the actors; the characters are nevertheless called Masks.

In early comic cinema, the Marx Brothers possess the qualities of a small *commedia* troupe. For all functional purposes, their faces are 'masked':[49] whether Groucho is called Otis P. Driftwood, or Rufus T. Firefly, he is always Groucho (just as Harlequin is always Harlequin and a *miles gloriosus* is always a *miles gloriosus*). The same is true of Chico, Harpo, and their regular foil, Margaret Dumont. The mirror scene in *Duck Soup* (1933, dir. Leo McCarey) shows that any individual with painted-on eyebrows and moustache (even the mute Harpo) will be mistaken for Groucho – a joke that can trace its origins back to the Aeacus-scene in Aristophanes' *Frogs*.[50] When characters are not so 'masked', and are played naturally and not individuated and made larger than life – for example, the lovers in *A Night at the Opera* (1935, dir. Sam Wood) played by Kitty Carlisle and Allan Jones – they are no longer memorable in this make-believe world. This is equally true of many early film actors: 'Chaplin's "tramp", Keaton's "wooden face", Harry Langdon's "Baby-face" are fixed and instantly recognizable figures, whatever social or psychological traits they may have to adopt for a particular story.'[51] Another feature of the Marx

---

[48] Johnstone (1981) 150 tells a story about the journalist Bill Richardson: 'he'd been asked to take part in a circus matinee as one of the clowns ... Once the make-up was on he became "possessed" and found himself able to tumble about, catch his feet in buckets, and so on, as if he'd been a clown in another incarnation. He stayed with the circus for some weeks, but he never got the same feeling without the make-up.'

[49] Similarly, 'Peking Opera make-up transforms the actor's face into a veritable mask' (Barba and Savarese (1991) 116).

[50] See Marshall (1993).

[51] Andrews (1993) 172.

Brothers' films is relevant to the relationships on the Plautine stage: while each Brother's appearance, speech mannerisms, demeanour, and relative age does not change from one movie to the next, the relationship between the characters they are playing can change, and does.

Among Plautine slaves there exists at least one instance where the same character recurs (*Pseudolus* and *Asinaria*). Different actors wearing the mask might create a different character, but anecdotal evidence from those who work with masks, indicates that completely different actors will produce similar (but not identical) characters when they put on the same mask.[52] To what extent characters, types, or masks were shared among Roman comic actors cannot be identified with certainty.[53]

For the audience, stock characters can evoke a stock response. Theatre composed of stock characters assumes audience familiarity with the types. Whether it is automatically to dislike a banker or a pimp – did the boys in ancient audiences boo stage villains? (*Pseudolus* 1082) – or to cheer the appearance of the running slave, a stock character or routine that must be identifiable to the audience immediately to have its effect. The appearance of a stock character must connote a specific set of qualities and (more importantly) values, at first sight. This is not to straitjacket the character. These stock types need not be completely predictable, but any individuation of the character is going to be done with these initial audience expectations as a platform: 'the characters are differentiated, rather than individualized'.[54] Lest we fear that such classifications are an exclusively modern preoccupation, we may note the many places listing character types from antiquity.[55] The audience recognised that these were repeated types.

Menander's characters were perceived to be naturalistic. A number of anecdotes from antiquity confirm the opinion that though masked, onstage, and speaking verse, they looked and acted like regular people doing regular things.[56] In contrast, at least some of Plautus' slaves are

[52] Johnstone (1981) 165.
[53] In both *commedia* and the Marx Brothers, masks were typically fixed with their actors. In Italy, a son might inherit a mask and its character from his father. The evidence adduced for doubling in Chapter 2 suggests this was not the case for Plautus.
[54] Duckworth (1952) 270.
[55] See, for example, Quintilian 11.3.74 (the omitted portion in the passage cited above), *Captivi* 57–8, *Heauton Timoroumenos* 35–40, *Eunuchus* 35–40, Horace, *Epistles* 2.1.170–74, and Ovid, *Amores* 1.15.17–18.
[56] Most obviously, there is Aristophanes of Byzantium's rhetorical dictum, 'O Menander! O Life! Which of you copied the other?' (Syrianus, *in Hermogenes* 2.23). What is lacking from the Greek fragments is a character of the extremes found consistently in Plautus. Menander has clever slaves, but for the most part they behave alike: none significantly individuated.

much more clearly defined individuals, even though that individualism is not tied to a character name or a play. This type of characterisation was probably adapted by the playwright from the *fabulae Atellanae*.

The 'Maccius' in Plautus' stage name may derive from the character Maccus of the *Atellanae*: 'it is in some sense a nickname, a pseudonym given to or adopted by the playwright for professional reasons'.[57] Every indication suggests that Maccus, a clown and a fool,[58] was the most popular of the Atellan characters.[59] The audience's sympathies are won by this character's vain efforts at self-advancement. It might be possible to connect Maccus the character in Atellan farce, with Titus Maccius our playwright: Aulus Gellius' claim (3.3.14) that Plautus began his career *in operis artificum scaenicorum* might mean Plautus began his theatrical career as an Atellan actor. To go from playwright to the character type represented by Pseudolus and Leonida is not a much bigger step. Such a claim can only be made tentatively, but it is possible that the physical appearance of the slaves, described so vividly in the text, points not to a description of Pollux's mask 22 (the Leading Slave), but to the Atellan mask of Maccus. Certainly, some blurring is taking place. An audience seeing the Roman version of Pollux's Leading Slave would create some association with the character of Maccus, since Maccus constitutes an element in the 'cultural literacy' of the average Roman theatregoer.[60]

I would press this further: that the mask-maker in Plautus' troupe, and the actor who later embodied the character, could consciously choose to represent certain physical features of Maccus when creating these slaves. The vivid description of these slaves will not correspond either to the particular mask of Pollux, nor to the more general type of generic Greek 'slave' mask (male with dark hair and beard). It is a separate thing, which will be perceived by a Roman audience as partaking of the Atellan character. This is not the mask of all Plautus' *servi callidi*, and many masks employed will more closely resemble the inherited Greek types. But, when the part represented a particular recurrent *callidus* who falls short of his own expectations (as Pseudolus and Leonida do), such blurring was possible. It may even be that a Maccus mask was used for these parts, though such an exact correspondence is not needed

---

[57] Gratwick (1973) 80.
[58] Perhaps a greedy fool, depending on the etymology preferred; see Kamel (1951) 92.
[59] This can be seen, for example, in the extant titles for (literary) *Atellanae*, which include 'Maccus', 'The Twin Maccuses', 'Maccus the Go-between' (*sequester*, perhaps 'the Trustee'?), 'Maccus the Soldier', 'Maccus the Maid', 'Maccus the Inkeeper', and 'Maccus the Exile'.
[60] I appropriate the term 'cultural literacy' from Hirsch, Kett, and Trefil (1987).

to establish that these characters have some connection with the Atellan Maccus.

We are now equipped to look at a particular stock character, the *leno* ('pimp'), not from any sort of sociological reality, but as an overblown, ridiculous, stock character, who was one shotgun in Plautus' dramaturgical arsenal. More than any other type, Plautus' pimps stand out as individuals, while still partaking of the stock type that revels in the excesses of cruelty, avarice, and power.[61] The Plautine corpus contains five pimps, three of whom are described in detail.[62] In a visual medium such as theatre, such description is not strictly necessary, since the audience can see the characters. Descriptions of Pseudolus and Leonida were shown to evoke a possible Atellan influence. The matter is not as straightforward with the pimps.

First is Ballio, the paragon of pimps from *Pseudolus*. His personality is clearly defined over the course of two scenes. In the first, a long *canticum* (133–229), he instructs his household slaves and his 'girls' on what they are to do on his birthday (see 165, 243, 775, 1237). The second scene defining his personality is the insult scene, in which Calidorus and Pseudolus, standing on either side of the pimp, hurl insults onto him, which are confidently and even proudly accepted (357–69). Ballio is a friend of long standing with

---

[61] Opinions are unanimous; sample verdicts from various plays can be found at *Curculio* 494–504, *Pseudolus* 974–7, *Rudens* 1284–5, and Terence, *Adelphoe* 188–9. The problems posed by pimps (who are properly understood to be slave dealers specialising in the market for sex: a contemptible but legal profession) are presented in purely Roman terms: we can be certain if a *pornoboskos* existed in the Greek original, it was nothing like the *leno* Plautus presents. The appearance of a Plautine pimp could reasonably be associated in an audience's mind with the traits and characteristics of a stock character. Real life does not contain such cartoonish extravagances of greed, but theatre can. Pimps have been denounced and it is their devotion to money and profit that makes them so hated. They have made a business of pleasure. Dordalus, the pimp in *Persa*, shows this with his sixfold use of the word *argentum* ('money') in four lines (*Persa* 422–5, a speech that would be equally at home with Misargyrides the banker at *Mostellaria* 567–653). The centrality of pimps to the very notion of Plautine comedy is shown by their prominence in a play's closing lines (*Persa* 858, and see *Poenulus* 1368–71).

[62] I am excluding the two *lenones* in Terence (in *Adelphoe* and *Phormio*) from this discussion, who are not presented in such a wild and exaggerated fashion (although see Hunter (1985) 72), nor am I considering the female version of the stock character, the *lena*, found in *Asinaria* and *Cistellaria*. Despite the apparent similarities, there exist fundamental differences between the *leno* and *lena* in terms of social position and relationship with the girl (see Willcock (1995) 20–24). All of the five Plautine pimps are interesting, and Segal (1987) 79–92 presents a detailed study of Dordalus from *Persa*. The final pimp, Lycus in *Poenulus*, is a much less nuanced character and serves more as a fall guy for the ruse. While he does not appear, the situation in *Epidicus* assumes a *leno* in the background of the story.

Pseudolus (233) and possesses his profession's characteristic obsession with money (265–8). Like Pseudolus, he appears conscious of his obligation to fulfil and exceed the expectations of his stock type.

Ballio's appearance is distinctive in three ways. First, his beard differs from what may be called the 'default' appearance for such a character – Pollux's description of the *pornoboskos* (mask 8) – which, like mask 7, is μακρογένειος ('with a long beard'); Ballio has *hirquina barba* (967, 'a goat's beard'), which Webster associates with mask 9, which is σφηνοπώγων ('with a wedge beard').[63] Second, when he moves, he steps sideways, moving like a crab (*Pseudolus* 955).[64] Comparison with *commedia* techniques and personal experimentation suggest that if an actor wants to move like a crab, movements are led by the knees. Everybody leads with one part of their body when they move: heroes lead with their chests, gluttonous merchants with their belly, and fools with their heads. There are consequences for each of these in other aspects of a character's physical appearance: for example, speed. To lead with one's belly slows movement considerably. To lead with one's knees, like a seedy villain, can lead to rapidly increased movement. If it is fair to apply this to Ballio, the pimp may well have been characterised by rapid, darting movements,[65] and may have possessed a (comparatively) lithe physique. In commedia, Pantalone (the lusty old man) also leads with his knees, and Ballio too is a *senex* (1190). Quintilian confirms the appropriateness of this for Ballio: *varicare supra modum et in stando deforme est et accedente motu prope obscenum* ('to place the legs wide apart is unbecoming if one stands still, and almost obscene if one moves in that posture').[66] The third distinctive feature in Ballio's appearance is the recalcitrant slave boy accompanying him (see e.g. 249). The comic by-play between these two is immediately suggestive: the sideways-skittering pimp eager to get to the forum, being continually held back by the low-status servant who is supposed to be leading him: this tension between urgency and delay characterises the whole play.[67]

Second is Cappadox, the pimp in *Curculio*. The least threatening of the Plautine pimps, what seems most striking about his personality is his soft

---

[63] Webster (1995) vol. I: 15.
[64] Compare Chalinus' line in *Casina*, *imitabor nepam* (443: 'I shall imitate a scorpion'). Despite the entries in the OLD and Lewis and Short, *nepam* here does not refer to a crab's movement, but suggests Chalinus is backing up to the stage wall like a scorpion (*nepa*) seeking shelter. This is a position for eavesdropping, as discussed in Chapter 4.
[65] Compare Quintilian 11.3.112, discussed in Chapter 2.
[66] Quintilian 11.3.125 (ed. Radermacher, vol. II: 352), tr. Dodwell (2000) 29 n. 44.
[67] Marshall (1996) and see Chapter 4.

spot for the *meretrix* Planesium (520–21). Planesium confirms that *bene et pudice me domi habuit* (698: 'he gave [her] chaste and kindly treatment at his house'). Nevertheless, his true pimply character soon re-emerges, as money trumps concern for restoring her family (528–30). As for appearance, Cappadox is sick, and this has made him green (231: *oculis herbeis*, 'with greenish gaze'). His illness is gastro-intestinal, and the size of his belly is noted by Curculio (230–33). Cappadox's own assessment of his health is more detailed (*Curculio* 220–22, 236–38):

> *nam iam quasi zona liene cinctus ambulo,*
> *geminos in ventre habere videor filios.*
> *nil metuo nisi ne medius dirrumpar miser.*
> *... lien enecat, renes dolent,*
> *pulmones distrahuntur, cruciatur iecur,*
> *radices cordis pereunt, hirae omnes dolent.*

> My spleen, like a girdle, binds my waistline as I walk;
> I feel I'm carrying twin sons inside my gut.
> My worst fear is that I'll burst open, up the middle
> ... My spleen's a killer, my kidneys hurt,
> My lungs are torn apart, my liver's racked with pain,
> My ticker's barely tocking, my whole belly aches.
>
> (tr. Smith)

It may even be that this description provides an internal reference to Plautus' *Amphitruo*, with line 221 referring metatheatrically but indirectly to the portly actor's previous role as the pregnant Alcumena. In all of this, though, it is the belly of the pimp that is emphasised. His pained, slow movements throughout the play do not evoke the pity they seek, but evince only disdain from the audience. While Cappadox's insides are obviously diseased, he takes great care for his external appearance. When a soldier calls upon all his weapons to help him, Cappadox invokes a different panoply altogether: *volsellae, pecten, speculum, calamistrum meum* | ... *meaque axitia linteumque extersui* (577–8: 'tweezers, comb, mirror, curling iron ... and my scissors, and linen rubbing towels'). This is the Cappdox paradox: a disgustingly bloated, morally reprehensible villain who is vain about his appearance and pities the girl he sells.

The third pimp is Labrax, from *Rudens*. Labrax exhibits a typical concern about his finances, magnified since his possessions have been lost in the sea. He is called *sceleris semen* (327: 'the sperm of villainy'), but by the finale exhibits genuine pleasure at the fact that Daemones has been reunited with his daughter (1365–6). Labrax looks nothing like Ballio or

Cappadox. He has the *forma* (1306: 'look') of a *mendicus* (1306: 'beggar'), which no doubt reflects the sea-washed clothes he wears throughout the play (549–50). Nothing distinguishes his beard (769). Before Labrax appears, Plesidippus has asked Daemones, *ecquem tu hic hominem crispum, incanum videris?* (125: 'whether you have seen a gray and curly-headed[68] man here'). Similarly, Trachalio describes Labrax, for whom he is searching (317–19):

> ecquem
> recalvom ac Silanum senem, statutum, ventriosum,
> tortis superciliis, contracta fronte?

> An old man, balding like Silenus
> Sturdy build, protruding paunch,
> With crooked eyebrows, forehead furrowed
> In a frown...?
>
> (tr. Smith)

Again, the details are precise. While balding, Labrax can still be identified by his gray curly hair. These features are in fact compatible with Pollux's description of the *pornoboskos* (mask 8), of which Webster notes that '[t]here is some general resemblance to the Papposilen and it is sometimes difficult to tell them apart'.[69] The brows of the *pornoboskos* may be asymmetrical. Nevertheless, 'all the examples recognised are bald, not 'balding" (ἀναφαλαντίας in Pollux).[70] Finally, the pot-belly (*ventriosum*, a word also found in the descriptions of the slaves at *Pseudolus* 1218 and *Asinaria* 400) of Labrax is associated with this mask on a number of gems, where the character also carries a stick.[71]

While Labrax is associated more closely to the Greek equivalent of the *leno* than is Ballio or Cappadox, other indications associate him with his jaw. Charmides asks (*Rudens* 543–4):

> iam postulabas te, impurata belua,
> totam Siciliam devoraturum insulam?

> Did you expect, you filthy animal,
> To gobble up the whole of Sicily?
>
> (tr. Smith)

---

[68] The word *crispum* can also mean 'wrinkly' or 'veined' (like marble), but Plautus uses it elsewhere only of hair.
[69] Webster (1995) vol. I: 15; the *Rudens* passage is adduced on p. 16.
[70] Webster (1995) vol. I: 15.   [71] Webster (1995) vol. I: 16.

Labrax has a wagging tongue (558: *lingua vivet*) and his name is the word for a voracious sea-bass, which gains additional nuance since he has recently suffered shipwreck. All this might suggest that Labrax leads his movement with his jaw. He and Charmides are cold, wet, in skimpy outfits, and are shivering (527–36). Labrax asks, *quid si aliquo ad ludos me pro Manduco locem?* | ... *quia pol clare crepito dentibus* (535–6: 'What if I rented myself at some games as Manducus? ... since, by Pol, my teeth chatter loudly'). The explicit reference to Manducus from the *Atellanae*[72] suggests the possibility that the Labrax mask comprises elements evoking both the Atellan Manducus and the Hellenistic *pornoboskos*. The Manducus mask may even have had a hinged jaw that could be opened so the character could swallow stage properties.[73]

Where Pseudolus and Leonida were shown to have a common origin possibly connected with the *Atellanae*, the same is certainly not true of Plautus' three pimps. Each is representative of the stock character of *leno*, but in terms of physical appearance, each is described in detail, and very obviously bears no visual similarity to any other. What is more, in the illustrated Terence manuscripts, 'characters of this order – Sannio in the *Adelphoe* and Dorio in the *Phormio* – wear masks of a new kind: bald with dark hair and a slave-mouth with no beard below it'.[74] This suggests at least one other look (*forma*) for the pimp.

How is all this to be reconciled with the *leno* as a stock character? The description of Labrax corresponds closely with the Hellenistic *pornoboskos*. Nevertheless, the script ties him to the Atellan figure of the jowly Manducus. With Pseudolus and Leonida, it was possible to suggest a connection between them and the Atellan mask of Maccus. Ballio and Cappadox do not correspond to the physical description of Labrax (and the Greek *pornoboskos*) or with each other: that all pimps perhaps lead movements with a different body part produces a number of additional small differences that are hard to isolate except through performance. But these two may also be tied to particular Atellan types.

The Atellan character that most obviously applies to Ballio is Pappus, the mask of an old man. One of the titles of an *Atellana* by Pomponius is *Sponsa Pappi* ('Pappus' Fiancée'), and so Pappus could appear in a farce

---

[72] Despite Lowe (1989) 168 n. 43, it is not right to see the reference here to 'a masked figure carried in processions' (see Festus (Paulus) 115 L) 'rather than a character of the Atellana'. An uninhabited mask is necessarily a secondary development and a theatrical audience would not make this association.

[73] See Juvenal 3.175–6 and Préaux (1962). Hinged jaws are also found on Indonesian frog masks.

[74] Webster (1995) vol. I: 15.

revolving around his virility. While there may be no direct causal connection, Pantalone, the equivalent *commedia* character, was often presented with a sharp, pointed beard, like Ballio's goatee. Nor are the other
old men in this play more 'Pappus-like' than Ballio: the two other *senes*
who appear, Simo and Callipho, are not distinguished physically in any
way in the text and appear themselves to be stock representatives of the
senex durus and the *senex lepidus*. Tentatively, then, I would suggest that
the relationship between Labrax and Manducus (textually explicit) is
analogous to the relationship between Ballio and Pappus (textually
implicit). Cappadox can also be accommodated into this scheme, and tied
to the Atellan character based on the belly, Dossennus.[75] A large gut and
slow movements are suggested for Dossennus by Horace's description of
Plautus himself: *quantus sit Dossennus edacibus in parasitis* (*Epistles* 2.1.173:
'what a Dossennus he is, among his greedy parasites'). However this line
is interpreted,[76] Dossennus is used as an image because of his associations
with the stock character of the *parasitus*. The equivalent *commedia*
character, *il Dottore*, happens also to share the foppish appearance with
Cappadox: *il Dottore*'s lace trim evokes Cappadox's curler and tweezers.
As with the other pimps, there appears to be a textually implicit association between Cappadox the pimp and one of the Atellan masks, even
though the mask is different in each case.

This problematises any sense of one-to-one correspondence between
mask and stock character. For what is demonstrably true of the *leno* is
conceivably true of any character on the Plautine stage. Plautus could
create a character that, through a combination of acting style, costume,
and mask, could be identified to some degree with a figure from the
Atellanae.[77] Finally, the *Curculio* example can be pushed a little further.
If Cappadox is associated with Dossennus, who is a glutton that can be
tied (albeit two centuries later) with 'greedy parasites', we can wonder
where this leaves Curculio in the scheme of things. Within the narrative,
he functions as a parasite: at 305–28, he delays in providing the information because he is famished, a stock routine for a parasite. This may
suggest that while Curculio is a parasite, he is not connected with the
Atellan Dossennus figure and may instead more closely resemble a

---

[75] Préaux (1962) rightly argues against Müller's equation of Manducus with Dossennus. The few
extant fragments from the literary period of *Atellanae* are insufficient for any negative case to be
made (contra Lowe (1989) 169 n. 46).

[76] See Beare (1964) 139.

[77] For similar elaborate descriptions of old men (Pappus), see Duckworth (1952) 90.

traditional Greek parasite, or indeed some other type. One inference we can draw from the association between Cappadox and Dossennus is that not every parasite was a Dossennus figure, despite Horace and Curculio's famished routine. Even raising this possibility leads beyond where speculation may reasonably take us, but Curculio's name is the word for the boll weevil – a different kind of parasite, but one with a very distinctive long, curved proboscis (and many of the characters in the play have animal-derived names: Leaena, Lyco, and perhaps Therapontigonus).[78] It is possible that the character Curculio was in performance not associated with the belly, but instead with his nose, since there was already a Dossennus figure in the play. Such a variation might lead to associations with another Atellan figure (Bucco, for example), but it is just as likely that any rigid categorisations are to be put aside in favour of a more flowing set of relationships between these characters, with each possessing a variety of literary and cultural influences, drawn from a variety of performance traditions.[79] In the end, these can be only suggestions, but they possess sufficienst plausibility to demonstrate that Plautus did not simply import his masking tradition. There were innovations, and any description of Roman masks cannot be directly transposed from a Greek model.

INDIVIDUALISED COMIC MASKS

It follows that masks would be, for the most part, individualised. The practical realities of masked acting in the theatre meant that the Roman comic playwrights manipulated the five basic mask types inherited from Greek New Comedy, and the audience's familiarity with certain stock characters from the *Atellanae* meant that the playwright could incorporate aspects of their mask types into his masks, thereby enriching the depth of character able to be represented. Other changes were possible during a performance: *Miles Gloriosus* 791–92 and 872 show that the hair on the

---

[78] Wiles (1991) 135–7. In my production of *Curculio* a special mask was made for the character with a long nose, which appeared either phallic or entomologically accurate, depending on one's knowledge of insects.

[79] In Chapter 4, I discuss the related issue of Curculio performing 'the running slave', a stock routine. The presence of two characters that can be seen in one way or another perhaps provides further evidence to an ongoing debate concerning the distinctions between the Greek *parasitos* ('sponger') and the Greek *kolax* ('flatterer'). Both character types apparently appeared in Menander's *Kolax* (see Arnott (1996a) 153–203) and in Terence's *Eunuchus*; see Brown (1992) 98–107 and Lowe (1989), who associates the parasite with the *Atellanae*. The example of *Curculio* could conceivably contribute to this debate.

mask could at times be altered. Once we recognise that some of the masks may have been individualised, there are consequences for other characters on stage and for the practical considerations of mask–making.

For example, in *Pseudolus*, Harpax appears seeking Ballio; Pseudolus has intercepted Harpax and pretends to be another of Ballio's slaves (636–9):

HARP.   *... sed quid est tibi nomen?*
PSEUD.   *servos est huic lenoni Syrus;*
        eum esse me dicam. Syrus sum.
HARP.   *Syrus?*
PSEUD.   *id est nomen mihi.*
HARP.   *verba multa facimus. erus si tuos domi est, quin provocas,*
        ut id agam quod missus huc sum, quidquid est nomen tibi?

HARP.   *... but what is your name?*
PSEUD.   (*to the audience*) The pimp has a slave called
        Syrus.
        I'll say I'm him. (*to Harpax*) I am Syrus.
HARP.   Syrus?
PSEUD.   That's my
        name.
HARP.   We're wasting words. If your boss is at home, why not
        call him out,
        So I can do what I was sent here for, whatever your
        name is.

Harpax's difficulty accepting the Pseudolus' pseudonym is puzzling. 'Syrus' is a typical slave name, and one well established in ancient comedy: characters with the name are found in Terence's *Adelphoe, Heauton Timoroumenos*, and as a female, Syra, in *Hecyra*, in Menander's *Epitripontes, Dis Exapatôn, Phasma*, and *Georgos*, and elsewhere in Plautus. Chrysalus in *Bacchides* 649–50 says:

> *non mihi isti placent Parmenones, Syri,*
> *qui duas aut tris minas auferunt eris.*
>
> I don't care for those Parmenos and Syruses
> who steal two or three minae from their masters.[80]

There is no obvious reason for Harpax's hesitancy in *quidquid est nomen tibi.*[81] Or is there?

---

[80] Tr. Hunter (1985) 66.
[81] This is why Lindsay follows Acidalius and assigns the clause to Pseudolus. Harpax is the one who is lost, though, and he needs to know with whom he is dealing.

Syrus is a relatively common slave name because its etymology derives from a place of origin, Syria. In *Truculentus* 530, Stratophanes says, *adduxi ancillas tibi eccas ex Syria duas* ('Look, I brought you two maids from Syria'). Many ancient slave names were produced this way. 'Thrax' signifies a slave of Thracian origin; the name 'Xanthias' was also given to Thracians because of their blonde or reddish hair; 'Geta' is another ethnic name from Thrace. In fact, in a Greek context, Pseudolus himself might be thought to be of Thracian origin: he is described as being *rufus quidam* ('a certain red-head', *Pseudolus* 1218), feature common to all the slaves in Pollux's catalogue except the Cicada.[82]

If Harpax's hesitancy indicates uneasiness, signalling a joke for the audience, we must ask under what circumstances can this exchange be funny. One answer is that this is an example of ethnographic humour. When a character on the Hellenistic or Roman stage identified himself as 'Syrus' he was assuming a name associated with a particular place of origin, and, by extension, with certain genetic characteristics. Masks could identify geographical origins: a mosaic of Menander's *Samia* shows a black *mageiros* and there is a black nurse called Giddenis in Plautus' *Poenulus* (1112–13), and an Ethiopian slave girl in Terence's *Eunuchus* (165–7, 470–71).[83] Similarly, the slave name 'Syrus' may here be associated with a particular type of slave mask: one with dark features, almost certainly dark hair, against which the red-headed Thracian would stand out in contrast, and about which no record has survived in Pollux's catalogue (which is to say that such a mask was not found among the particular collection that Pollux describes[84]).

There is therefore a joke when Pseudolus calls himself 'Syrus'. The name, however generic for a slave in comedy, is associated with particular ethnographic features, including dark hair. *Truculentus* 530 suggests there were female equivalents of the mask. Pseudolus' red-headedness, the first detail in his detailed description, is inconsistent with the name he gives himself, and this leads to Harpax's confusion and why he thinks *verba multa facimus*. In his survey of Menander's slave masks, MacCary believes 'the ethnic names – Getas, Sangarios, Syros, Syskos, Tibeios, Lydos – are not rendered appropriate by emphasis in characterization upon any national trait'.[85] There is, however, evidence for the addition of ethnic features to masks, to facilitate audience differentiation between

---

[82] See n. 22.   [83] See Snowden (1970) 163 and 314 nn. 40 and 41.
[84] For this account of the development of Pollux's catalogue, see Poe (1996) 311–12, 324–5.
[85] MacCary (1969) 294.

characters. Plautus here uses these details to get a laugh. A black mask seems to have been used in Terence's *Phormio*: Cicero, *pro Caecina* 10.27, thinks of the character as being black, though there are no indications of this in the text.[86] This points to an awareness of Terence's play from the stage, and provides clear if indirect evidence that Terence's plays were reperformed in the age of Roscius. More relevant to the present point, however, is the inference that features of ethnicity could be added to Roman comic masks without any textual indication. Such markers of ethnicity might even be independent of character names. A similar independence can even be seen employed on South Italian red-figure vases: every 'Xanthias' labelled on the vases wears a mask with black hair and beard.

In the absence of any certain artistic representations of Roman masks, we cannot say how much detail was represented on a mask. As an object functioning in the theatre, though, all that is important is what can be perceived at a distance by the audience. Plautus' troupe is willing to create striking theatrical effects by exploiting audience expectations of the mask. *Menaechmi* provides several clues in its design to facilitate the doubling of both brothers until the play's concluding scenes, when the brothers finally meet. Plautus spends most of the play having an actor wearing one mask play both brothers, only to reveal at the last moment that the troupe all along has had a second identical mask. *Miles Gloriosus* 138–53 suggested that this was the normal means of presenting twins in Roman comedy. Though they are not twins, the sisters in *Bacchides* could in practice wear identical (or almost identical) masks and still be distinguishable based on how the mask was animated by the different actors playing the roles.

Much more problematic are the masks of Philocrates and Tyndarus in *Captivi*. Both Philocrates and his slave Tyndarus have been taken captive, and in their servitude, they have switched identities (lines 37–9):

> *itaque inter se commutant vestem et nomina:*
> *illic vocatur Philocrates, hic Tyndarus;*
> *huius illic, hic illius hodie fert imaginem.*

> And so they have swapped clothes and names with each other:
> That one is called Philocrates, and this one Tyndarus;
> He has this one's form today, this one has his.

The prologue expresses concern that this is a matter that could be misunderstood by the audience (14), and we can be grateful for Plautus'

---

[86] Snowden (1970) 314 n. 42.

usual precision with demonstrative adjectives. The question is to what extent this concern is sincere. Might an audience actually be confused by this situation? The answer depends on how we understand 39: *imaginem*, the word also used at *Miles Gloriosus* 151 (and see *Amphitruo* 121, 125, and 141).

Both Philocrates and Tyndarus are in their mid-twenties (see *Captivi* 8, 20, 980–82), and, though captive and enchained, Philocrates is freeborn and one would expect that he would appear as an *adulescens*. His mask therefore contrasts with his costume, which through the ruse is that of a slave. Unusually in this play, Tyndarus is not marked as a slave (older, bearded) but is an age-mate of Philocrates. While also a captive, he possesses the *imago* of an *adulescens* when he dons Philocrates' clothes. There is considerable irony here. As the prologue reveals (17–21), Tyndarus is in fact the long-lost freeborn son of the *senex* Hegio.[87] By making the characters age-mates, the play allows Tyndarus to appear appropriately for the social position he will hold at the end of the play, once he has been recognised. This is not to deny that he has lived as a slave, and for some reason his freeborn name was Paegnium (984): a slave name in *Persa*, and (in its Greek form) the word for a sexual plaything – not the name of a freeborn citizen. The play works aggressively at blurring the categories of slave and free. The inherited Greek mask system does this already for young women. Here, in a play with no female characters, that ambiguity manifests itself in other ways.

Philocrates, too, is presented ambiguously, as a description of him makes clear (*Captivi* 647–8):

> *macilento ore, naso acuto, corpore albo, oculis nigris,*
> *subrufus aliquantum, crispus, cincinnatus*

> thin face, sharp nose, pale complexion, dark eyes,
> somewhat reddish-haired, curly with ringlets.

The reference to his hair, *subrufus aliquantum*, is problematic, since only slaves are red-headed in comedy.[88] Just as Tyndarus' presentation was

---

[87] Lindsay (1900) 114: 'It was absolutely necessary that the audience should know from the outset that Tyndarus was Hegio's long-lost son; for otherwise all the delicate irony of the situation in the scenes between Hegio and Tyndarus would be lost upon them, nor could they help being puzzled by the noble traits of the seeming slave's character.' While Lindsay underestimates the audience, his basic point is well founded.

[88] *Pseudolus* 1218; *Asinaria* 400, *Phormio* 51. Pollux's list suggests that red-headedness was common on slaves: of masks 21–27, all are red-headed except mask 21, the Pappos, who is a freedman, and mask 26,

made ambiguous by his beardlessness and birth name, so the red hair on an *adulescens* mask blurs a line normally preserved rigorously on the comic stage by combining physical features of slave and free. This probably required a special mask to be constructed for Philocrates. The conclusion that this is a play *ubi boni meliores fiant* (1034: 'where good men become better ones') accurately describes the action, but Philocrates' mask shows that free men captured in battle can assume qualities like any other slave. As *Captivi* engages with philosophical concerns concerning the naturalness of slavery, this mask demonstrates that no clear-cut solution exists. These ambiguities, of stagecraft and ethics, defy easy resolution.

Other possibilities have been raised. Leigh suggests that in performance Tyndarus and Philocrates also changed masks, and it is possible that *imago* can been understood this way.[89] The audience enjoys a position of superiority over all the onstage characters because of the information provided by the prologue, and this knowledge is reinforced by the masks. There is no need to destabilise character identity further by switching masks in this way, and since both are presented as *adulescentes* in any case, little is gained. Moore suggests the characters actually change masks by the end of the play.[90] This confuses the recognition too much, and the audience will be left only with the continuity of the actor (beneath costume and mask) to discern a critical element of plot. There are no instances in ancient comedy of an actor changing masks and not changing identities at the same time. Masks function as the primary marker of a character's identity, and it is consequently all the more important that each mask uniquely relates to a given character.

Plautus could use the mask system inherited from Greek performance to make an element of his narrative clear to the audience, reinforcing the situation described in the prologue. The audience will always know who was born free and who was born a slave. The same is not true, however, for female characters. The test case for this is the woman who is recognised as being other than she appears during the course of the play, an event that happens in *Cistellaria*, *Curculio*, *Poenulus*, *Rudens*, and in Terence's *Andria* and *Eunuchus*. It is not always citizenship (and concomitant eligibility for marriage) that is proved, though it may be. In Plautus, the

the Cicada, who has black hair and may be African (see note 22). In contrast, *rubicundum* ('flushed') can be used of slave or free: see *Rudens* 314 of an *adulescens*, *Pseudolus* 1219 of a slave, and *Hecyra* 440 in a deliberately confused description of a non-existent character.

[89] Leigh (2004) 84 and n. 101.   [90] Moore (1998b) 185–6.

true situation is rarely a mystery, since the fact is revealed in a prologue in every instance except *Curculio*.[91] This situation is often associated with the term *pseudokorê* ('false maiden'?), though the term is found only in Pollux and (given its uncertain etymology[92]) that term is best not used, except in reference to Pollux's catalogue. Nevertheless, in that catalogue two versions of the *pseudokorê* are listed among the female masks, and apparently distinguished only by hairstyle. Wiles suggests this mask represents a young woman whose circumstances are falsely understood, with the other masks used for *meretrices* who would not be so recognised over the course of the play: 'the mask . . . implies that she is the pseudo-virgin of the plot, the young man's mistress whom he has liberated from slavery, and certainly will marry at the end of the play'.[93] The question is not entirely moot, since *Curculio* (as the text stands) and the Terentian plays maintain the suspense of the recognition as the play unfolds. A codified mask system that was inflexible in this regard would have denied a Roman playwright the opportunity to present ambiguity or to create surprise.

Again, it becomes helpful to understand Pollux's list as describing the contents of one particular mask cabinet that he reads in structuralist terms. The order of the list acknowledges the five Hellenistic mask types. A troupe performing a play can use a mask they already possess or make a new one to accommodate the physical details that are found in the text of the play. Sometimes, this will seek a particular effect, as is achieved in the case of the slave girl Planisium in *Curculio*, whose appearance is marked as being *cum noctuinis oculis* (191: 'with owl eyes').[94] The play isolates one feature in an otherwise unmarked mask, and in practice an actor would select whatever young woman mask happened to have the largest, roundest eyes, and that this criterion would override the need to use a (supposed) *pseudokorê* mask.

Curculio has another joke involving the eyes of the mask: Curculio has emerged from the house with a slave, calling back to an imagined Phaedromus within. Only once he has emerged does he see Lyco the

---

[91] I do not believe this in itself is sufficient reason to believe that *Curculio* survives in an abridged form and that there was originally a narrative prologue, though that is generally held to be the case; see Fantham (1965) 85–8, Webster (1970) 220.

[92] LSJ translates 'a pretended maid' and cites Pollux 4.151. Such would be more appropriate perhaps for Chalinus' 'disguise' as a bride in *Casina*. See Gilula (1977).

[93] Wiles (1991) 206, and see 177–84.

[94] Wiles (1991) 137 notes how such a feature does not fit ancient concepts of beauty, but does correspond to the association of animal features with many of the characters in this play.

banker (390–94):

CURCULIO	*. . . attat, quem quaerebam. sequere me.*
	simulabo quasi non noverim. heus tu, te volo.
LYCO	*Unocule, salve.*
CURCULIO	*quaeso, deridesne me?*
LYCO	*de Coclitum prosapia te esse arbitror,*
	nam ei sunt unoculi.

CURCULIO	(*to audience*)
	Hey! The man I seek. (*to a slave*) Follow me.
	(*to audience*) I'll pretend I don't know him.
	He puts on an eyepatch.
	(*to Lyco*) Hey you,
	I want you.
LYCO	Hello, One-eye.
CURCULIO	Sir, do you mock me?
LYCO	I think you're from the family of the Cyclopes.
	They are all one-eyed.

Curculio goes on to brag that the injury was a catapult wound, to which Lyco suggests rather it came from being chased out of the kitchen – and Curculio confesses to the audience that this is indeed the most likely source of his imagined injury (394–8). Curculio adopts an eyepatch disguise, but he is not normally one-eyed (391: *simulabo*): this is his disguise as the soldier's freedman (*libertus*), Summanus (413–16, with the joke playing between an obscure god and bedwetting). The question becomes, when does Curculio disguise himself? While it is possible he wears an eyepatch as he appears, this loses the appearance of spontaneity achieved if the disguise is a panicked response to meeting Lyco unexpectedly. He sees the banker, and the character improvises a disguise based on what he has at hand.[95] Whatever solution is adopted, it parallels the staging of *Miles Gloriosus* 1306–9, where Pleusicles is also disguised as someone with one eye.

Masked acting necessarily involves a paradox, though. While many of the techniques are associated with conveying what is on the surface of the mask, the act of wearing a mask evokes the appearance of unanticipated depth of character. A masked actor is constantly negotiating between these poles, depending on the willing participation of the audience. How

---

[95] In our 1996 production, the actor took a cloth the size of a large napkin (with which Curculio had wiped his lips after his feast), and stuffed it in the eyehole of the mask, to create an instant (and very transparent) disguise, that of course was completely effective within the stage world.

this is accomplished is described by an exercise of Lecoq:

> After this first experience of masked performance, I ask the performers for the
> opposite of what the mask appears to suggest. For example, a mask whose face
> seems to present 'cretin' will at first be performed as just that. The character will
> be foolish, timid, clumsy. Next we consider what if the character might be
> knowledgeable, clever, sure of himself, supremely intelligent? Here the actor is
> performing what we call the *counter-mask*, revealing a second character behind
> the same mask, lending it a depth which is much more interesting. In this way
> we discover that people's faces do not necessarily fit what they are and that for
> each character there is a depth of field. A third stage can be reached with certain
> masks: to perform, in the same character, both mask and counter-mask.[96]

What Lecoq calls the 'counter-mask' is more satisfying for an audience,
but requires the actor to know both how his body appears in a given
mask, to be aware of that character and its effect on the audience, and to
play something opposed to those expectations. Every actor will respond to
a given mask differently, and consequently will produce a different
character, though the initial 'surface' character of the mask for each actor
might share many characteristics. This tension is also present with the half
masks of the *commedia*:

> The characters of the Italian comedy are constantly oscillating between two
> contradictory poles. Harlequin is, at one and the same time, naïve and cunning,
> the Captain is strong and scared, the Doctor knows everything and understands
> nothing, Pantalone is both an industrial boss, master of himself and helplessly off
> his head when in love. This duality, pushed to its limit, is a source of great
> richness.[97]

The richness of a masked performance lies in these tensions.

The mental demands of acting in a mask are therefore significant, and,
again, the mask cannot function in isolation. Noh acting, like acting in
Greece and Rome, rewards versatility, in the actor's ability to play a wide
variety of roles,[98] which further complicates the task. As the Noh actor
Akira Matsui says, 'The art is acting, not mask-wearing.'[99] But not any
mask can accomplish such effects, and the mask-maker needs to be an
artist. Lecoq praises Noh masks, which create the appearance of life
through the smallest movements: 'the greatest masks of all are those of the
Japanese Noh, where the slightest forward tilt of the head is sufficient to

---

[96] Lecoq (2001) 59.
[97] Lecoq (2001) 113, and, for Lecoq on the *commedia dell'arte* generally, 108–17.
[98] Johnson (1992) 24.   [99] Cited in Johnson (1992) 23.

lower the eyelids and convert the gaze from outward to inward!'[100] How the mask fits on the actor's head is also important:

> Like every other mask, a neutral mask should not adhere closely to the face. A certain distance should be preserved between the face and the mask, for it is precisely this distance which makes it possible for the actor to play. It must also be slightly larger than the face. The real dimensions of a face, as found, for example, on death masks, do not help the performer to find the register of play, nor to extend it to those around. This is true of all masks.'[101]

The fact that ancient masks appear to be slightly larger-than-life is therefore not only (or even primarily) associated with increasing visibility for the audience. It is rather a necessary component of the mask design to enable the character to come to life. Performance, as always, is the key: '[t]here is no point in contemplating the mask for hours, with heaven knows what mystic concentration, before performing. It must be jolted into life.'[102] This view runs counter to the conventional image in Greek and Roman art of an actor portrayed in contemplation of his mask. It is such images (which may represent only a moment; it is the viewer who assumes the actor has been there a long time) that lead to a mis-understanding of the profession of the masked actor. For only rarely will it be the case that an actor has only one mask.

Finally, we can turn to the practicalities for an actor of wearing such a mask. *Phormio* 209–12 consists of an exchange that has often been used to 'prove' that Roman comedy did not use masks. For it would appear that Antipho's face changes, offering for evaluation supposedly 'different' expressions to show his father that he is not afraid:

ANT.   *obsecro,*
          quid si adsimulo? satinest?
GETA.   *garris.*
ANT.   *voltum contemplamini: em*
          satine sic est?
GETA.   *non.*
ANT.   *quid si sic?*
GETA.   *propemodum.*
ANT.   *quid sic?*
GETA.   *sat est:*
          em istuc serva . . .

---

[100] Lecoq (2001) 60, and see Wiles (1991) 104.   [101] Lecoq (2001) 36, 38.   [102] Lecoq (2001) 55.

ANT.   No, please; what if I pretended – would that do?
GETA. Don't be silly.
ANT.   (*trying to look resolute*) Look at my face, both of you. Is that
       all right?
GETA   No.
ANT.   What about this then?
GETA   Nearly.
ANT.   Like this then?
GETA. That'll do. Now keep it up.[103]

Actual changing expressions are of course impossible on a fixed mask, and consequently some scholars have seen this passage as evidence against the use of masks.[104] Defenders typically invoke the appearance of motion and emotion that is often attested when an actor wears a mask:[105] and skilled performers can indeed make a mask seem to come to life, and express a range of emotions by combining head position with posture, gestures, and vocal inflection. This is not, however, what seems to be the case here.

Terence's passage has the appearance of very rapid back-and-forth exchanges between the characters: line 210 alone contains six speeches. By calling attention specifically to the face (*vultus*) and the rapidity of exchange, Terence is not allowing his actor to show the range of expression of which he is perhaps capable. But this does not eliminate the scene's entertainment value. Humour is achieved by having Antipho call attention to his facial expressions when his mask is immobile. 'Look at my face ... Is that all right?' he asks, indicating his mask's fixed expression. Geta tells him no, so Antipho quickly turns away, and turns back, displaying what by necessity is the same facial expression, saying 'What about this then?' The audience can see that nothing has changed, but this time Geta says 'Nearly'. Another spin and re-presentation from Antipho – 'Like this then?' – receives a confident response from his slave, 'That'll do. Now keep it up.' By calling attention to the unchanging nature of the conventional mask, Terence is able to evoke a sincere

[103] Tr. Radice (1976) 236.   [104] Gow (1912) 72 dismisses the example.
[105] Personal experience corroborates these claims. When students were shown a mask and asked 'Who is this?' or 'Describe this person', responses invariably focused not on physical characteristics, but on emotions and psychological states: 'he is sad'; 'he is angry'; 'he's a crazy person'; 'he's been hurt'. Even without an actor animating the mask, there is a willingness in the audience to interpret a mask as possessing an inner life. Indeed, this tendency is ridiculed by a fable of Aesop (*Fable* 27, and see Phaedrus 1.7), in which a fox sees a mask and is surprised that there are no brains inside.

metatheatrical laugh from his audience, as Antipho goes to face his father really no better prepared than he was to begin with.

Asinaria 837–41 present a similar joke, where a character is unable to change the mask's expression. The comic mechanism is therefore slightly more straightforward, while still calling attention to the mask the character wears. Argyrippus is speaking with his father Demaenetus:

ARGY.	*an tu me tristem putas?*
DEM.	*putem ego, quem videam aeque esse maestum ut quasi dies si dicta sit?*
ARGY.	*ne dixis istuc.*
DEM.	*ne sic fueris: ilico ego non dixero.*
ARGY.	*em aspecta: rideo.*
DEM.	*utinam male qui mihi volunt sic rideant.*

ARGY.	Why? Do you think I'm sad?
DEM.	Sad? You look as glum as if You'd just been hauled before the judge.
ARGY.	Don't talk that way!
DEM.	Don't act that way, And I'll no longer need to say it.
ARGY.	Look: I'm laughing. (*He gives a weak grin.*)
DEM.	How I wish My enemies would laugh so hard!

(tr. Smith)

Smith's stage direction is clearly what the situation expects. But how is 'a weak grin' to be accomplished with masks which cover the entire face? One solution, which amounts to the 'default' solution in a masked theatre, is to have the actor use the other variables available to him – his posture, vocal tone, hands, the angle light hits the face – to signify happiness in the natural way. I suggest, though, that it would be hard to represent a 'weak' smile this way, since any actor's movements would have to be clear enough to convey the emotion in the first place. A more obvious solution is for the actor to present himself as neutrally as he is able: specifically not to smile, while he says *em aspecta: rideo*. This would produce a visual joke where the actor's words are in clear contradiction to his disposition.

Because the mask functions in conjunction with the other resources brought by the actor to the stage, examples such as these begin to blur the distinction between physical aspects of the mask and how it is employed during performance. When successfully worn, the audience does not see the object, but only the character. Metatheatrical humour can disrupt this, but it is the power of the mask to hold and maintain audience attention: 'The wide-eyed gaze of the tragic [or comic] mask does not scatter or divide, but focuses and encompasses, compelling the attention of the entire theatre.'[106] The skill of acting in a mask can be learnt, and governs much of the way that we can envision stage action.

---

[106] Rehm (1992) 40.

CHAPTER 4

Stage Action

A play is written and then rehearsed, and the troupe has a contract from the magistrates to perform at a festival. These events probably occur in this order, but they need not. At an appointed time, the troupe makes its way to the recently constructed stage building, and gets ready to perform. There may have been some time between one form of entertainment and the next, and this will depend to a large extent on the purchases made by the magistrates. The *praeco* announces the play, blows a trumpet, and the crowd assembles. Ideally many will have stayed on from the previous performance: perhaps as the festival day wears on, slots in the venue programme become increasingly desirable. Then the play begins. After some time, it comes to an end, and the troupe's performance for the day is finished. The audience, which ideally has been loud and enthusiastic throughout, responds heartily to the appeal for applause that concludes a Roman comedy.[1]

A brief summary such as this, drawing primarily on the information gathered in Chapter 1, depends to a large extent on reasoned guesses, and continues to leave many questions unanswered. All pre-show activity was done to support what the audience saw onstage. Performance dynamics are not always obvious, and an examination of them further illuminates what the actors are actually doing onstage. Particularly since Roman comedy was written without stage directions, the ability to perceive stage action while reading a play is a vital skill for the modern reader.

All stage action is conditioned by acting style, and its primary determinant for Roman comedy results from wearing a mask.[2] The mask possesses no peripheral vision: this is true of the actor wearing the mask, but also of the character. The mask's gaze is focused, and consequently

[1] Every play by Plautus and Terence for which the ending survives contains an appeal to the audience in the play's closing lines for applause. The appeal can be a single word, as at *Miles Gloriosus* 1437, *plaudite* ('clap!'), or a few lines. See Hunter (1985) 41.

[2] See Marshall (1999a) for a full discussion.

159

the masked actor can direct the audience's attention to a particular point on the stage. This 'spotlight' effect is particularly valuable in an outdoor theatre, where it can accomplish many of the effects that modern theatre achieves through lighting. Resulting from this is a particular style of delivery where the direction a mask faces becomes very important. Clear, unambiguous head movement to the left or to the right is needed to indicate that a character is addressing an interlocutor. When a mask faces out (to the audience), the audience can readily accept that other figures on stage remain unseen, or that they cannot hear the character. The actor can negotiate between these three dominant facings (making sharp, ninety-degree turns by 'clicking' the head out, or clicking left or right) to create a variety of effects. This leads to a positioning of the actors on stage that emphasises ninety-degree angles: characters will tend to gravitate to the left or the right of one another rather than create depth in the stage picture by being upstage or downstage. These factors govern all other considerations of stage action.

FOCUS

Where the audience focuses its attention during the performance of a play is one of the principal concerns of all those involved in a production. This is part of the challenge of directing a play, and it is something that is controlled by a variety of factors, including the actors' position on the stage ('blocking'), their gestures, and their relationship with other objects on stage and with the audience. This point at which the audience directs its attention, constantly shifting throughout the play, is the 'focus'. At any given moment during a performance, the actors should know where the audience is expected to be looking; in my experience of directing, if the actors all know where the focus is, the audience will generally agree. The focus is usually a point in the demarcated performance area, but at times it might leave it, if (for example) an actor makes his way through the audience (as I believe happened at *Curculio* 280–98) or if an actor points at an individual spectator or indicates a specific location outside the performance space (as at *Curculio* 462–86).

Since the spectators cannot concentrate their attention on the entire performance space equally, some selection must be made. Part of the actors' job is to remove possibilities, so that the desired focus is evident. Often, the words spoken direct audience attention. At the conclusion of one speech, it must be clear to the audience which character speaks next. When the actors are quick at picking up their cues, the smooth transition from one voice to the next is accompanied by a movement of spectator gaze. A harmonious transition at a speech boundary creates a fluidity that makes watching the play easy for the audience. This is the purpose of the regularity of *stichomythia* in Greek tragedy, and there are analogous devices in Roman comedy. The audience expected monologues and soliloquies from certain characters,[3] and in these circumstances the focus fixes on them.[4]

To create a clear focal point is not only the work of the character speaking. Every person on stage contributes. Any distracting action or pose from a character not speaking threatens to upstage the speaker and thereby draw focus. It is imperative for actors on any stage to be aware of the focus, and to do so in character. If the character can hear what is being said – which is generally the case, unless he or she is the victim of eavesdropping – the mask can turn and face the direction of the speaker. If the character cannot hear what is being said, the actor will often choose to freeze or make small, slow gestures intended not to draw audience attention.[5] The use of masks serves to magnify whatever actions the actors take: when the actor supports the focus, the mask indicates this clearly to the entire audience; when an actor draws focus inappropriately, it is in the nature of the mask to call attention to itself. It is the other actors on stage who ensure that the audience always looks at the focus of the scene (which is typically the speaker).

Determination of focus is not merely a factor of who is speaking, however. Short speeches from a character can be designed entirely to support another character that the audience is expected to continue watching. In *Trinummus* 729–819, for example, Megaronides and Callicles are in conversation. Though Callicles speaks almost a third of the lines, almost everything he says is in support of Megaronides. Of his eighteen speeches in the scene (in Lindsay's text; Leo deleted some), twelve are less than a line in length and all but two complete a line of verse. In terms of the scene's rhythm, Callicles completes a metrical phrase much more often than he begins one. The scene's function is largely expository, and Plautus could have written this as a soliloquy, indicating the instructions Megaronides would give to his friend, or as a monologue with the friend present as a silent, nodding accomplice. As it is, the scene

---

[3] Duckworth (1952) 103–9.

[4] Compare Andrews (1993) 185: 'An essential part of the skill of a buffoon ... had always been that of holding the attention of an audience without help, often splitting himself into multiple characters or voices in order to do so.'

[5] Granted, these are modern choices, but there must be some analogous ancient equivalent.

keeps the focus on Megaronides but allows the plan to unfold with Callicles providing prompting questions to the character who holds the focus.

Other exchanges are more challenging than this, however. Beginning at *Persa* 544, there are four characters on stage: the *leno* Dordalus, the slaves Toxilus and Sagaristio, and Saturio's daughter, the last two of whom are dressed as Easterners. Toxilus is attempting to defraud Dordalus of money by selling him a free girl as a slave – an act of legal entrapment. The *virgo* has established her virtue (and the virtue of the Arabian girl she is playing; the two are deliberately blurred) in a survey of the vices which afflict cities (lines 554–60), but Dordalus needs to question her privately. Playing on Dordalus' greed, Toxilus offers no proofs of her being a slave and so must emphasise that she is foreign (hence the disguise) and consequently valuable. Indeed, so that there can be no legal recourse, Toxilus must insist that Dordalus enter into the contract freely: lines 591–8 show Toxilus holding back an over-zealous Dordalus because Toxilus feels there are not yet enough legal safeguards.[6]

Much of the scene blocks itself. From 544 to 575 there are two pairs on stage: Toxilus and Dordalus on one side and Sagaristio and the *virgo* on the other. The two stage doors represent Dordalus' house and that of Toxilus' absent master. Dordalus is probably standing in front of his house ('Dordalus' side'), with the supposed foreigners in front of the other house ('the Persian side'). The supposed Easterners give no indications that they see Toxilus and Dordalus, and so the scene functions like an eavesdropping scene (however, the actors could use gestures and quick head turns to indicate they were aware of the pimp's presence). From lines 561–75, the focus remains on the eavesdroppers except when they call attention to the *virgo*. When Toxilus asks *vin huc vocem?* (575: 'Do you want me to call [the Persian] over here?'), Dordalus responds, *ego illo accessero* ('I'll go there'). Whatever distance existed between the pairs is closed, and Toxilus addresses Sagaristio (576). In the conversation that follows (576–90) Sagaristio and Dordalus begin negotiating for the girl. Neither is willing to name a price: Dordalus does not want to overbid on uncertain merchandise, and Sagaristio wishes to secure as much as he can for his friend. At 591, Toxilus takes Dordalus back to Dordalus' side, so that their conversation can be thought by the audience to occur outside of

---

[6] This is a more plausible dramatic motivation than Toxilus deliberately endangering his scheme; the precise details of the legal situation remain vague but the implications are clear enough that exact correspondence with Roman (or Athenian) practice does not matter during performance.

the hearing of Sagaristio and the *virgo*. Throughout this exchange, the focus remains on Dordalus. How he responds to the situation is where the dramatic interest of the scene lies.

Now the complications begin. Toxilus leaves Dordalus' side, goes to the Persian side, and tells Sagaristio that Dordalus wishes to interrogate her (599). The focus moves with Toxilus: on receiving his answer, he returns to Dordalus' side and asks why he is standing there (600). Between 603 and 604 (not a speech boundary), Dordalus probably goes to the Persian side to speak line 604. He wishes to be out of Sagaristio's earshot, and so returns to his side (if he left; perhaps he raised his voice to deliver the line; in any case, the actor shifts the focus back to the Persian side momentarily) and tells Sagaristio to tell the girl to come to him (605). She does so as Sagaristio calls to Dordalus, *percontare, exquire quid vis* (606: 'Interrogate! Ask what you wish'). As she crosses, she carries focus with her. It is evident that Dordalus stands on the far side of the stage, because the *virgo* passes by Toxilus as she approaches Dordalus. The two speak at 606–8 but are not heard by Dordalus, but perhaps he wonders why she has stopped, for Toxilus then turns to him and tells him to stand back, which Dordalus does (609). Toxilus and the *virgo* are out of Dordalus' hearing for 610, but 611 is addressed to him. Dordalus withdraws to the Persian side, but Sagaristio does not accept the focus, and it stays with Dordalus and Saturio's daughter (612–13).

All movement has been micro-managed by Toxilus. At the beginning of the scene the focus could be divided between the two pairs: the reactions of Dordalus on one side were visually balanced with the virtuous daughter of Saturio in her exotic costume on the other. Toxilus shifts between the two, often bringing audience focus with him. At *Persa* 613, both Dordalus and the *virgo* are together, and the focus will rest on Dordalus' side of the stage until 659.[7] During the interview, Toxilus is hardly in the background. He addresses both characters, as well as the audience: at 622, he calls Saturio's daughter *callida* ('clever') – an adjective that one would expect to find (in a masculine form) applied to Toxilus himself. Determining Toxilus' movements here is not possible, precisely because he is not actively manipulating others. Perhaps he stays as close as he can to the cross-examination, or perhaps he continues to hop back and forth between the two stage areas, with his lines to the

---

[7] A consequence of this is that *exquire* (615: 'ask away') almost certainly is Toxilus speaking (so Leo) and not Sagaristio (so Lindsay). For Sagaristio to speak at this point would draw focus away from Dordalus' side, which otherwise remains the site of dramatic interest in the scene.

audience being delivered when he is on the Persian side. At 659, at least, he is on Dordalus' side, for it is then that all three move to the Persian side and rejoin Sagaristio to conclude the deal. The con is completed, though the scene continues. All of this movement is required by the text, and part of the intended effect is surely to make the ruse seem complicated. Both Dordalus and the audience are distracted by the required stage movements and so are more willing to leap to the conclusion of the contract. This is the play's most challenging scene to block, but through Plautus' careful use of deictic pronouns (which are always scrupulously precise) and Toxilus' careful engineering of the stage picture, there is in fact very little in this analysis open to variation.

Most Plautine plays have a scene of comparable complexity in terms of blocking, which in rehearsal occupies a disproportionate amount of time. In *Cistellaria*, one scene depends on the focus being a stage property, the *cistella* ('little box') of the title. This in itself is not unusual: the title of *Rudens* points to another scene where a property receives the focus, a trunk (936a: *vidulum*) that is attached to a rope on one side (938: *rudentem*) and a net on the other (942: *retem*). The tug-of-war between Gripus and Trachalio continues (see, e.g. 1030–32) but the focus of the scene for the most part remains with the *vidulus* itself, which contains the recognition tokens needed for the romantic plot.[8] In *Vidularia*, there was no doubt a similar scene where the *vidulus* was the stage focus, about which we now only know *plurimum luctavimus* (fragment IX, line 94: 'We wrestled a lot'), in the words of either Cacistus or Aspasius. The first appearance of the pot of gold at *Aulularia* 449 has a similar effect.[9]

Nevertheless, *Cistellaria* is unique for what it demands in terms of stage action. At *Cistellaria* 631 Melaenis, her maid Halisca, and Selenium come onstage. Melaenis produces the *cistella* for Selenium, *nam hic crepundia insunt* (635: 'for in here are [your] childhood toys'). She hands it to Halisca, and tells her to knock at Demipho's door (637). Whether Halisca moves or not, and regardless of where they are onstage, this clear instruction shifts the focus to one of the two doors. The playwright has tricked the audience, however, for it is the other door that opens, as Alcesimarchus leaves his house holding a sword (642) to deliver 639 (an apostrophe of Death that partakes of a suicide *lazzo* also found at *Asinaria*

---

[8] See Ketterer (1986c) 68 n. 12.

[9] See discussion in Chapter 1. This principle that name-scenes are also the scenes with the most complex stagecraft also holds true for *Asinaria*, if we take the 'ass' of the title to be Argyrippus carrying his servant Libanus (see lines 545–745), which is one level at which the title operates.

606–7).[10] His delivery is to the audience and consequently he does not see the women, who fear for his safety (*Cistellaria* 642–5):

MEL. *quid tibi est?*

SEL.   *Alcesimarchum non vides? ferrum tenet.*

ALC. *ecquid agis? remorare. lumen linque.*

SEL.   *amabo, accurrite,*
ne se interemat.

ALC.   *o Salute mea salus salubrior,*
tu nunc, si ego volo seu nolo, sola me ut vivam facis.

MEL. (*to Selenium*) What's wrong?

SEL. (*to Melaenis*) Don't you see Alcesimarchus? He's got a sword!

ALC. (*to himself*) Do you do anything? Lingerer! Leave the light!

SEL. (*to Melaenis and Halisca*) Please, run, so he doesn't kill himself!

ALC. (*to Selenium*) O my saviour, safer than the Saviour –
You alone ensure that I live, whether I wish to or not.

Something happens in 644 between these last two speeches. Selenium's plural imperative tells both Melaenis and Halisca to stop Alcesimarchus' suicide attempt, and since she is addressed next, it is probable that she rushes forward as well. What happens at this point is not clear. Perhaps all rush forward, they crash into one another, and Alcesimarchus catches Selenium, so that he can then call her his *salus*. He has not seen them until now (they have been eavesdropping). By line 646, Melaenis has regained some of her composure as she doubts his actual intentions. The confusion at this moment is great, as all four characters move around the stage. At 650 Alcesimarchus carries Selenium into his house, and at 652 Melaenis and Halisca follow them, leaving the stage empty, almost.

During the rush at line 644, Halisca dropped the *cistella*. Though it was unnoticed at the time, Lampadio finds the dropped property at 655–6: *sed quid hoc est, haec quod cistella hic iacet | cum crepundiis?* ('But what is this, this little box lying here with toys?'). This is the only time in Roman comedy that a significant object is left alone onstage. Unnoticed by the text, the plot requires that the object be dropped, left, and remain unnoticed by the characters. The narrow gaze of the mask helps the

---

[10] Terminology can be tricky, if we are to avoid negative connotations with the term 'stock routine'. The vaudeville term 'schtick', which suggests familiarity without the inorganic distancing of a 'stock routine', or the *commedia dell'arte* term *lazzo* might be more precise: it should be possible to assemble a catalogue of Plautine *lazzi* such as those which exist for Italian comedy in the sixteenth century (such as Gordon (1983)).

audience to accept that these characters fail to see the dropped object. While this sort of action is unparalleled, Plautus has fully visualised the stage action, and creates a moment where a stage property left alone onstage holds the audience focus, without a single line of dialogue in support: 'The positions of all the actors are at this moment dictated by the box.'[11]

Cistellaria and *Persa* both have scenes in which characters speak and are not heard by other characters on stage. Yet it is not the case that the characters are speaking 'aside', since vocal delivery in the mask is so stylised that naturalism cannot be said to be operating (and an aside presumes a normal mode of delivery that maintains the dramatic illusion[12]), nor are the characters speaking *sotto voce*: during an outdoor masked performance any 'stage whisper' is going to be loud, clear, and hardly distinguishable from normal delivery, except by overt gesture. We have seen how Plautus ensures the audience remains aware of the ever-moving focus. There are other techniques available to the playwright as he manipulates stage focus, the most obvious of which is when the focus is divided between two locations – the split-focus scene. Typically in Plautus the stage action presents characters onstage in two groups, with one character (or more) on one side of the stage, and one character (or more) on another side.[13] Given the mechanisms of vocal delivery in masks, it is likely that the groupings would be balanced, as was the case at *Persa* 544–75: having one grouping upstage of the other turns some masks away from the audience more than ninety degrees, reducing audibility and potentially confusing the interrelationships between characters.

Split-focus scenes typically take two forms. Sometimes, neither character is aware of the other. Two characters both face out, and address the audience unaware that the other is there, as at *Persa* 1–16, where both Toxilus and Sagaristio, though standing next to each other, face out and are unaware of each other's presence. *Persa* 1–16 atypically mirrors the action on both sides, as at Aristophanes, *Acharnians* 1095–1234.[14] The effect for the audience is like watching a tennis game: the focus shifts back and forth as the spectators anticipate where the focus will be next (*stichomythia* creates a similar effect in Greek tragedy). As first speaker, we expect Toxilus to take the lead, but it is Sagaristio who temporarily wins the role

---

[11] Ketterer (1986c) 35, and see 32–3 and 36.
[12] See Bain (1977), esp. 154–84, and, for delivery, Marshall (1999a).
[13] Fitzpatrick (1985) isolates a similar tendency in the *commedia dell'arte*.   [14] See Marshall (1997b).

of *callidus*, as he subsequently seeks to learn the source of his friend's affliction. The comedy of such a situation lies in its pretence and artificiality. Non-naturalistic delivery allows the audience to accept the characters' behaviour as normative within the dramatic world.

Eavesdropping creates a more common type of split-focus scene: the character or characters on one side of the stage are aware of the presence of those on the other side, but such awareness operates only in one direction. These scenes are easily established, as a Plautine fragment demonstrates: *sed leno egreditur foras; | hinc ex occulto sermonatus sublegam* ('But the pimp is coming outside; I'll overhear his speech from here secretly').[15] The word *hinc* does not refer to an upstage alleyway – the old view of the *angiportum* – but designates another side of the stage, perhaps slightly upstage (*Casina* 443), where the eavesdropper remains unseen by the other characters. The speaker remains fully visible to the audience, but hidden from the play's characters. The mechanism of eavesdropping allies the audience with the eavesdroppers, since both groups possess full awareness of the stage situation: this is one way the *servus callidus* creates rapport with the audience.[16] From the audience's perspective, both types of the split-focus scene divide the focus between two locations in the performance area, and expect the spectators to shift their attention back and forth between the two rigidly preserved areas.

If there is one aspect of Roman performance that resists even the most generous speculation, it is the use of gesture:[17] an actor's finger pointing at a character or object can direct focus more effectively than almost anything else the actor can do. There are three reasons for this difficulty. First, the evidence is late, and often of undeterminable date. Quintilian provides many examples of the application of theatrical gestures to the podium of the orator, but his reference point is the style of theatrical

[15] Scholars disagree where the fragment belongs: *Vidularia* fragment XX Leo; *Aulularia* fragment VII Lindsay.

[16] In this light, the eavesdropping scene at *Asinaria* 851–908, with Artemona and the Parasite spying on Demaenetus' dinner with Philaenium and Argyrippus, demonstrates how inverted the situation at the end of the play is. By having the *matrona* eavesdrop on the lusty *senex*, the stage picture disempowers him at exactly the time he asks to spend a night with his son's *meretrix*. The stage action works counter to the moral difficulties of the situation, so that at no point does the audience have the opportunity to consider the consequences of the proposed scenario (which would otherwise probably offend the sensibilities of many in the audience). Within an eavesdropping scene, Demaenetus' behaviour is seen as shocking, but due for inevitable punishment.

[17] See Graf (1991); De Jorio (2000) is valuable but is too positivistic about the continuity of meaning for a particular gesture over the centuries.

productions in the first century A D.[18] The manuscripts of Terence provide many illustrations purporting to derive from productions of Roman comedy, but precisely what they represent and to which century the original performance should be dated remain unknown.[19] Second, all gestures are, by definition, conventional. A culture agrees to the meaning of a given position of the hand, and the nuance is determined by cultural consensus. The semiotic value conveyed could as easily be attached to another gesture: there is nothing inherent in a circle made by my thumb and forefinger, with the remaining fingers raised and separated, that signifies things are 'okay'; that value has been fixed artificially, and its comprehensibility depends on pre-knowledge of its meaning. The meaning of any such cultural sign changes over time, and a premium is placed on the variability of such signs.[20] It would be more surprising if a gesture did not change its valence over time. Third, gestures represent a combination of both hand position and movement. Artistic representations (whether in illustrated manuscripts, vase-paintings, or terracotta figurines) necessarily lose the dimension of movement, and this obscures their nature. If I hold up my hand and face my palm towards someone approaching me on the street, this gesture can signify 'hello', 'goodbye', or 'stop' depending on the movement of my wrist and arm; nevertheless a photograph might not be able to distinguish the three gestures which would be easily and instantly communicated to anyone in my culture. While almost certainly Roman comic actors could employ culturally conditioned gestures signifying forcefulness, restraint, belligerence, compliance, etc. (to list the first four gestures Dodwell identifies),[21] I am sceptical that we can hope to ascribe a particular meaning to a given gesture for Roman stagecraft.

The loss of the understanding of gesture is particularly acute, because it would seem (judging from Quintilian) that quite elaborate hand gestures were employed. The techniques of *cheironomia* (the use of hand gestures, particularly in dance) cannot be recovered. This should not lead to despair, because while we may not know what gestures were employed in a given circumstance, we may feel confident that some gesture was used,

---

[18] Further, since we are removed also from Quintilian's world, the exact nature of the analogy can escape us. It is possible that he evokes gesture as used in mime.

[19] Dodwell (2000) is the most recent attempt to answer these questions; see also Jones and Morey (1931).

[20] Dodwell (2000) 61–5 in fact attributes the same meaning ('agreement, approval') to almost the same gesture: the hand is held in the same position but the wrist tilts back so that the palm faces up.

[21] Dodwell (2000) 40–60.

and we can trust that it was an appropriate one. Given the larger-than-life qualities that result from actors performing in masks, it is even likely that any gestures would be exaggerated when presented on the stage. Stylisation and local custom are key determinants of meaning: Lecoq describes 'the art of mime, which reaches its highest expression in Japanese Noh theatre, when the actor mimes his anger by means of a few vibrations of his fan'.[22] Part of the reason this works is that 'the *manner* in which a functional gesture is carried out can be universally interpreted if emotion is involved'.[23]

Gestures cannot be deduced from the text, and can often be counter-intuitive. This has no bearing on audience impact, as this claim about the *commedia* attests:

> when Pantalone falls into a rage and does a somersault, the spectators should not say: 'what a wonderful somersault!', but 'what an amazing rage!' To achieve this level of physical commitment and to justify this gesture, an extraordinary emotive charge is required, as well as perfect technique in the somersault.[24]

Here, though, gesture begins to blur into *lazzo: in fabulis iuvenum, senum, militum, matronarum gravior ingressus est, servi, ancillulae, parasiti, piscatores citatius moventur* (Quintilian 11.3.112: 'On the stage the gait of young men, of old men, of military characters and of matrons is somewhat slow; while male or female slaves, parasites and fishermen move with great agility'[25]). Quintilian presents stereotypes that largely coincide with stock characters: the *senex*, the *adulescens*, the *miles*, etc. He is not using stage terms precisely,[26] because his true interest does not lie with the stage.

There is also a level of common sense that must be kept in mind when thinking about gesture. While there was probably a gesture for speaking – Dodwell describes the *adlocutio* gesture 'in which the speaker crooks one or two fingers ... towards the person or persons addressed as if to hold his, or their, attention'[27] – this does not mean that every speaking character needs to make the gesture as he speaks. That would be too reductive. Gestures are not regulated so strictly, but are a means of enhancing communication available to the actors – communication both between dramatic characters and between actors and the audience. An actor may choose to use an appropriate gesture or not. If this conclusion seems to downplay the importance of gesture, that is because visual

---

[22] Lecoq (2001) 22.   [23] Hughes (1991) 12.
[24] Lecoq (2001) 116.   [25] Tr. Dodwell (2000) 28 n. 30.
[26] For example, Plautus does not typically use *iuvenis* and its cognates; *adulescens* would be expected.
[27] Dodwell (2000) 35.

evidence is likely to over-represent its use. Because static artistic media lose the dimensions of movement, speech, and time, there is a tendency to compensate through the depiction of something that can be represented: since the viewer cannot hear dialogue, or otherwise determine which character is speaking, a speaking gesture in the Terentian illustrations presents information that would be otherwise clear in a performance context.

Though precise gestures are not recoverable, it is possible to isolate something of what they might convey through Keith Johnstone's term, 'status'. Status represents a quality about the relationship between a person, particularly a dramatic character, and someone or something else. Status, a gradated scale from low to high, describes aspects of the way a character behaves:

Status is a confusing term until it's understood as something one *does*. You may be in low social status, but play high, and vice versa ... Status seems to me to be a useful term, providing the difference between the status you are and the status you play is understood.[28]

High status characters may be bold, confident, authoritative, and skilled. Low status characters may be shy, awkward, hesitant, or pass unnoticed. For Johnstone, 'status is basically territorial':[29] high status characters take up space when they sit down, low status characters keep their arms in their laps, minimising the space they occupy. A status dynamic exists whenever a character is onstage: when two characters interact, at any point one has higher status than the other. This can change over the course of a scene, where a character starts high status and ends low status: it can be argued that such transitions are a necessary part of interesting theatre.[30] Status dynamics are at work even when characters are alone onstage, as they relate to the space they are in, or to the audience. The neutral and uniform representation of the stage as a generic street means that typically Plautine characters are not lower status than the environment, though exceptions do exist: Harpax's hesitant entry in the unfamiliar city at *Pseudolus* 595–9 shows he is out of place, and the

---

[28] Johnstone (1979) 36, and 33–74, (1999) 219–31, and Marshall (1993) for status generally. Johnstone distinguishes 'social status' (what you are: a duchess, a tramp) from 'status' (what you play: haughty, reserved). When I teach status to actors and improvisers, I use the term 'social position' for the former, to avoid the verbal overlap.

[29] Johnstone (1981) 57.

[30] An alternative pattern to the scene of status reversal is the scene with two characters in competition, each trying to assert a higher status over the other.

unexpectedly familiar reception of Sosicles (Menaechmus II) as he wanders Epidamnus similarly keeps him continuously off his guard and therefore of lower status than his environment.

Status analysis provides a means to describe one of the most common situations in Roman comedy, the master–servant relationship. Slavery and other institutions of social stratification in the Roman republic establish differences of social position and prescribe an expected status relationship. A cornerstone of the western comic tradition is to invert these relationships by having servants play high status and masters play low – a relationship seen in Plautus' *servi callidi*, Molière's Sganarelle, and P. G. Wodehouse's Jeeves. The emphasis in status analysis is on what the actor does. An actor's gestures, posture, vocal quality, etc. cannot be recovered, but we can be confident that, in a given situation, one character behaves in a way appropriate to the status relationship, even though that might not coincide with the character's social position.

Status is a useful analytical device for actors and directors, but I introduce it here to emphasise the way that status differs from focus. The audience does not need to focus on the character with the highest status: more often than not, it is the actions of the lowest status character that are expected to be the point of audience attention. For example, *Miles Gloriosus* 1–78 establishes the nature of the vainglorious braggart Pyrgopolynices. Artotrogus, his parasite, is present, but is entirely subservient to the *miles*. One might expect the natural way to play such a scene would have the *miles* never formally acknowledge Artotrogus, but continually face the audience, maintaining high status and holding focus as much as possible, with Artotrogus as a low status servant fluttering and flattering around him. This is, indeed, the overt tenor of the scene. Central to the characterisation of the soldier, however, is the fact that this pretence slips occasionally. At lines 19–24, Artotrogus addresses the audience and tells them directly that the soldier's exploits are all false. This is the moment of status transition, after which the soldier will always have a lower status than the parasite. Metatheatrical address is an inherently high status activity in which a character is not even bound by the theatrical world, and the accompanying deflation of Pyrgopolynices' claims demonstrates an underlying status reality that works against the social positions of the characters. Artotrogus continues to anticipate his master's needs (as a good servant should), but the status relationship that emerges is one in which Pyrgopolynices appears dependant upon the sycophancy. Artotrogus' generous arithmetic (47: *recte rationem tenes*, 'that's some sum you have') and outrageous invention (58–9: *amant ted omnes mulieres*

neque iniuria | *qui sis tam pulcher,* 'all women love you, and no mistake –
since you're so pretty') demonstrate that he is in control of the situation.
This manifests itself in performance both by having Artotrogus regularly
receive focus, but also in the actor's stage mannerisms that show he is not
cowed by the *miles*. Since the deflation of Pyrgopolinices with him
unaware of its happening is the purpose of the scene, whenever the focus
rests on him after line 24, it settles on a low status character trying to act
high (the actor is then available to play both Sceledrus and Lurcio,[31]
different types of low status characters).

A final example shows how elements of status and focus combine. The
most challenging stage action in *Miles Gloriosus* occurs between 1216 and
1353, a passage framed on either side by a dialogue between Palaestrio and
Pyrgopolinices (1200–15, 1354–77). Acroteleutium and Milphidippa enter
(1216–26), and stage a conversation for the benefit of the eavesdropping
Pyrgopolinices. They explain what they are doing carefully to each other
and the audience, but out of the soldier's hearing. While the focus is split,
the normally high status position of eavesdropping is undermined by the
women's awareness and manipulation of the situation. The focus shifts
momentarily to the eavesdroppers (1227), establishing for the audience
that despite the women's awareness, the 'rules' of eavesdropping continue
to apply. Because this situation is carefully anticipated in the narrative,
the exchange can continue, with the women's conversation teasing the
oblivious soldier. Every time the focus shifts to him, his pride in what
they are saying deflates him further, and shows the success of the ruse.
Acroteleutium can make a prophetic joke about his body odour (1255–6);
she can see him (as he pretends not to be listening) but claims to be afraid
to approach (1260–62). Characters in the separate areas of the stage
can even address one another (1267: *vos volo,* 'I want you … ', says
Milphidippa; Pyrgopolinices answers, *et nos te,* ' … and we want you!').
The women arouse the soldier's ardour, and then depart (1280), leaving
him with Palaestrio on stage. As the women exit, Pleusicles, disguised as a
ship's captain, enters from the wing (1281), shifting the focus there. He
soliloquises (1284–91) and then speaks so as to be overheard (1292–7),
apparently establishing another false eavesdropping scene, until he turns
to the door. Palaestrio and Pyrgopolinices approach Pleusicles.[32] Because

---

[31] I accept Fleckeisen's proposal for this slave's name (against the manuscripts' Lucrio) not only to
help with scansion at 843, but because it is etymologically desirable for the drunken slave's name to
be associated with gluttony.

[32] Many other characters in the play also have polysyllabic plosive-prone names: Periplectomenus,
Philocomasium (*ph-* pronounced as an aspirated *p-*, as in Greek), and Milphidippa. Yet another

the focus is on Pleusicles, Palaestrio does not play high status (which could distract) but goes inside (1305), emerging with Philocomasium (1310), with attendants carrying her belongings.

Only Pyrgopolynices does not know Pleusicles' true identity, and in the exchange that follows (1311–53) the comedy depends on this, as Philocomasium is overly friendly with this supposedly anonymous captain. Overt public displays of affection are comically inappropriate at 1315–16, 1335–6, and 1345–6, and at each of them, the status of the lovers is raised and that of the soldier lowered as he fails to see through the increasingly implausible trick. None of this matters, of course:

Here too we have the inverse relation characteristic of the ad lib, in which the subordinate goal of the action serves mainly to act out comic business as inventively as possible. Nevertheless, the balancing act, however wanton, never signifies a real risk. Pleusicles could have behaved far more crazily; he'd still have got the girl in any case.[33]

The most awkward piece of stage action in the play occurs at *Miles Gloriosus* 1329–31:

PHIL.	*obsecro licet complecti prius quam proficisco?*
PYRG.	*licet.*
PHIL.	*o mi ocule, o mi anime.*
PAL.	*obsecro, tene mulierem,*
	ne adfligatur.
PYRG.	*quid istuc quaesost?*

PHIL.	Please, may I have a last embrace
	Before I leave you?
PYRG.	Yes, you may.
PHIL.	Oh, my dearest! Oh, my darling!
	(*Hurling herself at* PYRGOPOLYNICES, *she slips past him and faints into* PLEUSICLES' *arms.*)
PAL.	Watch out there! Catch the woman,
	Don't let her hurt herself.
PYRG.	What's going on?
	(tr. Smith)

level of the humour is operating purely on the fun of such names in the actors' mouths, which possess an inherent comedy (compare Margaret Atwood's claim: 'because, as you know, the P is the funniest letter in the alphabet' (Gzowski (1997), track 12). *Trinummus* 905–22 has similar fun with names beginning with C.

[33] Vogt-Spira (2001) 103, translated from Vogt-Spira (1995).

Smith's stage direction notes the awkwardness. Nixon instead has Philocomasium fall first on the soldier, and, as Palaestrio speaks at 1330–31, he is 'drawing her away and guiding her tottering steps to Pleusicles'.[34] Whatever happens, Philocomasium, holding focus, plays low status (asking for an embrace) but nevertheless ends up in her lover's arms. Nixon's stage direction places Palaestrio in a stronger position than he has had throughout this scene, while Smith's stage direction emphasises the implausible unpredictability of the event. However the swoon is managed, the Philocomasium actor must behave in a way unlike any other character in the play, while wearing a mask, and always ensuring that his character holds focus.

PACE

The action of a Roman comedy was performed continuously, and without any break.[35] There were no intermissions, and a play could last anywhere from an hour to more than two: when stage action, comic business, and audience reaction are factored into the running time of a show, an average of ten to twelve lines per minute proves to be a very quick pace.[36] The division of the extant Roman comedies into scenes and acts is the work of later ages and bears no connection to the original performance, to dramatic structure, to a second-century literary aesthetic, or to the relationship of the play to its Greek original. The overlap between Menander's *Dis Exapatôn* and Plautus' *Bacchides* shows that Plautus can remove a Greek act division completely. Indeed, the most natural structuring pattern to the *fabulae palliatae* is completely independent of entrances and exits. Nevertheless, act divisions continue to be published in modern texts, creating a false sense of the pace of ancient performance.

One of the most elusive quantities when staging a play is maintaining an appropriate pace. The energy and momentum created by the stage action communicates with the audience, and a well-crafted play can

---

[34] Nixon (1924) 271, italics removed.
[35] See the discussions at Conrad (1915), Weissinger (1940) 69–70, 77–83, Duckworth (1952) 98–101, and Beare (1964) 196–218.
[36] Running times in Plautine plays I have directed averaged 65 minutes for *Curculio* (729 lines), 80 minutes for *Asinaria* (947 lines), and 125 minutes for *Miles Gloriosus* (1437 lines). Though it is easy to read the text much faster than this, other factors can add up to one-third to the length of the running time, while still maintaining a very fast dramatic pace (by modern standards, which I take to be greater than ancient ones). In particular, these times include the actors' improvisational expansions, which comprise the most substantial contributions to the increased running time.

suggest an appropriate momentum to the actors and director. Horace indeed commends Plautus' mastery of pace, and by comparing his with that of Epicharmus in the early fifth century[37] implies that the playwright's mastery of this aspect exceeds that of the Greek authors of Old and New Comedy. In my experience directing Roman comedy for modern audiences, how the show can be 'tightened' is always the primary concern in the final rehearsals. Maintaining the momentum created by the narrative places great demands upon the actors. But it is not a matter of the actors delivering lines faster. The speed of delivery must never endanger clarity of enunciation, characterisation, or the proper timing associated with a joke. Rather, the most substantial gains are achieved by reducing the space between lines, by 'jumping the cues'. By one measure, the result of such work is minimal – running time might be reduced by three or four minutes (though I have known improvement of up to ten minutes); yet the consequence of this work for an audience is phenomenal. A breathless pace pulls the spectators along, and more actively involves them in the narrative. This is not a matter of rushing through the play: the actors can make pauses and luxuriate in their lines mid-speech, just not at a speech boundary. There is room for physical comedy, too, but again the loss of momentum is minimised when it occurs during a speech. When actors develop this habit in the delivery of their lines, it allows for them on occasion to take a beat at a speech boundary, which, because it varies the established tempo so obviously, is noticed by the audience.

This understanding of dramatic pace is subjective (just as the experience of it in the theatre is), but is supported by a cluster of examples, which demonstrate in different ways how Plautus has his actors maintain the pace of the performance. The plays possess a primary internal structure based on metre and music that affects the tempo of the play as it is experienced by both actors and audiences (see Chapter 5). First, though, it is necessary to understand the support mechanisms at work in performance which reinforce this dramatic structure. These mechanisms modulate between the audience's experience of time during the performance and the passing of time for the dramatic characters. On the one hand, the audience's experience of time possesses two dimensions: actual time and subjective time. Time passes inevitably as a play is acted. The audience experiences the play linearly, and cannot stop, go back, and

---

[37] *Epistles* 2.1.58: *Plautus ad exemplar Siculi properare Epicharmi*, 'Plautus [is said] to bustle, on the model of the Sicilian Epicharmus.'

re-watch an interesting, funny, or challenging scene in the way a reader can.[38] How the audience experiences time passing, though, is entirely subjective, and will vary from one spectator to the next. When the actors successfully modulate their pace, jumping on cues and maintaining an energy that can carry the audience with it, time seems to pass more quickly. There are other techniques that slow the experience of time passing, which at times (such as during a solo *canticum* or some other 'set piece') may be a desirable goal; but a faster pace is preferred.[39] On the other hand is the passing of time as experienced by the characters. Within the play, time is much more flexible. Offstage events may transpire more quickly than they would in real life. This, of course, is unexceptional, but does point to an 'Elasticity of dramatic time'[40] as it is experienced by characters in the play. Between *Menaechmi* 441 and 464, for example, Sosicles has time for lunch and sex with Erotium, and the brevity creates a humorous effect. The flexibility of dramatic time is occasionally apparent to the characters themselves: at *Andria* 474–5, when Simo hears Glycerium shouting within as she gives birth, he exclaims *hui! tam cito? ridiculum. postquam ante ostium | me audivit stare, approperat* ('Well! So soon? Ridiculous! After she heard I was standing before the door, she sped up!'). In Plautus, the most extreme dilations coincide with an 'empty stage' (as at *Menaechmi* 445) but in performance concerns for the audience's experience of time remain primary.

From time to time in Plautus the stage is 'empty', as when one character leaves and another enters with no interaction between the two. There may be anywhere between two and ten such empty stages in a play.[41] For example, at *Curculio* 370, Curculio, Phaedromus, and Palinurus enter Phaedromus' house, creating an 'empty stage' before Lyco enters to deliver line 371.[42] Since the three characters leave the stage through a door, and the banker Lyco enters by a wing, their paths do not cross, and consequently there does not actually need to be a moment when the stage is physically empty. Since Lyco's speech is delivered facing

---

[38] This fact is central to the analyses of Slater (2000).

[39] I should stress that this is not a factor of the play being a comedy. Exactly the same issues face the actors in a tragedy, where the maintenance of a quick pace is also essential. The final rehearsals of an ancient tragedy are spent the same way, tightening the cues so that the narrative mechanism can unwind itself more smoothly. In either case, the actors' technique remains the same, though the effect on the audience is different, as are the specific benefits of creating the pace.

[40] Duckworth (1952) 130, and see 127–32 and Beare (1964) 210–14.

[41] Beare (1964) 213, citing two in *Mostellaria* and *Andria*, ten in *Rudens* and *Adelphoe*. Empty stages are therefore a factor independent of author, date, or play length. While there is room for disagreement about some examples, Weissinger (1940) 86 provides a convenient checklist.

[42] Gilula (1996) 483 n. 9.

the audience, and in his mask the character is thought by the audience to have no peripheral vision, there is no need for the actors to jeopardise the play's momentum by introducing a pause.[43] Lyco speaks 371–83[44] and Curculio emerges from the house, calling back to those inside as he does so (384–5), before addressing the audience. In the minute or so of actual time that the audience has experienced with Lyco on stage, regardless of how it was experienced subjectively, much more time has passed for the stage characters, so that the professional parasite can have eaten a full meal and feel stuffed, almost (386–8). Perhaps the audience is meant to understand that an hour or two has elapsed between 370 and 371. However, it only becomes clear that time has passed at 384, at which point the audience needs to think back and reposition the soliloquy it has just watched in the mental picture of the play's chronology that is being built; in some instances (e.g. following the empty stage between 590 and 591), no explicit indication ever comes. This creates a problem, because in performance, two things are happening. The audience's perception of dramatic time may accept that at any empty stage 'time passes': the plays present no negative evidence to the supposition that the empty stage was a convention – an accepted shorthand for indicating something in the dramatic world, similar perhaps to the swirling hands on a clock face, once used for this purpose in twentieth-century cinema. Simultaneously, the actors must constantly be aware of the pace as the audience perceives real time passing. Since it is a convention, the stage action associated with the moments identified as an 'empty stage' can be almost anything, as long as it accords with accepted practice. We do not know what the convention was, but it is improbable that it would negatively impact upon the pace of the performance.

There are three ways that the so-called 'empty stage' can be treated in performance. The first is a simultaneous transition, with the entry and exit happening at the same time on different parts of the stage (as I described Lyco's entry at *Curculio* 371). The second possibility is a momentarily empty stage: a pause for a second or two might not interrupt the

---

[43] In my production of *Curculio*, the Phaedromus actor doubled as Lyco, a move contrived as a 'most difficult case' for lightning changes. In practice, the Phaedromus actor entered his house first and began his costume change assisted by those already backstage, while Curculio and Phaedromus performed an 'after you'/'no, after you' routine, enhanced by Palinurus' clowning. This effect is separate from the one described in the main body of the text, but both can exist simultaneously, appreciated to various degrees by different spectators.

[44] Bothe deleted line 374, and Leo also deleted 377–9; Lindsay keeps the whole speech. None of these excisions affects the present argument, except to enhance the effect described slightly. See also Zwierlein (1990) 251–3, who removes 374 but not 377–9.

momentum significantly. The third possibility is that the empty stage would be accompanied by an overt signal to the audience that time is passing, such as a musical interlude from the *tibicen*. This last possibility seemed attractive to scholars in the nineteenth and early twentieth centuries, whose theatrical tastes were conditioned both by the system of act breaks found throughout modern European theatre and by the prominence of naturalistic storytelling in the theatre of the time. This technique however presents the greatest threat to the maintenance of a smooth pace, as the actors risk losing the attention of the audience. Except for the pause at *Pseudolus* 573a, there is no positive evidence for this sort of interlude.[45] Even though it may be 'conventional', any interruption jeopardises the momentum.

By minimising the length of the interruption, the actors create an unresolved disjunction between real time as experienced by the audience and dramatic time as experienced by the characters. How we understand the spectators to handle such conflict is central to an appreciation of what Plautus is doing in his plays. For those audience members who notice the disjunction at *Curculio* 370, it is funny that Curculio has eaten a whole meal in the past minute, and such a conclusion predisposes the spectators to interpret other unreconciled disjunctions similarly. Besides, the comedy proceeds: immediately following this, Curculio adopts his 'One-eye' disguise (line 391), and the subject has changed. If the Plautine stage world is non-naturalistic,[46] the conflict of dramatic time persists, and is

---

[45] See Slater (2000) 108 n. 19. This is the only explicit reference to a pipe solo in Plautus (Beare (1964) 212–13; see Hunter (1985) 38–40), perhaps introduced because the Pseudolus actor needs a short break (Beare (1964) 228, and Paratore (1959)). More likely this is primarily a device to facilitate the introduction of a musical section, as with the pause between *Cistellaria* 630 and 631. It might also be funny. Humour could be played two ways. Perhaps Pseudolus returns straightaway, interrupting the soloist before the first bar is complete. It might be equally appropriate to lengthen the pause. The *tibicen* stops to indicate Pseudolus' return to the stage, and, when no one emerges, the music begins again for a reprise. The comic effect could be repeated many times: in the recording of the song 'Ice Cream Man' by Jonathan Richman and the Modern Lovers (*Modern Lovers Live*, 1977, track 4) the song itself is finished in three minutes. The track, however, lasts eight minutes and eleven seconds: the remainder consists of seven encores, over the course of which Richman repeats the full song, often introducing a verse with the words 'one more time'. Either option would be funny, and both would be meaningful to an audience that has been alerted to the tension that exists in *Pseudolus* between urgency and delay (see Marshall (1996)). In an informal conversation with Richman in 2003, he indicated to me that this was an unplanned routine and that this was the only performance in which the song was extended this way. He felt the comic effect from this improvisatory expansion interfered with the haunting nostalgia he wanted the song to evoke. However staged, there is no reason to see the interlude as a break in the performance.

[46] Among many other restrictions, naturalistic drama requires the audience's experience of dramatic time to be as close as possible to the actual passing of time. More scathing is Meyerhold's

reconciled only in the audience's imagination. If this is accepted as an appropriate way for Plautus to create humour, then the tendency towards the simultaneous transitions at an 'empty stage' (i.e. that the stage is never actually empty) is reinforced.

But this cannot always be the solution. Occasionally, as at the break between *Heauton Timoroumenos* 170 and 171, the stage needs to be empty. Chremes speaks (169–74):[47]

> *tempust monere me hunc vicinum Phaniam*
> *ad cenam ut veniat. ibo, visam si domist.*
> *nil opus fuit monitore. iamdudum domi*
> *praesto apud me esse aiunt. egomet convivas moror.*
> *ibo adeo hinc intro. sed quid crepuerunt fores*
> *hinc a me? quisnam egreditur? huc concessero.*

It's time to remind my neighbour Phania here to come over for dinner. I'll go and see if he's at home. (*he disappears into Phania's house and reappears almost immediately*) He didn't need reminding. They say he's been over at my place for some time. I'm the one who's keeping the guests waiting. I'll go straight in. But that's my door. Who's coming out? I'll stand aside here. (*he does so*)

Chremes creates an empty stage and, since it is he who next enters, the transition cannot be simultaneous. Either it is for a very short time without any other conventional marker (as Barsby suggests), or it is prolonged and accompanied by a marker. Whether the Greek original had an act break at this point is irrelevant: the lines must be interpretable in a Roman context, and, since the visit to Phania's house does not advance the plot (Phania is already at Chremes' house, where Chremes goes four lines later), we are obliged to seek a non-narrative reason for this exchange. The whole speech is addressed to the audience, and the last two lines introduce a familiar stock routine that serves as a lead-in to a very short split-focus scene (175–9). Other stage action is taking place: after Chremes begins line 174, his door opens and Clitipho emerges, still unseen by Chremes when he asks *quisnam egreditur?* The timing of the

---

assessment: 'The naturalistic theatre denies not only the spectator's ability to imagine for himself, but even his ability to understand clever conversation' (Meyerhold (1969) 27).

[47] Text and translation, Barsby (2001) vol. I: 194–5. Following the stage direction at 170 is the following note: 'This momentary vacating of the stage is awkward and unusual. It is likely that in the Greek original there was a divine prologue (omitted by Terence) between Chremes' disappearance and reappearance. It is also likely that Phania's house was conceived of as situated somewhere offstage in the Greek version; this passage is the only reason for placing it onstage in Terence' (194–5 n. 23).

entrance overlaps with a speech and does not occur at a speech bound-ary.[48] The effect of the empty stage is a transient one, and a lengthy interval at this point would confuse the momentum for the rest of the speech. More likely, this is Terence's joke: Chremes' near-instantaneous re-emergence from Phania's house gets a laugh, as does the fact that the trip was pointless in any case, as does the split-focus scene that follows.

This and general considerations of pace suggest the regular use of simultaneous transitions in Roman comedy, and only the shortest of pauses when that is not possible. Later in Terence's play, another empty stage pushes the limits of what is possible. At *Heauton Timoroumenos* 409, Antiphila, Bacchis, Clinia, and Syrus enter Chremes' house. Chremes appears at the same door, announcing *luciscit hoc iam* (410: 'now it is getting light'). Since this transition uses the same door, it cannot be simultaneous, but neither is a long pause required. Chremes' first words establish the necessary facts, and are presented in such a direct way that the audience has the opportunity to laugh at the contrast between dramatic time and actual time if the pause is very short. The outdoor venue does not offer the option of dimming the lights between lines 409 and 410, which would be the natural recourse in a naturalistic indoor theatre.

A possible exception occurs at *Aulularia* 627, when Euclio enters the temple and emerges to speak line 628, dragging Strobilus with him. As with Chremes' entrance at *Heauton Timoroumenos* 171, the instant re-appearance of the same character can serve a comic end. However, since in the play what transpires within the temple is a struggle, there is a way that a pause could be used without interrupting the play's momentum. If from within the temple there emerged comic sound effects indicating the struggle (effectively letting sound hold focus and constitute the needed onstage presence), the audience would have sufficient resources to pre-serve the play's momentum. Exaggerated noises – resounding crashes or the clanging of pots and pans[49] – in this context could yield a different

---

[48] Translators typically place the stage direction at the speech boundary, which can create a false sense of an empty stage. For entrance and exit announcements, see Duckworth (1952) 114–21.

[49] These examples are offered *exempli gratia*. In a comic context, the sound effects do not even need to be appropriate for a struggle, as Tregoweth (Treg) Brown regularly demonstrated in the sound effects he produced for Warner Brothers cartoons: 'in one sequence when Coyote got his foot caught in the line attached to a harpoon and was dragged willy-nilly across the desert floor over cacti, under boulders, bumping and slapping every obstacle possible, never once did Treg supply a logical sound effect: flying springs, breaking bottles, small explosives, human ouch'es and oof's, popping balloons, railroad crossing bells, and so on' (Jones (1989) 191). Comedy resides in the inappropriateness of sounds and what they suggest to each spectator's imagination.

comic result. We do not know that Plautus did this, but it remains a technique available to him that would not upset the principles of pace that have been discussed.

A similar example comes at *Menaechmi* 875. After Sosicles has feigned madness, the *senex* goes for a doctor. After he departs (perhaps beginning even as he is departing), Sosicles addresses the audience (876–81) and leaves, creating an empty stage. The *senex* returns immediately (882), followed by the doctor (889). This is funny in part because the whole exchange can occur in less than a minute of stage time. By having the *senex* emphasise the length of the wait (882–4), Plautus points to the haste in real time with which he has treated the offstage action. A formal 'time passes' device would minimise this effect.[50] Again, in *Cistellaria*, the *lena* Melaenis leaves the stage saying, *ibo domum, | atque ad parentes redducam Selenium* (629–30: 'I'll go home and return Selenium to her parents'). She exits, producing an empty stage, and returns to deliver the next line. The *tibicen* begins to play, and Melaenis' immediate return with her maid Halisca and the *meretrix* Selenium is funny, particularly in light of her first words, *rem elocuta sum tibi omnem* (631: 'Now I've told you everything'). The empty stage here happens to coincide with a change of metre and music, but this is different from an indication that time has passed; it is funnier to maintain the conflict between actual time and dramatic time.

Perhaps the best way to understand the importance of pace in the performance of a play is to look at how issues of timing affect a performance. My example is the opening 300 lines of *Persa*, though the conclusions concerning the tension that exists between urgency and delay are equally applicable to other plays.[51] Toxilus needs money: at *Persa* 117, he asks Saturio for *nummos sescentos* ('six hundred bucks'), the same amount that he had asked of Sagaristio at 36. At 52 Toxilus enters his house, saying *usque ero domi dum excoxero lenoni malam rem magnam* ('I will be at home continuously until I have cooked up some big trouble for the pimp'). Saturio's entrance to deliver the next line marks the play's first 'empty stage'. Since Toxilus leaves the stage through a door, and Saturio enters by a wing, this can be a simultaneous transition. Saturio addresses the audience in soliloquy (53–80), whereupon Toxilus emerges from his house, and tells the audience, *omnem rem inveni* (81: 'I solved the whole thing ... '; this echoes *Pseudolus* 574–89). Technically the door opens not at the speech boundary, but after 79; Toxilus emerges as line 80 is spoken

---

[50] For the passing of time offstage in Menander and Plautus, see Hunter (1985) 36–7 and 39.
[51] See Marshall (1996) for a discussion of these themes in *Pseudolus*.

(*sed aperiuntur aedes, remorandust gradus*, 'But the door is opening – I must slow my step') and speaks without any pause, maintaining the pace. The audience understands Toxilus' entry as the fulfilment of line 52, with the slave emerging as he has dreamed up a plan. Following their initial banter, it becomes clear that the two saw each other yesterday, before the play began: Toxilus has been asking everybody for money. Yesterday Saturio had said no, today Sagaristio had said no, so now he is asking Saturio again.

The telescoping of action here creates a sense of Toxilus' urgency in the play's opening ten minutes. This urgency could be communicated more quickly, but part of its dramatic effect is having the scene drawn out. Toxilus' goal is different from that of Plautus. How has Plautus used his time? Lines 1–16 constitute a split-focus scene, where the audience's attention is divided equally between the two characters. Even at this early point in the play, Toxilus is not fully himself: while both appear as slaves, Toxilus' doleful attitude and lovelornness is more appropriate for the *adulescens amans*, the 'young man in love', than for a slave.[52] Following some small talk (17–23), Toxilus reveals the play's main conceit: he is in love (24–5). When Sagaristio underlines the statement verbally with his question, *iam servi hic amant?* (25: 'So now slaves are lovers here?'), *hic* refers metatheatrically to the stage as much as it does to the dramatic setting of Athens. The terms of the contract for his beloved are explained (34–8), and there is the appearance of padding as Toxilus extracts a hard-hearted promise from Sagaristio to assist (39–52). Saturio then enters (in a simultaneous transition) and delivers a monologue on being a parasite (53–76). While very funny, its length plays against the urgency Toxilus had expressed. Finally, Saturio approaches the house of Toxilus' master (77–9). This directs focus to the door just in time for it to open from within, as Toxilus emerges (80). His first two lines are delivered to the audience (81–2); he notices the parasite briefly, as his mask clicks to the side and then clicks back to the audience for his explanation (83–4):

> *sed eccum parasitum, quoius mi auxiliost opus.*
> *simulabo quasi non videam: ita adliciam virum.*

> But there's the parasite whose help I need.
> I shall pretend I don't see him: that's how I'll entice him.

---

[52] Slater (2000) 31–44.

He then proceeds to call into the house to order some food to be prepared (85–9). Technically, this is not a split-focus scene, because both characters are aware the other is there. However, Saturio thinks that he is eavesdropping, and that it is a split-focus scene. When Toxilus proclaims (either calling into the house or 'as if to himself', as in Nixon's stage direction), *iam pol ille hic aderit, credo, congerro meus* (89: 'By Pol I think that pal of mine will be here right away'), there is no doubt the sentiment is intended for Saturio's ears. Lines 90–98 are scripted as if the eavesdropping continues, with Saturio delivering his lines to the audience as if he were unseen by Toxilus (e.g. 90: *me dicit, euge!* 'he means me – yippee!'). Toxilus even resolves the supposed split-focus scene with the accepted formula, *prope me hic nescio quis loquitur* (99: 'I don't know who is here speaking close to me').[53] The *lazzo* itself has already been used in the play (13), and its recapitulation here urges the audience to reinforce its previous enjoyment of the routine. The pseudo-*callidus* gives instructions to pseudo-servants in a pseudo-eavesdropping scene that recalls routines already used.

Saturio thinks he has high status. As a character he is free, and metatheatrically he is in the strong position of the eavesdropper. Toxilus trumps this by role-playing a familiar *lazzo* (the entering character speaking back to an unseen character within; *Curculio* 223–5). A variety of familiar techniques are used, manipulating focus in predictable ways. By varying the pace of the opening moment, introducing the element of urgency, altering the expectations of a stock character, and using stock routines in theatrically self-aware ways, Plautus clearly set the pattern for the rest of the play. Working contrary to these devices (each of which technically slows the revelation of information central to the plot) is the reference to the ongoing need for money that has occupied Toxilus for some time now (*Persa* 116).

A continued account of the play is not necessary. These techniques recur, and the emphasis on innovation persists. At *Persa* 159 explicit metatheatre returns with the reference to the *choragus* and rented *ornamenta*. A more sophisticated use of mirror-staging occurs at 200–50, this time between Paegnium, a young slave in the same household as Toxilus, and Sophoclidisca, slave to Lemniselenis whom Toxilus loves. Having established how mirror-staging works (1–16), Plautus develops the scene's potential. Each servant has emerged from his or her house and is heading to the other's with a letter. This movement could have been

---

[53] Marshall (1999a) 124 and n. 34.

accomplished in a single line (when Sophoclidisca returns to Dordalus' house, she does so during line 305). Plautus extends the scene to fifty lines, 'without materially advancing the plot – other than to establish that the two lovers are given to letter-writing'.[54] While the opening gesture is to create a split-focus scene (200–04), this is soon discarded as the mirror-staging creates parallelism and the characters interact. With paired speeches, Paegnium and Sophoclidisca are competing in *malitia* (238: 'baseness'), to see who is *peior* (237: 'slyer') – functionally this is a contest for higher status, determining who is a 'better' Plautine slave. Though incidental to the narrative, the scene is characterised by considerable haste, in a paradox that clearly appeals to Plautus: eighteen of the lines between 200 and 250 contain three or more speeches, which suggests that the back-and-forth rhythm of the conversation is very fast indeed.[55]

These vignettes establish the hierarchy of the play, in which Toxilus has command of his master's house since the master is away, with a network of slaves forming hierarchical ranks beneath him. Awkwardly fitting into this inversely stratified world are Saturio and, later, his daughter. Saturio is dependent on the welfare of the house, and that leaves him beholden to Toxilus. His willingness to profit from his daughter brings him into an uncomfortably close parallel with the play's only other free character, the *leno* Dordalus. Sagaristio returns with a soliloquy that seeks to characterise him in the role of the *servus callidus* (251–71); the monologue echoes Saturio's monologue at 53–80, and Plautus recapitulates the earlier comic business at the door. Following another status contest between Sagaristio and Paegnium (272–98), which incidentally also begins with a split-focus scene, Paegnium returns to the house of Toxilus' master, and enters mid-line in 298. By the caesura of line 300, the door opens again, with different characters emerging. With the audience focus on the door only recently moved back to Sagaristio, its sudden use in such a short space creates another theatrical surprise. All these effects are anticipated in the play's opening lines. Once established, they become part of the audience's shared experiences. Plautus is free to recapitulate these devices later in the play, and know that his audience will have the means to assess his developed use of the comic mechanism. In this way does he control the audience's experience of pace.

---

[54] Slater (2000) 35–6.   [55] For the effect of this rapid back-and-forth, see Hough (1970).

TONE

A related issue concerns the tone of Roman comedy: is there room for seriousness in Plautus?[56] The experience of an audience during the performance of a work is often very different from that of a reader. A performance possesses situational specificity. Parts of it are familiar to the audience: the atmosphere of the *ludi*, the linear experience of watching a play, and the source material in Greek New Comedy mean that there already exists a set of expectations that limit what 'going to a play' can mean. Parts are controlled by the troupe: focus, pace, and doubling conspire to ensure that the playwright has control over what the audience sees. All this unifies the audience's experience, creating a world that will resonate with a consolidated audience. The economic and social diversity of the audience itself exists in tension with this, and every performance strikes a slightly different balance in the compact made between performers and audience. The issue is much more complex than this, though, and further distinguishes the spectator's position from that of a reader of a play.

Performance reifies issues raised by the text. A reader's imagination does different things from what a spectator's does when presented with a character like the miser Euclio in *Aulularia*. Facial features are determined by the combined efforts of the mask-maker, actor, and director, and so inevitably Euclio will always look a little bit different from what the spectator would have imagined on his or her own; after the play, if it was successful, it may be hard for a spectator to imagine a miser ever looking any different from what he has seen. This is true even if the masking tradition did present rigidly codified representations of mask types (a supposition I argued against in Chapter 3): the actor's voice and somatype always yield a unique composite whole. Performance therefore presents physical limits on interpretability: not every possible interpretation of a play or a scene will withstand scrutiny in performance. A potentially serious issue like the beating of slaves or jokes about crucifixion could conceivably be played with equal effectiveness for over-the-top slapstick laughs or with deadly earnestness. The issue of violence on stage in Roman comedy is a genuine problem for modern western readers and audiences.[57] Slaves threaten to beat one another, and receive such threats from their masters, and the modern western sensibility recoils at the implications of this as a source of humour. There are however mitigating factors. The vocabulary in Roman comedy is

---

[56] Duckworth (1952) 272–304 considers these questions but does so purely from a literary perspective.
[57] A starting point for the discussion is Parker (1989).

standardised, which diminishes the language's shock value. Further, in
the republic, crucifixion was not a taboo concept associated for most
viewers with a particular historical event.

The degree of seriousness with which the matter was intended by the
playwrights cannot be determined. The reader can choose to imagine
either or both possibilities, or might never consider the issue. The spectator is presented with specific actions that lead towards a particular
interpretation. The troupe can choose to attempt to present such an issue
as ambiguous, which risks diversifying audience response to the issue – or
it may avoid making a decision at all (by choice to preserve ambiguity or
through ignorance of the potential difficulty). The audience might never
know that a decision has been avoided: it sees the performance and
interprets it in light of a given question; if the information is insufficient,
the spectator will create an answer out of the information available, or
decide to let the matter pass. This is important: actors always provide
further variables that contribute to the understanding of an issue even
when they are unaware of the issue's parameters; similarly, an audience
always takes the evidence presented as sufficient to form a complete
interpretation. While performance removes possible interpretations from
the audience, it cannot eliminate them all. There is always diversity within
the heterogeneous audience, and different spectators will isolate different
variables from what they have observed, creating a unique combination of
observed gestures, delivery styles, properties, masks, costume, blocking,
timing, plus a myriad of other ineffable but physically present details.[58]

Performance necessarily limits interpretation. At the same time, it
opens possibilities. When we read a play, our minds do not present a fully
developed world. Details not specifically mentioned in the text can be left
as blurry blotches in the mind's eye, attaining a more specific form only if
the text presents additional information. The practical concerns of
production do not impinge on our consciousness, because our minds can
adjust the imagined circumstances instantly. That is not the case with
performance. Because the actors occupy a physical space and pass real
time in their presentation of the play, performance operates by physical
laws, and allows no opportunity for retroactive revision. Stage action

---

[58] This also affects the diachronic analysis of the plays. Readers in different centuries and different
cultures project their own society's anxieties and concerns onto the plays, and read them in that
light. The same, obviously, affects my own preoccupations: what I see in Plautus is conditioned
both by what those scholars I have read see in him, and by my experience with 'comedy' in the
broadest possible sense, but also by my experience of making sense of these plays for students and
actors.

presents a diversity of signs, each of which conceivably connotes something different to each spectator. Every physical object carries with it a plurality of possible meanings that interact with the other physical objects on stage, but not everything will be noticed by each spectator, each of whom possesses a unique view of the performance area. The composite created in performance is never what was in the playwright's head but instead represents the combined actions and decisions made by all involved in the production in advance of the actual performance and during it. If this sounds unfathomable, that is because it is. For most in the audience, most of these details will not be isolated, but there is always something more to be noticed.

What this means for the tone of Plautine comedy is immense. We cannot know what all the decisions made were when Plautus' troupe was performing – indeed, we cannot know most of them: it is enough of a challenge to document such things in the modern world with video recording equipment. The plays possessed a physical reality when they were staged, and conscious decisions were made by the troupe concerning many issues. This means that for the original audience some interpretations of the play were actively encouraged, and others were discouraged or even precluded. Further, there existed a host of physical details that could provide additional means for the troupe to favour a given interpretation. There is no guarantee that the whole audience will accept this preferred interpretation, but, if the troupe wishes, it can draw the majority of spectators towards one conclusion.

How can we know what interpretative tendencies the troupe favoured? There are many choices, and the same piece of dialogue when read by different actors can evoke serious reflection or riotous laughter, or can shock with obscenities unnoticed in the other readings.[59] The issue of tone or seriousness provides a convenient and important locus for the discussion, because it concerns the audience's stake in the performance. By discussing 'stakes', we introduce the audience as a factor in the economic model of Rome's performance culture: as a term it represents

---

[59] For the most part, the text of Plautus does not present explicit obscenities. This does not stop actors and students from finding *double entendres* and opportunities for bawdy physical gesture. Gurlitt (1921) shocked scholars by finding obscenities that others had claimed never to notice, and his work has remained in undeserved obscurity. He is not always right, but some of his examples are convincing. Discussing the *commedia*, Andrews (1993) 201 writes: 'Visual evidence makes it clear that the level of vulgarity could be extreme, and the scenarios give an impression of repeated comic situations which we would now expect to amuse children more than adults.' Plautus can be played this way, too, and it remains possible that this effect was not downplayed in performance in antiquity. Mime, too, had a reputation for being bawdy.

what individual spectators have invested in the performance, in terms of time, money, intellectual effort, emotional energy, and, for those who travelled far to see the show, physical exertion. The force of some of these factors on a Roman audience is not great: magistrates defrayed economic costs, and the time spent was at a prestige event of the *ludi*, and consequently was not particularly costly. The greatest investment for a Roman audience was mental, in terms of intellectual effort and emotional energy, and it is here, in addition to the social dimension of being at the theatre, that the greatest rewards for the spectator lay. Humorous and comic elements fill the plays of Plautus, and their frequency and variety would seem to be designed to provide intellectual rewards for the entire audience, at a variety of levels. This is not to say that all the jokes are sophisticated or high-brow; rather, the nature of comedy's engagement with the individual spectator, whether through pun or pratfall, depends on the audience's ability to superimpose mentally both an expected state and an actual state and to recognise the resulting incongruity.

There are also emotional stakes for the audience: the standard plot of Greek New Comedy presents a romantic story, often of young love separated by obstacles and blocking characters that must be overcome. These are not cookie-cutter versions of the same story, but possess a great range, with each play presenting some unique twist on a deceptively simple starting point.[60] To what extent this affects the audience emotionally is uncertain: perhaps the audience did not care about the fate of the lovers at all. That seems improbable, however, given other clues that point to a degree of emotional engagement, including the 'numerous passages in which the characters discourse upon social and ethical problems'.[61] Nevertheless, the reverse can be argued persuasively: 'within the confines of Plautine theatre, members of the audience are constantly reminded that they themselves have an essential role in the dynamics of performance ... are directed to enjoy it from an amoral, comic perspective'.[62] Christenson considers the dynamics of performance, and sees a play that is devoid of any sustained emotional engagement for the spectators – this is what I take 'an amoral, comic perspective' to mean. *Amphitruo* and the presentation of Alcumena provide a particularly rich touchstone for this discussion,[63] but since so much of this play is problematic and exceptional, it is perhaps safer to base preliminary

---

[60] See Willcock (1995) 20–24.   [61] Duckworth (1952) 300.   [62] Christenson (2000) 33.
[63] See the discussions of Segal (1975), Perelli (1983), Phillips (1985), and Christenson (2000) for the recent development of this view of *Amphitruo*.

conclusions concerning the tone of Roman comedy on more representative plays.

Though the nature of performance can render some possible interpretations impractical, there are indications that seriousness of tone, sincere moral purpose, and emotional engagement had a part to play in Roman comic performance. Many of the themes that Duckworth lists in his discussion of tone are, in the end, ambiguous in their presentation, and could be played in performance either for laughs or with seriousness: 'wealth and poverty', 'love and marriage', 'master and slave', and 'the problem of education' (to take some of his section headings) are all present in various degrees in the plays: *Adelphoe* is explicit in its engagement with issues of childrearing and education, for instance,[64] but the question also bears on how we interpret Demaenetus' behaviour at the final celebration with Argyrippus and Philaenium in *Asinaria*, when he demands to spend the first night with his son's recently rented girlfriend (828–50), despite his earlier desire to help (64–83). These plays show that themes could receive radically varying treatments within a genre: a spectator leaving the theatre from *Adelphoe* might reflect on his own upbringing or parenting, but in *Asinaria* Demaenetus' threat is never taken seriously within the play by any except Argyrippus. Indeed, aspects of stagecraft (the eavesdropping that follows, the possible doubling of Demaenetus with Leonida, the abruptness with which the threat is introduced, etc.) argue that it is likely that other factors in the reification of the scene further mitigated against any seriousness being attached to Demaenetus' words. Different plays allow for different effects: 'Neither playwright is writing problem plays on social themes but inevitably, in the works of each, passages of serious thought occur and even the portrayal of characters in ludicrous situations may have an ethical function'.[65] While this can happen, it cannot be assumed as a general rule.

A clearer example comes in the case of the young women in the plays, where there are reasons to believe that Plautus wanted his audience to sympathise with their plight.[66] Saturio's daughter in *Persa* is a free citizen press-ganged into service by her father to imitate a foreign captive. Her dutiful service to her father endangers her marriageability, which is already threatened since her only dowry is his collection of joke books (388–96). It is hard to laugh at her situation, though humour exists all

---

[64] For a quick survey of the theme in this play, see Gratwick (1999) 13–15.

[65] Duckworth (1952) 273.

[66] The bibliography on the *meretrix* is immense, but some starting points are Schneider (1931), Fantham (1975), Gilula (1980), Wiles (1989), and Brown (1990).

around her. Saturio's selfishness is the emphasis of 329–99, and his daughter's piety magnifies that. Nevertheless, her characterisation is specific: most of what she says consists of gnomic wisdom that would surely appeal to the conservative elements in Plautus' audience (which may have been the majority, even given the festival context). Later, she presents a cogent meditation on the vices of urban living (549–60) and, in her cross-examination by Dordalus (615–57), proves herself both inventive and, through her careful choice of words and use of double meanings, honest.[67] Listening to her, Toxilus is impressed both at her ability to improvise convincingly in this context (they have not formally rehearsed this scene together, within the dramatic world), but also at her sophistication (639). The behaviour of the *virgo* can be measured against Saturio's scathing critique of the morals of contemporary Roman women (385–7, where the emphatically placed *nunc* 'now' and *hic* 'here' emphasise that the assessment extends beyond the dramatic world); the joke's success depends on his daughter being an exception to this tendency. Similarly, Dordalus' joke at her expense is much crueller if the audience feels some sympathy for her (656–7):

> *ne sis plora; libera eris actutum, si crebro cades.*
> *vin mea esse?*
>
> Don't cry, you'll be free soon enough, once you tumble a bit.
> Wanna be mine?

Dordalus is thinking only of money here, despite the additional nuance we might hear in *vin mea esse?*: like all *lenones* his concern is not with sex, but with the money he can gain from it. Nevertheless, it would be shocking for a Roman spectator to contemplate a free girl working her way out of slavery in this manner. This emotional involvement does not come at a cost for intellectual engagement: indeed, its presence can magnify the effect of other jokes. Cappadox, when he expresses genuine sympathy for his *meretrix* Planesium, becomes even more pathetic as an emblem of vice (*Curculio* 517–18, 522–3). An audience is consequently much more likely to feel some emotional involvement in the fate of Saturio's daughter than that of Planesium, who is not so foregrounded.

Similarly, Palaestra and Ampelisca in *Rudens*, as they flee the shipwreck and Labrax's clutches, consistently evoke audience pity, an effect that

---

[67] For the most recent discussion of the *virgo* in *Persa*, see Manuwald (2001), though there is no difficulty in the *virgo* being both clever and good. See also Lowe (1989).

could easily be enhanced by additional production elements, including costume, gesture, and (particularly in this case) musical accompaniment. Palaestra's initial entry at line 185 introduces music to the play, and the polymetric *canticum* continues until the two characters leave the stage at line 289.[68] Music can reinforce emotional connections with certain characters (some might say that is what music does best), but it does not do so of necessity. The collaborative efforts of the troupe may have produced a performance that favours such an interpretation, but there is a risk of overstatement. In *Stichus*, for example, the wives of the brothers Epignomus and Pamphilippus, Panegyris and her sister, never speak without some musical accompaniment. Nevertheless, their presence in the play is limited to a few scenes at the beginning of that play, and it is hard to believe that Plautus intends the audience to be as concerned with them as with the women in *Rudens*, whose welfare is an ongoing concern. For the audience, the stakes are much higher with the shipwrecked Palaestra and Ampelisca.

Plautus intended various effects in his characterisation of women in his plays, at times seeking to engage the audience emotionally (beyond the standard romantic narrative) and at times allowing for a more ambiguous or superficial presentation. Such inconsistencies may exist only for the reader: production decisions could draw an audience toward a more concrete conclusion than we can detect. Yet there is a place for seriousness in Plautus. Tonal variation can coordinate with other dramatic and metatheatrical effects to broaden the range of a play. However multi-layered the levels of comedy may be, there is always room for another dimension to be added, one of sympathy and emotional engagement with a pathetic character.[69] Characterisation throughout this process is crucial. The collective assessment of any character depends both on the presentation by the actor inhabiting the mask, but also on the reactions of other characters and the larger dramatic setting. The women in *Persa* and *Rudens* do not become uninteresting stereotypes in their moralising, but seem to offer a beacon of hope in how the actor presents them and in how other characters respond to them.

---

[68] Plautus' manipulation of music and metre are discussed in Chapter 5. Hunter (1985) 50–51 suggests metre was used to create seriousness in *Rudens*. Ketterer (1986b) 116, 132 n. 36, 37, and (1986c) 32, 35 discuss tone with respect to stage properties.

[69] I am using the term 'sympathy' in a restricted sense: not simply to mean the feeling of a common goal or purpose (the feeling I get when I root for Pseudolus or Wile E. Coyote), but rather the compassion of being affected by another's grief, which can exist fully in a fictional context.

Alcumena remains a problem case. Since Plautus does not have a uniform means of treating the portrayal of women in his plays but varies their personalities from one play to the next as he creates individuals able to arouse genuine interest within their individualised contexts, we cannot know what happened in *Amphitruo*. Much of her characterisation does seem to evoke pity, and conceivably could engage an audience on an emotional level: her speech and metrical features can be understood to encourage this conclusion. Against this, her pregnancy (physically represented on stage[70]), the play's concern with disguise and role-playing, and the artificial lengthening of the 'long night' (νὺξ μακρά, the title of a play by Plato Comicus that may have been Plautus' model) provide strong reasons why one might think Plautus expects only 'an amoral, comic perspective' from his audience. Our lack of knowledge concerning incidental performance decisions keeps the question open. But it is not an either/or proposition. The presentation of Alcumena could be sympathetic, or it could be exploited for comedy, but the gains from either of these unified presentations of her cannot be said clearly to outweigh the potential losses. The prominent place of all the characters in this play (which employs less role doubling than any other Roman comedy) suggests that Plautus is aware of what he is doing, and this leaves the possibility that Alcumena is deliberately presented in an ambiguous way, overdetermined by conflicting performance choices that invite the audience to treat her both as an object of fun and as a sympathetic heroine. Individual spectators will each strike a personal balance, as they reconcile the polyvalent clues provided by the actor. A conflicting, heterogeneous treatment of the play's moral pillar raises more questions for an audience than it answers, but represents the most sophisticated technique of characterisation Plautus employs.

ROUTINES

While there are times when Plautus has sought to achieve a serious tone as part of the diverse effect on his heterogeneous audience, the greater part of the comedies is filled with humorous routines on stock themes. These routines is familiar to most readers of the playwright, but their density and their function in the narrative and alongside it have not been explored to a degree that allows for generalisations to be made about stock routines in general. This double function is itself important. On the one hand, a comic routine is part of the story. By introducing a routine,

---

[70] Phillips (1985).

the playwright is telling the audience something about the characters and something about the dramatic world: these characters are likely to fall into certain modes of behaviour, and, once committed to a routine, they will see it through to its completion. This is one way stage characters differ from the real people in the audience: characters in Roman comedy lack foresight about their own actions, and a pattern, any pattern, provides a means for them to proceed. The end of a routine may come quickly, or it may be delayed. This flexibility is one of the most important features of a stock routine for an actor in performance, and provides the principal locus of improvisational expansion (see Chapter 6). On the other hand, comic routines operate alongside the narrative, which is to say that they often do not materially advance the story, and at times can be seen to delay the revelation of information. That is part of their fun. Properly performed this conflict will not concern the audience.

Whatever the origin of a particular routine, its purpose is to evoke laughter. It provides an audience with a recognisably familiar situation increasing the audience's vicarious participation in the plot. Stock routines exist in many forms in Plautus' comedy, and are often presented in series (a technique I have called 'shtickomythia').[71] Indeed, the successful pacing of the stage action presumes a smooth transition from one routine to the next. Routines can develop out of the physical conditions of the theatre itself, out of character, or out of cultural issues relevant to the audience. An example of the first of these categories is the *'quis hic loquitur?* scene Plautus uses to dissolve split-focus scenes.[72] Another would be the schtick associated with door-knocking in Greco-Roman comedy,[73] or the play on light and darkness at the opening of *Curculio*.[74]

Routines may also arise from the actions of a specific stock character. For example, the *servus currens* or 'running slave' is a stock routine, introduced in nine of Plautus' extant plays.[75] It is typical to see the *servus currens* described as a stock character, but strictly speaking this is not so. As a routine, the '*servus currens*' describes the actions of a character, often a slave, in a given scene; in contrast, the '*servus callidus*' is the character's identity throughout the play. The former is based on action, while the latter is tied to mask or occupation.[76] This type of routine developed for a

---

[71] Marshall (1999a) 127. [72] Marshall (1999a). [73] Brown (1995). [74] Arnott (1995).

[75] Law (1922) 31 n. 6, Duckworth (1936), Csapo (1987), (1989), (1993) with bibliography in the introductory note, at (1987) 399. As Csapo demonstrates, the running slave is paralleled in Greek New Comedy, and is not drawn from the Italian improvisatory traditions.

[76] This is true despite *Eunuchus* 35–40, where Terence includes the *servus currens* among comedy's *personae*, but his list of examples apparently combines stock characters with other plot elements. The problem is probably larger than this: Terence is not using the phrase *servus currens* or *miles*

typical narrative situation faced by a particular stock character, but becomes a routine that may in theory be performed by any character type. The parasite Curculio performs 'the running slave' at *Curculio* 280–302, though he is not a slave. Wiles suggests that he makes his way through the audience, further blurring any strict notion of the limits of the stage space.[77] The *servus currens* (as it has come to be called) is properly thought of as a routine that can be performed by a variety of character types. This may seem like a minor distinction, but in making it we see that Plautus can innovate in his application of routines: they are not unconsidered, throwaway devices. This juxtaposition of incongruous elements is similar to the presentation of Toxilus in *Persa* as a *servus amans*, where the stock character of the *adulescens amans* is combined with the mask of the slave, and Philocrates in *Captivi*, where a free *adulescens* is presented in the situation of a captive slave.

While it is probably not helpful to think of the prologue as a routine, there exists a similar ambivalence in its presentation.[78] Studies of the prologue typically consider the content of the speech rather than its mode of presentation to the audience. Part of its function is to provide narrative information about the plot (an *argumentum*), but it is not helpful to make the primary subdivision of prologues based upon whether or not an argument exists.[79] Prologues can amuse the audience in their own right; they help to establish a rapport between the stage world and the spectators early in the performance (with this may be included a *captatio benevolentiae*; they may also indicate specific events that will unfold, even if not every aspect of the narrative is revealed). Argumentative prologues are a means to enhance the audience's appreciation of what follows. None of these are necessary functions, and the prologue can be omitted. One need not posit lost prologues for *Curculio*, *Epidicus*, *Mostellaria*, *Persa*, and *Stichus*: even the confusions in *Epidicus* are

---

gloriosus as established adjective–noun pairs, but is using the modifiers as complements in his larger sentence structure. It is possible that none of his examples represent a stock character, but are dramatic events typically associated with a particular character type.

[77] Wiles (1991) 59–61. This technique proved very effective in my productions, for both Curculio's entrance and Leonida's entrance in *Asinaria*. In both cases, the actors naturally took objects belonging to the audience and turned them into makeshift props. These included purses, musical instrument cases, and in one instance a mountain bike.

[78] See also Leo (1912) 188–247, Abel (1955), Duckworth (1952) 211–18, and Beare (1964) 159–61.

[79] The narrative content is not completely unimportant, however, given the many variables involved in production discussed in Chapter 1. *Heauton Timoroumenos* 9 suggests that some in the audience did not know the name of the playwright; Cicero, *Lucullus* 20, suggests (for tragedy) they might not know the name of the play. These things cannot be taken as granted.

minimised by the additional interpretative information provided by stage action in a production.[80]

Of the plays with a prologue, there are apparently three possibilities for the actors in performance. The prologue can be delivered by a character in the play: Mercurius at *Amphitruo* 1–152, Charinus in *Mercator* 1–110, and Palaestrio in the delayed prologue at *Miles Gloriosus* 79–155 all speak in the *persona* they will adopt throughout the play, even if they show themselves aware of extra-dramatic information. In these cases, the actor wears his character's mask and costume as these lines are spoken. The prologue can also be delivered by an actor playing a divinity with no stage existence after their speech, though, as in Menander's *Dyskolos*, its presence may continue to be felt. These constitute a different category from the first: the Lar Familiaris in *Aulularia* 1–39, Auxilium in the delayed prologue in *Cistellaria* 149–202,[81] and Arcturus in *Rudens* 1–82. In this category we may also place the dialogue between Luxuria and Inopia at *Trinummus* 1–22, even though it possesses no argument and involves two characters. These also allow for innovative and creative costume decisions, creating a sense of spectacle early in the performance. Against these seven examples of prologues wearing mask and costume are seven 'impersonal' prologues, apparently lacking any individual identity. The longer examples include an argument (*Captivi* 1–68, *Menaechmi* 1–76, *Poenulus* 1–128, and *Truculentus* 1–94) and the shorter ones do not (*Asinaria* 1–15, *Pseudolus* 1–2,[82] *Vidularia* 1–16). For these prologues, a mask and costume would be potentially confusing for an audience, since no identifying features are given in the speech. The clearest solution is that proposed by Beare: 'In all probability he wore (if not the toga) the usual tunic, pallium and slippers, but *no mask*; and was therefore recognizable at once in speaking in his own person and on behalf of the dramatist.'[83] This same solution would then obtain for all of the prologues in Terence's plays,

---

[80] Duckworth (1952) 80–81 discusses and rejects Ritschl's theory that many prologues are post-Plautine. Once we accept a more fluid conception of the text in Plautus' day, the most cogent arguments against their authenticity disappear. A similar problem faces editors of Renaissance drama, where the prologue was not perceived to be an integral part of the play: 'the purpose of prologue and epilogue alike was to woo the first-performance audience ... and to petition the spectators, begging them to be indulgent rather than unkind. A play, having survived its first day and been "passed" by the audience, seems to have shed its stage orations which could then float free of the text, and so were easily lost before publication. ... A play in performance was by no means textually fixed' (Stern (2004) 122, and see 113–22).

[81] *Cistellaria* and *Miles Gloriosus* are the only Roman comedies with a delayed prologue, but the pattern is also found in Greek New Comedy, as in Menander's *Perikeiromenê*. See Schaaf (1977) 120–23.

[82] The authenticity of these lines does not affect the present argument.

[83] Beare (1964) 194. See also Saunders (1909) 30–36.

where the speaker is either impersonal or, explicitly, Ambivius Turpio. Of the two plays not considered, *Bacchides* is excluded from consideration because its opening is too fragmentary to know if a prologue existed; *Casina* 1–88 might belong to either of the last two categories, depending on whether or not one accepts Skutsch's proposal that the mention of Fides in line 2 would be accompanied by a gesture by the actor to himself.[84] If so, then *Casina* has a divine prologue, and if not, it is impersonal: in either case, the truth, lost to us, would be instantly identifiable to an ancient audience.[85]

The prologue is a dramatic mechanism that can be used by the playwright for a variety of effects: either as a lengthy introduction to a principal character, or as an eye-grabbing divine presence, or, most frequently, as a chance to look behind the mask and see the performer – yet another way Plautus and Terence use stage action to cement the rapport being built with the audience. This points to the staging of the codas that conclude the plays. Plays typically end with a direct appeal to the audience for applause. In the Plautus manuscripts, six plays explicitly ascribe the final lines to 'the troupe' (*grex* or *caterva*): *Asinaria* 942–7, *Bacchides* 1207–11, *Captivi* 1029–36, *Cistellaria* 782–7, *Epidicus* 732–3, and the final word of *Trinummus* 1189. Given the convention for the delivery of the prologue, it is possible that the clear ending was made clearer in performance, by having an actor remove his mask – a clear sign that the existence of the dramatic world was ending. Indeed, this may have been the case in every play. There is always a point where the narrative ends and the audience is asked for its approval. It is not inconceivable that the actor removed his mask to deliver *Amphitruo* 1146, *Casina* 1012–18, *Curculio* 729, *Menaechmi* 1162, *Mercator* 1025–6, *Mostellaria* 1181, *Persa* 857, *Pseudolus* 1334–5, *Stichus* 775, *Truculentus* 967–8. Of these sixteen examples (and to them we may add the two for which the ending no longer survives, *Amphitruo* and *Vidularia*), only *Trinummus* does not ascribe a continuous line to the unmasked actor. The *plaudite* (1189: 'clap!') provides sudden closure to a long play. This rapid one-word dénouement in fact characterises only long plays, and is found (without the ascription to *caterva*) at *Miles Gloriosus* 1437, *Poenulus* 1422, and *Rudens* 1423, where the last two words, *plausum date* ('give applause!') are

---

[84] Skutsch (1900) 272.
[85] The problems with the *Casina* prologue are notorious. Lines 5–20 refer to a remounting of the play at a time generally held to be a generation after the death of Plautus, i.e. in the time of Terence. This may be so, but the state of the Plautine text was sufficiently fluid that the revival could also have been in Plautus' own lifetime.

spoken outside of the dramatic narrative. In a theatre lacking the modern devices used to serve this end (the curtain and dimming lights), it would seem that this was enough to establish closure.

An unmasked speaker could be used to open a play (as in the impersonal prologues), and perhaps it was a customary means to conclude. Outside of these bookend functions, could an actor appear unmasked during a play? Only speculation is possible, but there are good reasons to think that, in one instance at least, this did happen. The appearance of the Choragus at *Curculio* 462–86 introduces a figure from the real world onto the dramatic stage, whose principal frame of reference is not Epidaurus where the play is set, but the forum in Rome. While this is clear to a reader of the play (because of character notations in the modern script), in performance there is a great disjunction at this entry. While dramatic characters know that they exist before an audience – this is evident in the metatheatrical references and attempts to establish a rapport, and in the stage action by the regular practice of facing 'out' – nowhere else are so many details from contemporary Rome introduced in such a short space. The existence of impersonal prologues means that the audience probably has some experience of receiving information from an unmasked actor. There is no sense of taboo arising from appearing unmasked, though it was unusual to do so while adopting another character outside of mime performances. Either the actor appeared wearing a mask representing one of the backstage personnel (assuming the troupe also employed stage managers) or the actor appeared unmasked, and delivered the lines in the same manner as an impersonal prologue (which, as it happens, is absent from this play). As so often, the staging decision that was instantly clear to an ancient audience remains elusive, though the latter seems more likely.[86]

A third way for routines to develop is from subjects that are a source of humour for the audience already. Arnott's surveys of 'Amorous Scenes in Plautus' and 'Love Scenes in Plautus'[87] show the range that a relatively elementary trope can possess when employed for comic effect. My example will concern references to literacy in Plautus, in what we may choose to identify as the *lazzo* of 'one person reading or writing for another', though variations do exist.[88] Since Roman literature is still a relatively new

---

[86] Slater (2000) 16–19 suggests *Epidicus* 81–103 is to be seen as a dialogue between an unmasked actor and his mask. This represents a much more aggressive theatrical innovation, and is not paralleled by *Curculio* 462–86.

[87] Arnott (1995) and (1997).

[88] The remainder of this chapter was written before Slater (2004) and has been left largely unaltered because of his use of it. Though our approaches differ, I believe the conclusions are largely complementary.

phenomenon, this routine represents humour about a new technology. In a world where the ability to read and write is suspect and not universal, jokes about literacy provide a release for societal apprehensions.[89]

The opening tableau of *Pseudolus* establishes Calidorus weeping over a letter he holds in his hands (10). He has had the letter for many days (9) and has done nothing, even though it establishes the fate of his beloved, and sets a deadline of tomorrow for her release (60). The repartee between Calidorus and Pseudolus allows a number of jokes. Phoenicium has bad handwriting (22–30) that only the Sibyl could decipher.[90] The mysterious ability of a letter to make someone absent appear present is the subject of further quick jokes, as Pseudolus teases Calidorus with *tuam amicam video, Calidore!* (35: 'I see your girlfriend, Calidorus!'), though the truth is soon revealed: *eccam in tabellis porrectam: in cera cubat* (36: 'look, she is drawn out in the letter: she lies in wax'). Eventually, Pseudolus reads the letter aloud (41–74), with occasional interrupting expostulations from Calidorus.

These outbursts serve to dramatise Calidorus' feelings for Phoenicium in that consciously artificial way of theatrical storytelling, but it also leaves uncertain whether Calidorus himself has read, or even has the ability to read, the letter. Phoenicium does appear later in the play, but only as a *muta persona*. It is only in the reading of her letter that the character is given any voice, and that voice comes from a middle-aged, bearded, pot-bellied slave. The art of reading aloud appropriates and recontextualises another's voice, and an actor is invited to discover ways to make this recontextualisation more entertaining. Does the Pseudolus actor adopt a falsetto, and read the letter with cooing tones? Calidorus does say *nam mihi videor cum ea fabularier* (62: 'for it seems to me I chat with her'). Or are Phoenicium's only words presented in the gruff and coarse voice of a slave?[91] Whatever the answer, Pseudolus' ability to read Calidorus' love letter confuses elements of sex and status, and grants Pseudolus a stage authority which he

---

[89] Slater (1996) documents Aristophanes' jokes about literacy, and demonstrates a similar suspicion in fifth-century Athens concerning literacy and magic use. Jokes about the internet, certain computer companies, and computer viruses similarly abound today (and are typically disseminated by computer!) in a way that jokes about less suspicious technologies, such as the telephone, do not.

[90] The passage also provides the *locus classicus* for describing handwriting as chicken-scratch (30). Clark (2001–2) argues that all handwriting on wax tablets looked like chicken scratch, which while true does not entirely remove the joke here.

[91] Very little can be said about vocal characterisation on the Roman stage. Pollux, *Onomasticon* 4.64, provides a technical vocabulary for light (= feminine?) and deep voices. There were some markers within the speeches that characterised the speaker's sex: 'In Plautus, men swear about equally ... by Hercules and by Pollux, and women swear about equally ... by Pollux and by Castor' (Nicolson (1893) 101; typography normalised).

will enjoy throughout the play. The letter also serves to set the plot of the play in motion. Using a letter to establish events antecedent to the play is accomplished elsewhere: Mnesilochus sent a letter to Pistoclerus (*Bacchides* 389–90); Epidicus claims there was a letter from Stratippocles to the music girl indicating that he had secured finances for her (*Epidicus* 251); and Palaestrio wrote a letter to his master (*Miles Gloriosus* 129–33).

This opening scene in *Pseudolus* is the only Plautine scene where a slave reads a letter for his young master. Typically, letters represent instruments of deception in these plays. Later in the same play, another letter is read aloud by Ballio (997–1014). The letter is from the soldier Polymachaeroplagides, but has been intercepted from his agent Harpax by Pseudolus and given to another slave, Simia, who is now pretending to be the real Harpax. Though he has not read the letter since it is sealed, Simia is eventually able to trick Ballio into saying the name of the soldier – Polymachaeroplagides – to confirm his assumed identity (982–91).[92]

In *Persa*, Toxilus, the *servus callidus*, wants a letter he wrote for his neighbour's slave, Sagaristio (459–61), which he will give to the *leno* Dordalus to read aloud (496–532). The letter purports to be from the absent master Timarchides, who does not appear as a character in the play, but it does provide evidence for the role Sagaristio adopts when he appears with Saturio's daughter (549). Toxilus even quotes the letter after it has been read: the girl supposedly comes *ex Arabia penitissuma* (541: 'from most remote Arabia', repeating a phrase from line 522 in the same metrical *sedes*).

A blocking character is also made to read a deceptive letter aloud in *Curculio*. Lyco the banker reads aloud a letter addressed to him

---

[92] In Plautus, no name ever receives quite the same attention as that of a soldier, whose bombastic onomastics reflect his character. In his opening scene of *Miles Gloriosus*, Pyrgopolynices feigns forgetfulness of the name of his former military commander, which is (allowing for slight manuscript variation) Bumbomachides Clutomistaridysarchides. It is precisely the manuscript variation of the soldier name in *Pseudolus* that catches my attention. The scene has Simia pretending to be Harpax, who has come to fetch the girl for Calidorus. Simia has the arranged recognition token, but, as Pseudolus discovers as he is eavesdropping on the scene, Simia does not know the name of the soldier, his supposed employer. Nor, since this is a Plautine soldier, can he reasonably guess the soldier's name (lines 983–91). Part of the joke comes from the fact that Simia is able to wrangle the name Polymachaeroplagides out of Ballio without attracting suspicion, and the repetition of the comic name surely enhances the effect. When Ballio says the soldier's name (in lines 988, 989, and again in line 999) it is always at a line end. Simia says the name only once, however, where it instead appears just before the caesura, in a line filled with resolutions. Is it not also possible that as Simia tries the name out in his mouth – and it does take practice to get it right – he slightly mispronounces it? This would add to the humour, and, if right, might demonstrate that the variant spellings of the name Polymachaeroplagides are due not to some scribal slip, but to the hesitant *servus callidus* and a moment of Plautine wit.

purporting to be from the soldier Therapontigonus Platagidorus (429–
36). We know Lyco can both read and write: he once filled four columns
in his ledger writing out the name of the soldier (409–10). When Therapontigonus Platagidorus does appear, he chastises Lyco for trusting
tablets (551). Earlier in the play, Curculio indicated he would tell Phaedromus what to write in the letter, but the offer is used merely to get the
characters offstage (368–9): Curculio will not write the letter himself,
because he will be eating (369). Here is a variant of the scene, where the
routine is avoided.

However, in *Bacchides* we have an instance of exactly what Curculio
avoids. Chrysalus, a slave, dictates a letter for his young master Mnesilochus to his father, as part of Chrysalus' scheme (726–53). Since the letter
purports to reveal Chrysalus' deceptive behaviour to the father, it is
important that the letter be in the young man's hand (730). This neatly
reverses the expected status dynamic, and perhaps explains the many
interruptions, as Mnesilochus is not used to writing, and so takes some
extra time (737). The ruse works, even though the letter is not read
onstage: Nicobulus does believe the letter – *aequomst tabellis consignatis
credere* (924: 'one ought to trust sealed tablets') – and so the letter
becomes the instrument of deception (934–5). The structure of this variation of the *lazzo* is clear. A *leno* (in *Pseudolus* and *Persa*), or a banker (in
Curculio) reads aloud a deceptive letter, which has either been obtained
under false pretences (as in *Pseudolus*), written by the *callidus* (as in *Persa*),
or dictated by him to his young master (as in *Curculio* and *Bacchides*).
The Plautine texts do not take advantage of every opportunity to use this
lazzo, but variations can be imagined. It would not, for example, be out
of place if in *Bacchides* the father Nicobulus, also a blocking character,
had read his deceptive letter aloud. Plays premised on the separation of
lovers can depend on the opening and reading of letters. Even if
letters need to be opened, *Trinummus* 793–5 reveal that letters may be
unsealed at customs, and that this may serve as an excuse for opening
another's mail.

Not all scenes involving literacy concern letters. Another variation of
the *lazzo* involves a parasite doing the writing for a rival lover, as part of a
larger effort to flatter him. In *Asinaria*, the parasite reads a contract to
Diabolus, stating the terms of the arrangement with the *lena* (746–809).
Diabolus, the rival lover in the play, codifies Philaenium's expected
behaviour. Terms suggested by Diabolus are omitted or added by the
parasite. Some of the terms themselves evoke literacy: letters are forbidden in Philaenium's house, because that is how lovers can enter

(761–3), and she must post a note on the door to this effect (760). Does this perhaps imply a suspicion of writing on the part of Diabolus that suggests his literacy is in question, as it was with Calidorus? Diabolus' parasite in *Asinaria* uses his ability to write to increase his master's estimation of him, even though its legalism drives Diabolus away from his intended goal.[93]

In *Miles Gloriosus*, Artotrogus is the parasite of Pyrgopolynices. He has tablets, anticipating his master's wishes, which – though nothing is written down (48) – are seen by the soldier to be markers of memory. Artotrogus miscalculates the sum of those the soldier has killed on campaign (38–49), and presumably does so deliberately: we are told $150 + 100 + 30 + 60 = 7{,}000$ (46), which overestimates the deceased by more than a factor of twenty, even assuming that the initial numbers are accurate. Does Pyrgopolynices know that the flattery is empty? His facility with numbers is probably so minimal that he may actually believe the total, even if the audience does not.

Of course, not all references to literacy are part of a standard comic routine. Literacy is implied for some characters through their word games. In *Mercator*, Demipho can spell *amo*, and knows the number of letters (303–4). This is part of a claim of rejuvenation, suggesting that the old man go back to school. In *Rudens*, Gripus and Labrax play word games on the single letter separating *medicus* ('doctor') and *mendicus* ('beggar'; 1304–6).[94] All of these instances also suggest a sufficient degree of literacy on the part of Plautus' audience to enable spectators to get the joke.

Literacy can serve other comic purposes as well, which at times can reveal elements of Roman social history. Sceparnio can read an inscription on a pitcher that shows it belonged in the temple of Venus (*Rudens* 478). It is assumed that free children are learning to read at age seven, for they have tablets with which to hit their pedagogues (*Bacchides* 440–41). Greeks in the forum could be stereotyped as always carrying books (*Curculio* 288–9). Sophoclidisca has worked for Lemniselenis for five years, which she believes is sufficient time for a sheep to learn its letters if

[93] On the exclusive contracts in *Asinaria* and *Bacchides*, see Ketterer (1986b) 103–4, 106–7, 108–11, and 129–30 n. 15.

[94] There is a similar joke at *Truculentus* 262–4, where Astaphium's *eiram* ('anger') is understood by Truculentus to be *eram* ('mistress'), a word that remains unspoken, though, somewhat confusingly, *eam* ('her') is spoken. The joke also plays on a double meaning of *comprime* ('press'). Astaphium declares, *dempsisti unam litteram* ('You removed a letter', line 264) whereupon the two proceed to etymologise Truculentus' name. This example seems much more recherché than *Rudens* 1304–6, but at least some of the audience must have been able to follow the exchange.

it went to school (*Persa* 172–4). This joke might suggest that the slave is literate, but need not do so: the joke can also be operating at the level of the actors. Later in *Persa*, Saturio's dowry for his daughter will be a collection of 600 Athenian jokes extracted from his joke books, of which he has several at home (390–396).[95] Syncerastus complains, as part of a diatribe against his *leno* master, that there are letters of all sorts (on wine-gifts) throughout the house, each with the giver's names a cubit high, so that the pimp will be regularly reminded of his benefactors (*Poenulus* 836–8). Elsewhere Plautus uses the same image for big writing: Gripus says he will advertise a lost chest with letters a cubit in height (*Rudens* 1294–6).

The written word represents an element of permanence in the very transient world of the Plautine stage. These examples reflect an attitude towards literacy in Plautus' audience, and demonstrate the comic possibilities of the written word in a performed medium. When these references are extended, and not just made as jokes in passing, they fit a structure that can be meaningfully identified as schtick, the *lazzo* of 'one person reading or writing for another', with its various permutations, and found in six of Plautus' plays.

---

[95] For joke books and the *scurra*, see Corbett (1986) 5–26. The emphasis in 395 that the jokes are Athenian and not Sicilian implies that there was some sort of Sicilian comedy (Epicharmus?) that was written down and available in Rome in the way that Athenian comedies also were.

CHAPTER 5

Music and Metre

MUSICAL STRUCTURE IN PLAUTUS

Even though act and scene divisions are found in the earliest manuscripts of Plautus and Terence, they possess no authority deriving from the playwright.[1] While Greek New Comedy was divided into acts (each play possessing four act breaks and therefore five acts, though this is hard to prove conclusively) and while Horace believed five acts to be the ideal, at least in tragedy (*Ars Poetica* 189–90), neither comic playwright structured his dramas on this principle.[2] Act divisions, when intended by the playwright, can serve a number of functions: they may indicate a pause in the action (as with the choral *entr'actes* signalled in the Menandrean manuscripts), or the passing of time within the narrative, or the blocking of a dramatic passage may allow the audience to consider it as a structural unit. None of these are relevant to Latin comedy. Roman comedies were presented continuously, without any breaks, and the elasticity of time is used on the Roman stage for comic effect, so any recognition of act divisions in performance would diminish the humour of the plays. There are even reasons to doubt an apparently explicit reference to a musical interlude within a play (*Pseudolus* 573a); nor can the presence of an empty stage be used to justify act divisions in Roman comedy.[3] There were patterns and structural units in the plays of Plautus, which are clear and meaningful for understanding the dramatic procession of each narrative.

---

[1] Duckworth (1952) 98–101. Such divisions were imposed as early as the first century BC. Before the Ambrosian palimpsest was read, there was no evidence for act divisions in Plautus before the 1500 edition of J. B. Pius.

[2] Beare (1964) 197–206, 208–12, 214–18, and see 340–46.

[3] Duckworth (1952) 99–100, Beare (1964) 212–13, and Moore (1998a) 246 discuss *Pseudolus*; Duckworth (1952) 98–101 and Beare (1964) 213–14 discuss empty stages, and see Chapter 4. Weissinger (1940) 86 provides a convenient hand-list, which, while it is possible to question individual examples, provides an independent measure of this variable.

My argument is building on the work of others,[4] and in many ways is simply reformulating metrical data through the filter of stagecraft and performance. Duckworth apologises for 'This somewhat technical analysis'[5] and since my analysis is building on his, a similar warning is perhaps in order here. We may take the following as established. Significant portions of every Roman comedy were accompanied by a *tibicen*, a musician playing a *tibia* about whom jokes could be made within the drama and whose identity was preserved prominently in the *didascalia*. In 1872, Ritschl and Bergk recognised that Roman comedy can be perceived in terms of alternating sections of verse which are accompanied and unaccompanied by the *tibicen*,[6] with every play ending with musical accompaniment. Every play follows this pattern, and (more importantly) this pattern can be perceived today because musical accompaniment was determined by metre: except as discussed below, the iambic senarius (*ia*[6]) was unaccompanied, and all other metres were accompanied.[7] Such a division exists logically prior to the customary threefold division associated with an actor's delivery of the lines: 'spoken senarii (S), "recitative" in the longer iambic and trochaic metres or in anapaests … (R), and *cantica mixtis modis* (C), "songs in mixed metres"; R and C were both accompanied by the piper, on stage as an "invisible" accompanist'.[8] Traditionally, S and R passages are associated with each other, since both are stichic (based upon a recurring metrical line of a predictable and describable form), and are separated from the '*cantica* proper' (which are non-stichic; the metre may change line by line).[9] Perceiving Roman

---

[4] See particularly Law (1922), Duckworth (1952) 362–4, 373–5, Moore (1998a), (1999).

[5] Duckworth (1952) 374.

[6] Ritschl (1877) 1–54 (first published 1871–2), Bergk (1872). Their independent arrival at the same conclusion is summarised by Moore (1998a) 245–6 and (1999) 131–3.

[7] For important 'introductory' discussions of such aspects of metrics in Roman comedy, see Questa (1967), Gratwick (1993) 40–63, 248–60 and (1999) 209–37. I use the following standard abbreviations for stichic metres: *ia*[6] iambic senarii; *ia*[7] iambic 'septenarius' (actually an iambic tetrameter catalectic); *ia*[8] iambic octonarius (iambic tetrameter acatalectic); *tr*[7] trochaic 'septenarius' (trochaic tetrameter catalectic); *tr*[8] trochaic octonarius (tetrameter acatalectic); *an*[4] anapestic tetrameter.

[8] Gratwick (1999) 231. Duckworth (1952) 373–4 uses the letter D ('deverbium') for senarii, R for 'recitative' metres and S ('song') for *cantica mixtis modis*. Neither system of notation is satisfactory, and both presume delivery styles for which there is inadequate information, but when needed, I employ Gratwick's system.

[9] For most of what I say in this chapter, the stichic metres are more important than the non-stichic *cantica*. Except as noted, I will accept the passages analysed by Questa (1995) as *cantica*. Lineation is slightly different from Lindsay's text (which also has a *conspectus metrorum*) but in no cases should there be confusion. Moore (2001a) 315 nn. 7 and 10 interleaves Questa's text for the *cantica* with Lindsay for other passages, which means his figures are different from mine. Alternate analyses of passages of *cantica* can be found in Braun (1970), and see Leo (1897).

comedy in terms of alternating accompanied and unaccompanied sections, grouping R and C since both were accompanied and separating them from S, underlies Moore's analyses, and prompts much of what I say here.[10] It is a distinction supported by markings of DV (for *deverbium*) and C (for *canticum*) found in some manuscripts, supported by Donatus, *Adelphoe praefatio* 1.7.[11]

An example will clarify. It is possible to describe the progression of the metrical structure of a play such as *Asinaria* (and consequently something of its musical structure) with the notation SCRSR:

Asinaria	1–126	ia^6	S
	127–38	various	C
	139–745	tr^7; ia^7; tr^7; ia^7	R
	746–829	ia^6	S
	830–947	ia^8; tr^7	R

Full song is only a minor part of the play (lines 127–38[12]), but it is clear that, whatever the actors are doing, the *tibicen* provides music to almost four-fifths of the play's lines, in two segments: lines 127–745 (619 lines) and 830–947 (118 lines). Both times the *tibicen* plays, more than one metre is represented.

Each juncture is important. Moore's analysis has concentrated on the transition from unaccompanied to accompanied passages.[13] The presence or absence of music is intimately connected with characterisation, with the lack of music being associated with traditional 'blocking' characters. The first unaccompanied passage (1–126) coincides with when the *senex* Demaenetus is onstage (though opening scenes are typically unaccompanied regardless of who is onstage); the second (746–829) is when the rival lover Diabolus is onstage.[14] Both times music starts, it is with

---

[10] For a detailed analysis of these labels, see Moore (forthcoming), ch. 2. This also undercuts a standard assumption on the dating of the plays, that they demonstrate an increasing number of *cantica mixtis modis*. This assumption has been thought to be generally true since Sedgwick (1925), but it will become clear that there are many ways in which the musical complexity of a passage can be established, and the formulation of Sedgwick's hypothesis deserves reconsideration. Dumont (1997) 46–8 doubts the validity of this principle for other reasons.

[11] See Moore (forthcoming), ch. 2. For a good, short overview of changes of metre in Plautus, see Gerick in Benz and Lefèvre (1998) 140 n. 36.

[12] See Questa (1995) 74–5. Though line 138 is tr^7, it completes the sentence begun in 136 and is considered part of the *canticum*. This and similar instances will affect the start and end points of several *cantica*.

[13] See e.g. Moore (1998a) 253.

[14] Actually, the last unaccompanied lines, 828–9, occur after Diabolus has left and the next scene has begun. The lines represent the transition to the final festivities, instructing stagehands (as silent

the appearance of the *adulescens* Argyrippus (127 and 830).[15] Plautus is in no way slavishly following convention in his use of music. In the characterisation of Demaenetus, for instance, we may note that surprise effects are created. In the opening scene, he is not the expected blocking figure of the *senex durus*, but (contrary to the musical indications) claims to wish to support his son's amatory endeavours (64–83); his true intentions are made clear only in the final musical scene when he demands the newly rented girl for the first night (847–8, and see 830–50). This is not what we expect, and while the audience does not support the advances of Demaenetus, there is some pleasure to be taken in the old man's schemes, and this pleasure is reflected in the music even though the scene presents the humiliation of the *senex*.

It is instructive to take these units and place them alongside another possible gauge of dramatic structure, the presence of empty stages. Weissinger suggests eight points in the play where the stage may be empty: strong breaks at lines 126, 248, and 503, and weaker breaks at lines 15, 544, 745, 809, 827.[16] His concern in making these distinctions is irrelevant to the present discussion, and (as discussed in Chapter 4) can be thought to be inconsequential for the performance of the play. It is sufficient to see these moments as junctures (of whatever weight) in the dramatic narrative. The three mandatory empty stages in fact reveal completely different relationships to the music of the play. After 126, the *tibicen* begins to play for the first time; after 248, the *tibicen* continues to play in accompaniment of tr^7; and after 503, the *tibicen* continues to play but the metre changes from ia^7 to tr^7. The others display a similar range. As at 126, the junctures at 745 and 827 mark the starting or stopping of the *tibicen*.[17] As at 248, the same metre continues after the juncture at 15

---

slaves) to position the table for the banquet, and are not sufficiently paralleled by *Mostellaria* 406–7 and *Rudens* 440–41; see also n. 17.

[15] See Moore (1998a) 250: 'After an unaccompanied prologue and opening scene, all of *Asinaria* is accompanied except for two consecutive scenes between Diabolus, the rival to the play's young lover, and his parasite.' The musical structure of the play would be thoroughly compromised if, as Havet has suggested, the *adulescens* in lines 127–248 were Diabolus and not Argyrippus (Havet (1905), endorsed most recently by Danese (1999) 59–66 and 76–8, and see 84–95; for a rebuttal of Havet's thesis, to which the present musical argument could be added, see Lowe (1992) 159–63).

[16] Weissinger (1940) 86.

[17] This assumes, with Weise and Leo, that lines 828–9 are an interpolation (see also Moore (1998a) 250 n. 8). I am not convinced that this is necessary. This is part of a very busy entrance, as the preparations for the onstage dinner party are brought out. For the *tibicen* to remain silent until the stage is set (and the characters quickly give instructions to the slaves) does not seem inappropriate to me, and allows the transition from one scene to the next to be accomplished with some business to cover the action. Once all is in place, the *tibicen* can start. If the lines are authentic, then there is an instance of music not coinciding with entrances, but in most respects the musical effect is the same.

and 809 (though both of these examples are unaccompanied). As at 503, the juncture at 544 represents a continuation of accompaniment, but in a different metre. At the very least this shows that any patterning of empty stages is unrelated to the musical structure of the play. Indeed, empty stages are secondary, especially since where and how many there are will always remain uncertain.

The musical structure of *Asinaria* is thus helpfully understood in terms of these five units, and at any of the junctures, Plautus can create significant effects that can lead to advances in the understanding of the play. Law suggests that particularly significant effects are achieved as music begins, as characters burst into song.[18] The pattern of all the plays, however, suggests that as a structural unit that repeats, it is more helpful to think in terms of an unaccompanied passage followed by an accompanied one. Every play ends with accompaniment, and this is always the end of a structural unit. It can be helpful therefore to think in terms of a breath, with the senarii being the inhalation, and the accompanied passage the exhalation. *Asinaria* then is made up of two such breaths, 1–745 (745 lines), and 746–947 (202 lines).[19] While Plautus' audience would not have used the term 'act', it is clear that in this play metre and music create two repeating structural units, each similar in shape though unique in form, that encompass the whole play, and would necessarily have been perceived by the audience as clearly as the act-dividing song of the chorus in Greek New Comedy.[20] Indeed, this would be the only repeating pattern available to an audience, and so it seems natural that the playwright and the actors would consider it as well. In this play, the second unit is shorter than the first one, and the effect of this is to provide a sense of the pace gradually quickening: again, the image of the breath usefully preserves the sense that shortening each successive unit adds to the level of excitement.

I call each of these structural units an 'arc', and each arc is composed of an unaccompanied passage (the 'rise' – to continue the metaphor – corresponding to the inhalation of the breath) followed by an accompanied passage (the 'fall', corresponding to the exhalation).[21] Further,

---

[18] Law (1922) 103–5, and see Moore (1998a) 246–7.
[19] In terms of the traditional act and scene divisions, these units divide at the beginning of act IV, scene i.
[20] In this respect my argument is similar to Primmer (1984) 16–20, 94–102, though there remain substantial differences in our methods.
[21] While I argue that the arc structure is explicit in the metrical patterns of the plays and would have been obvious to the ancient audience and performers, we do not know what the ancient terminology was. Terence, *Hecyra* 39, has the prologue declare *primo actu placeo* ('The first act went

both falls in *Asinaria* are 'complex', in that they comprise more than one metrical pattern (which may contain *cantica mixtis modis*, but need not). These metrical changes are significant in the experience of the play, but remain secondary compared to the difference created by the presence or absence of accompaniment. When only one metre is represented in an accompanied passage – a 'simple' fall – Plautus always uses tr^7. Any audience member who has seen a Roman play before will know this pattern and expect it. What the audience does not know is how many arcs a given play will have. It does not know when a play will end, but as each arc falls, the audience will be able to sense the impending arrival of the end of the unit, and as each new arc begins the audience is again involved in the construction of a new emotional, narrative, and musical unit. These are not the only structural units in the plays, but they are, I believe, the primary ones. Plautus can create patterns of *lazzi* strung together ('schtichomythia'), and there are other techniques employed by the playwright to deny a sense of absolute closure at each and every arc join. Still, this remains the only way to account for every play. The discussion so far is able to account for ten of the plays in Plautus' corpus.[22]

Asinaria is composed of two arcs of diminishing length: 1–745 (745 lines); and 746–947 (202 lines).[23] The first arc is by far the longest in Plautus.

Aulularia consists of four arcs of diminishing length: lines 1–279 (279 lines); 280–474 (195 lines); 475–660 (186 lines); and 661–833 (173 lines). The second arc begins with the entry of the slave Pythodicus, the cooks and (paradoxically, since it is unaccompanied) musicians from the market. The third begins with the entry of Megadorus, and we see that the beginning of an arc does not require an empty stage. Euclio is onstage at 475, though he remains unnoticed until 536 in an extended split-focus ('eavesdropping') scene. The continued presence of Euclio stitches the second arc to the third.

---

well', tr. Barsby (2001) 151), but he notes that Terence is not using the term *actus* in a technical sense – at least, not in our technical sense of 'act'. It is possible that Terence is describing the first 'movement' of the play, which could refer either to the opening scene or to the first arc as I have defined it.

[22] An abbreviated *conspectus metrorum* providing all the details relevant to this discussion is included as an appendix. It is essentially a simplification of Lindsay's *schema metrorum*, found at the end of each volume of his OCT, with each line entry corresponding to a passage of S, C, or R. I do not wish to push too far on the exact ratios and lengths of these arcs, since (a) line lengths can vary considerably, (b) there are undoubtedly some interpolations from a later period, which, while not as extensive as is suggested by Zwierlein, do exist (as at *Casina* 5–20), and (c) in performance the duration of a given line will be affected by speed of delivery, the nature of the musical accompaniment, and the presence of improvisational expansion. Still, the general trend evidenced by the manuscript tradition is worth documenting as precisely as possible.

[23] See also Moore (1998a) 250–51, 253.

Further, the fall of the third arc uses only one metrical form, the trochaic septenarius (tr^7), and does not possess the metrical variety seen in other musical passages (though this of course in itself constitutes variation).[24] It is a 'simple' fall. Euclio exits and re-emerges almost immediately following a short speech by the slave of Lyconides[25] (661–6), which begins the fourth arc. The slave's continued presence again stitches the two arcs together. The brief passage of *ia*[7] at 803–7 corresponds to a short soliloquy; the final *canticum* is a variety of trochaic lengths.

Captivi comprises three arcs: 1–360 (360 lines); 361–658 (298 lines); 659–1036 (378 lines). While the second is shorter than the first, the third is longer, an effect realised more fully in *Casina*. What is striking in this play is how closely bound the three arcs are. The transition between the first to the second at line 361 is not accompanied by an entry or an exit, but merely the turning of Hegio's attention from Tyndarus (who he thinks is Philocrates) to Philocrates (who he thinks is Tyndarus). The transition from the second to the third arc at 659 is accompanied by the arrival of the three non-speaking *lorarii*. This creates a seamlessness within the play, though as a structural unit the arc is still the clearest division.[26]

As with *Asinaria*, the play's arcs all possess a complex fall. Complex falls always contain at least one of the stichic metres, and often include a *canticum*. The fall of the final arc in *Captivi* is particularly elaborate, with seven discrete elements of various lengths:[27]

Captivi	768–90	*canticum*
	791–832	tr^7
	833–7	*canticum*
	838–908	tr^7
	909–21	ia^8
	922–9	*canticum*

It is typical (though by no means a fixed rule) that songs begin immediately after a spoken passage, at the apex of the arc – comic characters burst into song.[28] It is also typical for the decline in the arc to

---

[24] The final line of the arc, line 660, is not a 'septenarius' but an octonarius, i.e. it is not catalectic. This helps to provide closure to the structural unit. There are other isolated variants, each of which may represent problems in the textual tradition, noted in the appendix.

[25] See Lange (1973) for this character.   [26] Moore (1998a) 255.

[27] For the *cantica* in this passage, see Questa (1995) 132–7.

[28] Of the sixty-one passages of *canticum mixtis modis* identified and discussed by Questa (1995) which are preceded by some other passage (to take an impartial and largely agreed upon sample)

be gradual, from song to chanted recitative.[29] The fall in the final arc of
the *Captivi* consists of seven isolable passages, three of them *cantica*, each
of which in performance would possess a distinct and identifiable musical
character.

Casina possesses four arcs: 1–308 (308 lines); 309–423 (115 lines);
424–562 (139 lines); and 563–1018 (456 lines). While the joins of the arcs
can be tied to the movements of Olympio and Lysidamus, this does not
seem to be Plautus' emphasis. The second and third arcs both fall with a
passage of a single metrical form, tr^7. As with *Asinaria* and *Aulularia*, the
play begins with a first arc longer than the next two (I do not believe the
audience would perceive the second and third arcs, both of which have a
simple fall, as anything other than 'about the same length'). The structural surprise in this play is the huge length of the final arc (an effect
present to a lesser extent in *Captivi*). After a fairly short rise (563–620),
the audience is presented with the extraordinarily long *canticum* at
621–962, which embraces a range of metres and contains occasional
strings of (stichic) bacchiacs and anapaests, but does not re-establish the
more familiar iambo-trochaic stichic metres until the final passage of tr^7
(963–1018).[30] This is demanding for the actors, of course, but it also has
an effect on the audience, who are probably expecting a rapid dénouement, and a play of the length of *Curculio*, perhaps. As the *canticum*
continues, the audience becomes increasingly certain it is about to end,
which makes its prolongation all the more impressive. The effect would
have been very much like an Aristophanic *pnigos* or the breathlessness of a
Gilbert and Sullivan patter song, combining a sense of both exhilaration
and exhaustion as the level of humiliation for Lysidamus increases. When
the end does come, it is with a sense of visceral relief for everyone in the
theatre.[31]

Menaechmi consists of five arcs, each with a complex fall: 1–225 (225
lines); 226–465 (240 lines); 466–700 (235 lines); 701–871 (171 lines);
872–1162 (291 lines). More than any other Plautine play, *Menaechmi*

<hr />

forty-three are preceded by a passage of ia^6 and seventeen by tr^7, and one (beginning at *Truculentus*
209) by ia^7.

[29] Of the sixty-two passages of *canticum mixtis modis* identified and discussed by Questa (1995) which
are followed by some other passage, forty-six are followed by tr^7, nine by ia^7, and seven by ia^6.

[30] There is a short passage of ia^6 at 847–54, which Questa treats as part of the *canticum*. I see no need
to mark this as a (particularly) short rise. *Truculentus* 241–7 is another short ia^6 passage that is part
of a *canticum*, and other exceptional short passages of iambics exist.

[31] A related but ultimately less impressive form of prolongation of the end of a play can be found
when the tr^7 at the end of an arc are drawn out, as they are in the *Epidicus* (187 lines), *Mercator* (197
lines), and *Truculentus* (239 lines); see Moore (2001a) 332.

exhibits the most regular patterning of its arcs. The same pattern is evident in *Truculentus*, and it therefore seems to represent an alternate means of patterning arcs, rather than an exception to a usual pattern. Each juncture in *Menaechmi* is associated with Sosicles (Menaechmus II): the second, third, and fourth arcs begin with his entry; the fifth as he collapses after his feigned madness. The brief passage of ia^8 at 1060–62 corresponds to Menaechmus' final entry. As Moore writes, '*Menaechmi* thus offers Roman comedy's most effective use of musical accompaniment to contrast characters.'[32]

Mercator consists of four arcs: 1–224 (224 lines); 225–543 (319 lines); 544–666 (123 lines); 667–1026 (360 lines). Here the relationship of the arcs alternates (short-long-short-long), preventing the audience from ever determining a rhythm over the course of the play (and this may, in itself, constitute a desirable dramatic effect). The falls of the first two arcs are complex, and the falls of the second two arcs are simple (this is not unusual: no play begins with a simple arc; eight plays end with one).[33]

Miles Gloriosus consists of six arcs of diminishing length: 1–480 (480 lines); 481–812 (332 lines); 813–1093 (281 lines); 1094–1283 (190 lines); 1284–1377 (94 lines); 1378–1437 (60 lines). This is Plautus' longest play, and the use of ever shorter arcs helps the actors maintain the pace throughout the narrative. The rhythm of the falls of the arcs introduces some variation: the first, third, and fourth are complex; the second, fifth, and sixth are simple. The junctures are determined by the comings and goings of a different character each time: the entry of Periplectomenus at line 481, the entry of Lurcio at line 813, the exit of Milphidippa at 1093, the entry of Pleusicles at 1284, and the entry of the *puer* at 1378.[34]

Poenulus consists of five arcs: 1–409 (409 lines); 410–614 (195 lines); 615–929 (315 lines); 930–1303 (374 lines); 1304–422 (119 lines). There is a clear division in the unfolding of the narrative at line 930, the beginning of the fourth arc, when Hanno enters. The second and fifth arcs have simple falls, and as with *Mercator* there seems to be no pattern to the arc lengths. Both of the play's *cantica* begin with the entries of Anterastilis and Adelphasium (lines 210 and 1174), and it is not surprising that their departure at line 409 signals the end of the first accompanied passage and the first arc. The entries of Lycus at line 615 and Hanno at line 930 begin the third and fourth arcs. The transition to the final arc would seem to be an exception to the examples we have seen so far, occurring as it does

---

[32] Moore (1999) 138 and, on the play generally, see 136–41.
[33] See also Moore (1999) 141–3.   [34] See also Moore (1998a) 262–4.

mid-way through Antamonides' speech at line 1304. But it is precisely at this point that he decides to address Anterastilis and Hanno directly, ending the split-focus scene that had been in effect since he appeared onstage at line 1280. *Poenulus* contains a greater amount of ia^6 (both as a raw total and as a percentage of the whole) than is found in any other Plautine play. Even allowing for revisions in the play's ending (which represents a conflation of at least two separate performance events),[35] it is the least musical of Plautus' comedies.[36] Nevertheless, *Poenulus* follows the pattern established by the other plays.

Trinummus consists of five arcs of diminishing length: 1–391 (391 lines); 392–728 (337 lines); 729–997 (269 lines); 998–1092 (97 lines); 1093–1189 (97 lines). The accompanied passages alternate in metrical complexity: complex-simple-complex-simple-complex. The second arc begins with the exit of Lysiteles; the third begins with the exit of Stasimus, which follows shortly on an exit by Lysiteles at line 717; the fourth begins with the exit of the sycophant, who can be played by the Lysiteles actor. The same actor could therefore be used to mark these major divisions. The final arc begins with the final entry of Callicles at line 1093.[37] This is the only Plautine play in which all of the accompanied stichic passages are tr^7.

Truculentus consists of three arcs of approximately equal length: 1–321 (321 lines); 322–630 (309 lines); 631–968 (338 lines). Each arc has a complex fall. The junctures are defined by Diniarchus' first speech (he enters during line 320) and the exit of his slave Cyamus at line 630.[38] The fall of the first arc possesses some unusual features, in particular Astaphium's song at 209–55. This is the only *canticum mixtis modis* that is not an entry song, and the only song that immediately follows a passage of iambic septenarii.[39] That metre recurs from time to time during the song, too (lines 217–23, 237–40, 252–5), and there are a number of ia^6 (lines 224–7, 250), which I presume are also accompanied. However, while the *canticum* itself is unusual, it is wholly integrated into the overall accompanied movement from lines 95–321.

Half of the Plautine corpus fits the structural pattern I have suggested easily. The other plays demonstrate a more sophisticated use of metrical arcs, though the actual number of techniques used to introduce variation is quite small. To see how these plays hold together structurally, it is

---

[35] Maurach (1988) 210–13 argues that both extant endings are interpolated, and that the original ending is lost.
[36] See Moore (2004a).   [37] See also Moore (1998a) 266–8.   [38] See also Moore (1999) 146–9.
[39] Law (1922) 7.

necessary to abandon alphabetic order. Four of the twenty plays do not begin with a passage of *ia⁶* we have now seen to create the rise of an arc: '*Epidicus, Persa,* and *Stichus* begin with duets and the *Cistellaria* with a trio.'[40] The nature of the music (seen in the nature of the metres employed) is different in each case.[41] The three plays with duets may be discussed straightaway. The effect of this is to catch the audience unawares with the opening falling half-arc, creating a sense of excitement and interest abruptly.

Epidicus presents a challenging metrical structure,[42] but given our methodology it is easily analysed as a long falling half-arc, 1–305 (307 lines[43]); followed by two normal arcs: 306–81 (76 lines); 382–733 (352 lines). Each of the play's three falls is complex, and the length of the opening half-arc creates a parallel for the exhausting, exhilarating effect at the end of *Casina*. The first complete arc that follows it is the shortest seen so far – a quick catch-up breath following the long exhalation of the opening. Lines 306–81 constitute a short scene for Epidicus, framed by the exit of Periphanes (soon after that of Apoecides) and the entry of Periphanes (soon followed by Apoecides). It serves mainly to re-establish the rhythm the audience expects from Roman comedy, a pattern determined by the arc as a structural unit. While the playwright can play with the form, once the pattern is established, regardless of other elements of variation, it is always continued to the end of the play.[44]

Stichus seems tame in comparison. A falling half-arc, 1–154 (144 lines[45]), is followed by three arcs: 155–401 (247 lines); 402–640 (239 lines); 641–775 (135 lines). The three complete arcs are of diminishing length. Arc transitions are determined by the seemingly insignificant parasite Gelasimus: his entry at 155, his exit at 401, and his exit at 640 (alternately, the last two transitions might be governed by the entries of Stichus at 402 and 641).[46] During the revels that conclude the play, the joy is so great that it extends beyond the dramatic world into the theatre itself, and the normally

[40] Duckworth (1952) 373.
[41] Moore (2001a) 323–4 and n. 25; Moore (2004b) 320–21 finds thematic significance in the function of each of these musical exceptions.
[42] Duckworth (1952) 374. Note that if it were known that a narrative prologue in *ia⁶* had been lost from the beginning of the play, it would conform to a standard three-arc structure; see Duckworth (1952) 213–14.
[43] *Sic.* There is a probable lacuna of two verses between lines 189 and 190: see Duckworth (1940) 224.
[44] See also Moore (2001a).
[45] *Sic*, accepting the deletion of 48–57, lines omitted in the Ambrosian palimpsest, and identified as an alternate to 1–47 by Ritschl. If the lines were authentic (or had somehow replaced another passage of senarii) the situation would remain largely unchanged: a short falling half-arc is followed by four arcs (1–47, 48–154, 155–401, 402–640, 641–775).
[46] See also Moore (1998a) 259–60. Moore considers each accompanied and unaccompanied unit, not the arc pairs.

'invisible' *tibicen* is offered a drink by Sangarinus: from 715–18, the *tibicen* is encouraged to drink, which he has done by 722. I presume there is a pause in the music while the piper drinks, coinciding with Stichus' speech at 719–21. Later in the scene, the *tibicen* is again offered wine (762).[47] The piper again takes the drink, and this time the result is different. As he drinks, the lines that follow are unaccompanied, and therefore in ia^6.

This, it should not need to be said, is a joke. It would be perfectly possible to deliver a few tr^7 without music (719–21), but there is a laugh when the metre reverts to ia^6 for the seven lines while the *tibicen* drains his cup (once? twice?). The joke is metatheatrical, in that it has a character acknowledge the world of the actors, interrupting the flow of the narrative, which serves to pull the audience into the world of the play even further. Sangarinus addresses the actual *tibicen* of the play, whom the play's *didascalia* call Marcipor. While Marcipor drinks, it is physically impossible for him to play the *tibia*. Once he is done, he can do so again, for the final seven lines of the play. Marcipor is publicly being rewarded for his performance in a way that is expected: *Cistellaria* 785 tells the audience that following the performance *qui deliquit vapulabit, qui non deliquit bibet* ('he who messed up will be beaten; he who didn't will drink!'). It is generally taken that the referents in this sentence are actors who are slaves. In *Stichus*, however, the one known slave performer, the *tibicen*, has already begun his reward, and through this the audience gets a final laugh.[48] *Stichus* is also one of three plays that we know ended with *cantica mixtis modis* rather than with tr^7; the others are *Persa* and *Pseudolus* (the endings of *Aulularia* and *Vidularia* are lost).[49] All three of these scenes are moments in which a play concludes with slaves celebrating

---

[47] This passage shares many features with the end of Menander's *Dyskolos*, as noted by Brown (1990) 39–40, and see 47–8 for the metrical variety at the end of Greek plays. For the metatheatrical element in Menander's play, see Marshall (2002).

[48] This is not the only way the joke can work, and I am not sure one way is to be seen as 'more Plautine' than the other. It is possible that the slaves have brought on stage with them a non-speaking actor dressed as a *tibicen*, as the normal provider of musical accompaniment (and other delights) at a party. It is possible that Sangarinus offers this actor the drink, which is then mimed. The humour then comes from the fact that the real *tibicen*, Marcipor, stops playing while his onstage counterpart ceases to provide musical accompaniment within the narrative. This is more sophisticated, in that it paradoxically creates the metatheatrical rupture by preserving the 'convention' of musical accompaniment within the world of the stage, but it is evidently not unparalleled in antiquity: some South Italian red-figure vases show both actor–musicians and the real musicians playing for them; see Taplin (1993) 105–10. For actors dressed as *tibicinae*, compare Antamonides' claim (*Poenulus* 1416) that he does not want a pipe-girl because of the size of her cheeks and her breasts; *Aulularia* 332 suggests at least some *tibicinae* were overweight. This joke also provides some evidence that it was common enough for *tibicinae* not to wear a *phorbeia*.

[49] Possibly the original ending of *Poenulus* is lost. It would in any case have been in tr^7; see Moore (2001a) 332 n. 36.

their victories and being drunk in public. This combination, which may be seen as resonating particularly with the ludic spirit of the Roman festivals, seems sufficient to warrant the variation in structure.[50]

Does it therefore follow that other isolated ia^6 are similarly unaccompanied? Moore believes this,[51] but I remain unconvinced. In the case of other isolated ia^6, which in the case of *Stichus* both occur in the middle of a full *canticum*, the abrupt stopping of the musical accompaniment for a single sentence (as at 300) or sentence fragment (288a) lacks the richness of this humour. In these cases, it is better to see them as yet another of the varied measures Plautus was able to employ in the composition of his *cantica mixtis modis*, and that as part of a larger metrical system isolated ia^6 could be accompanied. In the same way that in time Menander's trimeters could be set to music, so here Plautus, recasting whatever was in the Greek original as polymetric *cantica*, can employ an isolated stichic verse form (or even a brief run, as at *Truculentus* 224–7) as part of the overall musical effect.

Persa is structured like *Epidicus* and *Stichus*. A short falling half-arc, 1–52 (52 lines); is followed by three arcs: 53–328 (276 lines); 329–672 (344 lines); 673–858 (186 lines). Each unit has a complex fall. While the first full arc is not particularly short, it is shorter than the arc that follows, which in turn is longer than the one that follows it. The first and second arcs begin with Saturio's entrances at 53 and 329. The final one begins once Dordalus is tricked, signalled by his exit from the stage to get money to pay Sagaristio. As discussed, the presence of slaves drinking publicly explains the use of *canticum* to conclude the play. Of greater interest is the fall of the second arc, the complex accompanied passage 470–672.

The *canticum* (470–500)[52] ends with a short passage of ia^6 (501–12) whereupon the (expected) tr^7 begin. No sooner have they begun however (513–19) when again a short passage of ia^6 intervenes (520–27) before the trochaics continue until the end of the arc (528–672). These are not additional cases of metatheatrical humour involving the *tibicen*. Instead, both of the intervening ia^6 passages (501–12 and 520–27) occur when the pimp Dordalus reads a letter. The act of reading is given a special status

---

[50] See Duckworth (1952) 326–37. In the case of *Stichus*, however, the seven lines that follow the drink taken by the *tibicen* hardly constitute anything other than punctuation for the metatheatrical joke: it is possible that some in the audience would interpret them in terms of the musician being unable to establish the rhythm due to the effects of alcohol, though this is an effect more usually associated with bacchiacs (Tobias (1980) 14).

[51] Moore is explicit, e.g. at Moore (1998a) 255, 258, (2001a) 329–30 n. 33, (2004a) 155–6, (forthcoming) chs. 1 and 2.

[52] Questa (1995) 293–5.

within the play because reading a document on stage requires precision and depends upon the audience being able to follow the nuances of the written word. The Diabolus scene in *Asinaria* similarly depends upon reading and writing, and as we have seen also is written in unaccompanied *ia*[6]. When a character has to read on stage, the structural pattern created by the arc can be temporarily suspended.[53] Once this is recognised, *Persa* too behaves predictably.

Pseudolus consists of four arcs: 1–393 (393 lines); 394–766 (373 lines); 767–997 (231 lines); 998–1335b (338 lines). The first three are of diminishing length; the last is longer and concludes with a celebrating slave song. All possess complex falls involving *cantica*. The first and second junctures are marked by the exit of Calidorus at 393 and the entry of the *puer* at 767. The third juncture occurs at a moment of stage reading: the pimp Ballio begins to read a letter sent to him by the soldier Polymachaeroplagides. Unlike *Persa*, the music does not re-establish itself until 1103 with Harpax's return to the stage. The act of reading cancels the music. Similarly, Pseudolus' reading of Calidorus' letter at 41–4, 51–9, and 64–73 are all part of an unaccompanied scene. The pattern is thus completely typical, despite the 'interlude' at 573a, which creates no meaningful juncture in performance or in the unfolding of the narrative.[54]

Bacchides, when complete, probably possessed six arcs: 1–108 (total length undeterminable);[55] 109–499 (391 lines); 500–72 (73 lines); 573–760 (188 lines); 761–996a (236 lines); 997–1211 (215 lines). Had it survived complete, *Bacchides* would rival *Miles Gloriosus* as the longest play.[56] The arcs vary considerably in length, with all but the second and third possessing complex falls. Again, the arc junctures correspond with character movements: the second arc begins when Lydus enters; the third begins when he exits; the fourth begins when the parasite enters; the fifth begins when Mnesilochus exits. The final arc begins when the *senex* Nicobulus reads a two-line tablet. As in *Pseudolus*, the act of reading onstage cancels

---

[53] So, implicitly, Moore (2001b) 270, chart 3: '501–512 and 520–527 unaccompanied for reading of letter'. For the play generally, see Moore (2001b).

[54] Marshall (1996) 37. Nor is there need to follow Moore (1998a) 246 in believing there are 'likely' interludes at *Cistellaria* 630 and *Trinummus* 601 (or at *Heauton Timoroumenos* 873): in all of these places, the actor leaves, the *tibicen* begins to play, and the actor can re-enter immediately, as discussed in Chapter 4. For *Pseudolus* generally, see Moore (1998a) 264–6.

[55] Such a claim involves assumptions concerning the authority of the traditional order of the fragments, some of the key issues concerning which are outlined by Barsby (1986) 93–4. If all the *ia*[6] fragments belong to a scene preceding the *cantica* fragments (which is a possibility), the situation is as I describe it here. If there is more variation, a total of six and a half or even seven arcs is possible.

[56] Barsby (1986) 93.

the music (rather than temporarily suspending it, as in *Persa*), and *ia*[6] continue until 1075.

Curculio consists of four arcs: 1–215 (215 lines); 216–370 (155 lines); 371–634 (264 lines); 635–729 (95 lines). The play exhibits straightforward metrical alternation: the first and third arcs are long and each possesses a complex fall; the second and fourth arcs are short and each possesses a simple fall. The first two junctures are determined by the entries of two blocking figures, Cappadox the pimp at 216 and Lyco the banker at 371, and the exit of Phaedromus in the line preceding each entry. The final transition which begins the fourth arc is different, however. The scene presents the *adulescens* Phaedromus, the *meretrix* Planesium, Curculio, and the *miles* Therapontigonus, who has been cheated of his girl. In the wild confusion that ensues, the young lovers ask the soldier a question (629–31, 634):

> PHAED. *miles, quaeso te ut mihi dicas unde illum habeas anulum,*
> *quem parasitus hic te elusit.*
> PLAN.   *per tua genua te obsecro,*
> *ut nos facias certiores . . .*
>   *. . . fac me certiorem, obsecro.*

> PHAED. Soldier, I ask you to tell me where you got that ring,
> which the parasite here tricked you out of?
> PLAN. (*falling to his knees in supplication*)
>   By your knees, I beg you,
> So that we may know for sure . . .
>   . . . Let me know, I beg you.

The origin of the ring has already been the subject of discussion, and the lovers have already questioned Curculio (599–609). To this entreaty, Therapontigonus responds (635–6):

> THER. *ego dicam, surge. hanc rem agite atque animum advortite.*
> *pater meus habuit Periphanes.*
> PLAN.   *hem, Periphanes!*

> THER. I will tell.
> (*to Planesium*) Get up.
> (*to everyone*)   Listen up and pay attention.
> *Pause.* (*The music stops, everyone turns to listen, including the* tibicen.)
> (*significantly*) It belonged to my father Periphanes.
> PLAN.   What!
>   Periphanes!

I have included full stage directions to make clear what must happen in performance.[57] The transition from the end of one arc to the beginning of another, with the associated transition from an accompanied metre to an unaccompanied one, comes at the moment of *anagnôrisis*. Planesium's response, echoing the name (which hitherto has remained unmentioned), underlines the significance of the soldier's seemingly ordinary statement. Certainly long-lost siblings and recognition tokens are a staple of New Comedy, but in this case Plautus has used the metrical structure of the drama to create his surprise effect. By emphasising the moment, it is clear that the news that Therapontigonus and Planesium are siblings is a revelation, and has not been anticipated earlier in the play in a prologue that now is lost (the precise details are spelled out in 637–61). To create this special effect (the revelation of a dramatic surprise), Plautus must stitch two arcs together more closely than in any of the instances we have seen so far. The situation is not completely unparalleled. As with the scenes of reading, the transition to ia^6 is effected for the presentation of significant information.[58] *Poenulus* 1304 begins a new arc within a speech, and in *Stichus* we saw how the end of accompaniment could be used to create a metatheatrical joke with the *tibicen*. In this case, the otherwise innocuous call for attention at 635 is emphasised by the sudden musical silence that precedes it.

Mostellaria consists of four arcs, of diminishing length: 1–407 (407 lines); 409–746 (359 lines);[59] 747–992 (246 lines); 993–1181 (189 lines). The first three arcs have a complex fall. Plautus makes significant efforts to stitch the arcs together to reduce the abruptness of the transitions. The first juncture occurs after the departure of Philolaches. While his last speech is in 406, the fact that the music continues through the end of 407 before reverting to iambics provides textual indication that his departure is slowed somewhat. When he leaves, the music stops, and Tranio continues his soliloquy. The second transition is also unusual. It follows immediately upon a *canticum*, though the *canticum* ends with some stichic iambics: 741–5 are ia^8, 746 ia^7, and 747–82 ia^6. The *canticum* winds down, then, with a brief series of shortening iambic lines until it stops after 746. This is a new technique, and one that Plautus does not seem to have used elsewhere; but, as with *Curculio* 636, it does serve to emphasise the successful supplication of Simo by Tranio, concluding at

---

[57] See also Moore (1998a) 249.
[58] For this and other uses of the ia^6 see Hunter (1985) 48.
[59] *Sic.* There is no line 408 in Lindsay's text.

746. The third arc concludes with the departure of the slaves Phaniscus and Pinacium at line 992. *Mostellaria* shows Plautus combining a typical pattern of diminishing arc length with some less conventional means of linking the arcs together.

Cistellaria possesses significant lacunae that obscure the arc structure. Nevertheless, it would appear from the extant fragments that it possessed a half-arc, followed by five arcs, which must be considered individually. The play begins with accompaniment: 1–119 present three singers in a complex fall that immediately involves the audience (119 lines).[60] The departure of the *meretrices* Selenium and Gymnasium at 119 initiates the first full arc, 120–253. A lacuna prevents determining the full length (it is more than 134 lines long), but it would appear to possess a simple fall, since 231–53 are all tr^7. The second arc seems to be represented by two long fragments, one in ia^6 (273–304) from the rise, and one in ia^7 (305–73a) from its fall. While only one metre is represented in the fall, there have been no examples of a simple fall in any metre other than tr^7, and so it seems likely that we should assume some metrical variety and a complex fall in this arc (which will have been longer than the 101 lines indicated).[61] The third arc, 374–535, may have begun with the arrival of the *lena*, but we cannot tell. Lines 374–408 are all ia^6 and come from the arc's rise. Lines 449–535 show both ia^8 and tr^7, and so attest to a complex fall (in an arc more than 162 lines long): 449–52 will be the end of a longer passage of ia^8; the iambics in 463–4 are corrupt.

The arrival of the slave Lampadio at 536 initiates the fourth arc, 536–746 (211 lines), which again possesses a complex fall. The final metre represented in this arc is ia^7, which we have seen Plautus use in *Mostellaria* to create a smooth transition from one arc into another. As in *Curculio*, an unexpected recognition involving tokens is occurring, not anticipated in the play's prologue (149–202). While perhaps it is not as cleanly accomplished as in *Curculio* and lacks the metatheatrical joke, the silencing of the music comes immediately after Phanostrata identifies herself with the words, *ego sum illius mater, | quae haec gestavit* ('I am the mother of her who had these [tokens]', 745–46) and the effect is clear. The revelation of this news (quickly confirmed by an identification of where she lives) stuns all in the theatre, the music stops, and then she

---

[60] See Moore (2004b).
[61] When Terence, writing a generation later, does introduce simple falls employing a metre other than tr^7, he uses ia^8, and not ia^7 as here.

continues to speak, beseeching Halisca to reveal where the tokens came from (747–8).[62] The revelation of this significant information continues in iambics, as the final, very short arc 747–87 (41 lines), gets underway. Demipho enters and joins Lampadio on stage as the music begins for the last time. He asks *quid hoc negoti est, quod omnes homines fabulantur per vias | mihi esse filiam inventam?* (774–5: 'What's this news, that absolutely everyone is talking about in the streets, that my daughter has been found?'), and the audience enjoys a final laugh, since the news has spread instantly (and without any obvious messenger).[63]

   Amphitruo presents similar difficulties, with its lacuna between lines 1034 and 1035.[64] Nevertheless, it would appear to have possessed six arcs: 1–462 (462 lines); 463–860 (398 lines); 861–973 (113 lines); 974–1034 and fragments I–VI (more than 67 lines); fragments VII–XIX and 1035–1130 (more than 117 lines); 1131–46 (16 lines). The third and the sixth arcs have simple falls. The second arc begins when Mercurius enters, and the third begins when Jupiter enters. The fourth, which has a very short rise, begins after the first line of a soliloquy by Jupiter (973), but since this is the line following Alcumena's departure, this probably indicates that her departure was slowed somewhat, as at *Mostellaria* 406–7: she is, after all, pregnant.[65] The sudden end of the *ia*⁶ at the peak of the arc coincides with Mercurius' re-appearance, this time performing the routine of a *servus currens* (line 984). What follows is a complex fall, as Mercurius' *ia*⁸ (984–1005) are replaced by *tr*⁷ (1009–34 and fragments I–VI).

   However, lines 1006–8 are *ia*⁶. Here is the end of Mercurius' speech, which is directed out to the audience (1005–8):

> sed eccum Amphitruonem, advenit; iam ille hic deludetur probe,
>   siquidem vos voltis auscultando operam dare.
>   ibo intro, ornatum capiam qui potis decet;
>   dein susum ascendam in tectum ut illum hinc prohibeam.

---

[62] Line 747 begins *sed quaeso ...* ('But I ask you ...'), and it is perhaps not fanciful to compare the use of *sed* at the beginning of *Poenulus* 1304: both indicate the beginning of a new arc part way through a character's speech.

[63] Nixon (1917) vol. II: 181 assumes an empty stage after 773, with Lampadio re-emerging immediately to signal that 'An hour has elapsed'. Weissinger (1940) 86 marks this as a possible empty stage, with a question mark. It is much funnier and instantly comprehensible in performance to play the incongruity of the situation, reinforced by the addition of music.

[64] See also Christenson (2000) 56–7.

[65] Phillips (1985).

But here's Amphitruo – he's coming! Now right here I'll trick him completely . . .

(*The music stops. Pause.*
Mercurius approaches the audience as if to let them in on a secret.)
. . . if only *you* will hearken to my plan.
I'll go inside and get costumed as a drunk.
Then I'll climb up on the roof to keep him away from here.
                    (*Exit Mercurius.*
The music begins, with a different tune, as Amphitruo enters.)

As in *Curculio*, the end of the music enables the character speaking to reveal significant information. In this case, the information is crucial, since nowhere else in the Plautine corpus does a play require the use of the upper roof. The troupe has engineered a surprise effect for the audience involving the unique disposition of stage resources, and the momentary pause in the music provides the necessary information for the spectators to appreciate it.[66] In previous cases where significant information is revealed (as in *Curculio*), the musical effect inaugurated a new arc. Here, Mercurius' intentions represent only a brief pause in the musical scene.

While fragmentary, the fifth arc apparently began with Alcumena's return to the stage, since she speaks fragments VII–IX. The sixth arc, the shortest in Plautus, begins with the appearance of Jupiter on the palace roof (or otherwise *ex machina*); his speech is answered by three short trochaic lines from Amphitruo, as he claims to accept the situation. Christenson notes that 'the god's appearance is strictly unnecessary',[67] since all has been resolved by line 1130 in any case. As in *Cistellaria*, the short final arc is humorous in its brevity. The effect for an audience is both to create a joke (as the meaningful structural unit is deflated by its small size) and to create the sense of an encore – a bonus 'scene' affirming the play's closure.[68]

Rudens, the final play to be considered, is built with seven arcs, more structural units than any other play: 1–441 (441 lines); 442–592 (143 lines[69]); 593–779 (187 lines); 780–1190 (411 lines); 1191–1226 (36 lines); 1227–1337 (101 lines); 1338–1423 (86 lines). Arcs 2, 5, and 7 possess a simple fall. The second arc begins two lines into Ampelisca's soliloquy (lines

---

[66] Moore (1998a) 252 sees another purpose in these lines: to more clearly delineate Mercurius' *servus currens* scene from the rest of the play. Both functions may be at work.
[67] Christenson (2000) 315 suggests the possibility of a crane, but this is not needed.
[68] See also Moore (1999) 143–6.
[69] *Sic.* In Lindsay's text, one line is numbered 442–50.

440–57), which begins after Sceparnio's departure. *Mostellaria* 406–7 provides a parallel for the metre reflecting a slow departure of an actor,[70] and since Sceparnio has been free with his hands in the preceding scene (*Rudens* 419–39), an extended delay as he continues to grope Ampelisca would be comically appropriate. When he leaves, Ampelisca's speech continues as the new arc begins. But it is also significant that when the speech continues, it signals some aggressive stagecraft as she looks offstage (to the wing? into the audience?) and describes in detail what she sees,[71] the arrival of the shipwrecked Labrax and Charmides. Perhaps the relating of offstage action, unseen by the audience, was thought to be challenging enough that ia^6 would facilitate its comprehension. The exit of Charmides at 592 and the entry of Daemones at 593 mark the transition into the third arc, and the exit of Trachalio at 779 marks the transition to the fourth arc. The fifth arc is quite short (1191–1226), particularly given that it does not come at the end of a play. However, its content reveals why the playwright would choose to mark off these lines as a discrete structural unit. Daemones enters and during his soliloquy gives the arc its full rise and, as he shouts inside his house to his wife, initiates its fall. Such a change is unusual, and signals to the audience that this will (likely) be a short arc, encouraging the audience to wonder why. This serves to focus the audience's attention on the scene, which, as Trachalio appears, quickly devolves into one of concentrated verbal humour, in which the word *licet* ('OK') is spoken seventeen times (1212–26, with two more in 1225, *infelicet* and the cognate *licentia*). Indeed, the joke was expected to be so successful that it is recapitulated in the sixth arc at 1269–79, where the word *censeo* ('I imagine') in various forms appears nineteen times.[72] The sixth arc begins when Gripus enters at 1227, and continues until Labrax begins to swear an oath at 1338. Gripus dictates the terms of the oath, to which Labrax agrees. As he dictates, the music stops: the precision of the wording makes this exchange function exactly as a scene involving reading would (like the letter in *Pseudolus*), and in this way it perhaps comes closest to the scene in *Asinaria* in which Diabolus dictates his prospective contract to his parasite.

Plautus employs only a few techniques as he structures his narratives. Nevertheless, with them he is able to create a great degree of variation, so

---

[70] See also n. 17 on *Asinaria* 828–9.
[71] The closest parallel for this scene is Euripides, *Theseus*, fr. 382K.
[72] Smith (1991) 297–9 and 301–2 capture the essence of these scenes perfectly.

that no two extant plays are the same. The arc structure, with its regularity established by the spoken iambic rise and the musical fall, provides
a pattern into which the narrative is placed (again, 'rise' and 'fall' are
terms derived from the image of the arc, and are not inherent in the
nature of musical accompaniment). The benefit of this analysis is that it
describes the play in units that we know must have been perceptible to
the original audience. Six of Plautus' plays possess four arcs, but this is
certainly not a rule: two, two and a half, three (twice), three and a half
(twice), five (three times), five and a half, six (three times), and seven arcs
are also attested. The audience does not know in advance how many arcs
a play will have. The extra-long opening arc in *Asinaria* is particularly
striking; in *Casina*, the extra-long final arc similarly rewards the audience.[73] As the audience is carried along the undulating current of the play,
the end of the arc is not a necessary conclusion in itself, but a means of
driving the narrative ever forward towards the play's resolution.

Arcs are an integral part of the structure of Roman comedy, and are far
more meaningful in a performance context than the act and scene divisions in the manuscripts. What the arcs mean for the playwright, however, is equally important. For as he adapts the Greek source play, all of
his changes are made fully aware of this structural pattern. Roman
translation practice in the middle republic fully expected that a change in
language would also entail a change in metre, and there is no required
correlation between the arc divisions and the act divisions in the Greek
source play. But the arcs are not all easily separable units, and the
playwright possesses several techniques to smooth the transition from one
arc to another. In performance the smooth progress of the play depends
upon there not being great structural rifts. It is perfectly legitimate to see
an alternating structure of unaccompanied and accompanied passages, as
Moore does, and to note that some of the most striking effects are
accomplished as music begins.[74] My reading is that the playwright
(typically) is deliberately not placing major narrative divisions at the
primary structural breaks, and that this reinforces the play's overall unity.

---

[73] Eight arcs in Plautus last longer than 400 lines, and only the 456-line arc in *Casina* comes at a play
end. *Amphitruo* (462 lines), *Asinaria* (745 lines), *Miles Gloriosus* (480 lines), *Mostellaria* (407 lines),
Poenulus (409 lines), and *Rudens* (441 lines) all come at the beginning of a play; *Rudens* also has a
411-line arc in its middle.

[74] Moore (1998a) 257–8: 'while almost all Plautus' changes to and from iambic senarii … occur at
the entrance or exit of a character, those entrances and exits often do not correspond with major
new directions in the plot … More often, major units of action comprise a pairing of
accompanied and unaccompanied passages, usually with the accompanied passage beginning the
unit.'

It is the pair of passages (unaccompanied, accompanied) that were seen as a unit. Arcs reflect one way that the play hangs together, but there are others, such as the use of stock routines: the 'musical structure' (if such it can be called – it is only a skeletal musical outline, providing a hint of the music's rhythm; but it is the best we can do) is an independent complement to comic schtick.

Many variables control the nature of accompaniment in Plautus' composition process, and the matter of causation should not be misattributed. In the preceding discussion, an explanation was often presented for the transition from one arc to another, often tied to a character's entry or exit. But I have not sought to demonstrate that these are the most important entrances or exits to the narrative of the play, nor do I believe that one causes the other. To use the first example of an arc juncture considered, it is neither the case that the entry of Diabolus and his parasite at *Asinaria* 746 (or the exit of Argyrippus, Libanus, Leonida, and Philaenium at 745) causes the music to stop and the new arc to begin; nor does the end of an arc cause Leonida to leave and the merchant to arrive. Nor does this need to correspond to an act division in the Greek original, though it may well do so. The playwright at all times carefully and creatively balances his use of music, stock comic routines, character entrances and exits, and the relationship to the Greek original. This is never a mechanical or automatic process.

For all their differences, Terence's plays are built using exactly the same arc structure.[75] *Adelphoe*,[76] *Heauton Timoroumenos*,[77] and *Hecyra* each possess six arcs; *Phormio* has seven; *Eunuchus* has eight; and *Andria* has ten. Two of the arcs in *Andria* (384–403 and 524–37) are very short, and these are also distinctive in that, unlike the Plautine practice, their falls do not contain any tr^7, a metre represented in the fall of every Plautine arc. Instead ia^8 are used, as indeed they are in the simple fall of *Phormio* 748–819, which also has no trochaic component.[78]

Emerging from this discussion is an assumption that the audience receives and processes accompanied passages differently from the way it does unaccompanied passages. This is intuitively true, and would be easy to support by appeal to psychological and musicological studies. Plautus'

---

[75] A convenient and clear 'Metrical Analysis' for Terence's plays is found in Barsby (2001) Vols. I: 445–52, II: 369–75. This information is therefore not repeated in the appendix.

[76] See Moore (1999) 149–51.

[77] See Moore (1998a) 268–71.

[78] Iambic octonarii are the only stichic metre Terence uses numerically more often than Plautus: there are about 420 such lines in Plautus, and 870 in Terence (Beare (1964) 328).

practice of using ia^6 for key elements of plot (including prologues) means that Plautus expects that some in his audience will not be able to process accompanied passages fully.[79] The additional layer of (musical) information adds complexity and perhaps means that rhythmic and musical effects could at times overshadow the verbal content of the passage. Consequently, musical passages might be received impressionistically by some spectators.

STICHIC METRE AND SONG

The metrical virtuosity of Roman comedy is central to an appreciation of the audience's experience during performance. Metrical differences (which necessarily correspond to musical differences) are one of the principal resources available to the playwrights for creating emotional effects. Rough totals demonstrate the relative frequencies of particular metres in Plautus:[80]

ia^6	c. 8,200	(37.6%)	unaccompanied
tr^7	c. 8,800	(40.6%)	accompanied
ia^7	c. 1,300	(6.1%)	accompanied
ia^8	c. 420	(1.9%)	accompanied
other	c. 3,000	(13.8%)	accompanied

Plautus exhibits 'wide variations from play to play'[81] and not much can be gleaned from these figures in isolation, except that on average over 60 per cent of a play was accompanied.

In both Plautus and Terence, ia^6 and tr^7 represent the principal quantitative metres used in each play. Unlike Plautus, Terence uses the senarius more frequently: c. 3,100 ia^6 against c. 1,300 tr^7. This ratio is misleading, however, because Terence uses other stichic metres with greater regularity, particularly ia^8, and alternates between them much more frequently than Plautus does, which replicates much of the effect of the Plautine *cantica*, which are otherwise almost absent from Terence's

---

[79] Moore (2004a) 144 suggests it is possible to grasp the plot of *Poenulus* by reading only the senarii.

[80] See Duckworth (1952) 362–70, Beare (1964) 327–8, Gratwick (1999) 232. Since there are many ways that such totals can be reached, the totals given here are only approximate (particularly since lines are not of equal length), and represent only a consistent summary of the totals of previous scholars.

[81] Gratwick (1999) 232.

plays.[82] The use of music is equally important to Terence, though it is expressed in a different way.

While I have tried to emphasise the difference between tr^7 and ia^6 in terms of musical accompaniment, in their basic form they are similar. Though the use of 'feet' in describing these verse forms dates to antiquity, such language obscures the fact that the metres are almost identical to each other:[83]

$$x - x - x \mid - x - x - \smile - \qquad (ia^6)$$
$$- x - x - x - x \mid - x - x - \smile - \qquad (tr^7)$$

Following the caesura, there is no difference in the verse structure; before the caesura, tr^7 is the same as ia^6 with $- x -$ at the front. In Roman comedy, the audience registered the cretic rhythm ($- \smile -$) that concludes each of these stichic measures. While both ia^6 and tr^7 admit to a great degree of variation (as long syllables are resolved into two short syllables, and any anceps syllable may be realised as one short, one long, or two short syllables), the audience continually anticipates this expected conclusion to the line as an assurance that the rhythm continues properly. Even if the expectation is subconscious, for over three-quarters of a Roman comedy, this aural key is present (in both accompanied and unaccompanied metres) and is the surest indicator of the verse form.,

It is easy to complicate the experience as we try to account for minor variations that, in performance, are passed over in less than a second. Study of such moments potentially demonstrates what assumptions were in the mind of the poet as a given line was written, but there is no way of knowing whether the poet thought in these terms explicitly: a violation of Meyer's Law or Luch's Law[84] may simply have felt intuitively 'wrong' to the author and the audience. Indeed, Cicero (*Orator* 51.173) recognises

---

[82] The brief exceptional passages are *Andria* 481–6, 625–38, and *Adelphoe* 610–17.

[83] I do not wish to pursue the technical aspects of this representation, when excellent introductions to Plautine metre exist in easily accessible commentaries: Willcock (1987) 141–61, Gratwick (1993) 40–63 and 248–60, Barsby (1999) 290–304, and see Raven (1965) and Questa (1967). In brief: $\smile$ represents a short syllable; $-$ represents a long; x represents an anceps ('doubtful') syllable that can be realised as either short or long; $\mid$ marks caesura or diaeresis in the line, where there is always a word end (if it is true that podic analysis is not helpful, the distinction between these terms vanishes). The final element in any line, and often before a caesura, is *indifferens* – it may appear as either a long or a short; for simplicity, these have not been marked.

[84] Together these constitute 'the central rule of Plautine metric' (Gratwick (1993) 56, italics removed).

this, albeit condescendingly:

in versu quidem theatra tota exclamant, si fuit una syllaba aut brevior aut longior; nec vero multitudo pedes novit nec ullos numeros tenet nec illud quod offendit aut curat aut in quo offendat intelligit; et tamen omnium longitudinum et brevitatum in sonis sicut acutarum graviumque vocum iudicium ipsa natura in auribus nostris collocavit.

... in the case of poetry ... the whole audience will hoot at one false quantity. Not that the multitude knows anything of feet, or has any understanding of rhythm; and when displeased they do not realize why or with what they are displeased. And yet nature herself has implanted in our ears the power of judging long and short sounds as well as high and low pitch in words.[85]

When the verse form provides regular, predictable, and obvious aural cues, it is these that determine its acceptability in performance.[86] This is particularly true since neither of these verse forms (as opposed to the dactylic hexameter, for example) is isochronic: if we assume that two shorts are roughly equivalent in duration to a long (a supposition authorised by the way long syllables resolve),[87] ia^6 may occupy between 18 and 23 short-syllabic units, and tr^7 between 23 and 29 such units.[88] Gratwick's discussion of reading Plautine verse aloud rhythmically[89] emphasises the onset of the final cretic rhythm, which further encourages an audience to notice and appreciate the regularity of the closing cadence. While we cannot know the nature of the musical accompaniment to the delivery of tr^7, it would be very unlikely that the *tibicen* would work against what the playwright is expecting from his actors' delivery. The problem of isochronicity will return when we consider exactly what the *tibicen* does during a performance.

That alternate long syllables should receive particular emphasis is a conclusion from another aspect of Gratwick's analysis. He compares the

---

[85] Text and translation, Hubbell (1962) 452–3. See also Cicero, *de Oratore* 3.196.

[86] Cicero, *Stoic Paradoxes* 3.26, describes actors mispronouncing syllables and getting booed off the stage (this is perhaps the fate of the comic actor Eros at Cicero, *pro Q. Roscio comoedo* 30).

[87] The equation of two short syllables with one long is approximate, but is mostly accurate in terms of the metrical structure. Musically, things are different. Greek musical texts 'show us long syllables being occasionally protracted to the value of three or (in the later texts) four shorts' (West (1992) 132). However, the situation is not as haphazard as Dionysius of Halicarnassus suggests at *de Compositione verborum* 64 (2.42.15 UR): West continues, 'we find one example of a final closed syllable ... being treated as long within the verse, and there are two or three instances of this happening at verse end [i.e. being treated as a syllable *indifferens*]. We do not find any case of a long syllable being shortened.'

[88] Gratwick (1993) 46–8 and 60–62 in particular phrases the problem in terms of isochronicity.

[89] Gratwick (1993) 61.

expected appearance of feet of a particular shape (i.e. whether they are iambs with three short-syllabic units, or spondees with four; $\smile -$ or $- -$) if they were distributed randomly, with what is actually observed, in the first 400 complete senarii from *Menaechmi* and *Adelphoe*.[90] His results demonstrate both that Plautus and Terence think of the iambic metron as having the usual form $- - \smile -$ rather than $x - x -$ (further undermining the value of thinking of the senarius as being composed of six 'feet'),[91] and that Plautus is not altering the use of a particular metre to individualise the speech patterns of characters, except possibly in rare instances: the iambic metron exhibits these features regardless of the character type speaking. What type of metre a character uses is part of their presentation,[92] particularly with other verse forms.

Unsurprisingly, other stichic metres are related. The addition of an iambic metron ($x - x -$) to ia^6 produces ia^8, used occasionally by Plautus but with much greater frequency by Terence:[93]

$$
\begin{array}{ll}
x - x - x \mid - x - x - \smile - & (ia^6) \\
- x - x - x - x \mid - x - x - \smile - & (tr^7) \\
x - x - x - x - x \quad - x - x - \smile - & (ia^8)
\end{array}
$$

The diaeresis need not be present, but when it is, it is strong enough that the metre may as well be two iambic dimeters ($2 \times ia^4$):[94]

$$
\begin{array}{ll}
x - x - x - x - x - x - \smile - & (ia^8) \\
x - x - x - \smile - \mid x - x - x - \smile - & (ia^8)
\end{array}
$$

This is typical in the longer stichic metres, and shows that more than eight elements (most of which theoretically might resolve into two shorts) represents an upper limit for either the actor or the audience in terms of what gets processed as a unit. The addition of one element to the beginning of the tr^7 has meant that the break point in the line has been moved back one element as well. This again suggests that the caesura was recognised in some way in the delivery of the lines, but it also shows that ia^8 has a very different 'feel' than ia^6 and tr^7. Though a relatively rare

---

[90] Gratwick (1993) 257–60, (1999) 233–7.

[91] This is an important conclusion, but since comparative analyses have not been done on other stichic metres, it is clearest for this overview to mark the syllables as anceps.

[92] For *Adelphoe*, see Gratwick (1999) 232.

[93] This is the metre that Terence would eventually introduce to create a simple fall in his arcs, using a metre other than tr^7 for perhaps the first time.

[94] Raven (1965) 63, 65, 67, Willcock (1987) 152–3.

rhythm, Plautus uses it for an effect that 'stands out for its frequency, [and] is best described as comic or heroic exaggeration, and occurs when the usually disreputable or pompous character comes on stage extolling his exploits or abilities.'[95] The rhythm of ia^8 with its balanced caesura means that 'iambic octonarii ... are farcical, ridiculous, exaggerated' and are particularly suited for boasting slaves.[96]

When this balance is removed, the effect of the line is changed. The iambic septenarius (ia^7) removes the mandatory short syllable from the second last element of the ia^8 line:[97]

$$x - x - x - \smile - \mid x - x - x - \smile - \qquad (ia^8)$$
$$x - x - x - \smile - \mid x - x - x - - \qquad (ia^7)$$

As with all the stichic metres, there is a strong and necessarily audible ending to the line that is distinctive: used in the *Atellanae*,[98] it has been called 'a rollicking rhythm',[99] though Moore believes ia^7 'slow the pace of performance' for key comic scenes (such as *Asinaria* 545–745).[100] Plautus concentrates his use of this metre in particular plays, with over half of Plautus' use found in *Asinaria* and *Miles Gloriosus*, which have comparatively little *cantica*, and *Rudens*, which has some of Plautus' richest songs.[101] It is also used distinctively in the first arc of *Truculentus*. Further

---

[95] Tobias (1980) 15, who then lists the examples of 'heroic' octonarii, which 'account for about 75% of Plautus' iambic octonarii': *Amphitruo* 153–8, 180–218, 248–62, 984–1005, 1053–85, *Aulularia* 413–14, *Bacchides* 925–78, 987–8, *Captivi* 516–24, 770–80, 909–21, *Persa* 3–12, *Pseudolus* 185–93, *Stichus* 274–308. With 127 ia^8 verses total, *Amphitruo* represents almost a third of Plautus' use of this metre.

[96] Tobias (1980) 16. Nine of the fourteen passages listed in the previous note are in the mouths of slaves.

[97] Raven (1965) 69, 71. Lindsay (1922) 275 says 'the sure examples of absence of Diaeresis are less than one in twenty ... The consequence is that the Septenarii of Plautus have an unretarded, lively movement that makes them very pleasant reading.'

[98] Marius Victorinus, *Ars Grammatica* 3.12 (Keil (1961) vol. VI: 135, lines 25–7): *frequens hoc comicis metrum, et praecipue antiquae comoediae scriptoribus, nostri quoque Plautus et Caecilius et Turpilius non aspernati sunt, Atellanae autem scriptores appetiverunt* ('This metre is often in the comic poets, and especially in the authors of Old Comedy; also our Plautus and Caecilius and Turpilius did not spurn to use it; but the Atellan authors strove to use it'). Assuming Victorinus (or his source) knows something about *Atellanae*, this passage apparently presents a chronological development from (Greek) Old Comedy to Roman New Comedy and on to Atellan authors. This would suggest that he is referring to literate *Atellanae* (post-Turpilius, who died 103 BC according to Jerome), and not their improvised precursors. Indeed, 17 of the 314 lines from literate *Atellanae* considered by Frassinetti (1967) 145–6 are iambic septenarii. This is just over 5 per cent, less than Victorinus' emphasis (*appetiverunt*) would expect, but perhaps our sample is not representative. We are not in a position to affirm that the metre was used in improvised *Atellanae* (it may have been taken over directly from Plautus), but the possibility remains.

[99] Duckworth (1952) 368.   [100] Moore (2004a) 157.   [101] Law (1922) 8.

variations of these long lines may be found in the *versus reizianus* and the tr^8, which occur less frequently.[102]

Aristotle considered the Greek iambic trimeter closest to ordinary speech, and the senarius is its Latin form.[103] Because of their similarities, all of these iambo-trochaic rhythms, then, partake in some sense of the rhythms of natural speech, an effect enhanced by the freedom that each form allows. Nevertheless, at no point can we forget this is poetry. The rhythms are rigidly patterned, and often further bound by the presence of musical accompaniment. However, as Wright observes in his discussion of Shakespeare's iambic pentameter (another verse form often equated with natural speech),

> sooner or later, playwrights are bound to absorb two inescapable facts about dramatic verse. First, the paradox that in the theatre … verse becomes *in*visible, unmeasured by the eye. Second, it comes to us not in silence from a page we read with our eyes and imagine ourselves speaking, but sounded by human voices other than our own.[104]

The spectator cannot see a shift in metre coming on the page but must be guided aurally by the actor and musician. Acoustic cues (in the form of distinctive line ends) are essential, even if an individual audience member is not following the rhythms consciously. When a new rhythm is introduced, the audience must feel the shift, and will perceive characters and events differently as a result. Wright's 'paradox' exists because the verse is continual, and so it stops being an object of attention in itself, and becomes a patterning device to serve the playwright's ends. The second component is just as important, for it is beholden upon the actors always to speak the verse clearly, audibly, and intelligibly. This is a challenge in any theatrical tradition, but in an outdoor festival context employing masked actors the problem is particularly acute. Even for an engaged and attentive audience, there are always obstacles hindering clear and effective delivery. The rhythms of the poetry must be respected by the actor, and not exaggerated, for it is only through his delivery that the audience can appreciate the playwright's structure. The actor must appear natural, but

---

[102] The *reizianus* also has affinities with anapaests (Questa (1967) 245).

[103] Aristotle, *Poetics* 1449a24–6, *Rhetoric* 1404a32, and see Cicero, *Orator* 55.184: *at comicorum senarii propter similitudinem sermonis sic saepe sunt abiecti, ut nonnumquam vix in eis numerus et versus intellegi possit* ('But the senarii of comedy are often so lacking in elevation of style because of their resemblance to ordinary conversation that sometimes it is scarcely possible to distinguish rhythm and verse in them'; text and translation, Hubbell (1962) 460–63).

[104] Wright (1988) 91–2.

not naturalistic, which of course would not be possible in any case given the theatrical and performative context: 'it is a naturalness embedded in a highly figured medium'.[105]

Nowhere is this patterning more evident than in the *cantica mixtis modis*. Each arc makes its fall (by definition) to the accompaniment of the *tibia*, and in these accompanied passages there are typically modulations between metres, often including passages that exhibit considerable metrical variety using metres other than the repeating iambo-trochaic patterns we have examined. There has been considerable debate as to whether these *cantica* were 'sung' or not, in part because there is no way definitively to know.[106] 'Speech' and 'song' are neurologically distinct means of producing sound, and a large number of intermediate vocal mechanisms exist that complicate the matter further.[107] While I believe that 'song' is appropriate in the context of Plautus' *cantica*, there are other measures that guarantee a distinct mode of delivery for these passages. What marks the *cantica* as distinct from the accompanied stichic metres is the fact that the verse form does not repeat (except for stichic anapaests, discussed below). There is no default rhythm, and here, more than anywhere else in a Roman comedy, the delivery of the lines is likely to be precisely aligned with the music of the *tibia*. The audience will never know what rhythm will exist in the next line to be delivered, and virtuosity – that of the actor, of the musician, and of the playwright – is on prominent display.

Plautus uses *cantica* to entertain the audience, but also to define characters. Cooks, soldiers, and parasites seldom sing,[108] but female characters are given a disproportionate amount of lyrics. Within the accompanied passages the *cantica* were in some way 'elevated' in their delivery. *Cantica* can be used to represent the extremes of emotion; they can serve as a 'showpiece' for the lead actor;[109] and they can lend an additional prominence to otherwise minor characters, such as Leaena in *Curculio*, Phaniscus in *Mostellaria*, Ptolemocratia in *Rudens*, and Cyamus in *Truculentus*. They

---

[105] Wright (1988) 230.

[106] In favour of sung *cantica* are Lejay (1925) 11–28 and Duckworth (1952) 369–75; arguing that such a case cannot be made is Ritschl (1877) 22–33. See also Moore (1998a) 247 and n. 5.

[107] List (1963). Even Livy 7.2.10 was confused about how accompanied passages were delivered; there is no need to follow his implausible belief that a *cantor* delivered all accompanied lines from backstage. Beare (1964) 220 provides a charitable summary: 'At all events it seems clear that Livy regarded the canticum as something which required a special vocal effort, greater than what was needed for the diuerbium'.

[108] Collart (1970).

[109] Moore (2001a) 318 suggests this for the opening song of *Epidicus*.

are not, in the end, separable from the play, however. Law describes '[a] group of eighteen cantica, or about a quarter of the whole number ... in which there seems to be no break either in situation or subject-matter but which are completely fused with the following lines'.[110]

In this context, we can consider briefly three verse forms found amongst the *cantica*: cretics, bacchiacs, and anapaests. The effect in performance of bacchiacs and cretics is remarkably different from that which is created by the tendency towards alternating long and short syllables, as found in iambo-trochaic metres. Both the cretic metron ($-\smile-$) and the bacchius ($\smile--$) occupy roughly five short-syllable lengths, which can in many instances be expanded to six ($---$, a molossus). There are, for example, three basic forms of the bacchiac tetrameter:

$$x--x-\mid-x--x-- \qquad (ba^4)$$
$$x--x--\mid x--x-- \qquad (ba^4)$$
$$x--x--\smile\mid--x-- \qquad (ba^4)$$

Plautus has about 560 bacchiac lines,[111] either of this form, or in some straightforward variation (dimeter, syncopated, and catalectic forms all exist). While short strings of bacchiac verses exist (e.g. *Pseudolus* 244–8), it is unlikely that the audience identified this as a stichic metre. Rather, what they perceive is the repeated long syllables that led Lindsay to suggest it was 'a metre admirably suited to Roman "gravitas"'.[112] Tobias agrees – 'bacchiacs suggest *gravitas* or *dignitas*, either real or parodied' – and notes in particular that 44.7 per cent of Plautus' bacchiac lines are delivered by female characters, an amount disproportionate to the number of lines given to women in the plays overall (16.2 per cent).[113]

Similarly, cretic lines (of which there are about 400) exhibit related patterns, sometimes with a diaeresis after the second metron:

$$-x--x--x--x- \qquad (cr^4)$$

Trimeters, dimeters, and monometers also exist, and podic analysis of the lines is of limited value for understanding what an audience perceives,

---

[110] Law (1922) 11.
[111] Tobias (1980) 9 says 558. Beare (1964) 332 says 400, but this is probably an accidental confusion with the total of cretic lines on page 333.
[112] Lindsay (1922) 289. Moore (2004a) 152 observes that of the *cantica* described by Questa (1995), eighteen begin with bacchiacs, and nineteen begin with anapaests.
[113] Tobias (1980) 16 and 9; and, generally, see 10–15.

since line- end is not distinguished aurally. If we compare cretic tetrameters to bacchiacs, the similarities emerge:[114]

$$x - - x - - x - - x - -\qquad (ba^4)$$
$$- x - - x - - x - - x -\qquad (cr^4)$$

Consequently, Duckworth has difficulty isolating the function of the cretic: 'Cretics too have a variety of uses, ranging from battle description ... to the portrayal of intoxication; expressions of emotion are frequent: joy..., confidence..., grief..., feigned terror ..., despair ....'[115] Because there is often not time for an audience to perceive aurally what the line structure is, any distinction between the two will likely depend on the tone and pace of the accompanying music. Whatever rules Plautus is using to combine measures, for the audience it is all part of the larger *canticum*.

In contrast to all of the metres discussed so far, anapaests represent a rhythm which the modern western ear can easily appreciate, because it is isochronic.[116] The anapaestic metron ($\smile\smile \_ \smile\smile \_$ though at times a dactyl can be found, and so $\smile\smile \smile\smile \smile\smile$, but this suggests a freedom that is not exhibited) always occupies four short-syllable lengths. There are about 500 anapaestic lines in Plautus,[117] and typical line lengths are the dimeter, the 'octonarius' (= tetrameter) and the 'septenarius' (= tetrameter catalectic):

$$\smile\smile \_ \smile\smile \_ \smile\smile \_ \smile\smile \_\qquad (an^4)$$

$$\smile\smile \_ \smile\smile \_ \smile\smile \_ \mid \smile\smile \_ \smile\smile \_ \smile\smile \_\qquad (an^8)$$

$$\smile\smile \_ \smile\smile \_ \smile\smile \_ \mid \_ \smile\smile \_ \smile\smile \_ \_\qquad (an^7)$$

The regular caesura in the long lines and the roughly equal duration of each metron mean that they naturally fall into halves. Anapaestic lines are often associated with movement. Both earlier in Greek drama, and throughout Seneca, they are a metre of the chorus, often unhelpfully

---

[114] Beare (1964) 333.
[115] Duckworth (1952) 370–71.
[116] Augustine, *de Musica* 6.26–8 relates isochronicity to the pleasures of listening to music. For anapaests generally, see Boldrini (1984).
[117] Duckworth (1952) 369. Representative passages may be found at *Aulularia* 713–26, *Bacchides* 1076–1108, 1149–1206, *Cistellaria* 203–29, *Persa* 168–80, *Pseudolus* 230–42, *Rudens* 220–28, *Stichus* 309–29, *Trinummus* 256–300, and 820–42.

labelled 'marching anapaests'. This does suggest that movement on the comic stage, at least when this metre was being employed, could adopt a formal regularity, a clockwork rhythm maintained by the predictability of the measure (when the line was employed as a stichic metre, and not as an isolated line in a larger *canticum* system). The regularity of anapaests means that they can be delivered more quickly, too, and so they are appropriate for excited outbursts. Second, 'Latin anapaests of this type are characterized by a marked lack of harmony between metrical rhythm and the word accent.'[118] When regularity is introduced in one aspect of the poetry, it is taken away in another.

All of this patterning is deliberate. Plautus revels in various ways of patterning human speech, and provides his actors with many different metrical opportunities, each of which have implications for the play's music, the actor's characterisations, and the audience's processing of the dramatic narrative. The selection of a verse form is never random and it is never mindlessly transported from the Greek original. Plautus' metrical genius is the ability to pattern the play he is writing on both the macro-level (the arc structure) and the micro-level (accomplishing effects line-by-line). A central component of the audience experience of Roman comedy, songs are not to be seen as diversions from the main business of the play, as has often been done even by their defenders.[119] Roman comedy simultaneously integrates humour operating at a great many levels, one of which is the enthusiasm and excitement produced by metrical variety. Any efforts we make to appreciate 'the more austere pleasures of meter'[120] will be rewarded.

THE *TIBICEN* AND COMIC DELIVERY

For some in the audience, the most memorable contributor to the performance would be the *tibicen*, the musician who accompanied the performance on the *tibia* ('pipe').[121] The instrument was normally played in pairs, with each pipe fingered by a different hand. Though the

---

[118] Duckworth (1952) 369. In n. 18 he cites Lindsay's observation that this shows 'that Plautus was a quantitative, not an accentual, poet, and did *not* assign too high a place to the reconciliation of accent and ictus' (Lindsay (1922) 397).

[119] Law (1922) 62 talks of 'songs on stereotypes and wholly irrelevant themes ... used to fill time intervals'; this can never be helpful.

[120] Wright (1988) 97.

[121] There is no completely acceptable translation of *tibia*, an instrument that probably uses a double-reeded mouthpiece, like the Greek *aulos* (which was the instrument accompanying Greek drama) and the modern oboe. On the instrument generally, see Reinach (1919).

didascalia to *Stichus* and to Terence's plays record the name of the musician prominently, the *tibicen* was a slave, and the practical economics motivating a Roman theatre troupe's decisions suggest this slave was probably owned by someone in the troupe.[122] Not only is the familiar musician always available for the preparation of a play, but he could also be subcontracted for additional performances, supplementing the troupe's overall income.

The *tibicen* was a liminal figure, part of the performance but equally not part of the dramatic world the performance creates. The division is not absolute, as the final lines in *Stichus* demonstrate, but for the most part the function of the *tibicen* is to enhance the separateness of the performance. It also reinforces the architecture of the play, by helping to normalise the verse forms spoken by the actors, and by establishing the principal structural patterns so that the arcs are immediately discernible to an audience. These are both theatrical (non-diegetic) functions, separate from diegetic music within the dramatic narrative, though the *tibicen* had a part to play here too.[123] It is possible that at times the *tibicen* was called to provide accompaniment for onstage musicians: some female love interests in Roman comedy are *tibicinae*, and it is possible that they appeared on stage with their (prop) instrument, requiring genuine musical accompaniment. It is also possible the *tibicen* was required to imitate other instruments, such as the lyre: unusually, the love interest in *Epidicus* is a *fidicina* ('lyre-girl'). Moore sees this as 'more refined'[124] within the world of the play, but it is also, in terms of stagecraft, much more aggressive. Perhaps then the *fidicinae* in *Eunuchus* and *Phormio* are following Plautus' dramaturgical innovation, rather than exhibiting an aspect of Terence's refinement.

There are a great number of questions concerning the *tibicen* for which it would be nice to have certain answers. Cicero, *pro Murena* 26, claims that the wanderings of lawyers in court were *tibicinis Latini modo* ('in the style of a Latin *tibicen*', Quintilian 7.1.51). Most take this to mean that the *tibicen* followed the actors singing as they moved about the stage in Roman drama (a similar inference may be drawn from Horace, *Ars Poetica* 215), though this is not the only interpretation of the passage

---

[122] The later existence of guilds of *tibicines* (e.g. *Corpus Inscriptionum Latinarum* 6.2584) means that not all pipers were slaves, though perhaps in theatrical contexts this was the norm.

[123] Plautus plays with the diegetic/non-diegetic disctinction at *Mostellaria* 933–4, where Phaniscus claims (within the narrative) not to hear a *tibicina*, even though the metre is *tr⁷*, and therefore accompanied by the *tibicen*.

[124] Moore (2001a) 328 n. 30.

possible: the distinction might be between Latin pipe-players and Roman ones, and in any case he is referring to the theatre in his day.[125] No melodies survive from Roman drama and we do not know the feel of the music the *tibicen* played. The Greek *aulos* and the *tibia* were by c. 200 BC probably two names for the same instrument; they are in any case functionally equivalent, and the Hellenistic *aulos*-fragments are very similar to the *tibiae* from Pompeii. The *tibia* was able to create a range of sounds that could evoke a variety of emotions from the audience: 'the pipes were thought capable of imitating all sounds and voices, and as a result they were also deemed the most mimetic of instruments'.[126]

Even the nature of the instrument has many uncertainties. The *tibicen* had available to him several types of *tibia* from which to choose. The *didascalia* to Terence's plays demonstrate the variety available: *Andria* was allegedly performed *tibiis paribus dextris vel sinistris* ('on equal pipes, either left or right');[127] *Heauton Timoroumenos*: *tibiis inparibus deinde duabus dextris* ('on unequal pipes and then two rights'); *Eunuchus*: *tibiis duabus dextris* ('on two right pipes'); *Phormio*: *tibiis inparibus tota* ('on unequal pipes throughout'); *Hecyra*: *tibiis paribus tota* ('on equal pipes throughout'); *Adelphoe* (and also Plautus' *Stichus*): *tibiis sarranis tota* ('on Tyrian pipes throughout'). Donatus offers different readings for *Eunuchus*, *Phormio*, and *Adelphoe*, and the manuscripts offer variants for *Phormio*, so there is little reason for confidence even if we knew what these variables represented.[128]

The right-hand pipe seems to have been a straight cylinder; it is sometimes claimed that the left-hand pipe was longer (and therefore lower in pitch), but firmer evidence would be nice. When one of each was used (*tibiae inpares*, 'unequal pipes'), this was perhaps the 'Phrygian' style (*tibiae Phrygiae*). Servius equates *tibiae sarranae* (as in *Adelphoe*) with *tibiae pares* (as in *Hecyra*), but given that *Eunuchus* calls specifically for two *dextrae*, perhaps 'Tyrian' implies specifically two *sinistrae*. *Andria*, and perhaps *Hecyra*, apparently allow for some choice (though *Andria*, since it was only mounted once during Terence's lifetime, presumably did not avail itself of this choice: re-mountings of these plays were contemplated by someone). Most striking is the change that is indicated by

---

[125] Trimalchio is similarly confused about the meaning of the expression at Petronius, *Satyricon* 53, when he asks his piper to play in Latin.

[126] Csapo (2004) 219.

[127] This is the reading of one manuscript of Donatus, accepted by the OCT of Terence; the *didascalia* for *Andria* are lacking.

[128] Tansey (2001) 41–2 suggests that Donatus' didascalic information can refer to post-Terentian revivals.

the word *deinde* for *Heauton Timoroumenos*: presumably the *tibicen* changes his pipe arrangement during one of the passages of ia^6, but we cannot know the musical reason or the effect.[129] Despite the apparent precision that this information provides us, much is still unknown: what the instruments sounded like, how they were played in pairs, what notes were played, whether they doubled the rhythms and melodies of the actor's voices, and at what point (or how many times) musicians switched instruments during performances.

There is no question that the *cantica mixtis modis*, which constitute showpiece elements in the fall of an arc, required intense rehearsal so that both actor and musician clearly could present the melody with its rapidly changing rhythms for an audience that possessed no means of expecting recurring patterns even if they were present. Given the pressures required for mounting a production, if the *tibicen* was able to compose accompaniment for the accompanied iambo-trochaic stichic metres spontaneously in performance, then the rehearsal process could be streamlined considerably, though not eliminated. This is what I suggest happened. The process of composition in performance ('improvisation') provides a buffer for all performers of these passages. Vocal melody will not equate with the notes of the music played on a one-to-one basis – indeed it cannot, because the 'score' has no independent existence before it is played. The *tibicen* will set and maintain the pulse of the line and provide an emotionally appropriate musical background, exhibiting for the actor a more or less predictable character, alongside which his voice can deliver his lines. This in no way diminishes the virtuosity of the *tibicen* who must constantly be aware of his musical performance, what the actors are doing, and the musical and metrical structure of the play – his prominence in the *didascalia* is justly earned.[130] The *cantica* interrupt the improvised element of the music for a carefully rehearsed number that is more musically demanding (with complex, alternating metres) and therefore, for an audience, more spectacular, but which represent, for the musician, a performative activity that is less intellectually demanding, or at least one that is demanding in a different way.

---

[129] Many interesting possibilities exist: perhaps the *tibiae sarranae* were products of Carthage, and represent a recent import to Rome when used in *Stichus* (Palmer (1997) 48–9).

[130] Non-dramatic musical fragments are equivocal. While generally some variation of accompaniment for stichic measures is suggested (West (1992) 209), the hymn preserved at *Supplementum Epigraphicum Graecum* 30.390 (= Pöhlmann and West (2001) 19) suggests a standard melody, no doubt allowing for some variation, was at times used.

Moore believes that the *tibicen* employed a technique of circular breathing, the uninterrupted exhalation of air required to play the didgeridoo and sometimes employed by a wide variety of wind instrumentalists.[131] While the suggestion is not inherently improbable, it perhaps makes unduly literal Roman concerns against the interruption of musical performance in a religious context and in favour of constant music during sacrifices.[132] A number of details (such as the large cheeks of *tibicinae* in *Poenulus* 1416) are ultimately neutral on the question: while a large air reservoir would be useful for circular breathing, that is not its only function for an instrumentalist. At *Mercator* 125, *perii, animam nequeo vertere, nimis nihili tibicen siem* ('I'm dying! I can't turn my breath – I would be a really lousy piper'), the Acanthio actor is performing a running slave routine, and, as he catches his breath, compares himself to a *tibicen*. Certainly the phrase *animam vertere* looks as if it could mean 'to breathe circularly'.[133] However, the context does not expect Acanthio to do this. The phrase cannot simply mean to breathe in and out, though it is likely he is huffing and puffing as part of the comic routine; what he lacks rather is breath control, the ability to modulate his breath in the way a trained musician does.

More promising is the question of the composition of the music. Donatus, *de Comoedia* 8.9–10, tells us:

cantica vero temperabantur modis non a poeta sed a perito artis musicae factis … eius qui modos faciebat nomen in principio fabulae post scriptoris et actoris superponebatur

Indeed, the songs were moderated with melodies not from the playwright but by someone skilled in the art of musical composition … At the beginning of a play

---

[131] Moore (forthcoming), ch. 1.

[132] See, e.g. Pliny the Elder, *Natural History* 28.11, and Cicero, *de Haruspicum Responso* 23. Csapo (2004) discusses some of these issues as they relate to the Greek world. Further, Moore's argument works against his belief that individual senarii in accompanied passages always or regularly indicate moments when the music stops. For, even if it later becomes clear that the unaccompanied line is a senarius and therefore need not have associated music, the audience will notice in the first instance that the music has stopped. If circular breathing were used by the *tibicen*, then it seems unlikely that the playwright would taunt the audience with the possibility of some supposed sacrilege at a point where the dramatic characters are creating a separate effect. I have argued that in most cases the isolated senarii do not represent a break in the music, so the point becomes moot. That does not necessarily imply, however, that circular breathing must have been used. Music can be continuous and still possess rests and momentary silences that are a natural part of the creation of rhythm and melody.

[133] I am unable to find any parallels for the phrase. Enk (1932) vol. II: 33 suggests that Acanthio is merely saying he cannot 'catch his breath' (*'animam recipere, i.e. efflare et renovare'*) but this fails to explain the reference to the *tibicen*.

the name of the one who made the melodies [appeared] after the playwright and was placed before the actors.[134]

The prominence given to *tibicines* in the *didascaliae* suggests the musical specialist was the *tibicen* himself. But the notion of composition typically implies in modern western culture a fixed musical score, and no visual representation of a musician (in the Greek or Roman stage performance) suggests that musicians had music in front of them while they played. There is no indication that scores were ever used during performance in antiquity, even though the surviving music can be very complex, and over the length of a play would amount to a great deal of music. Musical notation can preserve melodies, but it was not a cue during performance.

Advancing beyond this picture, though, is not straightforward. What I envisage happening in performance is this. Each of the iambo-trochaic metres had a different style of accompaniment associated with it. The metrical form determined the rhythm, and the *tibicen* composed the melody in performance as the actors sang so as to complement the actors' lines. The same melody would not need to repeat identically with each line, but the tonal range, the beat, and perhaps other aspects of the accompaniment were determined by the metre so that it was not neces- sary for each line to be rehearsed perfectly in advance of the performance. The various ways of arranging the *tibiae* could affect the tonal range, timbre, resonance, etc., but in essence (leaving aside changes in fingering, etc.) the *tibicen* is doing the same thing for each metrical form regardless of his instrument's arrangement: different combinations of pipes increase the audience's perception of the music's versatility, and need not repre- sent greater difference for the musician than a switch between a tenor and an alto saxophone (though with the *tibia* the musician is playing two instruments at once).[135] Each different metre could have different styles of accompaniment depending on the arrangement of the instrument. The key aspect of my interpretation is that much of a play's music is improvised, composed in performance before a live audience in coop- eration with the actors and their delivery of the playwright's lines.

It follows that a trained ear in the audience should be able to identify a passage's metre based upon the music coming from the *tibicen*. Music for ia^7 will sound different from music for tr^7, and ia^8 will be different again, and this musical cue was available also for the actors, reinforcing the

---

[134] Wessner (1902–8) vol. I: 30–31.
[135] Huge differences remain possible. It could be that pipes had different *modi* (attunements), and switching pipes meant switching scales (not tonal range, necessarily, but tonal arrangement).

play's performative structure. It also suggests that the music changes noticeably as the metre does: this means that in those arcs that possess a complex fall, the music will exhibit at least two distinct characters, and often many more. Once a metre was established (particularly in passages of tr^7, since their rhythm is the most familiar to the actors) the *tibicen* would be free to add a wide range of flourishes and other ornamentation because of the high degree of predictability involved in the technique of musical composition. The improvised music is not random, but probably operated with a minimal degree of variation of a regularly repeating melodic line.

For the actor, some questions remain. Because we do not know what the voice did during accompanied passages, the relationship between it and the music of the *tibia* cannot be identified. It is often suggested that the actor delivered accompanied stichic lines as a form of 'recitative' or chanting, mid-way between speech and song, in which case the actor could replicate the melodic contours produced by the *tibia* to some degree. This is also the case if we think of the lines as 'song', and the question is not applicable if the lines were 'spoken', delivered in the same vocal mode as the unaccompanied senarii. If spoken, the music would principally provide emotional colouring to the context and telegraph to the audience an aspect of the play's dramatic structure, but these functions are present to some degree regardless. Whatever the actor did, the *tibicen* could emphasise the four principal beats in the tr^7 line, vocal emphasis supported by musical emphasis. It seems probable that the music of accompanied stichic verses in Roman comedy provided appropriate emotional colouring, identification of the spoken metre and reinforcement of its pulse, the opportunity for distinctive ornamental flourishes, and, perhaps, a discernable melody that could be followed by the actor's voice.

Does this mean the actor is following the music, or is the *tibicen* following the poetry? Both are possible. The actor must deliver the lines, which in some sense are written down, which might suggest the musician follows him. The reverse implies that what the actor says is fixed to such a degree that the musician always knows what the actor is about to say (with all that implies both for rehearsal, and for the musician's memory, concentration, and alertness during performance). Neither situation seems to me likely to pertain as a rule.

The question is important because it links to the problem of isochronicity. Because the iambo-trochaic measures do not possess a fixed length (the number of short-syllable time units can vary), any increase or decrease in the total length of the line by the actor (by consciously or subconsciously substituting a word that scans as an iamb for a word that scans as a spondee, for instance) could potentially throw off the music. The two easy ways of extricating oneself from this straitjacket are improbable in a performance context. The first involves the musician knowing the words the actors will say verbatim and using that as a template for the music, which is then played. The degree of precision in performance required and the amount of rehearsal that this implies make this inherently implausible. Nor is it sufficient to suggest the music isolates only the four principal beats of the line, and that it could be said of other syllables, 'just as in English verse, they are merely "spacers" to which some notional standard compromise time value may be assigned'.[136] Gratwick suggests that 'there are simple answers to these questions'[137] but he does not consider the implications for musical accompaniment, and some additional reckoning is needed.

Musical improvisation is not easy, but it is possible. My experience as an improviser in modern unscripted comedy has demonstrated that a whole range of models of performance can exist here. The musician might provide a standard, fixed musical form (such as a 12-bar blues on guitar), within which the singer follows the easily identifiable rhythm and melody. This structure through its predictability contains little risk for the performers. Alternately, an improviser can provide the melody, and the musician does his best to reinforce and support the way the improviser performs. The best improvisation, however, presupposes no fixed rules. Performers used to working with one another give and take with a synergy that allows the creativity of all parties to be realised. Almost paradoxically, both parties lead cooperatively, each listening for cues from the other. Plautus' script provides an element of control: the actors and the *tibicen* know the plot, the arc structure and metrical changes, and rehearsed *cantica*. This removes much of the unpredictability arising from composition in performance. It makes no sense to ask 'how free was the *tibicen* in his elaborations?' because there is no musical score to which elaborations are made (or it was such a simple repeated rhythmic line that expected flourishes and elaboration). Rehearsal would be needed for *cantica mixtis modis*, but the rehearsal time allotted to a play's music is

---

[136] Gratwick (1993) calls this 'The English solution' (47), and he believes (rightly) such a proposal 'will not do' (48). See also West (1992) 137–42 for a different means of addressing the problem, involving the prolongation of certain syllables.

[137] Gratwick (1993) 48; the answers are on 60–62.

greatly diminished when it is realised that accompanied stichic metres expect a pre-defined type of musical accompaniment.

Most of the metres used are non-isochronic, admitting a great variety of temporal lengths. Even if musical accompaniment could be used to standardise the tempo for certain metres (as with Gratwick's 'English solution'), there will be times when the tempo fails to remain constant due to stage action or comic business. This will be even more true for unaccompanied ia^6. The pace within a given speech changes from one line to the next, and an above-average number of long syllables may mean the line is slowed in delivery; equally, if a steady beat is maintained, the effect may give the impression of haste. Either is possible.[138] Each level of delivery will possess a different dynamic that can be correlated to the degree of freedom available to the actor while delivering the lines. The presence of musical accompaniment, even when the dynamic allows for improvisatorial interchange between the singer and the musician, presents some limits on the actor's freedoms, and more limits will exist when the metre is not stichic. This is not to say that there cannot be jokes involving comic timing in *cantica*, but it does mean that such jokes must be carefully rehearsed since all aspects of rhythm and tempo are strictly governed by the irregular music. Humour concerning delivery is part of the musical composition.

Passages in accompanied, stichic metres are increasingly free. Because most of these lines are non-isochronic, the presence of a give-and-take dynamic between actor and musician means that each must be subject to the other's performative expectations. The musician will tend to reinforce the music and metrical structure, while the actor has an obligation to the audience to deliver the lines meaningfully, which entails preferring the demands of syntax and grammar. Humour from comic timing can be rehearsed and determined by the playwright and director, but can also be introduced by the actor(s) and musician working together. For example, the long passage of ia^7 at *Asinaria* 545–745 contains a great deal of comic business: the triumphant celebration of the two slaves; the appearance of the young lovers and the ensuing eavesdropping scene; the teasing of the lovers by the slaves and the subsequent inversion of status, as Argyrippus supplicates Leonida; the by-play with the bag of money; and Argyrippus physically carrying Libanus, in a scene that evokes both the character's name ('Silver-horse') and the play's name ('The Ass Comedy'). Essentially, this is all schtick: the action necessary for the plot could be

---

[138] Compare MacDowell (1971) 162.

accomplished in a single line – 'Master, here is the money you need.' The empty stage that follows comes at the end of the long first arc, and it seems hard to imagine that, despite the regularity of the metre, it would have been possible to determine in advance the precise timing of this incredibly diverse and lengthy passage. The riding scene particularly would require a degree of flexibility in the musical performance (and in the interaction between actors and musicians). There must exist a mechanism that would allow both the actors and the musician to alter the pace and timing of the delivery to accommodate the stage action as needed or desired.[139]

Timing cannot be reduced to a single variable. It is not merely the amount of space left between the set-up and the punch-line of a joke, but is a product of the rapport established between a performer and the audience. The tempo of delivery, the amount of detail in the narrative, the presence of rhythmic and formulaic patterns in speeches all help to determine aspects of timing, but so do the size and composition of the audience, its familiarity with and comfort in the performance venue, and the actor's character and stage presence. It is not something measured on a clock, but is something that becomes defined over the course of a performance as the actor's relationship with the audience develops. Timing depends on an innate quality of the performer, but it is also something that experience can refine, as the performer learns how to maximise audience response.

The successful timing of some types of jokes depends on the regularity provided by the metre. Both *Rudens* 1205–26, in which first Trachalio and then Daemones complete lines begun by the other with the word *licet*, and 1265–80, where the joke is recapitulated with forms of *censeo*, are passages of tr^7. As speeches are tossed back and forth within the line (in these passages, lines 1215, 1268, 1271, 1274, 1276, and 1278 each have four speeches or parts of speeches within them), what is being demonstrated is the actors' ability to follow the metre (and the *tibicen*) while dealing with the sense of the exchange, the tempo established by the music, and other features of the verse such as hiatus, elision, and change of speaker.[140] The comic potential of these scenes lies in the almost clockwork way that the

---

[139] Further affecting matters is the possibility of percussionists working with the *tibicen*. Cicero, *pro Caelio* 65, mentions *scabilla* ('foot-clappers') used to end a mime. Known in the Greek world, but not clearly attested earlier in the republic, *scabilla* were used for percussion and to keep time. Additional musicians would affect the actor–*tibicen* relationship, but not enough is known to say more.

[140] Hough (1970).

characters can insert the one word over and over into an otherwise rigorously controlled dialogue. The audience knows that they are able to do so because the scene is scripted, but through the use of timing and the appearance of spontaneity, this fact becomes less salient than the impressiveness of the actors' abilities to maintain the pace. Exactly the same factors are at work in *Pseudolus* 357–68, where Calidorus and Pseudolus hurl insults at Ballio, each of which he confidently accepts. Four, five, or even six speeches per line occur, but the comedy emerges not only from the evident status inversion as insults are accepted as badges of honour by the pimp, but by the mechanical regularity of the insults. Whether the scene was performed quickly, with Calidorus and Pseudolus escalating both pace and volume, or if it were slow and controlled throughout, as if a verbal chess match were being waged, the rhythm of the speeches regularized by the musical accompaniment enhances the comedy.[141]

There is momentum in the verse.[142] Some comic motifs were not confined to a given metrical form. Scenes of door-knocking, for example, could be accommodated to any metrical structure,[143] but we may imagine that their performance would vary considerably depending on the nature of musical accompaniment. There are many factors at play, if only we consider them. It remains incumbent upon us as interpreters of the genre to think in terms of the effects the music has on performance and the way that comedy is created in Roman comedy.

---

[141] Ballio was a showcase role for the actor Roscius in the 60s and 50s BC, who as he grew older needed the *tibicen* to play slower (Cicero, *de Oratore* 1.254). For Roscius as an actor, see Garton (1972) 169–88. In the Warner Brothers cartoon *Rabbit Seasoning* (1952), Bugs Bunny and Daffy Duck go through their 'Duck Season'/'Rabbit Season' debate at both tempos.

[142] Wright (1988) 141 describes the effect of mid-line speaker change (*antilabê*) on the delivery of Shakespearean verse, equally applicable to Roman comedy: *antilabê* 'impels the speeches forward. Although pauses do occur … their tendency is to obscure the meter, so normally the characters must keep completing each other's lines without undue delay.'

[143] Brown (1995) 82–4 discusses a number of such scenes in Plautus, and provides a hand-list at 87 nn. 34 and 35.

CHAPTER 6

Improvisation

DEGREES OF SCRIPTEDNESS

Improvisation allows for variation in acting, so that even if the same
scenario is seen more than once it is possible to see a different
version of it each time.

Riccoboni, *Histoire du Théâtre Italien* (1728)[1]

Few theatrical concepts are as easily misunderstood as improvisation, and
the variety of current theatre practices that use the name further confuses
the matter. Improvisation can be used to create a script that is then
rehearsed; it can be a tool for actors to improve a scripted performance;[2] it
can also be used as a theatrical metaphor to describe fully scripted
moments that have the appearance of being created *ex tempore*. All of these
functions, however, are derived from improvisation as a means of creating
a performance without a script. Improvisation distinguishes itself from
scripted theatre by not having a fixed text that the actors have memorised
in advance of the performance. We can easily grant that 'The lack of
verbatim memorisation does not necessarily imply its contrary, spontaneous chaos.'[3] What it does imply, however, is not obvious.

Improvisation is a process of composition in which the moment of
composition coincides with the moment of performance. Improvisation
is not a genre of theatre, but a process for generating theatre in any of a
number of genres. This does not mean that the improviser is unprepared,
but it does mean that verbatim memorisation is not a factor. Difficulties
arise in part from the several contexts in which improvisation may be
invoked. For example, in an otherwise exemplary study of ethno-
musicological improvisation, the author suggests that because 'Schubert
wrote down certain of his works rapidly and ... without working and

---

[1] Richards and Richards (1990) 204.   [2] See Lecoq (2001) 29–65.   [3] Fitzpatrick (1995) 28.

reworking them very much, [this] could lead us to regard his musical thinking as basically improvisatory.'[4] As a description of a process of composition that might work as a metaphor, but it fails to recognise the fundamental congruence of composition and performance which defines improvisation.

In most western drama, the actors have heard the words they are saying in performance before, just as they have heard the words being spoken by other actors – this is a function of the rehearsal practice, as well as the fact that plays typically have a run, and are performed over several nights. Even in this context, there are a number of possible practices that may fall under the rubric of improvisation that are useful to isolate, if we are better to understand what occurred during a *palliata*. The distinction between scripted and unscripted performance is not a simple binary polarisation: it is a continuum with many possible gradations.[5] One way to think of this is to consider a line representing degrees of 'scriptedness' in a performance:

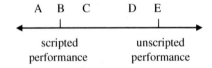

Any pictorial representation is going to be, to some degree, inaccurate. This picture represents one aspect of the nature of the production, and I am not assigning specific values to points on the line. What is important is the relationship that can be drawn between different points; the line is not representing many other variables that operate, including the quality of the performance, its success, or the degree of work involved in preparation. Let point B represent whatever we think of when we imagine a 'standard' scripted performance: actors have been given a published script in advance; it has been rehearsed under the guidance of a director; lines have been learned and are delivered in front of an audience to the best of the actors' ability, more or less faithfully to what was prepared in rehearsal, in order to create some sort of dramatic 'truth'. However we conceive of such a scripted performance, this is obviously not the extreme of the continuum: the line extends, and there is room in either direction of the scale.

---

[4] Nettl (1974) 10–11.   [5] Fitzpatrick (1995) 41–4.

There are a number of factors that might take a production and move it to the left on the scale, towards point A, reducing the number of unscripted elements. A play might be tightly blocked, with the actors having been given very precise notes about their movements by the director or through the playwright's stage directions. In a musical, the accompaniment provided by the orchestra sets the rhythm, pitch, and tempo of delivery, further scripting what the actor can do. Many plays with a long production history carry with them cultural associations with which any performer engages (consciously or unconsciously) that further script the performance and the audience reaction to it. Dame Edith Evans's representation of Lady Bracknell in act I of Oscar Wilde's *The Importance of Being Earnest*, and in particular her memorable delivery of a single line ('A handbag?') on stage and in the 1952 film, have served to define the role so completely that anyone else tackling it is measured against this performance by much of the audience.[6] Plays with only a single actor might exist further to the left along the line, since additional elements of variation created by the relationship between actors during a performance are absent. In 1908, Edward Gordon Craig first proposed his notion of the *Über-marionette*.[7] Imagining the ideal actor as being capable of perfectly representing the desires of the director or author as if he were a theatrical puppet served as a critique against the egism of the actors of his day. For our purposes, it suggests that one can continue to increase scriptedness, and that a 'scripted performance' (point B) is not in itself an extreme. Craig's notion might be perceived to be an attempt to define the extreme limit of an examination of this sort, as indeed does film, which can consistently repeat identical performances; it is not self-evident, however, that either of these represents an ideal.

Similarly, one can imagine many factors that might take the 'standard' scripted performance (point B) and move it to the right on the scale, towards point C, increasing the number of unscripted elements. Failure on the part of the actor to correctly deliver a line constitutes one means of unexpectedly deviating from the script. Touring shows might possess less formal blocking so that the play might be adapted to multiple venues. Sometimes a lack of formal preparation is signalled explicitly to the audience, perhaps by indicating that the play has been 'workshopped'. In addition, all of the minute variables that can change a performance from

---

[6] Fifty years later, Dame Judi Dench's *sotto voce* delivery of the line in Oliver Parker's 2002 film received comment in almost every review.

[7] *The Actor and the Über-marionette*, see Craig (1911) 54–95, originally published in 1908 in the second issue of *The Mask*.

one night to the next can shift a scripted performance further to the right of the line. Even such apparent minutiae as when an actor draws a breath while delivering a line can have repercussions for an audience interpreting the work as a whole. Such variations may exist in the thousands or tens of thousands for any given performance; nevertheless some actors carefully rehearse when they breathe while delivering certain speeches.

All of this, however, is clearly different from what most people think of in terms of improvisation. What Johnstone calls 'pure improvisation',[8] point E in the diagram, is a type of performance in which there is no script: literally, not one of the actors knows what any other will say in a scene, and the dialogue, movements, etc., are created at the moment of performance. Obviously, such a performance involves risks for the actor, but a group of performers properly prepared ('rehearsed' is not the right word) can develop techniques to minimise that risk. One set of techniques has been developed by Keith Johnstone for his improvised show, *Theatresports*.[9] Johnstone's model emphasises cooperation between the improvisers, and, using these techniques, it is possible to create unscripted theatre that from an audience's point of view is at times indistinguishable from scripted theatre.[10] While they cannot be seen as universally viable, Johnstone's techniques may be situated in a historical perspective. Theoreticians of the *commedia dell'arte*, for example,

forbid an actor to speak at the same time as another and to leave the performance space before his interlocutor has finished his response, since in the first case overlapping would render both utterances unintelligible, and in the second case the absence of the stimulus-emitting actor would cause a loss of continuity and consequently of textual coherence.[11]

These techniques are not the only means of producing pure improvisation, and even using them there are ways in which degrees of

---

[8] Johnstone (1981) 27.   [9] Johnstone (1981) 33–142, Johnstone (1999) 55–129.

[10] In some circumstances this might be seen as a desirable pursuit, though I have known audience members at an improvised show to feel cheated when they think that they have in fact witnessed scripted theatre.

[11] Pietropaolo (1989) 168. There are problems with the 'stochastic composition process' Pietropaolo advocates: while there is an element of back-and-forth between performers, the response given to an offer is not drawn from a fixed list that pre-exists the offer. Instead, there are many possible responses to any offer, some of which may be familiar, some of which may be appropriate, some of which might pre-exist as a potential response that finds itself appropriate given the nature of the offer. One of these is selected, and becomes the next offer.

scriptedness may increase, and a given performance might be pulled to the left on the line in the diagram.

Scriptedness can be introduced in a variety of ways. All improvisers will possess much that will allow them, if they so choose, to present as unscripted something they have in fact memorised or rehearsed: a joke, a speech, or even an physical expression or a particular way of reacting to a situation can constitute mini-scripts. While often indistinguishable from the rest of the scene, the method of production is in fact different – it is prepared – and an audience member watching such an actor over the course of several performances will notice such repetitions. These additions are obviously undesirable in a scene purporting to be improvised, but there is not a great distinction between this and the words spoken in most ordinary conversations. Much of everyday speech, including that in an improvised scene, is scripted: the mini-scripts in an improv scene contribute to the creation of a sense of verisimilitude for the audience. At the level of the scene, there is a variety of means that keep the performance to the left of pure improvisation, at point D on the line. One of these, common in modern improv, is the use of audience suggestions:[12] by asking for a suggestion from the audience and then successfully incorporating it into a scene, the improviser can 'prove' that the scene is truly improvised. Soliciting suggestions can help to create a stronger rapport with the audience, as some spectators try to devise suggestions intended to stump the performer. All this may benefit the performer, but it does prevent pure improvisation, by introducing another kind of script. Any delay in the implementation of a suggestion, even if it is only thirty seconds, pulls the performance even further to the left on the line, and the result starts to be indistinguishable from a poorly rehearsed scripted performance. Finnegan describes an oral composition being aggressively workshopped before eventually reaching the moment of performance in the Gilbert Islands.[13] This shift manifests itself not only in terms of the means of production – actors consult with one another and choose avenues they believe will be most productive, creating a rudimentary script – but also from the perspective of the audience. While the scene remains superficially similar to pure improvisation, what constitutes a successful performance changes when a script like this is in place. Actors may similarly impose restrictions upon themselves to introduces

---

[12] The procedure is criticised by Johnstone (1999) 25–30 as being unhelpful for achieving pure improv.

[13] Finnegan (1992) 82–3. See also Nettl (1974) 4–5, where he describes the vision songs of the North American Plains Indians.

scriptedness, by deciding to improvise a scene in verse or to music, or defining the scene as a quest or a love scene, etc.[14]

An important aspect of this dynamic is the presence of risk for the actor. In a typical scripted performance, the risk for the actor is low: he knows his lines, has been directed adequately and knows from rehearsals what the other people onstage are likely to do. A key component of acting involves appearing to be delivering lines as if they were produced spontaneously. In an unscripted performance, the risk for the actor appears to be much greater. No script and no rehearsal (in the traditional sense) means that the actors are in the same position as the characters they are playing: neither knows what will happen next in the scene. That translates into a dynamism that is communicated to the audience because the audience knows that the risk is real: at any point the scene could in fact veer horribly off course (and in that possibility lies a good part of the fun for the audience). The challenge is in part limited only to perceptions however, for the audience, knowing that unscripted theatre presents these risks, is in most cases forgiving when they occur. The actual risk for the actor is minimised, but the perception of risk allows the scene to have its effect. Neither mode is better than another, but different degrees of scriptedness create their rapport with the audience in different ways. In a performance that is partly scripted and partly improvised, the perception of risk can operate as if the show were fully improvised. Because the scene may go awry at any moment as unscripted elements are introduced, the actors can enjoy the benefits of an unscripted performance while in fact operating for the most part in a scripted environment.

Scriptedness also exists at the level of the overall performance. A variety of modern improv shows frame all the scenes in the context of a sporting match:[15] two or more teams compete against one another for points, and this creates a format to which the audience knows how to respond.[16] The use of these frame narratives forms another script, patterning the sequence of scenes. With televised improvisation the decision to broadcast only part of the proceedings, editing the less successful scenes, provides a further cushion for the improvisers and constitutes a form of after-the-fact scripting (again reducing the level of risk). 'Scripts' do not need

---

[14] Many standard improv games are listed in Johnstone (1999) 130–274, 302–19, and 362–8, but not all of these are meant for public performance. See also Spolin (1983).

[15] Johnstone (1999) 1–24, 320–36.

[16] This is part of the success behind the *Theatresports* model, adapted in the United States as *Comedy Sportz* and Britain as *Whose Line is it Anyway?*, and it is also found in Quebec's *Ligue Nationale d'Improvisation*, which employs the frame of Canadian ice hockey.

to be written to constitute a means of shifting the performance towards point D on the line.[17] Other large-scale frame narratives exist.[18] No place on the line need require more or less preparation by the performers. As one moves closer to point A on the diagram, there may be a tendency towards increased amount of time for preparation, but rehearsal times at any place may be long or short.[19]

Another feature of pure improvisation is that it is a composite creation. Authorship cannot be ascribed to a single individual: I would hesitate to assign an actor any responsibility for a character's lines spoken in an improvised scene: they are the product of the group functioning as a corporate unit. A similar tension exists in jazz music between the ensemble and the soloist.[20] In the give-and-take of unscripted performance the whole is very much larger than the sum of the parts.[21] I believe the originality of Roman comedy is the direct result of this collaborative process.

The concept of pure improvisation requires this detail because most modern theatregoers have experience with scripted theatre, and unscripted theatre is not seen to have an equal performative value or to possess the possibility for the same dramatic range. I have been discussing comedy, and improv is generally thought to lend itself to humour, but it need not. Seasoned improvisers can create meaningful and powerful

---

[17] Given this, there remains some room to the right of point E on the line, since even with pure improvisation there exist 'rules' (often unspoken) that continue to govern the behaviour of the performers, and these can also be perceived in terms of a script (such a rule might include an agreement not to physically harm one's fellow improvisers, etc.).

[18] E.g. Johnstone (1981) 65. Using almost exactly this structure my improv group in Edinburgh on several occasions staged 45–60 minutes shows in 1991–2.

[19] Similarly, approaching point E, the Edinburgh performances mentioned in the previous note were only possible after two years of weekly improvised performances – while the shows themselves had no real rehearsal (two dry runs with a much smaller audience), the success was determined largely by several hundred hours' shared experience improvising in front of audiences, with both successes and failures along the way.

[20] See, for example, Ingrid Monson in Clark (2000) 120–24.

[21] My use of 'performance' excludes ordinary non-theatrical interactions. What I am describing is more explicit in its identity as a performance. One might speak of the existence of a series of frames (selling tickets, using a stage, wearing a mask) that mark an exchange as performative in some sense. The important distinction is that a performance opens itself to evaluation by those outside of the frame. Many question the existence of pure improvisation, not believing it is possible for an actor to go on stage not knowing what words are going to be said, but this is precisely what happens in ordinary (non-performative) conversations on a regular basis. What is surprising about improvisation is the apparent vulnerability of the actors who improvise in this manner, because of the lack of control that each actor possesses: 'It's weird to wake up knowing you'll be onstage in twelve hours, and that there's absolutely nothing you can do to ensure success' (Johnstone (1981) 27–8). There exist techniques that can minimise this sense of vulnerability, but for pure improvisation, part of the goal for the performers is to appear to be working with an element of risk. The presence of an evaluating body (the audience) distinguishes performance and means that, in any given case, a performance may be more or less successful.

dramatic scenes as well. Johnstone is part of a tradition that includes more familiar names such as Jacques Lecoq, Dario Fo, and Jerzy Grotowski, all of whom are key figures in the development of modern improvisation, and all of whom could be accommodated into the structure I have been discussing.[22] When improvisation is seen as an alternate means of producing theatre, we are in a better position to appreciate the middle ground. For it is between points B and E on the line that a number of types of performance may be situated, and it is here that I suggest Roman comedy belongs. There is no single point along the line where we can say that a given performance (or type of performance) stops being scripted and starts being improvised. Different people approaching a given performance will produce different conclusions: 'the lines that different cultures might draw between "fixed" composition and improvisation will appear at different points of a continuum'.[23]

Many types of performance possess elements of improvisation, and each exists somewhere near the middle of the line, blending scripted and unscripted elements. Fitzpatrick calls this a 'flexible' performance, a term which allows him to emphasise that 'in many cultures oral and written processes happily cohabit and complement each other'.[24] In each case, there are elements that can be identified as operating as a script. What is important for our appreciation of Roman comedy is to recognise that each negotiates a unique means of blending scripted and unscripted elements: there is no best way of achieving this balance.

The *commedia dell'arte* provides another example of a performance blending scripted and unscripted elements. Though the precise nature of Italian improvisation continues to be debated, no one would deny that the *commedia* was 'a mixed oral-literate process'[25] combining many theatre practices. Patterning devices are used, such as *lazzi*,[26] the stock routines available to each character that may be employed in various situations, and *generici*,[27] model speeches for each character type, which could be rehearsed (perhaps even memorised) and inserted as desired into an improvised conversation.[28] Patterning the overall narrative is the *scenario*, plotting entrances, exits, and the bare minimum of action that is

---

[22] For an overview of the place of these men in modern improvisation, see Frost and Yarrow (1990) 61–92.

[23] Nettl (1974) 7.

[24] Fitzpatrick (1995) 29. For flexible performance, see Fitzpatrick (1995), and especially 7–46: 'Oral Performance and the *Commedia dell'arte*'.

[25] Fitzpatrick (1995) 44.   [26] Gordon (1983).   [27] Henke (2002) 43–5.

[28] This was a standard characteristic of *il Dottore* ('the Doctor') for example, which Shakespeare appropriated for Holofernes in *Love's Labour's Lost*.

required in a scene.[29] The earliest manuals on *commedia* acting prescribe techniques that are cogent advice for an improviser today:

above all the actor must be careful not to speak when his partner is holding forth ... and before responding he should allow the one speaking to reach the end of his sentence ... Further, it is important for the actor to remember that when he is speaking on the stage alone he must cease as soon as he is joined by another speaking character ... It is prudent however not to enter until the other actor is about to conclude his speech: that conclusion can be signaled by the speaker ... making some easily understood gesture. But it is better to agree the moment of entrance, than to disturb the flow.[30]

Cecchini's advice is in some ways very elementary: the actor is to accept the ideas of the other improviser, not to interrupt with words or an entrance, but to seek fluidity in the presentation; he may consequently expect the same in return. This is a fundamentally cooperative model of improvisation: 'actors, singly and in teams, were constantly drawing on an accumulated stock of existing repertoire'.[31] Similar ideas can be found in modern improvisation.[32] The result of such a performance can be spectacular and can lead to exaggerated and idealistic claims. Writing in the seventeenth century, Gherardi claims 'The Italian comedians learn nothing by heart; they need but to glance at the subject of a play a moment or two before going upon the stage.'[33]

Jazz improvisation too is formed from building blocks:[34] the arrangement functions like a script even though it need not be written out: 'arrangement begins the moment something is agreed upon in advance ... it is not possible to speak of arrangement in jazz without mentioning improvisation'.[35] There are the influences of (known) previous performances of a piece as well as the performer's knowledge of harmonic structures (which is essentially the grammar of music). Operating beside these is an etiquette that exists during a jam session that governs the behaviour of the improvisers.[36] An individual's self-indulgence comes at the expense of the corporate product. Restraint is

---

[29] See Salerno (1967) and Cotticelli, Heck, and Heck (2001). Fitzpatrick (1995) 82–3 believes the scenarios are 'unreliable indications of performance practice, precisely because they had been through the possibly contaminating process of edition for publication ... '.

[30] From Cecchini, *Frutti* (1628), cited in Richards and Richards (1990) 201.

[31] Andrews (1993) 181.   [32] See Johnstone (1981) 94–100.   [33] Cited in Duchartre (1966) 30–32.

[34] Nettl (1974) 14–15.   [35] Berendt (1992) 159–60.

[36] This is partially described by Lippincott in Clark (2000) 116–20. There is much of value in Feather (1965) 209–44. See also Lippincott in Clark (2000) 118–19.

rewarded. Pietropaolo, describing *commedia dell'arte*, misses the point when he writes 'A performer must ... decide whether to surprise the audience by producing the least expected response or to give them exactly what they expect along with the pleasure that comes with the sense of having made an accurate prediction.'[37] This should not be a balanced choice: 'the least expected response' is never the right decision for an improviser, because it is self-indulgent. To appear creative, the improviser must give the audience what it wants before it knows it wants it.

Each model of improvised performance creates a unique means of blending scripted and unscripted elements. Berendt tells the following story about the recordings of Charlie Parker:

Of the four masters of Parker's 'Cool Blues,' recorded in immediate succession on the same day (only the final one was approved by Parker), three were put on the market under different titles: 'Cool Blues,' 'Blowtop Blues,' and 'Hot Blues' – and to a certain degree they are all different 'pieces.'[38]

The inverted commas around the final word betray the author's acknowledgement that vocabulary developed for scripted performance is inadequate. The difference between these recordings is greater than different interpretations of a traditional piece of music, though even here tempo, timbre, and dramatic effect can vary between performances. To the performer, these were all versions of the same song; to the audience, the differences were considerable and individuated the various recordings. The piece is perceived differently because it lacks a written, textual identity. Similarly, modern recording technology allows direct comparison of the 'same' work by a performer. Nettl describes his experiences with a Persian musician: 'When confronted with the concrete evidence of the recordings, he admitted the existence of the differences, but not their significance, and implied that the essence of what he performed in a *dastgah* is always the same.'[39] Here, the notion of what is being performed is not defined by verbatim repetition. Modern audiences return to weekly improvised performances. Exactly this degree of variation may be evident in Plautus, with the troupe performing the same play on successive days, but the audience seeing different performances, even though each purports to be a rendering of the same Greek original.

Further, an improvised work cannot be separated from its performers. Each performer's contribution to the whole is individualised, and in a

---

[37] Pietropaolo (1989) 172.   [38] Berendt (1992) 159.   [39] Nettl (1974) 8.

work that is created by a group, the identity of the work created draws from each individual's resources, but is not limited by them. It is possible to provide a musical score of different ways jazz musicians perform 'the same tune'.[40] There is an overlap here between the notions of a composer and an interpreter (in the Plautine context, between the playwright and actor – every improvising actor is part playwright).[41] This is because in jazz, the song is not defined by the score: '*How High the Moon* is not simply the melody ... found on the sheet music, but a harmonic ski-trail along which ten thousand musicians have traveled. The improvisational bases of jazz are not melodies, but chord structures.'[42] Furthermore, each individual's 'voice' is distinctive. Each improviser has a personal repertoire of skills. In jazz, this is the performer's 'sound'; in *commedia*, it includes the *lazzi* one performs well; for Homer (if we also consider the spontaneously composed epics of Greece), it is the bard's personal toolkit of *formulae*. This repertoire emerges spontaneously only for oneself. Once performed, however, it enters into the public domain to be adapted, alluded to, or appropriated by subsequent performers. Reference to these antecedents can be more or less direct, but all introduce a degree of scriptedness to the work. Nettl discusses the relationship of the improvised work to the model in terms of 'audibility': some antecedents are more audible than others.[43] The melody followed by the jazz musician will typically have a high degree of audibility (the audience is supposed to recognise the song), but the existence and employment of straightforward chord progressions will be 'minimally audible' for most in the audience. For Plautus, the explicit or implicit acknowledgement of a precedent in Greek New Comedy leads the audience to concentrate on that level, even in the absence of a direct experience of the model. This gives Plautus' actors a great deal of freedom with what they choose to incorporate into the performance, as well as a built-in means of distancing the result from themselves.

All these performance types – modern improv, *commedia dell'arte*, jazz, Homeric epic – exist somewhere in the middle of our hypothesised line measuring degrees of scriptedness; they are all blended performances. None of these can be situated precisely (e.g. by saying that jazz is more or less scripted than Homer), and there will be variation from one performer to the next, and even between given performances of the 'same' work.

---

[40] Berendt (1992) 154–5. [41] Berendt (1992) 156–7. [42] Feather (1965) 210.
[43] Nettl (1974) 16–17.

Each type of performance strikes its balance in a unique way, negotiating a unique set of variables. There is no 'right' formula.

This is not the case with Greek theatre, where there are reasons to believe actors were given a written part, and choruses were trained by the *didaskalos* (director) from a full written script.[44] Fifth-century comedy might introduce a (disposable) joke on the day of the performance, and it might subsequently enter into the written tradition.[45] There is nothing to indicate that Athenian performance was subject to significant unscripted variations: indeed, for a chorus to be at all successful, it must exist at the extreme left of the line, as choristers perform carefully rehearsed words, music, and choreography. This is not to say that improvisation might not have been a tool contributing to the final script. The famous anecdote about Menander (Plutarch, *Moralia* 347e–f) might be interpreted to suggest that he first devised something akin to a *scenario* as used in the *commedia*:[46]

> λέγεται δὲ καὶ Μενάνδρῳ τῶν συνήθων τις εἰπεῖν, 'ἐγγὺς οὖν,
> Μέναδρε, τὰ Διονύσια, καὶ σὺ τὴν κωμῳδίαν οὐ πεποίηκας;'
> τὸν δ' ἀποκρίνασθαι, νὴ τοὺς θεοὺς ἔγωγε πεποίηκα τὴν
> κωμῳδίαν· ᾠκονόμηται γὰρ ἡ διάθεσις δεῖ δ' αὐτῇ τὰ στιχίδια
> ἐπᾷσαι'...

The story is also told that one of Menander's intimate friends said to him, 'The Dionysian Festival is almost here, Menander; haven't you composed your comedy? Menander answered, 'By heaven, I have really composed the comedy: the plot's all in order. But I still have to fit the lines to it.'

Possibly Plutarch is right to infer from this that playwrights – Menander, at least – valued dramatic action (τὰ πράγματα) more than the words spoken. Regardless, this is discussing the process of composition and not the nature of the performance itself.

Given this continuum, I suggest the plays of Plautus represent another form of blended performance. They are not fully scripted like their

---

[44] See Marshall (2004) for rehearsals of Greek drama.

[45] E.g. Aristophanes, *Ecclesiazusae* 1154–62, where the chorus asks the judges not to condemn their play because it has been selected to appear first. Since the order of performances in the dramatic competitions was selected randomly at the beginning of the festival, the line itself is part of the scene which cannot have predated the performance by more than a few days. However, the rhetoric of the passage is such that the playwright might very well have written other lines to accommodate other allotments of position. The comic playwright might as easily complain about the disadvantages of performing last, or being caught somewhere in the middle.

[46] Text and translation, Babbitt (1936) 506–07.

(purported) Greek models, but neither are they examples of pure improvisation. In striking a balance among the many genres that Plautus allowed to influence his drama, the playwright has created something that produces theatre in a completely different way from his explicit model, Greek New Comedy. Part of his inheritance from mime and the *fabulae Atellanae* is an understanding of the mechanisms associated with improvisation. Recognising this challenges notions of what the Plautine text represents, and it establishes a discontinuity between the New Comedy of Greece and the *palliata*.

TEXT AND SCRIPT

An equally fundamental discontinuity exists between the 'script' of the performance (what words were heard by an audience when the play was initially performed, whether or not they actually existed in a written form) and the 'text' of a *palliata* (the words that are attributed to the author in the extant plays as they survive). Roman comedy, drawing on an eclectic range of performance traditions that combine scripted and unscripted elements, problematises the oral/literate division in a way that has not been adequately acknowledged.[47]

The manuscript tradition to the Renaissance provides a text, which apparently comprises the twenty-one plays (including the mutilated *Vidularia*) of the *fabulae Varronianae*, those plays selected by the scholar and poet Varro (116–27 BC) from the approximately 130 titles circulating under Plautus' name which had not had their authorship impugned by any previous scholar.[48] This emphasis on unanimous unexceptionability in all likelihood condemned many plays that originated in Plautus' troupe, and perhaps preserved some that did not, though this possibility is seldom raised. Indeed, much of Varro's ground had already been worked by Accius, writing in the second century BC. He identified twenty-five plays as Plautine, but excluded *Colax* ('The Toady') and *Commorientes* ('Partners in Death'), plays Terence identified as Plautine

---

[47] The methodological problem is addressed in part by Andrews (1993) 174: 'From a purist point of view, there can be no *commedia dell'arte* text on which we can base any arguments. Since the actors improvised, whatever that may turn out to mean, from an outline scenario, they used no written script. Whenever we find a written script that looks as if it might be informative, then by definition it is no longer improvised and therefore no longer *commedia dell'arte*. This logical dilemma makes us rely, to a degree which is in theory dangerous, on personal judgment, even on hunch.'

[48] See Gratwick (1993) 4–6.

(*Eunuchus* 25,[49] *Adelphoe* 7). Other non-Varronian plays, such as *Saturio* ('Tubby') and *Addictus* ('The Debt-Bondsman') were connected to biographical details of Plautus by Aulus Gellius 3.3.14, writing in the second century A D. While these biographical details are probably false inferences arising from the plays,[50] the attribution long after Varro of the titles to Plautus shows that their spuriousness was not universally accepted.

The plays were performed in the centuries after Plautus' death, which Cicero dates to 184/3 BC (*Brutus* 60). Throughout this period, the text surely changed to some degree either through error or deliberate alteration. Such alterations could take the form either of excision (reducing a play's length, cutting lines, scenes and/or parts) or through interpolation (the introduction of additional material to the text, beefing up certain parts, perhaps to gratify a particular actor). From our perspective today, it would be very difficult to identify instances of excision, since even apparent lapses of sense and continuity can typically be explained within the context of a comedic narrative.

The study of interpolation was given new life in 1990, when Zwierlein published the first of four volumes on the text of Plautus.[51] Zwierlein believes Plautus suffered massive interpolation in the century after his death, and that at times over a third of any script might be due to a post-Plautine reviser (*das Bearbeiter*).[52] Zwierlein assumes Plautus is presenting 'faithful' adaptations of Greek plays, and so any perceived deviations from this standard, or from the perceptions of an ideal of Latinity[53] are blamed on the reviser. Many in the nineteenth century held a similar position, but that was before papyrus fragments of Menander had been published. Since we do not possess any complete Greek originals of extant Roman plays, generalisation about what is possible in Greek New

---

[49] *Colax* is attributed both to Plautus and to Naevius, raising the possibility of joint authorship, revision, or (most likely) an absence of our notion of what constitutes a script for performance.

[50] For this tendency in ancient biography, see Lefkowitz (1981).

[51] Zwierlein (1990), (1991a), (1991b), (1992). A generous appreciation of Zwierlein's approach can be found in Jocelyn (1993) and (1996).

[52] Of the five plays discussed in detail by Zwierlein's volumes, *Poenulus* loses 190 of 1422 verses (13.4 per cent), *Curculio* 42 of 729 (5.8 per cent), *Miles Gloriosus* 340 of 1433 (23.7 per cent), *Pseudolus* 277 of 1335 (20.7 per cent), and *Bacchides* 465 of 1265 (38.3 per cent). Some of the problems in these lines might be attributed elsewhere, and on some verses Zwierlein is surely correct. But the standard of judgment used is so rigorous and artificial, that all the conclusions must be approached with the greatest scepticism. (Line totals come from Lindsay (1903). Because of the difference in line lengths, and the variability of line lengths in the *cantica*, the ratios can only be approximate.)

[53] Quintilian 10.1.99 approves Varro's approval of Aelius Stilo's *bon mot* that if the Muses wished to speak Latin, they would sound like Plautus: *licet Varro Musas, Aeli Stilonis sententia, Plautino dicat sermone locuturas fuisse si Latine loqui vellent.*

Comedy must remain speculative. In assessing Zwierlein's project, however, we must notice that it is precisely in *Bacchides*, the one play for which the best evidence exists to determine Plautus' techniques of adaptation, that the activity of the hypothetical reviser is greatest. By this standard, if more Greek New Comedy survived, more of Plautus' text would be attributable to the reviser.

Our texts of Plautus are not the scripts used by the actors, as Zwierlein correctly recognised. But even this does not address the true difficulties in understanding what we mean by the text of Plautus. If we accept that it is possible (at least in theory) to remove the accretions and alterations of time introduced in the intermittently attested manuscript tradition, the consequences of the process of compiling an edition, and the interpolations and possible excisions of the late republic, the question remains: does this then give us Plautus' text? The answer is no.

From the perspective of performance criticism, what we mean by 'the text' is what words the actors said while performing the play – the script of the show. In most modern dramatic productions (because we live in an age of the printing press, photocopiers, cheap paperbacks, word processors, and high literacy), 'the script' is distributed to actors before or during the rehearsal period; the words said onstage correspond, except for minor slips, with the words pre-existing on the printed page. The basic skill of a modern stage actor in the West today entails the ability to reproduce a quality performance night after night. But this is not the only measure of a successful performance.

If we allow for a different means of producing a play, a number of crucial aspects of the performance context change. Here are a few possibilities, each of which seems to me more likely than not to be true. The play perhaps did not exist in a complete written form before it was performed: it may have had only a skeletal outline, like the *scenario* of the *commedia dell'arte*. Actors perhaps did not see the whole script, but only their own parts (as were used in later Roman performances of tragedy). Verbatim presentation perhaps was not seen as the criterion for a good performance, but rather that a considerable degree of variation was tolerated from one performance to the next. Variations between performances were perhaps preserved in writing, perhaps through a process of dictation by the actors to a scribe after a successful run. Multiple recordings of a single play, containing substantial variations from each other, perhaps existed and were circulating in Plautus' lifetime, all of which had originated from live performances by Plautus' troupe.

Western society is almost entirely literate and possesses a logocentric bias that privileges the written text. This was not the case in republican Rome. When we remove our literate expectations of this society – even allowing for individuals to possess multilingual literacy, as Plautus himself did – what remains is a culture where 'performance' can adopt a much more fluid identity. Plautus is writing (or 'writing') transitional texts that combine elements both of the literate and of the pre-literate. Rome was rich with unscripted, improvisatory performance genres, and Plautus had no reason not to adopt techniques from these traditions into his plays.

The transmitted text need not correspond exactly to the words spoken in any performance of a play, nor need it correspond (for the most part) to the words spoken in every performance of the play. Improvisation as a mode of producing a text is a fundamentally different thing than the scripted appearance of spontaneity exhibited by some Plautine characters, particularly the *servi callidi* ('clever slaves'), that constitutes 'improvisation' only within the dramatic world, but not as a genuine means of composition for the performers of the play. It is never possible to document 'the script' as the troupe performs it until after the audience has departed. For Plautus, performance necessarily precedes text.

This creates a genuine ontological problem concerning what a play of Plautus is. 'The script' may never have existed as a physical document, and consequently the ideal of textual criticism – the recovery of the words written by Plautus himself – may be impossible even in theory because at least part of the process of composition of the *fabulae palliatae* was done at the moment of performance. This is not quite the situation in Terence, where the playwright distances himself from improvisatory traditions and makes it clear that he remains at arm's length from the production – though it would be rash to take all his characters say in the prologues at face value, and we cannot know that in performance the plays were not altered by actors used to performing in the hybrid tradition described.

While it is necessary to cite the plays in discussing Roman comedy, 'the text' will only ever be an approximation of what was experienced in the theatre. The plays are still products of the original performances, and any given passage may provide insight into the nature of performance in the Roman republic. The analysis of any given play, however, does change, since it must recognise that the content of the performance is fluid, and any given passage has the potential to be altered as part of the normal production practice. This means that structuring patterns, such as metre and stock routines, become even more important.

IMPROVISATION IN PLAUTUS

I suggest that the performance of Plautus will have contained moments of improvisation.[54] This should not in itself be an improbable claim. The influence of mime and *fabulae Atellanae* extended to an awareness of means of composition different from that of scripted theatre. Rome had no relevant scripted theatrical traditions: the introduction of drama to the celebration of *ludi* was still recent, and audience expectations will have been predicated on an understanding of a variety of different performance genres. One way to think about it is this: we know *Stichus* had a run of at least three days in 200 BC, though this need signal nothing more than the debut in Rome – other performances at other venues outside Rome may perhaps be added. Lindsay's text measures the play at 775 lines. I believe that when a Roman audience saw the play at the *ludi Plebeii*, they saw a performance that in all likelihood contained more lines of verse than this. More importantly, I believe that if any in the audience came to see the play the following day, they would have seen a different number of lines performed. Possibly, if the weather was cold and the audience unforgiving, fewer lines might be delivered. Our text represents something that might have occurred in performance, and it is conceivable that it corresponds to a particular performance. It does not however represent all performance variations that existed, or were possible. Despite such variations, Plautus' troupe would think of each performance as presenting the same play. Improvised variations do not create a new script, though it is possible that a successful unscripted moment might be re-incorporated in subsequent performances under the right conditions, at which point it would have the status of something partially scripted. To prove this is impossible, but the reverse is just as unprovable. Since what we mean by improvisation represents a considerable range of attitudes towards scriptedness, it is more important to establish the likelihood that there is some degree of improvisation than to isolate precisely what that degree is. I would probably credit a greater degree of unscriptedness in Plautine

---

[54] Goldberg (1995) is perhaps the best discussion of true improvisation in Plautus, though our conclusions differ. I am happy to see some of the ideas in this section anticipated by Goldberg (2004), an excellent paper that I saw only after final revisions to the manuscript had been made; his examples are drawn from *Cistellaria*.

performance than many, but what matters is that what we have documented in the text of Plautus is a record of a blended performance.

Discussions of Plautine improvisation suffer because they lack a clear
sense of what improvisation means. Slater's discussion, first published in
1985, provided the necessary groundwork:

> Neither the literary (scripted) nor the improvisational playwright exists in a pure
> form ... In Plautus the two roles are merely two ends of a spectrum ...
> Improvised theatre per se cannot be scripted. It does, however, behave in certain
> recognizable ways ... Various actions, some abortive, some successful, follow
> and interrupt one another.[55]

So far so good: but what follows demonstrates this is not what Slater
isolates: 'All these features of improvisation can be imitated in scripted
theatre. Therefore, when I speak of improvisation, I mean Plautus' literary imitation of these features of improvisational theatre.'[56] For Slater,
the plays of Plautus are fully scripted dramas that emulate features of
improvisation. While he acknowledges the continuum between 'scripted'
and 'unscripted', for him the character improvises, not the actor playing
the character. The merits of Slater's analysis are many. No one today
would deny that Plautus' plays are in some sense about the theatrical
process (i.e. they are metatheatrical), and that characters are aware of
themselves as characters: 'Improvisation and metatheatre seem to me
intimately related.'[57]

My contention goes further. Characters 'improvise' within the plays
because the performance milieu of the Roman republic expected actors
to improvise, not only in mime and *fabulae Atellanae*, but in *fabulae
palliatae* as well. All three genres were blended performances, and while
there was typically a larger scripted element in the *palliatae* than in the
other dramatic forms, there remained real opportunities for the actors to
improvise as part of their comic performance. A consequence of this is
that what we think of as the text of Plautus achieved its 'final' form
(barring post-Plautine interpolations and copying errors) after the play
had been performed. Goldberg disagrees:

> Plautus' plays were not themselves improvised in any technical sense. They were
> performed according to scripts that have not only survived, but declare by their
> very existence the primacy of the author's role in the theatrical life of his
> time ... The very name 'Plautus' had ... 'drawing power' ... Those interested

---

[55] Slater (2000) 9.   [56] Slater (2000) 9–10.   [57] Slater (2000) 12 n. 29.

in the 'metatheatrical' aspects of Plautine comedy rightly observe an impromptu element in his plots, but this is not the same thing as true improvisation. The critical trope cannot be taken literally.[58]

I believe the critical trope must be taken as a meaningful possibility within the theatrical context, so that its representation within the dramatic world can also be meaningful. Unless there is a point of reference familiar to the audience, the literary representation of the effect will not make sense. This does nothing to diminish the 'drawing power' of the name Plautus: he remains the creative genius behind the plays, and continues to guide and direct his actors. Not all improvisational performances are equal, and a strong directorial hand provides a necessary counterpart to unscripted creativity. The freedom of improvisation does not diminish the fact that Plautus is behind it all, though it is easy in our text-based culture to see this as somehow lessening his authorial control. Rather than being 'an illusion of the play's construction',[59] I believe the improvisational quality is properly understood to be the means of producing the success of these comedies.

Plautus is crafting a play, constructed from different pieces over time with the help of his associates, and not simply 'writing' a document that remains unchanged. A circularity remains that defies certain proof for either side of the argument, since evidence for improvisation must come from the written texts themselves. Nevertheless, if there was improvisation as part of the production practice – if the length of a play could vary from one performance to the next – there should exist some textual indication, in the same way that the oral–formulaic origins of the Homeric poems can be perceived. There are three classes of evidence that contribute to an understanding of the question, and one class that has been used which does not. The positive evidence comes in the form of doublets, elastic gags, and expectations of the actors. The negative class, which I shall consider first, comprises narrative events.

The role of improvisation has been prominent in recent scholarship emphasising the function of native Italian elements in the development of Roman comedy.[60] Two publications by Eckard Lefèvre have identified many discrete elements that Lefèvre believes find their natural home in

---

[58] Goldberg (1995) 36. Compare Barsby (1995) 65: 'Insofar as these [improvisatory routines] appear in Plautus, they will have been adapted for a fully scripted drama, but we may nonetheless be able to detect their improvisatory ancestry.'

[59] Goldberg (1995) 37.

[60] Among the many studies produced are Lefèvre (1982), Stärk (1989), Lefèvre, Stärk, and Vogt-Spira (1991), Lefèvre (1995), Benz, Stärk, and Vogt-Spira (1995), Lefèvre (1997), (2001), and a series of

Stegreifspiel ('improvisation').[61] Each element is equivocal, however, because each could naturally develop and exist in a scripted context as well. Even if these devices could be demonstrated to originate in an unscripted milieu, none needs to exist in an improvised context.

Lefèvre fails to distinguish consistently between improvisation in performance, the playwright's use of improvisatory techniques in the scripting process, and the literary imitation of improvisation. It makes no sense to claim an exclusive or proprietary relationship between improvisation and metatheatre,[62] audience address,[63] the moral deficiency of characters,[64] satire,[65] intrigue,[66] verbal wrangling,[67] or amusing comments:[68] narrative content can handily exist in scripted or unscripted theatre (and, in the case of intrigue, may more naturally require a pre-scripted narrative) as the presence of all of these elements in modern literary drama attest. It is wrong to suggest the *servus currens* belongs to the improvised tradition when he is clearly attested in the Greek New Comic tradition,[69] and this conclusion can be easily extended to comic business involving other characters.[70] Similarly, some elements Lefèvre identifies exist because of other aspects of dramatic production. Performance conditions in Rome generally encouraged the prominent use of monologues[71] (as transitions and to facilitate doubling, to smooth over

---

edited volumes on individual plays including Benz and Lefèvre (1998), Baier (1999a), Faller (2001), and Auhagen (2001).

[61] Lefèvre (1999) 16–45, (2001) 98–130. The former study regularly asks, with particularly leading rhetoric, 'where is *x* most at home?' (*Wo ist der* x *beheimatet?*).

[62] *Metatheater*: Lefèvre (1999) 20–24, (2001) 99–101.

[63] *Aparte* ('asides'): Lefèvre (2001) 115–17. The term 'aside' presumes a naturalistic form of delivery, which we have seen is not applicable to Plautus. Characters speaking to the audience directly can remain unheard by other characters onstage if they so wish.

[64] *Moraldefizit*: Lefèvre (1999) 24–6.

[65] *Satire*: Lefèvre (1999) 26–9, (2001) 101–4.

[66] *Intrige*: Lefèvre (1999) 29–31.

[67] *Streit-Szenen*: Lefèvre (1999) 34–9. *Streit-Gespräche*: Lefèvre (2001) 107–13.

[68] *Komische Kommentare*: Lefèvre (1999) 39–41.

[69] Lefèvre (1999) 31–2. See Csapo (1987) and (1989). As Zagagi (1995) 80 emphasises, 'Some recent attempts to detect Plautine improvisations are based on an idealized picture of New Comedy (and Greek drama in general), which takes it for granted that repetition of scenes and motifs for purely comic purposes and inconsistency in characterization and plot movement are utterly alien to the Greek sources.' This important observation helps us avoid easy traps of ascribing to the unknown *Atellanae* features which are fully present in extant Greek comedy. Zagagi (1995) provides a detailed examination of many Menandrean passages that anticipate the style of comedy found in Plautus. To these may be added Menander's *Perinthia*, where the slave takes refuge at an altar, anticipating *Mostellaria* 1094–1180, and see *Rudens* 760–61 and *Heauton Timoroumenos* 975–6.

[70] *Koch-Gerenne* ('cook running around') and *Euclio-Gerenne*: Lefèvre (2001) 104–7.

[71] *Einzel-Szene* ('solo scene'): Lefèvre (1999) 43–4. *Monologe*: Lefèvre (2001) 113–15. See also the discussions of the characterisation of stock characters, particularly slaves and parasites, which is also

Greek act divisions, etc.), the artificiality of time and place,[72] and a clear mechanism to indicate the end of a play.[73] The prominence of plots involving look-alikes and disguise[74] (again related to intrigue) cannot be associated with masked acting of necessity, but was clearly also part of the scripted Greek tradition. Finally, Lefèvre claims an improvisational origin for elements that are distinctive of Plautine style but possess no necessary relationship with improvisation, particularly with the aggressive use of metaphor.[75]

For the most part, Lefèvre isolates narrative elements as if they belong most appropriately in a particular genre; we do better to say that they are most at home in 'comedy'. Dramatic action is not a sign of improvisation, nor is the stage action expected of actors in every dramatic text:

All performances give actors things to do as well as things to say, and Plautine scripts were especially good at building stage directions into the text and creating opportunities for added business. We need not fall back on the example of Atellan farce to explain the presence of such antics in Plautus or why Roman audiences would enjoy them.[76]

Improvisation is not a theatrical genre but is a means of producing a dramatic text. Narrative elements, and incidental production elements such as how the end of the play is indicated, have no bearing on the means of producing the words spoken on stage. Closer to the mark is an earlier study, which examined six Plautine plays and in which means of production played a more prominent role,[77] emphasising structural elements, such as paratactic composition, a repetitive structure, and the relative lack of importance of unity of plot, with the corresponding autonomy of individual scenes that this implies.

All of these may be claimed to arise out of improvisational techniques (in performance or as part of the scripting process), as may inconsistencies of characterisation, stereotyped comic characters, and the regular

---

accomplished mainly through monologues: *Sklaven-Spiegel*, Lefèvre (2001) 129; *Sklaven-Spiegel und Parasitentum*, Lefèvre (1999) 32–3.

[72] *Irrealität der Zeit und des Orts*: Lefèvre (1999) 41–2, (2001) 129–30.

[73] *Schluß-Gong* ('concluding gong'): Lefèvre (1999) 44–5.

[74] *Doppelgängertum und Verkleidung*: Lefèvre (1999) 16–20. On page 19 Lefèvre cites Duckworth (1952) 168: 'Trickery and impersonation, the ludicrous fooling of one person by another, are characteristic of low comedy and existed ... in the pre-literary Italian farces.' Duckworth's prejudices ('low comedy') imply a hierarchy of scripted over unscripted performance, and it is disingenuous to use this as evidence for the improvisational origins of impersonation.

[75] *Metaphern-Exuberanz*: Lefèvre (2001) 117–29.

[76] Goldberg (1995) 36.

[77] Lefèvre, Stärk, and Vogt-Spira (1991).

exploitation of recurrent situations for traditional routines and comic schtick. Regardless, many of these features only become apparent through the analysis of a written text. In performance, when a play is experienced linearly by the audience, with timing governed by the actors and a plurality of other performance elements contributing to the sum of what the spectators have available as they develop their interpretations, paratactic patterns seem intuitively natural and repetition is an ideal means to reinforce key motifs and narrative points. Strong individual scenes can easily hold their own amongst a unified plot, but this is an artificial polarisation, and another gradated scale would more accurately reflect what is possible here. Strong memorable scenes that could stand alone possess an inherent dramatic interest whether in a scripted or an unscripted form: witness the title scenes in the arbitration of Menander's *Epitrepontes*, the tug-of-war of *Rudens*, Libanus riding Argyrippus in *Asinaria* 545–745, or (in *commedia*) the dentist scene of Flamminio Scala's *Il cavadente*, 'in which Arlecchino masquerades as a traveling dentist and unnecessarily extracts most of Pantalone's teeth'.[78] Balancing these contrasting modes of production is a challenge, but there are ways in which an understanding of improvisational techniques explains features in the Plautine texts and provides creative opportunities (and not limitations) for the performers.

The first class of evidence indicating improvisation in performance is the presence of doublets in the text. Here is the beginning of a monologue by Libanus at *Asinaria* 249–53:

> *Hercle vero, Libane, nunc te meliust expergiscier*
> *atque argento comparando fingere fallaciam.*
> *iam diu est factum quom discesti ab ero atque abiisti ad forum,*
> *igitur inveniundo argento ut fingeres fallaciam.*
> *ibi tu ad hoc diei tempus dormitasti in otio . . .*

> By Herc, Libanus, now it is best to rouse yourself
> and trot out a trick to procure some cash.
> It's a while now since you left your boss and went to the forum
> so that you might trot out a trick then to find some cash.
> You slept there undisturbed until this time of day . . .

Libanus continues his self-address, but in these opening lines we can see lines 250 and 252 contain the same information in a slightly different construction and mostly the same vocabulary, which is why Guietus

---

[78] Andrews (1993) 195. The reader may choose to see this list either as presenting the items in chronological order or in an order of decreasing scriptedness.

deleted line 252 (accepted by Leo but not Lindsay). While 252 *igitur* seems awkward, either line is viable between 249 and 251; following 250, 252 is redundant, but it is not obviously inferior to 250. It is also unlike something that one would expect from an actor's interpolation: it does not build on already established ideas, but merely repeats them with mostly the same words.

I propose this doublet is a performance variant. In performance, the actor would speak either line 250 or 252 (or a third line like it), but never both. The manuscripts preserve one of two things. Possibly the choice for the performer is between lines 249–50 and 251–3, either of which could be followed by 254–5, in which Libanus' self-address continues as he banishes the dullness of his mind:

> a. *Hercle vero, Libane, nunc te meliust expergiscier*
> *atque argento comparando fingere fallaciam.*

> b. *iam diu est factum quom discesti ab ero atque abiisti ad forum,*
> *igitur inveniundo argento ut fingeres fallaciam.*
> *ibi tu ad hoc diei tempus dormitasti in otio ...*

This preserves the surviving manuscript order, and merely provides a different origin for the waking imagery that continues into the subsequent lines. As alternates each has merits. Lines 249–50 names the character again, emphasising the self-address; 251–3 instead emphasise the offstage location. The second possibility would see the doublet purely with the repeated line, and with a transposition of 251 and 250, maintain both the character's name and the information about the forum:

> *Hercle vero, Libane, nunc te meliust expergiscier*
> a. *atque argento comparando fingere fallaciam.*
> b. *igitur inveniundo argento ut fingeres fallaciam.*
> *iam diu est factum quom discesti ab ero atque abiisti ad forum,*
> *ibi tu ad hoc diei tempus dormitasti in otio ...*

The tradition became increasingly dependent upon a literary conception of text and preserved both lines. Line 251 was moved to where it would at least make grammatical sense, even if it remained aesthetically challenged so close to 250. Identifying such otiose lines as performance variants is preferable to seeing them as later interpolations.

This has several implications. First, whatever was said, there is no direct consequence for any of the other actors in the play. Since the lines come in a soliloquy and affect only the speaking character (i.e. they are not a cue for action by someone else), none of the variants would be actively missed in performance. Second, both versions did not exist in writing before the play's performance, and perhaps neither did. The actor learned some line (which probably had the verb *fingere* in some form taking *fallaciam* as a direct object, and *argento* in an ablative absolute clause) and spoke something appropriate when the time came. Third, the measure of a successful performance did not depend on the actor repeating the line verbatim. Performance variants are found with too much frequency in Plautus to allow us to suggest this is an accidentally preserved slip rather than an established practice. Fourth, however the actor became familiar with his lines (using parts, perhaps), our manuscripts represent a text consolidated following the initial run of the play at the *ludi*. Pre-existing texts may have played a part in this process, but the recording process was alive to the possibilities of variant performance inherent in a living theatre tradition that permitted some degree of improvisation. Fifth, neither of the variants is more correct or 'better' than the other. It may be that one possibility (a. or b. in either example) was realised in performance before the other: this is a question of priority (which cannot be answered), but is irrelevant to the result of the recording process. It may even be that one of the possibilities preserved was never even spoken before an audience, but represents a revised version, added by the playwright after the performance, and kept alongside something an actor said. Sixth, the process of textual consolidation took place after the initial run of the play but before the memory of the show had faded. My experience with improvisers is that pure improv scenes can be memorially reconstructed reliably for about a week after the performance. Plautus' actors performed in a blended tradition and possessed some form of preliminary texts, and ancient memories were no doubt better than modern ones, on average. Allowing a variation of two orders of magnitude due to these effects, the process could perhaps take place within two years, at a maximum. Such reconstructions need some if not all of the actors from the performance present and participating in the process.

This view does not denigrate the contribution made by improvisation. Indeed, the play cannot be said to be 'written' until after it has been performed. There is a corollary: the plays of Plautus contain lines that did not originate with the playwright. However much of the original script did make it into the final record of the performance, the verses our manuscripts preserve include improvisatory expansions and variants that originated in the collective of the theatrical troupe: the text preserves the theatrical tradition over the literary tradition. A similar phenomenon has been described for the Shakespearean text: 'if it is a performing text we are dealing with, it is a mistake to think that in our editorial work what we are doing is getting back to an author's original manuscript'.[79] Indeed, 'most literature in the period, and virtually all theatrical literature, must be seen as basically collaborative in nature, and ... Shakespeare can be distinguished from most other playwrights only because he was in on more parts of the collaboration'.[80] This is precisely the position of Plautus as I see it.

Armed with this model, one discovers many examples of performance doublets. Of exactly the type we have seen is *Pseudolus* 1136–9:

HARP. *heus, ubi estis vos?*
BALL.   *hic quidem ad me recta habet rectam*
                viam.
HARP. *heus, ubi estis vos?*
BALL.   *heus, adulescens, quid istic debetur tibi?*
                bene ego ab hoc praedatus ibo; novi, bona scaevast mihi.
HARP. *ecquis hoc aperit?*
BALL.   *heus, chlamydate, quid istic debetur tibi?*

HARP. (*calling to the door*) Hey, where are you?
BALL. (*to audience*) He has a straight path
        straight to me!
HARP. (*knocking at the door*) Hey, where are you?
BALL. (*to Harpax*) Hey, young man, what are
        you owed from there?
        (*to audience*) I will leave here rich with loot. I know: my
        omens are good.
HARP. (*knocking at the door*) Will any one here open up?
BALL. Hey, cloak boy, what are
        you owed from there?

Fleckeisen deleted line 1137 since it is composed of elements of both lines 1136 and 1139.[81] In performance, however, the scene is easily playable and the repetition merely reinforces the stage action. But it is possible that again we have a performance variant, where the actors could speak merely line 1137, or expand the door-knocking with the addition of Ballio's audience address, and speak lines 1136 and 1138–9:

[79] Orgel (2002) 2.   [80] Orgel (2002) 4–5.
[81] Zwierlein (1991b) 206–13 excises lines 1132–5 and 1138–9.

a. HARP.   *heus, ubi estis vos?*

   BALL.   *hic quidem ad me recta habet rectam viam.*
           bene ego ab hoc praedatus ibo; novi, bona scaevast mihi.

   HARP.   *ecquis hoc aperit?*

   BALL.   *heus, chlamydate, quid istic debetur tibi?*

b. HARP.   *heus, ubi estis vos?*

   BALL.   *heus, adulescens, quid istic debetur tibi?*

The different versions of the descriptions of Ballio's crablike movement in line 955 (Varro preserves a significantly different reading from the manuscripts) are naturally seen as a performance variant;[82] possibly the 'extra' *meretrix* in Ballio's song allow *Pseudolus* 218–24 to be seen as a doublet of lines 209–17.[83] Even when the prologue in *Poenulus* 123–8 announces he must change costume, the manuscripts preserve the necessary information twice:

> *ego ibo ornabor; vos aequo animo noscite.*
> *hic qui hodie veniet, reperiet suas filias*
> *at hunc sui fratris filium. dehinc ceterum*
> *valete adeste. ibo, alius nunc fieri volo:*
> *quod restat, restant alii qui faciant palam.*
> *valete atque adiuvate, ut vos servet Salus.*

Well, I must go and get into my costume. Follow our plot patiently. He [the Carthaginian] who arrives to-day will discover his daughters and this nephew. Now then farewell and stand by us. I am going, I must become another man. As for what remains, others remain to make it clear. Fare ye well and show us favour, so that Salvation may keep you safe.[84]

The subject of line 124, *qui* ('who'), refers back to *is* ('he') in line 121. Line 123 interrupts this flow. Again, we have a performance variant:

> a. *ego ibo ornabor; vos aequo animo noscite.*
> b. *hic qui hodie veniet, reperiet suas filias*
>   *at hunc sui fratris filium. dehinc ceterum*
>   *valete adeste. ibo, alius nunc fieri volo:*
>   *quod restat, restant alii qui faciant palam.*
>   *valete atque adiuvate, ut vos servet Salus.*

---

[82] Zwierlein (1991b) excises lines 954–5.

[83] Zwierlein (1991b) 90–98 excises lines 218–29. Because this passage is part of a *canticum*, however, it more likely represents two versions of the song, and not a record of a moment of spontaneous improvisation in performance.

[84] Translation by Nixon, slightly adapted.

Regardless of how the actor announces he will change costume, the final two lines of the speech remain the same, and can constitute a meaningful cue for the entry of the first actors.[85] A doublet of a different sort can be seen in Terence, *Heauton Timoroumenos* 48–50 and *Hecyra* 49–51. The repetition of these three lines verbatim has led most to excise them from *Heauton Timoroumenos*, especially since one manuscript omits lines 48–9. However, for the spectator attending the performance in 163, it is not certain that the repetition of this straightforward trope would be noticed by any of those who had been in the audience of *Hecyra* two years before, and a repetition of the lines would probably remain unnoticed.

Doublets exist: one way or another, we must account for their presence. I believe variation arising from improvisation represents the most economical way of understanding their origin. There are other explanations. The presence of doublets in the text of Shakespeare is sometimes argued to originate with printers' errors, resulting from when they failed to notice the author's marks indicating deletion. This is not a viable explanation in the pre-printing world of republican Rome. Zwierlein raises textual issues with all the passages I have used as examples, and for him these are the product of a late second-century reviser. However, he is unable to explain plausibly what motivates the reviser. Performance variants remain a more economical hypothesis, based on these and other examples. The absence of variants in other passages does not mean that another passage is somehow purer or more literary. Performance variants are revealing something about the text as a whole, not just about the particular sections. If the entire play was subject to improvisatory expansion, this has left traces at occasional points in our text. Some performance variants have been preserved, but they do not exhaust the opportunities for expansion or omission by the actors in performance. Some passages in Roman comedy were more strictly moderated by metre and music that would make improvisatory expansion more difficult.[86]

---

[85] Zwierlein (1990) 221–2 excises lines 124–7. Another doublet from *Poenulus*, lines 917–22 and 923–9, is symptomatic of a larger rearrangement of the text. Since the latter passage places Agorastocles in the forum and not at his house, the variant attests to alternative stage movement earlier for the Agorastocles actor. Immediately following these passages, the 'Punic' spoken at Hanno's entrance forms another doublet: 930–39 and 940–49; see also Krahmalkov (1970).

[86] For this reason I cannot believe Barsby (1995) 67: 'A good example of a monologue which seems to be expandable *ad libitum* and could thus be left to the actor to improvise is Ballio's long address to his slaves ... which goes on for nearly a hundred lines (133–229).' The metrical variety of this passage suggests rather a carefully rehearsed *canticum* – precisely the place where improvisational expansion is least likely to be found. When Zagagi (1995) 85 describes the Plautine *cantica* as the place 'where improvisation is most likely to have occurred', this makes very different assumptions about the nature of musical accompaniment.

But for the stichic metres, both accompanied and unaccompanied, variation in the moment of performance would have been possible for a trained improvisor.[87]

The examples so far have all been relatively small-scale alterations that would not represent a significant alteration of the action. The second class of evidence operates on a larger scale, with 'elastic' gags or modular units:[88] 'such modular components are a sign of improvisation technique, of a mode of performance in which an actor's existing repertoire of jokes, long and short, can be adapted and inserted into any plot with which they do not actually clash'.[89] Vogt-Spira uses a similar image in his description of Acanthio's slow revelation of information at *Mercator* 120–88, following his entry as a running slave:

> One might speak of a paradoxical reversal, for the transmission of information, the goal of the scene and critical for the whole plot, serves in the local context simply as the basis for a comic device. This can, rather like a soap-bubble, be extended or 'blown up' as long as the actors can think of something amusing. We ought therefore not to speak of a slowing down, since nothing is actually being delayed; rather the progress of the action is temporarily unimportant.[90]

Curculio does the same thing as Acanthio at *Curculio* 299–335, following his running-slave entry. The *Curculio* example is less than half the length of the *Mercator* passage, but the nature of improvisation and modular construction mean that in performance, the *Curculio* passage might be similarly extended. The beginning of Acanthio's routine has him complaining of physical ailments (*Mercator* 123–5): a variation on this subroutine is found at *Curculio* 309–10, itself echoing *Curculio* 216–22, with Cappadox's initial entry.

As with the performance variants, the presence of expandable comic routines diagnoses something about the entire play, not merely about the given passage: 'The elastic gag cannot have been the only characteristic of the unwritten dramaturgy of improvised comedy. Nevertheless, when it is found in a written script, it is a useful sign of the presence or influence of

---

[87] English-language improvisers I have worked with can, with practice, improvise unaccompanied verse scenes in iambic, trochaic, and anapaestic rhythms.

[88] Andrews (1993) 175–85. At 266 n. 17 he suggests that the technique is applicable to Plautus but provides no details.

[89] Andrews (1993) 181.

[90] Vogt-Spira (2001) 101, translated from Vogt-Spira (1995). This scene again partakes of the tension between urgency and delay observed in *Pseudolus* at Marshall (1996) and *Persa* in Chapter 4.

professional [improvisatory] practice.'[91] While it would not nearly be as straightforward as these examples, a similar analysis could suggest the two endings of *Poenulus* were derived from performance variations, at a larger scale of composition again, perhaps from two performances by the troupe, in order to account for a change in casting.[92] Accepting that any passage might receive unscripted expansion in performance, there is no longer a need to assume textual variations are 'unauthorised' or necessarily postdate Plautus. Of course, individual cases may do so: text preserves in a written form something which was not written in origin, but which developed in the moment of performance. With a blended script, all variants, realised and unrealised, are equally valid. This brings us to the third class of evidence.

The strongest reason to accept an element of improvisation in the performance of the plays of Plautus is that, when social context is also considered, the alternative is much more unthinkable. While the conventional assessment of Plautus' plays as scripts for performance serves to make the Roman comedians very much like the playwrights writing in Europe since the sixteenth century, the world that produced the plays was very different. The intersecting effects of literacy levels, production costs, and time constraints on rehearsal point to a blended performance being more viable economically. The performing *palliata* troupe had incentives from a variety of areas to keep costs down in the production of its plays. Troupes received contracts with at times less than three weeks for pre-production activity. A rigid sense of 'the text' works against this. The traditional model of Plautine performance requires all the members of the troupe to be fully literate, and expects the troupe to possess at the least five or six written parts for the play that was about to be performed, which would then be memorised and rehearsed. Scribal copying and verbatim memorisation represent a wasteful use of both preparation time (both must precede useful rehearsals) and financial resources (both have cash costs associated with them). Further, the limited field of vision provided by a mask means that the actor must be 'off book' before the mask can be used in rehearsal.

A well-prepared group of actors able to improvise within an established repertoire of gags and routines could offset these negative consequences, so that on receiving a contract serious rehearsals in masks could begin within days. The skills of an actor had to include the ability to compose

---

[91] Andrews (1993) 185.
[92] Contrast the positions of Maurach (1988), and Zwierlein (1990) 60.

verse spontaneously in a variety of metrical and musical registers – a difficult skill, but one that can be trained and one which would come more naturally in a society where literacy levels remained low and the notion of a 'text' or of proprietary authorial rights was altogether absent. Once learned, the actors retain the skill for future performances. In the mime contest between Decimus Laberius and Publilius Syrus, part of Julius Caesar's means of smoothing over the tensions with Laberius was to improvise an iambic senarius (Macrobius, *Saturnalia* 2.7.8, and Suetonius, *Julius Caesar* 39.2): the single verse from an amateur dramatist (Caesar had written an *Oedipus* in his youth) points to the skill possessed by all professionals, the ability spontaneously to produce passable verse. Plautus provides a literary imitation of this pure improvisatory activity in *Persa*.[93] This is not to say that the entire troupe was illiterate: casting concerns suggest that two or three actors shouldered the majority of a play's lines, and perhaps only they received written parts in advance of the contract being awarded. Streamlining the demands on time and money, however, represents a substantial gain for the troupe, and means that all actors did not need to possess an extraordinary education before entering the profession. There are other consequences. Self-indulgence remained a risk for Plautus' actors, as the responsibility for reining in excesses (at least in later improvising traditions) usually lies with the actor himself. For any given performance, a precise running time will not have been known in advance. Conceivably, a troupe could throw off the day's schedule slightly by unreasonably extending its performance.

If a written text of a dramatic work exists prior to performance, we can call this (in some sense) a script: whether a fully scripted play with individual lines assigned to particular actors or characters, an outline *scenario* as used in *commedia dell'arte*, or an order of performance as seen on *P. Berol.* inv. 13927, the written object is available to guide, direct, and in some ways limit what the actors do onstage. If a written text of a dramatic work comes into existence after a performance, the object possesses a fundamentally different identity: it becomes a transcript. Assuming the individual or individuals recording the transcript are aware of the performance, then what is documented may contain elements devised in performance, revisions of unsuccessful material, performance variants, etc. – what scholars of Renaissance drama call 'memorial

---

[93] Marshall (1997b), describing a scene in trochaic septenarii.

reconstructions' of the performance event. These transcripts can even choose to ignore or expunge elements derived from performance, creating a self-consciously 'literary' text.

The distinction between 'script' and 'transcript' isolates when the document achieves its final form. Our tendency has been to see the plays of Plautus as scripts: written in advance of performance, translated and adapted from other Greek scripts. When we say the *fabulae Atellanae* never achieved a literary identity until the first century BC, we mean before this point there were no scripts possessing enough detail that were seen to have lasting value after the performance. Whatever outlines or prop lists were used, there was not enough connection that they possessed 'literary' value. The transition to the written *Atellana* meant that a fuller script existed in advance of the production. It could consequently be given to actors other than the author who could then remain apart from the world of the stage, like the knight Decimus Laberius until he received Caesar's request. By the first century a script could pre-exist performance: performance did not significantly alter the written text.

A step towards this change may indeed have been taken by Terence. While he had a patron in Ambivius Turpio, Terence was less directly involved with the preparation of a play for performance than Plautus had been. What he provided for the troupe may indeed have looked very much like the surviving scripts. What we cannot say, though, is how 'faithful' Turpio and the other actors were in their stage representation of Terence's work. From a performance perspective, this is not necessarily a significant loss, because the audience would not have been able to say how faithful Turpio and his actors were either. The audience is only presented the play as a performed entity, and has no access to the performance documents used by the actors as they prepared. This did not stop improvisation, but it does suggest that varying attitudes began to emerge in the second century. Even for Cicero, there remained a place for improvised comments in drama: in a letter to Atticus (14.3) Cicero indicates a desire to hear spontaneous remarks at the theatre, and in *pro Sestio* 120–23, he describes how the famous actor Aesopus improvised lines while performing a tragedy. Again, this emphasises that improvisation is not a genre of theatre, but is a means of producing works in any of a number of theatrical genres. For Aesopus and Cicero, even tragedy in the first century BC did not preclude improvisation.

The earliest playwrights in Rome operated on a cusp, as the technology of writing and increasing trade across the Mediterranean revolutionised their culture. Most forms of cultural expression were affected, and theatre was no exception. Plautus and his contemporaries drew together performance genres and produced an amalgam of the literate (Hellenistic New Comedy, translated from the Greek) and the pre-literate (mime and *fabulae Atellanae*). Economic pressures from all sides encouraged innovation and efficiency in the development of the theatrical product. One of the consequences of this was blended performances that combined scripted and unscripted elements.

Some of the actors may have been illiterate and consequently 'their approach to creating "scripts" and memorizing them for performance would be different from the methods adopted by anyone who could read and write'.[94] Plautus could read and write. Plautus, the *poeta* and *architectus* of the comedies, was fully versed in the literary conventions of the Greek world, probably mediated at least in part from the South Italian performance tradition, and he combined this with aspects of the unscripted traditions native to Italy. Molière seems to have sought a similar balance in his (scripted) plays: he spent time outside of Paris, touring his shows in less urban settings, where he 'must have observed a particular rhythmic structure which was adopted by improvising actors, and seen that it had a theatrical validity in its own right which could be turned back into a written script'.[95] While *palliatae* troupes were balancing contracts for performances at *ludi*, preparing plays for production, and carrying on the various other activities of their lives, their previous plays were consolidated into a written form.

Plautus had taken a Greek literary play, and had rendered it into Latin. There was probably a master-copy of some sort in existence before the performance. He, or someone else, would have prepared parts, so that the principal actors in the company would be able to begin to prepare their roles. There may also have been property lists, mask lists, notes of cues for offstage sound effects, and conceivably notes of some sort or another for the *tibicen* reflecting the arc structure. The tendency to argue that certain plays lacked any Greek model does a disservice to the literary side of the composition.[96] The *fabula palliata* requires at least this in advance of production. This was not the end of the composition process, though: key scenes were sculpted in rehearsal and in performance before an audience. Changes were made spontaneously according to the actor's perceptions of audience response, the festival environment, the activities

---

[94] Andrews (1993) 176, describing performers in *commedia* troupes.
[95] Andrews (1993) 185 and see 171–2.
[96] See especially Goldberg (1978), Stärk (1989), and Lefèvre, Stärk, and Vogt-Spira (1991).

of fellow actors, prepared comic routines, and the demands of the script. The collaborative oral component was an integral part of the creation process.[97] The goal was not verbatim performance, but something more responsive to audience expectations: 'In memorizing and performing the sequence, the stress would lie on conveying the information and/or getting the laugh, rather than on repeating the words identically every time.'[98] Spontaneity is rewarded for the improvising actors, and they possessed skills to enhance that ability.[99] Creativity and inventiveness were expected of them during the performance, and this provided a meaningful component to the creation process.

At some time after the end of the *ludi*, a record of the performance was made. The playwright himself was almost certainly actively involved in this process. We cannot say what the motivation was for this activity. There was no extensive book trade in Rome, and it is anachronistic to assume all performances yearn for literary status. There is a clear way whereby Plautus' reputation or pocketbook would be enhanced by his plays attaining the status of 'literature'. The stage was where he worked and earned his living (Aulus Gellius, *Attic Nights* 3.3.14). There are advantages for a troupe in the creation of permanent texts. Textual consolidation can offer benefits within the context of blended performances. Principally, a transcript of the performance (edited, with additions and subtractions drawn from the experiences of the actors) can serve as a record of what happened on stage. Improvisation can at times be brilliant, but no performance is ever unforgettable, and some record of what occurred on stage could serve as the basis for future performances of the same play. It would not prescribe what was said on stage, but could document, with variants, what had once worked, to allow a more nuanced remounting of the play under the same conditions – another blended performance where the play would again be subject to improvisational expansion – easier and that much more nuanced. The transcript would be available to serve as a script for a future performance, where it would receive exactly the same treatment at the hands of the actors as the documents that had pre-existed the first staging had received.

---

[97] Again the *commedia* points to a potentially analogous circumstance: 'despite the fact that we have, mostly in manuscript form, around 800 of the scenarios the actors used as a skeletal framework for their performances, there is almost no evidence of any other written materials. . . . this scarcity in itself is a strong indication that the actors were relying on oral memory rather than literate recording and memorizing from the written record' (Fitzpatrick (1995) 16).

[98] Andrews (1993) 176.

[99] Johnstone (1981) 75–108 provides one set of guidelines for teaching spontaneity.

Such a document remains in the first instance a tool for the playwright himself, though what then exists is a tool that others can use as well. If this process of consolidation never happened for the scenarios of the *commedia dell'arte*, with the stage antics preserved written in full, part of the reason is to be found in the different attitude to the written word before the performance. The outline provided by a scenario was much more schematic than the translation of Greek New Comedy that the Roman troupe used as its preliminary document. The written word remained central to the creation of the *palliata*, and was part of every stage of its performance history. But the documents created were fluid, able to respond to the exigencies of the stage and the realities of performance and stagecraft in an ever-changing theatrical context.

Following Plautus' death, remountings of his plays did take place, and an increasingly literate world no doubt treated the transcripts differently. The text was not fixed: discussions of the early textual history of Plautus emphasise that the second century was a time of great variability, 'mouvance' in Deufert's term.[100] This no doubt happened, but the problem has been overstated. There was no 'text of Plautus': all written versions of the plays were transitional documents, intended as guides for future performances and not meant to be treated as unalterable icons fixed for all time. If the texts were changed in various ways in the later second century, that was nothing compared to the degree of change Plautus himself introduced into his plays.

Theatre is an event, when actors and audience come together to create fictional worlds that can charm, delight, instruct, and challenge. Titus Maccius Plautus, writing at a time when Rome was expanding its horizons geographically, socially, and intellectually, brought together scripted and unscripted elements in a composite genre that combined Greek and Roman performance traditions, yielding a fusion of several levels at which humour operated. The resulting comedic structure set the pattern for European and North American comedy to the present day. The most distinctive features for the original audience when the plays were performed, would have been the rough edges. These plays acknowledged they were plays, and the characters made it clear they wanted to make their audience laugh. Routines and shorter gags were presented for the audience's delight, forged on the stage producing laughs that might never be repeated. It was a healthy, vibrant, comic tradition that rewarded the

---

[100] Deufert (2002). Other important studies of this period, with varying conclusions, include Lindsay (1904) 2–23, Jocelyn (1987) and (1984), and Zwierlein (1990) and his subsequent studies.

innovative and bold performers who told romantic plots of young lovers with slapstick, aggressive physical comedy, and evocative wordplay. The tension and dynamism arising from the intersection of script and spontaneity was what characterised the *fabulae palliatae*, but most of the evidence for it is lost to us today. If it is to be recaptured, it is only through our learning what the plays tell about the moment of performance. The stagecraft resources, the production context, the demands placed on actors and musicians, and the structural elements in the plays that make the narrative real for an audience gathered to see a show – this is where Plautus' raw comedy achieved its purpose.

Appendix: *Conspectus Metrorum Plautinorum*

The following overview of the metrical structure of Plautus emphasises the changes of metre and the arc structure described in the main text. For *cantica mixtis modis*, I have followed the designations of Questa (1995), not questioning his designation of anapaestic passages, etc.; references in square brackets are to appropriate pages in Questa (1995). For all stichic metres, I have followed the numeration in Lindsay's text (1904–5), which contains a more detailed *schema metrorum*; occasional variants have been noted. The symbol • designates a 'simple fall' in an arc, in which the *tibicen* provides accompaniment only for trochaic septenarii (tr^7). S = 'senarii' (unaccompanied iambic senarii); C = 'canticum' (accompanied mixed metres); R = 'recitative' (accompanied stichic metres).

AMPHITRUO

arc 1	1–152	S	ia^6
	153–79	C	[60–61]
	180–218	R	ia^8
	219–47	C	[62–3]
	248–62	R	ia^8 (253–4 tr^7)
	263–462	R	tr^7
arc 2	463–98	S	ia^6
	499–550	R	tr^7
	551–85a	C	[64–7]
	586–632	R	tr^7
	633–53	C	[68–9]
	654–860	R	tr^7
arc 3	861–955	S	ia^6
	956–73	• R	tr^7
arc 4	974–83	S	ia^6
	984–1005	R	ia^8

	1006–8	S	ia^6 – see text
	1009–fr. vi	R	tr^7
arc 5	fr. vii–x	S	ia^6
	fr. xi–1052	R	tr^7
	1053–85	C	[70–71]
	1086–1130	R	tr^7
arc 6	1131–1143	S	ia^6
	1144–6	• R	tr^7

ASINARIA

arc 1	1–126	S	ia^6
	127–38	C	[74–5]
	139–380	R	tr^7
	381–503	R	ia^6
	504–44	R	tr^7
	545–745	R	ia^7

arc 2	746–829	S	ia^6
	830–50	R	ia^8
	851–947	R	tr^7

AULULARIA

arc 1	1–119	S	ia^6
	120–60	C	[78–81]
	161–279	R	tr^7
arc 2	280–405	S	ia^6 (393 tr^7)
	406–48	C	[82–5]
	449–74	R	tr^7
arc 3	475–586	S	ia^6
	587–660	• R	tr^7 (660 tr^8)
arc 4	661–712	S	ia^6
	713–30a	C	[86–7]
	731–802	R	tr^7
	803–7	R	ia^7
	808–18	R	tr^7
	819–33	C	[88–9]

BACCHIDES

arc 1	27–34	S	ia^6 – see text
	1–26	C	[92–3]
	35–108	R	tr^7
arc 2	109–367	S	ia^6
	368–499	• R	tr^7
arc 3	500–25	S	ia^6
	526–72	• R	tr^7
arc 4	573–611	S	ia^6
	612–70	C	[94–9]
	671–760	R	tr^7 (673 eup.)
arc 5	761–924	S	ia^6
	925–96a	C	[100–7]
arc 6	997–1075	S	ia^6
	1076–1206	C	[108–21]
	1207–11	R	tr^7

CAPTIVI

arc 1	1–194	S	ia^6
	195–241	C	[124–7]
	242–360	R	tr^7

arc 2	361–84	S	ia^6
	385–497	R	tr^7
	498–540	C	[128–31]
	541–658	R	tr^7
arc 3	659–767	S	ia^6
	768–90	C	[132–3]
	791–832	R	tr^7
	833–7	C	[134–5]
	838–908	R	tr^7
	909–21	R	ia^8
	922–9	C	[136–7]
	930–1036	R	tr^7

CASINA

arc 1	1–143	S	ia^6
	144–251	C	[140–49]
	252–308	R	tr^7
arc 2	309–52	S	ia^6
	353–423	• R	tr^7
arc 3	424–514	S	ia^6
	515–62	• R	tr^7
arc 4	563–620	S	ia^6
	621–962	C	[150–75]
	963–1018	R	tr^7

CISTELLARIA

	1–37	C	[178–81]
	38–58	R	ia^7
	59–119	R	tr^7
arc 1	120–202	S	ia^6
	203–28	C	[182–3]
	231–53	R	tr^7
arc 2	273–304	S	ia^6
	305–73a	R	ia^7 – see text
arc 3	374–408	S	ia^6
	449–52	R	ia^8 – see text
	453–535	R	tr^7 – see text
arc 4	536–630	S	ia^6
	631–70	R	tr^7
	671–703	C	[184–7]
	704–46	R	ia^7

arc 5	747–73	S	ia^6
	774–87	• R	tr^7

CURCULIO

arc 1	1–95	S	ia^6
	96–157	C	[190–95]
	158–215	R	tr^7
arc 2	216–79	S	ia^6
	280–370	• R	tr^7
arc 3	371–461	S	ia^6
	462–86	R	tr^7
	487–532	R	ia^7
	533–634	R	tr^7
arc 4	635–78	S	ia^6
	679–729	• R	tr^7

EPIDICUS

	1–195	C	[198–211]
	196–305	R	tr^7
arc 1	306–19	S	ia^6
	320–40	C	[212–13]
	341–81	R	ia^7
arc 2	382–525	S	ia^6
	526–46	C	[214–17]
	547–733	R	tr^7

MENAECHMI

arc 1	1–109	S	ia^6
	110–34	C	[220–21]
	135–225	R	tr^7
arc 2	226–350	S	ia^6
	351–68	C	[222–3]
	369–465	R	tr^7
arc 3	466–570	S	ia^6
	571–603	C	[224–7]
	604–700	R	tr^7
arc 4	701–52	S	ia^6
	753–74	C	[228–9]
	775–871	R	tr^7

arc 5	872–98	S	ia^6
	899–965	R	tr^7
	966–89	C	[230–33]
	990–94	R	tr^7
	995–1005	R	ia^8
	1003–6	C	[234–5]
	1007–59	R	tr^7 (1007 tr^8)
	1060–62	R	ia^8—see text
	1063–162	R	tr^7

MERCATOR

arc 1	1–110	S	ia^6
	111–28	R	ia^8 (117 tr^7)
	129–40	C	[238–9]
	141–224	R	tr^7
arc 2	225–334	S	ia^6
	335–63	C	[240–41]
	364–498	R	tr^7
	499–543	R	ia^7
arc 3	544–87	S	ia^6
	588–666	• R	tr^7
arc 4	667–829	S	ia^6
	830–1026	• R	tr^7

MILES GLORIOSUS

arc 1	1–155	S	ia^6
	156–353	R	tr^7
	354–425	R	ia^7
	426–80	R	tr^7
arc 2	481–595	S	ia^6
	596–812	• R	tr^7
arc 3	813–73	S	ia^6
	874–946	R	ia^7
	947–1010	R	tr^7
	1011–93	C	[244–51]
arc 4	1094–1136	S	ia^6
	1137–1215	R	tr^7
	1216–83	R	ia^7
arc 5	1284–1310	S	ia^6
	1311–77	• R	tr^7

arc 6 1378–93 S ia^6
  1394–1437 • R tr^7

MOSTELLARIA

arc 1 1–83 S ia^6
  84–156 C [254–9]
  157–247 R ia^7
  248–312 R tr^7
  313–47 C [260–263]
  348–407 R tr^7

arc 2 409–689 S ia^6
  690–746 C [264–9]

arc 3 747–82 S ia^6
  783–804 C [270–71]
  805–57 R tr^7
  858–903 C [272–5]
  904–92 R tr^7

arc 4 993–1040 S ia^6
  1041–1181 • R tr^7

PERSA

  1–52 C [278–83]

arc 1 53–167 S ia^6
  168–279 C [284–91]
  280–328 R ia^7

arc 2 329–469 S ia^6
  470–500 C [292–5]
  501–12 S ia^6 – *see text*
  513–19 R tr^7
  520–27 S ia^6 – *see text*
  528–672 R tr^7

arc 3 673–752 S ia^6
  753–858 C [296–307]

POENULUS

arc 1 1–209 S ia^6
  210–60 C [310–13]
  261–409 R tr^7

arc 2 410–503 S ia^6
  504–614 • R tr^7

arc 3 615–816 S ia^6
  817–22 R ia^8 (821–2 ia^7)
  823–929 R tr^7

arc 4 930–1173 S ia^6 (1165 tr^7)
  1174–1200 C [314–19]
  1201–25 R tr^7
  1226–73 R ia^7 (1226 ia^8)
  1274–1303 R tr^7

arc 5 1304–97 S ia^6
  1398–1422 • R tr^7

PSEUDOLUS

arc 1 1–132 S ia^6
  133–264 C [322–35]
  265–393 R tr^7

arc 2 394–573a S ia^6
  574–603 C [336–9]
  604–766 R tr^7

arc 3 767–904 S ia^6
  905–50 C [340–45]
  951–97 R tr^7 (997 ia^8)

arc 4 998–1102 S ia^6
  1103–35 C [346–9]
  1136–1245 R tr^7
  1246–1335b C [350–59]

RUDENS

arc 1 1–184 S ia^6
  185–289 C [362–71]
  290–413 R ia^7
  414–41 R tr^7

arc 2 442–558 S ia^6
  559–92 R tr^7

arc 3 593–614 S ia^6
  615–63 R tr^7
  664–81a C [372–3]
  682–705 R ia^7
  706–79 R tr^7

arc 4 780–905 S ia^6
  906–62b C [374–5]
  963–1190 R tr^7

arc 5	1191–1204	S	ia^6
	1205–26	• R	tr^7

arc 6	1227–64	S	ia^6
	1265–80	R	tr^7
	1281–1337	R	ia^7

arc 7	1338–56	S	ia^6
	1357–1423	• R	tr^7

STICHUS

	1–47	C	[382–5]
	48–57	S	ia^6 – see text
	58–154	R	tr^7 (67 ia^8)

arc 1	155–273	S	ia^6
	274–330	C	[386–91]
	331–401	R	tr^7

arc 2	402–504	S	ia^6
	505–640	• R	tr^7

arc 3	641–72	S	ia^6
	673–82	R	ia^7
	683–761	R	tr^7 (702–5 ia^8)
	762–8	S	ia^6 – see text
	769–75	C	[392–3]

TRINUMMUS

arc 1	1–222	S	ia^6
	223–300	C	[396–403]
	301–91	R	tr^7

arc 2	392–601	S	ia^6
	602–728	• R	tr^7

arc 3	729–819	S	ia^6
	820–42a	C	[404–7]
	843–997	R	tr^7

arc 4	998–1007	S	ia^6
	1008–92	• R	tr^7

arc 5	1093–1114	S	ia^6
	1115–19	C	[408–9]
	1120–89	R	tr^7

TRUCULENTUS

arc 1	1–94	S	ia^6
	95–129	C	[412–15]
	130–208	R	ia^7
	209–55	C	[416–21]
	256–321	R	tr^7

arc 2	322–447	S	ia^6
	448–64	C	[422–3]
	465–550	R	tr^7
	551–630	C	[424–31]

arc 3	631–98	S	ia^6
	699–710	R	tr^7
	711–29	C	[432–3]
	730–968	R	tr^7

References

Abel, K. 1955. *Die Plautusprologe*. Mülheim-Ruhr.

Adams, J. N. 1982. *The Latin Sexual Vocabulary*. London, Duckworth.

Allen, W. 1959. 'Stage Money (*fabam mimum*, Cic. *Att.* I, 16, 13)', *Transactions of the American Philological Association* 40: 1–8.

Anderson, W. S. 1993. *Barbarian Play: Plautus' Roman Comedy*. Toronto, University of Toronto Press.

Andrews, R. 1993. *Scripts and Scenarios: The Performance of Comedy in Renaissance Italy*. Cambridge, Cambridge University Press.

Arnott, P. D. 1961. 'Greek Drama and the Modern Stage', in W. Arrowsmith and R. Shattuck (eds.), *The Craft and Context of Translation*, 113–28. Austin, University of Texas Press.

Arnott, W. G. 1967. 'The Disassociated Actor', in G. L. Beede (ed.), *Greek Drama: A Collection of Festival Papers*, 40–51. Vermillion, Dakota Press.

　　1968. 'Alexis and the Parasite's Name', *Greek, Roman and Byzantine Studies* 9: 161–68.

　　1989. 'Gorgias' Exit at Menander, *Dyskolos* 381–92', *Zeitschrift für Papyrologie und Epigraphik* 76: 3–5.

　　1995. 'Amorous Scenes in Plautus', *Papers of the Leeds International Latin Seminar* 8: 1–17.

　　1996a. *Menander II*. Cambridge, MA, Harvard University Press.

　　1996b. *Alexis, The Fragments: A Commmentary*. Cambridge, Cambridge University Press.

　　1997. 'Love Scenes in Plautus', in J. Axer and W. Görler (eds.), *Scaenica Saravi-Varsoviensia*, 111–22. Warsaw, DiG.

Auhagen, U. (ed.). 2001. *Studien zu Plautus' Epidicus*. Tübingen, Gunter Narr.

Babbitt, F. C. 1927. *Plutarch: Moralia*, vol. I. Cambridge, MA, Harvard University Press.

Baier, T. 1998. '*Les Captifs*: Eine Plautus-Nachahmung Jean Rotrous', in Benz and Lefèvre (1998) 165–93.

　　1999a. *Studien zu Plautus' Amphitruo*. Tübingen, Gunter Narr.

　　1999b. '"On ne peut faillir en l'imitant": Rotrous *Sosies*, eine Nachgestaltung des plautinischen Amphitruo', in Baier (1999a) 203–37.

　　2004. *Studien zu Plautus' Poenulus*. Tübingen, Gunter Narr.

Bain, D. 1977. *Actors and Audience: A Study of Asides and Related Conventions in Greek Drama.* Oxford, Oxford University Press.

    1979. 'Plautus vortit barbare', in D. West and T. Woodman (eds.), *Creative Imitation and Latin Literature,* 17–34. Cambridge, Cambridge University Press.

Barba, E. and N. Savarese. 1991. *A Dictionary of Theatre Anthropology: The Secret Art of the Performer.* New York, Routledge.

Barchiesi, M. 1970. 'Plauto e il metateatro antico', *Il Verri* 31: 113–30.

Barsby, J. 1982. 'Actors and Act-Divisions: Some Questions of Adaptation in Roman Comedy', *Antichthon* 16: 77–87.

    1986. *Plautus: Bacchides.* Oak Park, IL, Bolchazy-Carducci.

    1995. 'Plautus' *Pseudolus* as Improvisatory Drama', in Benz, Stärk, and Vogt-Spira (1995) 55–70.

    1999. *Terence: Eunuchus.* Cambridge, Cambridge University Press.

    2001. *Terence,* 2 vols. I: *The Woman of Andros, The Self-tormentor, The Eunuch.* II: *Phormio, The Mother-in-Law, The Brothers.* Cambridge, MA, Harvard University Press.

Barton, I. M. 1972. 'Tranio's Laconian Key', *Greece and Rome* 19: 25–31.

Beacham, R. C. 1991. *The Roman Theatre and its Audience.* Cambridge, MA, Harvard University Press.

Beare, W. 1964. *The Roman Stage: A Short History of Latin Drama in the Time of the Republic,* 3rd edn. London, Methuen.

Bennett, S. 1997. *Theatre Audiences: A Theory of Production and Reception,* 2nd edn. London and New York, Routledge.

Benz, L. and E. Lefèvre (eds.). 1998. *Maccus barbarus: Sechs Kapitel zur Originalität der Captivi des Plautus.* Tübingen, Gunter Narr.

Benz, L., E. Stärk, and G. Vogt-Spira (eds.). 1995. *Plautus und die Tradition des Stegreifspiels.* Tübingen, Gunter Narr.

Berendt, J. E. 1992. *The Jazz Book: From Ragtime to Fusion and Beyond.* 6th edn, rev. Gunther Huesmann. New York, Lawrence Hill.

Bergk, T. 1872. 'Ueber einige Zeichen der Plautinischen Handscriften', *Philologus* 31: 229–46.

Bernabò-Brea, L. 1981. *Menandro e il teatro greco nelle terracotte liparesi.* Geneva, SAGEP.

Bernstein, F. 1998. *Ludi publici: Untersuchungen zur Entstehung und Entwicklung der öffentlichen Spiele im republikanischen Rom.* Stuttgart, Franz Steiner.

Bieber, M. 1961. *The History of the Greek and Roman Theater,* 2nd edn. Princeton, Princeton University Press.

Boldrini, S. 1984. *Gli anapesti di Plauto.* Urbino, Pubblicazioni dell'Università di Urbino.

Bonaria, M. 1965. *Romani Mimi.* Rome, In Aedibus Athenaei.

Bradley, D. 1992. *From Text to Performance in the Elizabethan Theatre.* Cambridge, Cambridge University Press.

Brandon, J. R. 1992. *Kabuki: Five Classic Plays.* Honolulu, University of Hawaii Press.

Braun, L. 1970. *Die Cantica des Plautus*. Göttingen, Vandenhoeck and Ruprecht.

Briscoe, J. 1981. *A Commentary on Livy, Books XXXIV–XXXVII*. Oxford, Oxford University Press.

Brook, P. 1968. *The Empty Space*. New York, Atheneum.

Brown, P. G. M. 1987. 'Masks, Names, and Characters in New Comedy', *Hermes* 115: 181–201.

    1990. 'Plots and Prostitutes in Greek New Comedy', *Papers of the Leeds International Latin Seminar* 6: 241–66.

    1992. 'Menander, Fragments 745 and 746 K-T, Menander's *Kolax* and Parasites and Flatterers in Greek Comedy', *Zeitschrift für Papyrologie und Epigraphik* 92: 91–107.

    1993. 'The Skinny Virgins of Terence, Eunuchus 313–17', in H. D. Jocelyn and H. Hunt (eds.), *Tria Lustra*, 229–34. Liverpool.

    1995. 'Aeschinus at the Door: Terence *Adelphoe 632–43* and the Traditions of Greco-Roman Comedy', *Papers of the Leeds International Latin Seminar* 8: 71–89.

    2002. 'Actors and Actor-managers at Rome in the Time of Plautus and Terence', in Easterling and Hall (2002) 225–37.

Buck, C. H. J. 1940. *A Chronology of the Plays of Plautus*. Baltimore, Johns Hopkins University Press.

Calder, W. M. 1975. 'The Size of the Chorus in Seneca's *Agamemnon*', *Classical Philology* 70: 32–35.

Carney, T. F. 1963. *P. Terenti Afri Hecyra*. Pretoria, The Classical Association of Rhodesia and Nyasaland.

Chalmers, W. R. 1965. 'Plautus and His Audience', in T. A. Dorley and D. R. Dudley (eds.), *Roman Drama*, 21–50. London, Routledge.

Chiarini, G. 1989. 'La rappresentazione teatrale', in P. F. G. Cavallo and A. Giardina (eds.), *Lo spazio letterario di Roma antica*, vol. II: 127–214. Rome, Salerno.

Christenson, D. M. 2000. *Plautus: Amphitruo*. Cambridge, Cambridge University Press.

Clark, A. (ed.). 2000. *Riffs and Choruses: A New Jazz Anthology*. London, Continuum.

Clark, J. R. 2001–02. 'Early Latin Handwriting and Plautus' "Pseudolus"', *Classical Journal* 97: 183–89.

Coarelli, F. 1977. 'Public Building in Rome between the Second Punic War and Sulla', *Papers of the British School at Rome* 45: 1–23.

    1983. *Il foro Romano*, vol. I: *Periodo arcaico*. Rome, Quasar.

    1985. *Il foro Romano*, vol. II: *Periodo repubblicano e augusteo*. Rome, Quasar.

Cohee, P. 1994. 'Instauratio sacrorum', *Hermes* 122: 451–68.

Cohen, A. R. 1999. *Role Doubling as a Dramatic Technique in Greek Tragedy*. Dissertation, Stanford University.

Collart, J. 1970. 'Le soldat qui ne chante pas (quelques remarques sur le rôle du miles chez Plaute)', in *Mélanges M. Durry* (*Revue des Etudes Latines 47 bis*), 199–208. Paris.

Conrad, C. C. 1915. *The Technique of Continuous Action in Roman Comedy.* Dissertation, Menasha.

Corbett, P. 1986. *The Scurra.* Edinburgh, Scottish Academic Press.

Cotticelli, F., A. G. Heck, and T. F. Heck. 2001. *The Commedia dell'Arte in Naples: A Bilingual Edition of the 176 Casamarciano Scenarios,* 2 vols. Lanham, MD and London, The Scarecrow Press.

Craig, E. G. 1911. *On the Art of the Theatre.* London.

Csapo, E. 1987. 'Is the Threat-monologue of the *Servus currens* an Index of Roman Authorship?', *Phoenix* 41: 399–419.

　　1989. 'Plautine Elements in the Running-slave Entrance Monologues?', *Classical Quarterly* 39: 148–63.

　　1993. 'A Case Study in the Use of Theatre Iconography as Evidence for Ancient Acting', *Antike Kunst* 36: 41–58.

　　2004. 'The Politics of the New Music', in P. Murray and P. Wilson (eds.), *Music and the Muses: The Culture of 'Mousike' in the Classical Athenian City,* 207–48. Oxford, Oxford University Press.

Csapo, E. and W. J. Slater. 1995. *The Context of Ancient Drama.* Ann Arbor, University of Michigan Press.

Cunningham, I. C. 1971. *Herodas' Mimiamboi.* Oxford, Oxford University Press.

Damen, M. 1985. *The Comedy of Diphilos Sinopeus in Plautus, Terence, and Athenaeus.* Dissertation, University of Texas at Austin.

　　1988. 'Actors and Act-Divisions in the Greek Original of Plautus' *Menaechmi*', *Classical World* 82: 409–20.

　　1989. 'Actor and Character in Greek Tragedy', *Theatre Journal* 41: 316–40.

　　1992. 'Translating Scenes: Plautus' Adaptation of Menander's *Dis Exapaton*', *Phoenix* 46: 205–31.

　　1995. 'Actor, Character and Role in Chrysalus' Trojan Aria (*Bacchides 925–978*)', *Text and Presentation* 16: 24–31.

Danese, R. 1999. 'I meccanismi scenici dell'Asinaria', in R. Raffaelli and A. Tontini (eds.), *Lecturae Plautinae Sarsinates,* vol. II: *Asinaria,* 49–95. Urbino, Quattro Venti.

Davis, C. B. 2003. 'Distant Ventriloquism: Vocal Mimesis, Agency and Identity in Ancient Greek Performance', *Theatre Journal* 55: 45–65.

De Jorio, A. 2000. *Gesture in Naples and Gesture in Classical Antiquity.* Bloomington, Indiana University Press.

De Lorenzi, A. 1952. *Cronologia ed evoluzione Plautina.* Naples.

Della Corte, F. 1975. 'Maschere e personaggi in Plauto', *Dioniso* 46: 163–93.

Deufert, M. 2002. *Textgeschichte und Rezeption der plautinischen Komödien im Altertum.* Berlin, de Gruyter.

Dodge, H. 1999. 'Amusing the Masses: Buildings for Entertainment and Leisure in the Roman World', in D. S. Potter and D. J. Mattingly (eds.), *Life, Death, and Entertainment in the Roman Empire,* 205–55. Ann Arbor, University of Michigan Press.

Dodwell, C. R. 2000. *Anglo-Saxon Gestures and the Roman Stage.* Cambridge, Cambridge University Press.

Duchartre, P. L. 1966. *The Italian Comedy*, trans. R. T. Weaver. New York, Dover.

Duckworth, G. E. 1936. 'The Dramatic Function of the *Seruus currens* in Roman Comedy', *Classical Studies Presented to Edward Capps*, 93–102. Princeton, Princeton University Press.

1940. *Epidicus*. Princeton, Princeton University Press.

1952. *The Nature of Roman Comedy: A Study in Popular Entertainment*. Princeton, Princeton University Press. (2nd edn, 1994, with a Foreword and Bibliographical Appendix by R. Hunter. Norman, OK (= Duckworth (1952) and Hunter (1994)).

Dumont, J. -C. 1997. 'Cantica et espace de représentation dans le théâtre latin', in B. Le Guen (ed.), *De la scène aux gradins* (PALLAS 47), 41–50. Toulouse, Presses Universitaires du Mirail.

Easterling, P. and E. Hall (eds.). 2002. *Greek and Roman Actors: Aspects of an Ancient Profession*. Cambridge, Cambridge University Press.

Elm, D. 2001. 'Plautus' Persa und Della Portas Trappolaria', in Faller (2001) 287–301.

Enk, P. J. 1932. *Mercator*. Leiden, A. W. Sijthoff.

Ernout, A. 1932–61. *Plaute, Comédies*, 7 vols. Paris, Les Belles Lettres.

Faller, S. (ed.). 2001. *Studien zu Plautus' Persa*. Tübingen, Gunter Narr.

Fantham, E. 1965. 'The *Curculio* of Plautus: An Illustration of Plautine Methods in Adaptation', *Classical Quarterly* 15: 84–100.

1968. 'Terence, Diphilus and Menander: A Reexamination of Terence *Adelphoe* act II', *Philologus* 112: 196–216.

1975. 'Sex, Status, and Survival in Hellenistic Athens: A Study of Women in New Comedy', *Phoenix* 29: 44–74.

1982. 'Quintilian on Performance: Traditional and Personal Elements in *Institutio* 11.3', *Phoenix* 36: 243–71.

1989. 'Mime: The Missing Link in Roman Literary History', *Classical World* 82–3: 155–68.

2002. 'Orator and/et actor', in Easterling and Hall (2002) 362–76.

Feather, L. G. 1965. *The Book of Jazz, From Then till Now*. New York, Horizon.

Finnegan, R. H. 1992. *Oral Poetry: Its Nature, Significance, and Social Context*. Bloomginton, Indiana University Press.

Fitzpatrick, T. 1995. *The Relationship of Oral and Literate Performance Processes in the Commedia Dell'Arte: Beyond the Improvisation/Memorisation Divide*. Lewiston, Edwin Mellon.

Fraenkel, E. 1960. *Elementi Plautini in Plauto*, trans. F. Munari. Florence, La Nuova Italia.

Frank, T. 1932. 'Two Notes on Plautus', *American Journal of Philology* 53: 243–51.

Franko, G. F. 2004. 'Ensemble Scenes in Plautus', *American Journal of Philology* 125: 27–59.

Frassinetti, P. 1967. *Atellanae Fabulae*. Rome, in Aedibus Athenaei.

Frost, A. and R. Yarrow. 1990. *Improvisation in Drama*. New York, St Martin's.

Gaiser, K. 1972. 'Zur Eigenart der römischen Komödie. Plautus und Terenz gegenüber ihren griechischen Vorbildern', *Aufstieg und Niedergang der römischen Welt*, vol. I: 2, 1027–1113. Berlin, de Gruyter.

Garton, C. 1972. *Personal Aspects of the Roman Theatre*. Toronto, Hakkert.

Gentili, B. 1979. *Theatrical Performances in the Ancient World: Hellenistic and Early Roman Theatre*. Amsterdam, J. C. Gieben.

Gilula, D. 1977. 'The Mask of the Pseudokore', *Greek, Roman and Byzantine Studies* 18: 247–50.

  1978. 'Where did the Audience Go?', *Scripta Classica Israelica* 4: 45–49.

  1980. 'The Concept of the *bona meretrix*: A Study of Terence's Courtesans', *Rivista di Filologia e Istruzione Classica* 108: 142–65.

  1981. 'Who's Afraid of Rope-Walkers and Gladiators? (Ter. *Hec.* 1–57)', *Athenaeum* 59: 29–37.

  1985–88. 'How Rich was Terence?', *Scripta Classica Israelica* 8–9: 74–78.

  1989. 'The First Realistic Roles in European Theatre: Terence's Prologues', *Quaderni Urbinati di Cultura Classica* 62: 95–106.

  1993. 'The Crier's Routine (Plaut. *Asin.* 4–5; *Poen.* 11–5)', *Athenaeum* 81: 283–87.

  1996. 'Choragium and Choragos', *Athenaeum* 84: 479–92.

Goldberg, S. M. 1978. 'Plautus' Epidicus and the Case of the Missing Original', *Transactions of the American Philological Association* 108: 81–91.

  1995. 'Improvisation, Plot, and Plautus' *Curculio*', in Benz, Stärk, and Vogt-Spira (1995) 33–41.

  1998. 'Plautus in the Palatine', *Journal of Roman Studies* 88: 1–20.

  2004. 'Plautus and his Alternatives: Textual Doublets in *Cistellaria*', in Hartkamp and Hurka (2004) 385–98.

Goold, G. P. 1959. 'First Thoughts on the Dyscolus', *Phoenix* 13: 139–60.

Gordon, M. 1983. *Lazzi: The Comedy Routines of the Commedia dell'Arte*. New York, Performing Arts Journal Publications.

Götte, K. 2001. 'Plautus' Persa als Inspiration für John Lylys Mother Bombie', in Faller (2001) 273–86.

Gow, A. S. F. 1912. 'On the Use of Masks in Roman Comedy', *Journal of Roman Studies* 2: 65–77.

Graf, F. 1991. 'Gestures and Conventions: The Gestures of Roman Actors and Orators', in J. Bremmer and H. Roodenburg (eds.), *A Cultural History of Gesture from Antiquity to the Present Day*, 36–58. Ithaca, Cornell University Press.

Gratwick, A. S. 1973. 'TITVS MACCIVS PLAVTVS', *Classical Quarterly* 23: 78–84.

  1982. 'Drama', in E. J. Kenney and W. V. Clausen (eds.), *The Cambridge History of Classical Literature*, vol. II: *Latin Literature*, 77–137. Cambridge, Cambridge University Press.

  1993. *Plautus: Menaechmi*. Cambridge, Cambridge University Press.

  1999. *Terence: The Brothers*, 2nd edn. Warminster, Aris and Phillips.

Green, J. R. 1997. 'Deportment, Costume and Naturalism in Comedy', *Pallas* 47: 131–43.

2006. 'The Persistent Phallos: Regional Variability in the Performance Style of Comedy', in F. M. J. Davidson and P. Wilson (eds.), *Greek Drama III: Papers for Kevin Lee*, 141–62. London, Institute of Classical Studies.

Grenfell, B. P. and A. S. Hunt. 1903. '413. Farce and Mime', *Oxyrhynchus Papyri* 3: 41–57.

Gruen, E. S. 1990. *Studies in Greek Culture and Roman Policy*. Leiden, Brill.

1992. *Culture and National Identity in Republican Rome*. Ithaca, Cornell University Press.

Gurlitt, L. 1921. *Erotica Plautina: Eine Auswahl erotischer Szenen aus Plautus*. Munich, Georg Müller.

Gzowski, P. 1997. *The Morningside Years CD* (bound with *The Morningside Years*). Toronto, McClelland and Stewart.

Halford, A. S. and G. M. Halford. 1956. *The Kabuki Handbook*. Tokyo, C. E. Tuttle.

Handley, E. W. 1965. *The Dyskolos of Menander*. London, Methuen.

1968. *Menander and Plautus: A Study in Comparison*. London, H. K. Lewis.

1975. 'Plautus and his Public: Some Thoughts on New Comedy in Latin', *Dioniso* 46: 117–32.

Hanson, J. A. 1959. *Roman Theater-Temples*. Princeton, Princeton University Press.

Harsh, P. W. 1937. 'Angiportum, Platea, and Vicus', *Classical Philology* 32: 44–58.

Hartkamp, R. and F. Hurka (eds.). 2004. *Studien zu Plautus' Cistellaria*. Tübingen, Gunter Narr.

Havet, L. 1905. 'Etudes sur Plaute. *Asinaria* I: La Seconde et la troiscème scènes et la composition générale', *Revue de Philologie* 29: 94–103.

Henke, R. 2002. *Performance and Literature in the Commedia dell'Arte*. Cambridge, Cambridge University Press.

Hinard, F. 1976. 'Remarques sur les praecones et le praeconium dans la Rome de la fin de la République', *Latomus* 35: 730–46.

Hirsch, E. D., J. F. Kett and J. S. Trefil. 1987. *Cultural Literacy: What Every American Needs to Know*. Boston, Houghton Mifflin.

Hoffer, C. 1877. *De personarum usu in P. Terenti comoediis*. Halle.

Hough, J. N. 1970. 'Rapid Repartee in Roman Comedy', *Classical Journal* 65: 162–67.

Hubbell, H. M. 1962. *Cicero. Brutus, Orator*. Cambridge, MA, Harvard University Press.

Hughes, J. 1991. 'Acting Style in the Ancient World', *Theatre Notebook* 41: 2–16.

Hunter, R. L. 1979. 'The Comic Chorus in the Fourth Century', *Zeitschrift für Papyrologie und Epigraphik* 36: 23–38.

1985. *The New Comedy of Greece and Rome*. Cambridge, Cambridge University Press.

1994. 'Foreword and Bibliographical Appendix', in G. E. Duckworth, *The Nature of Roman Comedy*, 2nd edn, iii and 465–71. Norman, Oklahoma University Press.

Huys, M. 1993. 'P. Oxy. LIII 3705: A Line from Menander's *Periceiromene* with Musical Notation', *Zeitschrift für Papyrologie und Epigraphik* 99: 30–32.

Jackson, J. 1962. *Tacitus: The Histories*. Cambridge, MA, Harvard University Press.

Jocelyn, H. D. 1967. *The Tragedies of Ennius: The Fragments*. Cambridge, Cambridge University Press.

1984. 'Anti-Greek Elements in Plautus' *Menaechmi?*', *Papers of the Liverpool Latin Seminar* 4: 1–25.

1987. 'Studies in the Indirect Tradition of Plautus' *Pseudolus* (II)', *Filologia e forme letterarie: Studi offerti a Francesco della Corte*, vol. II: 57–72. Urbino, Quattro Venti.

1993. Review of Zwierlein (1990), *Gnomon* 65: 122–37.

1996. Review of Zwierlein (1991a), *Gnomon* 68: 402–20.

2000. 'The Unpretty Boy of Plautus' *Pseudolus* (767–789)', in E. Stärk and G. Vogt-Spira (eds.), *Festschrift für Eckard Lefèvre*, 431–60. Hildesheim, Georg Olms.

Johnson, M. 1992. 'Reflections of Inner Life: Masks and Masked Acting in Ancient Greek Tragedy and Japanese Noh Drama', *Modern Drama* 35: 20–34.

Johnston, P. A. 1980. '*Poenulus* I, 2 and Roman Women', *Transactions of the American Philological Association* 110: 143–59.

Johnstone, K. 1981. *Impro: Improvisation and the Theatre*, corrected edn. London, Routledge.

1999. *Impro for Storytellers*. London, Faber and Faber.

Jones, C. 1989. *Chuck Amuck: The Life and Times of an Animated Cartoonist*. New York, Farrar, Straus, and Giroux.

Jones, L. W. and C. R. Morey. 1930–31. *The Miniatures of the Manuscripts of Terence Prior to the Thirteenth Century*, 2 vols. Princeton, Princeton University Press.

Jory, E. J. 1967. 'PAIS KOMOIDOS and the DIA PANTON', *Bulletin of the Institute of Classical Studies* 14: 84–90.

1986. 'Gladiators in the Theatre', *Classical Quarterly* 36: 537–39.

1988. 'Publilius Syrus and the Element of Competition in the Theatre of the Republic', in N. Horsfall (ed.), *Vir Bonus Discendi Peritus: Studies in Celebration of Otto Skutsch's Eightieth Birthday*, 73–81. London, Institute of Classical Studies.

Kamel, W. 1951. 'The Fabula Atellana and its Stock Characters', *Bulletin of the Faculty of Arts, Cairo* 13: 89–97.

Kauer, R. and W. M. Lindsay. 1926. *P. Terenti Afri Comoediae*. Oxford, Oxford University Press. (Reprinted, 1958, with additions by O. Skutsch.)

Kehoe, P. H. 1984. 'The Adultery Mime Reconsidered', in D. F. Bright and E. S. Ramage (eds.), *Classical Texts and their Tradition: Studies in Honor of C. R. Trahnam*, 89–106. Chico, CA, Scholars Press.

Keil, H. 1961. *Grammatici Latini*. Hildesheim, Georg Olms.

Ketterer, R. C. 1986a. 'Stage Properties in Plautine Comedy I', *Semiotica* 58: 193–216.

1986b. 'Stage Properties in Plautine Comedy II', *Semiotica* 59: 93–135.

1986c. 'Stage Properties in Plautine Comedy III', *Semiotica* 60: 29–72.

King, T. J. 1992. *Casting Shakespeare's Plays: London Actors and their Roles.* Cambridge, Cambridge University Press.

Krahmalkov, C. 1970. 'The Punic Speech of Hanno', *Orientalia* 39: 52–74.

Kurrelmeyer, C. M. 1932. *The Economy of Actors in Plautus.* Graz, Deutsche Vereins-Druckerei.

Lange, D. 1973. 'The Number of Slave Roles in Plautus' *Aulularia*', *Classical Philology* 68: 62–63.

Law, H. H. 1922. *Studies in the Songs of Plautine Comedy.* Dissertation, Menasha.

Lecoq, J. 2001. *The Moving Body: Teaching Creative Theatre.* New York, Routledge.

Lefèvre, E. 1982. *Maccus vortit barbare: Vom tragischen Amphitryon zum tragikomischen Amphitruo.* Wiesbaden, Franz Steiner.

1995. *Plautus und Philemon.* Tübingen, Gunter Narr.

1997. *Plautus' Pseudolus.* Tübingen, Gunter Narr.

1999. 'Plautus' Amphitruo zwischen Tragödie und Stegreifspiel', in Baier (1999) 11–50.

2001. *Plautus' Aulularia.* Tübingen, Gunter Narr.

Lefèvre, E., E. Stärk, and G. Vogt-Spira (eds.). 1991. *Plautus barbarus: Sechs Kapitel zur Originalität des Plautus.* Tübingen, Gunter Narr.

Lefkowitz, M. R. 1981. *The Lives of the Greek Poets.* London, Duckworth.

Leigh, M. 2004. *Comedy and the Rise of Rome.* Oxford, Oxford University Press.

Lejay, P. A. A. 1925. *Plaute.* Paris, Boivin.

Leneaghan, J. O. 1969. *A Commentary on Cicero's Oration* De Haruspicum Responso. The Hague, Mouton.

Leo, F. 1895–96. *Plauti Comoediae*, 2 vols. Berlin, Weidmann.

1897. *Die plautinischen Cantica und die hellenistische Lyrik.* Berlin, Weidmann.

1912. *Plautinische Forschungen zur Kritik und Geschichte der Komödie*, 2nd edn. Berlin.

Lindsay, W. M. 1900. *The Captivi of Plautus.* London, Methuen.

1904. *The Ancient Editions of Plautus.* Oxford, J. Parker.

1904–05. *T. Macci Plauti Comoediae*, 2 vols. Oxford, Oxford University Press. (Revised, 1910, with addenda and corrigenda.)

1922. *Early Latin Verse.* Oxford, Oxford University Press.

List, G. 1963. 'The Boundaries of Speech and Song', *Ethnomusicology* 7.1: 1–16.

Llarena i Xibillè, M. 1994. *Personae Plautinae.* Barcelona, Publicacions de la Universitat de Barcelona.

Lowe, J. C. B. 1989. 'The *virgo callida* of Plautus, *Persa*', *Classical Quarterly* 39: 390–99.

1990. 'Plautus' Choruses', *Rheinisches Museum für Philologie* 133: 274–97.

1992. 'Aspects of Plautus' Originality in the *Asinaria*', *Classical Quarterly* 42: 152–75.

1995. 'Plautus' "Indoor Scenes" and Improvised Drama', in Benz, Stärk, and Vogt-Spira (1995) 23–31.

1997. 'Terence's Four-Speaker Scenes', *Phoenix* 51: 152–69.

Lowe, N. J. 2000. *The Classical Plot and the Invention of Western Narrative.* Cambridge, Cambridge University Press.

Ludwig, W. 1959. 'Von Terenz zu Menander', *Philologus* 103: 1–38.

MacCary, W. T. 1969. 'Menander's Slaves: Their Names, Roles and Masks', *Transactions of the American Philological Association* 100: 277–94.

1970. 'Menander's Characters: Their Names, Roles and Masks', *Transactions of the American Philological Association* 101: 277–90.

1971. 'Menander's Old Men', *Transactions of the American Philological Association* 102: 303–25.

1972. 'Menander's Soldiers: Their Names, Roles and Masks', *American Journal of Philology* 93: 279–98.

MacDowell, D. M. 1971. *Aristophanes: Wasps*. Oxford, Oxford University Press.

1994. 'The Number of Speaking Actors in Old Comedy', *Classical Quarterly* 44: 325–35.

Maidment, K. J. 1935. 'The Later Comic Chorus', *Classical Quarterly* 29: 1–24.

Marshall, C. W. 1993. 'Status Transactions in Aristophanes' *Frogs*', *Text and Presentation* 14: 57–61.

1994. 'The Rules of Three Actors in Practice', *Text and Presentation* 15: 53–61.

1996. 'Plautus' *Pseudolus*: The Long and the Short of it', *Text and Presentation* 17: 34–38.

1997a. 'Comic Technique and the Fourth Actor', *Classical Quarterly* 47: 77–84.

1997b. 'Shattered Mirrors and Breaking Class: Saturio's Daughter in Plautus' *Persa*', *Text and Presentation* 18: 100–09.

1998. 'In Seneca's Wings', in J. P. Bews, I. C. Storey and M. R. Boyne (eds.), *Celebratio: Thirtieth Anniversary Essays at Trent University*, 86–95. Peterborough, Ontario, Trent University.

1999a. '*Quis Hic Loquitur?* Plautine Delivery and the "Double Aside"', *Syllecta Classica* 10: 105–29.

1999b. 'Some Fifth-Century Masking Conventions', *Greece and Rome* 46: 188–202.

2000a. 'Female Performers on Stage? (PhV 96 [RVP 2/33])', *Text and Presentation* 21: 13–25.

2000b. 'Location! Location! Location!: Choral Absence and Dramatic Space in Seneca's *Troades*', in G. W. M. Harrison (ed.), *Seneca in Performance*, 27–51. Swansta.

2002. 'Chorus, Metatheatre, and *Dyskolos* 427–441', *Scholia* 11: 3–17.

2003. 'Casting the *Oresteia*', *Classical Journal* 98: 257–74.

2004. '*Alcestis* and the Ancient Rehearsal Process (*P. Oxy.* 4546)', *Arion* 11.3: 28–45.

Mattingly, H. B. 1957. 'The Plautine *didascaliae*', *Athenaeum* 35: 78–88.

1960. 'The First Period of Plautine Revival', *Latomus* 19: 230–52.

Maurach, G. 1988. *Der Poenulus des Plautus*. Heidelberg, Carl Winter.

McCarthy, K. 2000. *Slaves, Masters, and the Art of Authority in Plautine Comedy*. Princeton, Princeton University Press.

McKeown, J. C. 1979. 'Augustan Elegy and Mime', *Proceedings of the Cambridge Philological Association* 25: 71–84.

McLeish, K. 1976. *Roman Comedy*. London, Macmillan.

McMillin, S. and S. MacLean. 1998. *The Queen's Men and Their Plays*. Cambridge, Cambridge University Press.

Meyerhold, V. E. 1969. *Meyerhold on Theatre*, trans. E. Braun. London, Methuen.

Millar, F. G. B. 1984. 'The Political Character of the Classical Roman Republic', *Journal of Roman Studies* 74: 1–19.

Milnor, K. L. 2002. 'Playing House: Stage, Space, and Domesticity in Plautus' *Mostellaria*', *Helios* 29: 3–25.

Moore, T. J. 1991. '*Palliata togata*: Plautus, *Curculio* 462–86', *American Journal of Philology* 112: 343–62.

    1994. 'Seats and Social Status in the Plautine Theatre', *Classical Journal* 90: 113–23.

    1998a. 'Music and Structure in Roman Comedy', *American Journal of Philology* 119: 245–73.

    1998b. *The Theater of Plautus: Playing to the Audience*. Austin, University of Texas Press.

    1999. 'Facing the Music: Character and Musical Accompaniment in Roman Comedy', *Syllecta Classica* 10: 130–53.

    2001a. 'Music in *Epidicus*', in Auhagen (2001) 313–34.

    2001b. 'Music in *Persa*', in Faller (2001) 255–72.

    2004a. 'Music in a Quiet Play', in Baier (2004) 139–61.

    2004b. 'Meter and Meaning in *Cistellaria* II', in Hartkamp and Hurka (2004) 319–33.

    forthcoming. *Music in Roman Comedy*.

Moorehead. 1953–54. 'The Distribution of Roles in Plautus' *Menaechmi*', *Classical Journal* 49: 123–27.

Muecke, F. 1986. 'Plautus and the Theatre of Disguise', *Classical Antiquity* 5: 216–29.

Naumann, M. 1976. 'Literary Production and Reception', *New Literary History* 8.1: 107–26.

Nesselrath, H.-G. 1985. *Lukians Parasitendialog*. Berlin, de Gruyter.

Nettl, B. 1974. 'Thoughts on Improvisation', *Musical Quarterly* 60: 1–19.

Nicoll, A. 1931. *Masks, Mimes, and Miracles: Studies in the Popular Theatre*. London, George G. Harrap.

Nicolson, F. W. 1893. 'The Use of *Hercle* (*Mehercle*), *Edepol* (*Pol*), *Ecastor* (*Mecastor*) by Plautus and Terence', *Harvard Studies in Classical Philology* 4: 99–103.

Nixon, P. 1917. *Plautus II: Casina, the Casket Comedy, Curculio, Epidicus, The Two Menaechmuses*. Cambridge, MA, Harvard University Press.

    1924. *Plautus III: The Merchant, The Braggart Warrior, The Haunted House, The Persian*. Cambridge, MA, Harvard University Press.

Oakley, S. P. 1998. *A Commentary on Livy Books VI–X*, vol. II (Books VII and VIII). Oxford, Oxford University Press.

Obbink, D. 2001. '4546. Euripides, *Alcestis* 344–82 with Omissions', *Oxyrhynchus Papyri* 67: 19–22.

Olson, K. 2003. 'Roman Underwear Revisited', *Classical World* 96: 201–10.

Orgel, S. 2002. *The Authentic Shakespeare, and Other Problems of the Early Modern Stage*. New York, Routledge.

Palmer, R. E. A. 1997. *Rome and Carthage at Peace*. Stuttgart, Franz Steiner.

Pansièri, C. 1997. *Plaute et Rome, ou, Les ambiguïtés d'un marginal*. Brussels, Collection Latomus.

Paratore, E. 1959. 'Il flautista nel *DUSKOLOS* e nello *Pseudolus*', *Rivista di Cultura Classica e Medievale* 1: 310–25.

Parker, H. N. 1989. 'Crucially Funny, or Tranio on the Couch', *Transactions of the American Philological Association* 119: 233–46.

Perelli, L. 1983. 'L'Alcmena plautina, personaggio serio o parodico?', *Civiltà Classica e Cristiana* 4: 383–94.

Phillips, J. E. 1985. 'Alcumena in the *Amphitruo* of Plautus: A Pregnant Lady Joke', *Classical Journal* 80: 121–26.

Pickard-Cambridge, A. W. 1968. *The Dramatic Festivals of Athens*. Oxford, Oxford University Press.

Pietropaolo, D. (ed.). 1989. *The Science of Buffonery: Theory and History of the Commedia Dell'Arte*. Ottawa, Dovehouse.

Poe, J. P. 1996. 'The Supposed Conventional Meanings of Dramatic Masks: A Re-examination of Pollux 4.133–54', *Philologus* 140: 306–28.

Pöhlmann, E. and M. L. West. 2001. *Documents of Ancient Greek Music: The Extant Melodies and Fragments*. Oxford, Oxford University Press.

Porter, J. R. 2004. 'Aristophanes, *Acharnians* 1118–21', *Greece and Rome* 51: 21–33.

Potter, D. S. 1999. *Literary Texts and the Roman Historian*. New York, Routledge.

Préaux, J. G. 1962. 'Manducus', in M. Renard (ed.), *Hommages à A. Grenier* (Collection Latomus 58), 1282–91. Berchem-Brussels, Latomus.

Prehn, B. 1916. *Quaestiones Plautinae*. Breslau, Nischkowsky.

Prescott, H. W. 1910. 'Three *Puer*-Scenes in Plautus, and the Distribution of Rôles', *Harvard Studies in Classical Philology* 21: 31–50.

1923. 'The Doubling of Rôles in Roman Comedy', *Classical Philology* 18: 23–34.

1932. 'Criteria of Originality in Plautus', *Transactions of the American Philological Association* 63: 103–25.

1934. Review of Kurrelmeyer (1932), *Classical Philology* 29: 350–51.

1937. 'Silent Roles in Roman Comedy', *Classical Philology* 32: 193–209.

Primmer, A. 1984. *Handlungsgliederung in Nea und Palliata: Dis Exapaton und Bacchides*. Vienna, Österreichische Akademie der Wissenschaften.

Purcell, N. 1983. 'The *apparitores*: A Study in Social Mobility', *Papers of the British School at Rome* 51: 125–73.

Questa, C. 1967. *Introduzione alla metrica di Plauto*. Bologna, R. Pàtron.

1970. 'Alcune strutture sceniche di Plauto e Menandro', *Entretiens sur l'antiquité classique XVI: Ménandre*, 181–215. Geneva, Fondation Hardt.

1995. *Cantica: Titi Macci Plauti*. Urbino, Quattro Venti.

2001. *Casina*. Urbino, Quattro Venti.

Radice, B. 1976. *Terence: the Comedies*. New York, Penguin.

Rambo, E. F. 1915. 'The Significance of the Wing-Entrances in Roman Comedy', *Classical Philology* 10: 411–31.

Raven, D. S. 1965. *Latin Metre: An Introduction*. London, Faber and Faber.

Rawson, E. 1993. 'Freedmen in Roman Comedy', in R. Scodel (ed.), *Theater and Society in the Classical World*, 215–33. Ann Arbor, University of Michigan Press.

Rehm, R. 1992. *Greek Tragic Theatre*. New York, Routledge.

Reich, H. 1903. *Der Mimus: ein Litterar-Entwicklungsgeschichtlicher Versuch*. Berlin. Weidmannsche Buchhandlung.

Reinach, T. 1919. 'Tibia', in C. Daremberg and E. Saglio (eds.), *Dictionnaire des antiquités grecques et romaines* V: 300–32. Paris, Hachette.

Reynolds, R. W. 1946. 'The Adultery Mime', *Classical Quarterly* 40: 77–84.

Richards, K. and L. Richards. 1990. *The Commedia dell'Arte: A Documentary History*. Oxford, Blackwell.

Richardson, L. 1992. *A New Topographical Dictionary of Ancient Rome*. Baltimore, Johns Hopkins University Press.

Ringler, W. A. 1968. 'The Number of Actors in Shakespeare's Early Plays', in G. E. Bentley (ed.), *The Seventeenth-Century Stage: A Collection of Critical Essays*, 110–34. Chicago, University of Chicago Press.

Rosivach, V. J. 1983. 'The *aduocati* in the *Poenulus* and the *piscatores* in the *Rudens*', *Maia* 35: 83–93.

 2000. 'The Audiences of New Comedy', *Greece and Rome* 47: 169–71.

Rouse, W. H. D. 1975. *Lucretius: De Rerum Natura*, rev. M. F. Smith. Cambridge, MA, Harvard University Press.

Russell, D. A. 1968. 'The Origin and Development of Republican Forums', *Phoenix* 22: 304–36.

 2001. *Quintilian: The Orator's Education*, vol. V (Books 11–12). Cambridge, MA, Harvard University Press.

Rusten, J. and I. C. Cunningham. 2002. *Theophrastus: Characters; Herodas: Mimes; Sophron and Other Mime Fragments*. Cambridge, MA, Harvard University Press.

Sage, E. T. 1935. *Livy IX: Books XXXI–XXXIV*. Cambridge, MA, Harvard University Press.

Salerno, H. F. (ed.). 1967. *Scenarios of the Commedia dell'Arte: Flaminio Scala's 'Il teatro delle favole rappresentative'*. New York, New York University Press.

Sandbach, F. H. 1982. 'How Terence's *Hecyra* Failed', *Classical Quarterly* 32: 134–5.

Saunders, C. 1909. *Costume in Roman Comedy*. New York, Columbia University Press.

 1913. 'The Site of Dramatic Performances at Rome in the Times of Plautus and Terence', *Transactions of the American Philological Association* 44: 87–97.

Schaaf, L. 1977. *Der Miles gloriosus des Plautus und sein griechisches Original. Ein Beitrag zur Kontaminationsfrage*. Munich, W. Fink.

Schanz, M. and C. Hosius. 1927, repr. 1966. *Geschichte der römischen Literatur*, 3 vols. Munich, C. H. Beck'sche.

Schechner, R. 1969. *Public Domain: Essays on the Theatre*. Indianapolis, Bobbs-Merrill.

Schneider, K. 1931. 'Meretrix', *Realencyclopädie der classischen Altertumswissenschaft* 15.1: 1018–27.

Schönbeck, H.-P. 1981. *Beiträge zur Interpretation der plautinischen 'Bacchides'*. Düsseldorf, Peter Mannhold.

Schumacher, C. 2000. 'Would you Splash Out on a Ticket to Molière's Palais Royal?', *Theatre Research International* 25: 248–54.

Schutter, H. E. 1952. *Quibus annis comoediae Plautinae primae actae sint quaeritur*. Groningen, De Waal.

Sedgwick, W. B. 1925. 'The Cantica of Plautus', *Classical Review* 39: 55–58.

  1949. 'Plautine Chronology', *American Journal of Philology* 70: 376–83.

Segal, E. 1975. 'Perché Amphitruo', *Dioniso* 46: 247–67.

  1987. *Roman Laughter: The Comedy of Plautus*, 2nd edn. New York, Oxford University Press. (1st edn, 1968.)

Shackleton Bailey, D. R. 2000. *Valerius Maximus: Memorable Doings and Sayings*. Cambridge, MA, Harvard University Press.

Sheets, G. A. 1983. 'Plautus and Early Roman Tragedy', *Illinois Classical Studies* 8: 195–209.

Sifakis, G. M. 1967. *Studies in the History of Hellenistic Drama*. London, Athlone Press.

  1979. 'Boy Actors in New Comedy', in G. W. Bowerstock, W. Burkert and M. J. C. Putnam (eds.), *Arktouros: Hellenic Studies Presented to B. M. W. Knox*, 199–208. Berlin, de Gruyter.

Sinfield, A. 1983. 'The Theatre and its Andvences', in A. Sinfield (ed.), *Society and Literature 1945–1970*, 173–97. London, Methuen.

Skutsch, F. 1900. 'Ein Prolog des Diphilos und eine Komödie des Plautus', *Rheinisches Museum für Philologie* 55: 272–85.

Slater, N. W. 1996. 'Literacy and Old Comedy', in I. Worthington (ed.), *Voice into Text*, 99–112. Leiden, Brill.

  2000. *Plautus in Performance: the theatre of the Mind*, 2nd edition. Amsterdam, Harwood Academic. (1st edn, Princeton University Press, 1985.)

  2004. 'Staging Literacy in Plautus', in C. J. Mackie (ed.), *Oral Performance and its Context*, 163–77. Leiden, Brill.

Smith, I. 1967. 'Their Exits and Reentrances', *Shakespeare Quarterly* 18: 7–16.

Smith, P. L. 1991. *Plautus, Three Comedies: Miles Gloriosus, Pseudolus, Rudens*. Ithaca, Cornell University Press.

Snowden, F. M. 1970. *Blacks in Antiquity: Ethiopians in the Greco-Roman Experience*. Cambridge, MA, Harvard University Press.

Spolin, V. 1983. *Improvisation for the Theater: A Handbook of Teaching and Directing Techniques*. Evanston, IL, Northwestern University Press.

Stambaugh, J. E. 1988. *The Ancient Roman City*. Baltimore, Johns Hopkins University Press.

Stärk, E. 1989. *Die Menaechmi des Plautus und kein griechisches Original.* Tübingen, Gunter Narr.

Stern, T. 2004. *Making Shakespeare: From Stage to Page.* London, Routledge.

Tanner, R. G. 1969. 'Problems in Plautus', *Proceedings of the Cambridge Philological Society* 15: 95–105.

Tansey, P. 2001. 'New Light on the Roman Stage: A Revival of Terence's *Phormio* Rediscovered', *Rheinisches Museum für Philologie* 144: 22–43.

Taplin, O. 1993. *Comic Angels and Other Approaches to Greek Drama through Vase-Paintings.* Oxford, Oxford University Press.

Taylor, L. R. 1935. 'The *Sellisternium* and the Theatrical Pompa', *Classical Philology* 30: 122–30.

   1937. 'The Opportunities for Dramatic Performances in the Time of Plautus and Terence', *Transactions of the American Philological Association* 68: 284–304.

   1966. *Roman Voting Assemblies from the Hannibalic War to the Dictatorship of Caesar.* Ann Arbor, University of Michigan Press.

Tobias, A. J. 1980. 'Bacchiac Women and Iambic Slaves in Plautus', *Classical World* 73: 9–18.

Trendall, A. D. 1967. *Phlyax Vases*, 2nd edn. London, Institute of Classical Studies.

Vogt-Spira, G. 1995. 'Traditionen improvisierten Theaters bei Plautus', in B. Zimmermann (ed.), *Griechisch-römische Komödie und Tragödie*, 70–93. Stuttgart.

   2001. 'Traditions of Theatrical Improvisation in Plautus: Some Considerations', in E. Segal (ed.), *Oxford Readings in Menander, Plautus, and Terence*, 95–106. Oxford, Oxford University Press.

Webster, T. B. L. 1970. *Studies in Later Greek Comedy*, 2nd edn. New York, Manchester University Press.

   1995. *Monuments Illustrating New Comedy*, 3rd edn, revised and enlarged by J. R. Green and A. Seeberg, 2 vols. London, Institute of Classical Studies.

Weinberger, W. 1892. 'Beiträge zu den Bühenalterthümern aus Donats Terenzcommentar', *Wiener Studien* 14: 120–30.

Weissinger, R. T. 1940. *A Study of Act Divisions in Classical Drama.* Scottdale, Mennonite Publishing House.

Welch, K. 1994. 'The Roman Arena in Late-Republican Italy: A New Interpretation', *Journal of Roman Archaeology* 7: 59–80.

   2003. 'A New View of the Origins of the Roman Basilica: The Atrium Region, Graecostasis, and Roman Diplomacy', *Journal of Roman Archaeology* 17: 5–34.

Wessner, P. 1902–08. *Aeli Donati Commentvm Terenti*, 3 vols. Leipzig, Teubner.

West, M. L. 1992. *Ancient Greek Music.* Oxford, Oxford University Press.

Wiemken, H. 1972. *Der griechische Mimus: Dokumente zur Geschichte des antiken Volkstheaters.* Bremen, Carl Schünemann.

Wiles, D. 1989. 'Marriage and Prostitution in Classical New Comedy', in J. Redmond (ed.), *Themes in Drama. II: Women in Theatre*, 31–48. Cambridge, Cambridge University Press.

1991. *The Masks of Menander: Sign and Meaning in Greek and Roman Performance.* Cambridge, Cambridge University Press.

1997. *Greek Theatre Performance: An Introduction.* Cambridge, Cambridge University Press.

Willcock, M. M. (ed.). 1987. *Plautus: Pseudolus.* Bristol, Bristol Classical Press.

1995. 'Plautus and the *Epidicus*', *Papers of the Leeds International Latin Seminar* 8: 19–29.

Wilson, L. M. 1938. *The Clothing of the Ancient Romans.* Baltimore, Johns Hopkins Press.

Wilson, P. 2000. *The Athenian Institution of the Khoregia.* Cambridge, Cambridge University Press.

Wiseman, T. P. 1995. *Remus: A Roman Myth.* Cambridge, Cambridge University Press.

Wright, G. T. 1988. *Shakespeare's Metrical Art.* Berkeley, University of California Press.

Wright, J. 1974. *Dancing in Chains: The Stylistic Unity of the comoedia palliata.* Rome, American Academy.

1993. *Plautus' Curculio.* Norman, University of Oklahoma Press.

Wüst, E. 1932. 'Mimus', *Realencyclopädie der classischen Altertumswissenschaft* 15.2: 1727–64.

Zagagi, N. 1995. 'The Impromptu Element in Plautus in the Light of the Evidence of New Comedy', in Benz, Stärk, and Vogt-Spira (1995) 71–86.

Zwierlein, O. 1990. *Zur Kritik und Exegese des Plautus I: Poenulus und Curculio.* Stuttgart, Franz Steiner.

1991a. *Zur Kritik und Exegese des Plautus II: Miles gloriosus.* Stuttgart, Franz Steiner.

1991b. *Zur Kritik und Exegese des Plautus III: Pseudolus.* Stuttgart, Franz Steiner.

1992. *Zur Kritik und Exegese des Plautus IV: Bacchides.* Stuttgart, Franz Steiner.

Index Locorum

General Index

acting styles 61, 87, 92–4, 159
  antilabê 244
  comic timing 243–4
  delivery 164–6, 195, 196–8, 204, 227, 230–6
  See also under individual plays, metrical
    structure of
actors,
  boy 94
  maximum number on stage at once 122–5
  social status of 86–7
  star parts 116–20
altar, stage 38–40, 42, 53–4, 68
Ambivius Turpio *see* Turpio
angiportum 54–5, 107–8
arc structure 205–7, 222–5
  see also under individual plays, metrical
    structure of
Atellanae ('Atellan Farces') 5, 7, 28, 146, 229
  scripted 6–8, 275
audience 73–82
  boys in 75
  emotional engagement of 188–9
  segregation of 77–8
  size of 37, 79–81

Brook, Peter ix

Caecilius, *Plocium* ('The Necklace') 4, 22
calendar, misalignment of 17
cancelli (barriers) 48
choragus 26–9, 62, 122, 183
cinema, 35, 73, 79, 137–8
Circus Flaminius 47
Comitium 45–8
  use of Rostra 44
commedia dell'arte 137–40, 154, 169,
  248, 252–53, 255, 259, 266, 274, 277
costumes 56–66
  renting 26–7
  use of padding 64–5
  see also under doubling, 'lightning changes'

Craig, E. Gordon 132, 247–58

Diphilus *see under* Plautus, *Commorientes*
disguise 59–61
doors 49–50, 52–4
doublets in performance *see* improvisation
doubling
  impact of small parts 100–1
  in Greek theatre 94–5
  in *Menaechmi* 105–7, 149
  in *Pseudolus* 99, 101–4
  in Rome 95–8
  'lightning changes' 98, 100, 108–9, 117–9, 121,
    124, 177

eavesdropping 55, 103, 141, 161–2, 167, 172, 183,
  189, 199, 208, 242
elastic gags *see under* improvisation
Elizabethan theatre practices 23, 27, 34–5, 109,
  116, 127, 195, 244, 274–5

fabulae
  Atellanae see *Atellanae*
  Palliatae see *Roman Comedy*
  Praetextae 15
  Tabernariae 14
  Togatae 14
focus
  split-focus scenes 166–7
forum Romanum 40–4

Gaius Naevius *see* Naevius
gesture 91–2, 167–70
gladiators 23–6, 40, 43–4, 48, 78
Goldoni, Carlo 106

Herodas 7

improvisation 6–8, 245–56, 260, 263–74
  degrees of scriptedness 246–57